PRAISE FOR

BEAUTIFUL

JIM KEY

D0951614

"A classic. . . . *Beautiful Jim Key* is a window into a lost world."
—*Nashville Scene*

"A captivating literary excavation of lost Americana."
—*Publishers Weekly* (starred review)

"Beautiful Jim Key may be the biggest celebrity you've never
heard of—until now."
—*Winston-Salem Journal*

"A wonderful true story of an extraordinary horse and an equally
extraordinary man."
—Berry Gordy

"Rivas performs an important service by bringing this story to light
and reminding us how it was almost lost."
—*Knoxville News-Sentinel*

"A wonderful slice of American life at the turn of the last
century. . . . Rivas deserves praise."
—*Contra Costa Times*

"Like Laura Hillenbrand's *Seabiscuit,* this brilliantly re-created history
of Beautiful Jim Key is destined to become a classic."
—David Geffen

"For years, many thought the story of Beautiful Jim Key and his
trainer, Dr. William Key, was a tall tale. . . . Rivas weaves these stories of
horse and trainer together while placing them in the context of their
times, as Laura Hillenbrand did in *Seabiscuit,* offering a narrative that
is even more exciting than a tall tale because every word is true."
—*St. Petersburg Times*

Bradley K. Ross

ABOUT THE AUTHOR

MIM EICHLER RIVAS has worked as an author, coauthor, and ghostwriter on more than twelve nonfiction books, including the *New York Times* bestseller *Finding Fish*. She lives with her family in Hermosa Beach, California.

BEAUTIFUL JIM KEY

The Lost History of the
WORLD'S SMARTEST HORSE

MIM EICHLER RIVAS

 Harper   *An Imprint of HarperCollinsPublishers*

Grateful acknowledgment is made to the following for permission to reprint the photographs in this book: Annie Mott Whitman Collection of Jim Key Materials, Manuscripts Section, Tennessee State Library and Archives: insert pages 1 top, 2 top, 3, 6 left, 7 top and bottom, 9, 10 bottom, 11 top, and 12–13; David Hoffman Collection: insert pages 1 bottom, 2 middle and bottom, 10 top, 11 bottom, and 14; collection of Mim Eichler Rivas: insert pages 4 and 16; MSPCA-Angell, Boston, Massachusetts: insert page 5 bottom; St. Louis Public Library: insert pages 5 top and 6 right; Tennessee State Library and Archives, from the *Official History of the Tennessee Centennial Exposition:* insert page 8. The images on page 15, top and bottom, originally appeared in *Master St. Elmo: The Autobiography of a Celebrated Dog* by Caro Senour.

To the memory of my father, Eugene Eichler,
a peacemaker, who demonstrated throughout
his forty-six years of life that with kindness,
wisdom, a good joke, and a story or two
hardened minds can be opened,
and the world can be changed for the better.

What he loved in horses was what he loved in men,
the blood and the heat of blood that ran them.
All his reverence and all his fondness and all the
leanings of his life were for the ardenthearted
and they would always be so and never be otherwise.

—CORMAC MCCARTHY
All the Pretty Horses

CONTENTS

AUTHOR'S NOTE

THIS IS THE TRUE STORY of an American hero who rose to international renown at the turn of the last century and who, in his short twenty-three years of life, helped spur a significant shift in human consciousness. What made this individual different from other great men and women who change the course of history is that he was neither man nor woman. Beautiful Jim Key was a horse. An *educated* horse. Together with his owner/teacher/best friend "Dr." William Key—an ex-slave from Shelbyville, Tennessee, a Civil War veteran, horse whisperer, self-taught veterinarian, entrepreneur, and one of the most recognized African-Americans of his day—Jim Key helped launch a worldwide animal rights movement through an international network of humane societies. His contribution was to transform what was once considered a radical fringe element into a mainstream concern and to make kindness toward animals a cornerstone of civilized existence.

Beautiful Jim Key was to the humane movement exactly what every important cause needs. He was a star. Years before horses like Dan Patch, Man O'War, Seabiscuit, and Secretariat became revered household names, Beautiful Jim Key trailblazed his way into stardom and set the standard for animal celebrities forever after. Yet unlike his fellow equine stars, Jim was famous not because of his speed or his beauty. He was, without a doubt, a paragon of physical grace, a heartthrob, and a matinee idol. At a press party on November 30, 1897, during a private exhibition at Field's Stables at 156 East Twenty-fifth Street in Manhattan—assembled to announce Jim's Broadway debut—a reporter for the *New York Times* was smitten with his "expressive eyes" and the "suggestive tosses of his finely formed head." Indeed, it was the press who first dubbed the mahogany bay "Beautiful." But his good looks didn't make him an icon.

Jim was beloved because he was smart. During nine years of continuous exhibition, he demonstrated inexplicable abilities to read, write, spell, do math, tell time, sort mail, use a cash register and a telephone, cite Bible passages, and engage in political debate. Known as the "Marvel of the Twentieth Century" and "The Greatest Crowd Drawer in America," he was seen by an estimated ten million Americans. The rest of the public settled for second best, following his comings and goings, as well as the controversies that swirled around him, in nonstop headlines in most major newspapers. Legions of fans bought his souvenir programs and buttons, publicity photographs, and postcards. They collected specially minted Beautiful Jim Key pennies, danced the "Beautiful Jim Key" two-step, wore Jim Key gold pinbacks in their collars, and competed in Beautiful Jim Key essay contests, while one million children signed the Jim Key Pledge: "I promise always to be kind to animals." Meanwhile, the proceeds from his performances and merchandise funded scores of local, state, and national animal protection organizations, and also made Jim and his human associates wealthy beyond their dreams.

A hundred years later, this amazing saga has seemingly vanished from the pages of history. When a 1904 vintage promotional pamphlet relating elements of this story first crossed my radar, what confronted me was a mystery. Why had I never heard of it? Yet why did it seem remotely familiar, like a flash of déjà vu or a long-lost memory asking to be remembered? Where had the history gone? Why had it resurfaced now?

Initial research very quickly turned up a wealth of documentation that provided answers. But other questions emerged, questions that plagued Beautiful Jim Key even at the height of his career. Was his act a hoax? Were ten million Americans taken for a ride? On the other hand, if Bill and Jim were faking it, what kind of an elaborate system allowed them to pull it off?

These questions will be explored on the pages ahead. In order to both validate this story and allow readers to determine what processes were or weren't at work, I have resisted my storytelling temptation to invent scenic details and dialogue as texture to this narrative. Dialogue in quotation marks is quoted from actual sources; scenes described in detail are likewise taken from detailed documents, except in those instances where I have added connective tissue between events when certain moments have been suggested by sources but can still be considered speculative.

Readers may come to different conclusions about whether Jim's ability to nonchalantly subtract a $1.69 purchase from two dollar bills and deliver change in correct coins to the recipient was a function of performing a well-designed trick or whether he was capable of deductive reasoning and critical thinking. Clearly, there were reasons why Jim and his entourage seemed always to be in a race for their lives to overcome hurdles of prejudice, skepticism, and competition. There are other reasons why the notion of humanlike animal intelligence touches off a powerfully resistive public nerve—now as then. Yet what is evident, in any case, is that Beautiful Jim Key definitely *appeared* to be able to do all that was claimed of him.

That he *appeared* to have an I.Q. equivalent to that of a twelve-year-old human and to have mastered academics equivalent to a sixth-grade level was essential in his ability to open and change the public mind. This, more importantly, leads to the questions at the heart of what Dr. William Key and Jim Key accomplished. How were they able, in nine short years, to bring about a transformation of thinking, forging connections that transcended age, economic background, race, and species, all across the country, at a time when few were genuinely concerned about the welfare of animals? Moreover, what were the individual and cultural crosscurrents that shaped them as crusaders for a simple message: the power of kindness—toward our fellow human beings, toward all creatures, and toward the earth itself—trumps all others?

During the late 1800s, a time that called forth for a being like Beautiful Jim Key, animal rights activists—many of the same groups who promoted such outlandish ideas as women's suffrage, racial equality, conservation, literacy, the humane reform of labor, welfare, schools, and prisons—were generally viewed as radicals and kooks. Troublemakers. In a kind of spooky rerun, current advocates for animal and environmental protection—in fact, most progressive organizations—are once again being labeled extremists and nuisances. "Special interest groups."

In an age of terror, war, and plagues—by no means exclusive to our times—the values of nonviolence, tolerance, kindness, and the quest for peace on our fragile planet seem to have fallen into disrepute.

Maybe that's why this story has resurfaced now. It's possible that a horse and a man of color from Tennessee have as much to teach us today as they did at the turn of the last century. Maybe more.

AUTHOR'S NOTE

BEAUTIFUL
JIM KEY

1

Prehistory

Saturday, April 30, 1904.
The Louisiana Purchase Exposition, Opening Day.

MISS ALICE ROOSEVELT parted the seas of fairgoers as she paused to smooth her skirt, making sure, as she always did, that it had just the right swing. With her gaze fixed ahead at her destination, the unusual Silver Horseshoe Building, the President's daughter continued along the Pike, the exposition's mile-long amusement area. Gone was her trademark expression of boredom. On her way to preside at an Opening Day performance given by the smartest horse in the world, Alice appeared to be positively delighted.

Neither Alice nor her escort, Ohio congressman Nicholas Longworth, had yet to witness the horse in action, but they had certainly read his press and heard enough claims about the Celebrated Educated Arabian-Hambletonian to understand why he was expected to be the top draw on the Pike.

This stretch of marketplaces and attractions, she could see, didn't have the expansive grandeur of the rest of the fair. Architecturally, there was no comparison. Thus far, the Pike was an unfinished hodgepodge, while the main exhibit areas seemed to be perfectly realized visions. They radiated in avenues and plazas to provide spectacular views of the main Festival Hall—one part Louis Quatorze and three parts fairyland—along with the euphoric Cascade Gardens pumping ninety thousand gallons of water per minute into geysers and fountains that spilled over plunging falls lit by green glass steps, offsetting the futuristic fantasy of the Palace of Electricity, which turned megawattage into visual evidence that the planners had truly outdone themselves.

Earlier that day, exposition president David Francis had welcomed the first flanks of what would total 200,000 Opening Day visitors. The weather itself was miraculous. It had been cold and stormy for weeks in St. Louis, with black skies and oppressive winds almost causing Francis and fellow officials to delay the date of the opening. After they decided to take the risk and open, rain or shine, the city nervously awoke at dawn that Saturday to a pale fog. By early morning, the sun broke through, sending the temperature and humidity rising, and basking the World's Fair in a jubilant golden mist.

Alice Roosevelt and Congressman Longworth were on hand to listen as John Philip Sousa and his band played "Louisiana" while simultaneously, back in Washington, D.C., in the East Room of the White House, Alice's father, President Theodore Roosevelt, was joined by an assembly of ambassadors and ministers from around the globe, his cabinet, justices of the Supreme Court, president pro tem of the Senate, and the Speaker of the House. The President was then handed a golden key, which he ceremoniously turned to trigger a telegraphic transmission that moments later in St. Louis unleashed the electricity required to raise and unfurl flags of all nations, thus starting the machinery of the Louisiana Purchase Exposition.

"Open ye gates!" shouted David Francis, after the cries of the crowd had subsided. "Swing wide ye portals! Enter herein ye sons of men! Learn the lesson here taught and gather from it inspiration for still greater accomplishments!"

Trumpeting the fair's themes of progress and education, Francis made no apologies for the unfinished construction of the Pike. Rather, he promoted the manner in which he and fellow planners had looked for a way to elevate the carnival atmosphere associated with amusement and midway areas by envisioning it as a "living color page of the world." Anything foreign or different was a go: food, beverages, rides, shows, souvenirs, creatures, and humans. But ironically, as the months ahead would prove, for all its otherness, the Pike became the soul of the Exposition, the mingling and mixing pot that was becoming America. It was the meeting place of the fair, to be immortalized in song and film, where the nation responded to the call to "Meet Me in St. Louis."

The mile-long Pike was so called in tribute to its trek across time and space that reached at its zenith the stratosphere of the North Pole (but only took twenty minutes to climb), echoed by the dominating snowcapped Alpine peaks at the avenue's eastern border. As an unmistakable precursor to Disneyland's Matterhorn, the Alpine heights were complete with medieval castles, peasants singing Tyrolean folk songs, a mammoth cyclorama enclosed within the mountains' caves, and a heart-racing tram ride up the slopes, on which the Piker (any visitor to the Pike) could observe the lay of the land.

Even though construction hadn't been completed by Opening Day, Alice and her escort and most of the 200,000 fairgoers who poured onto the Pike at noon, could see the magical domain shaping up. Due west of the Alpine Heights was the Irish Village with the Blarney Stone Theatre, Irish dancing maidens, and the Great Dublin Army Band playing Celtic music, while an adjacent concession, Under and Over the Sea, used lights and scenery to evoke the Jules Verne–inspired experience of a submarine ride to Paris with a return by airship. This was still considered futuristic, even though five months earlier at Kitty Hawk the Wright Brothers had taken their machine-powered Flyer on her maiden voyage.

Below France, the Streets of Seville were so painstakingly recreated by Mrs. Hattie McCall Travis, the only female concessionaire on the Pike, that the massive undertaking was reported to have killed her before completion. Next came the Hagenback Animal Paradise with a glamorous assortment of animals to rival any of P. T. Barnum's menageries, displayed not behind bars but simply with mosquito netting to separate spectators and animals. From there, the Piker could travel toward Mysterious Asia, past the wares and snake charmers in the Taj Mahal marketplace, under the carved and gilded gateway to the Japanese gardens, through the Chinese Village, into the Moorish Palace with its wax museum display of anthropological history, to Cairo and Constantinople, amid roaming elephants, monkeys, camels, and donkeys.

Competing for attention were such attractions as the very popular Filipino Village with its cast of hundreds, the Palais du Costume exhibit at the Paris Pavilion, the assembly of authentic representatives of fifty-one different Native American tribes, the Abbey Battle Cyclorama with scenic representations and live reenactments of America's famous battles, a ride through the Galveston Flood, the

New York Fire Station theatre extravaganza with illusions that made a building burst into flame, and an indoor boat tour through the Six Days of Creation—from "Let there be light!" to a finale in Eden. There were the scientific concessions not to be missed, such as the hospital wing that exhibited newly invented incubators (with real preemie infants, live nurses and doctors), the Magic Whirlpool ride, which took passengers across an enchanted lake and over plunging waterfalls, and the novel Scenic Railway Pavilion, where trains could be boarded for other destinations at the fair.

The Pike was to stir some of the biggest newsmaking events that took place over the course of the exposition. One such event occurred later in the summer when an enterprising concession-aire—facing low sales of hot tea at his café—came up with the mad-cap idea of pouring the tea over glasses of ice. Before long, iced tea was the beverage of choice across much of a sweltering and not yet air-conditioned nation. The heat provoked a second innovation, for which at least three of the fifty ice cream vendors on the Pike claimed credit. When the demand for ice cream dishes and spoons exceeded the supply, one, two, or all three of these concessionaires concocted a method of baking waffle cookies in conical shapes. By the end of the summer, ice cream cones were an American institution. The portable cornucopias cut down on utensils and allowed fairgoers to continue spending money and visiting other attractions while they walked and licked their ice cream. Using the tongue with such abandon was still a rather risqué public act, even with waning Victorian values, but it was made respectable by the liberating atmosphere of the Pike.

But the event that truly became the gossip of the season was an encounter on Opening Day during an American Humane Education Society benefit performance given in the Pike's quirky Silver Horseshoe Building, a pseudowestern-styled piece of architecture with a four-story facade rising up in the shape of a gigantic horseshoe around which tiled letters declared it the home of THE MOST WONDERFUL HORSE IN THE WORLD. The encounter, of course, was between Beautiful Jim Key and his guest of honor, Miss Alice Roosevelt, who seldom did anything that went unnoticed.

Almost from the moment, three years earlier, when her father ascended suddenly from the vice presidency to become president, following McKinley's assassination, the seventeen-year-old became known as Princess Alice. She was royalty, on her way to becoming what many consider the first female American celebrity of the twentieth century. Strikingly pretty, brunette and bright-eyed, with a high-bred, turned-up nose and full pouting lips, she managed to stir up so much public frenzy that she was lampooned in a *Chicago Tribune* political cartoon that showed crowds in the stands at a horse race, looking not at the track but in every other direction, with a caption reading "Alice, where art thou?"

Every public sighting drew reams of ink. Her face was described as artfully animated. The gossip pages of the *San Francisco Call* dubbed her petite nose "saucy," her chin as firm and round, her body as a "slender, supple, lissome figure expressing youth and life in every line," and her fashion genius was attested to by her ability to attain the right fit of her bodice, the perfect tilt to her hat. Her life story—she was an independent heiress to the fortune left to her by her mother, Alice Lee (Teddy Roosevelt's first wife), who had died just days after giving birth—made Princess Alice that much more compelling.

But she was not famous because of her childhood troubles or because she was beautiful and inordinately rich. She was famous because she was her father's daughter—fearless, blessed with an irrepressibly rebellious spirit, a gregarious, barbarous wit—and was such an original that her favorite pale gray/blue color was eventually named "Alice blue." She was endlessly forgiven for smoking wherever she pleased, for racing a motorcar from Newport to Boston (not the daintier electric horseless carriage most female drivers preferred, but the noisier, faster gas-run automobile), for traipsing around the White House with her pet garden snake wrapped around her arm, for jaunting off to foreign destinations whenever she liked, and for her bold disdain of anything or anyone who struck her as boring or too much of a do-gooder. When a frustrated adviser once implored Teddy to control her, Roosevelt's famous reply was: "I can do one of two things. I can be President of the United States, or I can control Alice. I cannot possibly do both."

Instead, in a canny PR move, Teddy encouraged his daughter to be of service as his emissary to certain affairs of state he was unable to attend, a role she played masterfully. In that capacity she had come to the Louisiana Purchase Exposition to preside in her father's place during the Opening Day festivities on the Pike.

Alice's name had been romantically linked to a handful of eligible sons of the European nobility (and it was assumed with her money and her family's political might, she would certainly want to marry a title) as well as several young American bluebloods. But Congressman Nicholas Longworth, thirty-five years old to her twenty, was not yet considered to be one of Alice's suitors. Not that he was an unlikely candidate. Besides being from a prominent Cincinnati family, he was a Republican, as was Alice's father; he was a Harvard graduate and a member of Harvard's very exclusive Porcellian Club, as was her father. Longworth had also been moving quickly up the political ranks and seemed to have a promising future (eventually making him Speaker of the House). He was known in some circles to have a propensity to be a womanizer and to have a propensity to drink, but neither traits were necessarily political liabilities, and what seemed to make up for those or any other shortcomings was his virtuosity at the violin. Hearing him play, gentlemen removed their hats in awe; ladies swooned. In another day and age, he would have been a rock star.

In front of the Silver Horseshoe Building, a receiving committee comprised of world's fair officials and some of the well-known members of Beautiful Jim Key's entourage waited anxiously in the rising noonday heat until they finally spotted Miss Alice Roosevelt, on Longworth's arm, "comin' down the Pike," as the saying soon to be coined went. Among the greeting committee were Jim's two grooms, brothers Stanley and Sam Davis, both in their early twenties, from Shelbyville, Tennessee, where the Equine King had been born and bred. There was also the much-publicized Monk, the smallish, scruffy stray dog who had become Jim's self-appointed bodyguard and traveling companion. Then there was the celebrity horse's famous promoter, Albert R. Rogers, who stepped forward to greet the President's daughter and Congressman Longworth before ushering them through the archway into the packed auditorium.

Inside, as Rogers led Alice and Nicholas down to their front-row seats, the temperature and humidity had risen to summerlike highs in an auditorium packed well over its capacity. A noisy buzz of anticipation already running through the crowd was amplified with excited comments spurred by Miss Roosevelt's presence. Energy, heat, and the loud volume of voices conspired to become intolerable.

Then: a hush. On a stage that was set as part classroom and part business office, with a bizarre string of what looked like garlands of garlic but were actually five thousand rabbit's feet dangling above the stage, Dr. William Key seemed to materialize without an entrance. Standing quietly, he commanded an instantaneous silence. The program described him as mulatto, and in that mix his skin had the tint of a seasoned penny, with bloodlines of black, white, and Native American in his features. With his long white hair and beard in the style of General Custer, Doc Key was dressed in fashionable equestrian attire. He stood with the bearing of an aristocrat and took in the audience with a piercing intensity—all creating an aura of a tall, powerful man, even though his wiry frame was average to slight. Just as mesmerizing was his voice—soft and rich in texture, yet large and resonant enough to fill the hall. The voice of a horse whisperer. Like a cool breeze sweeping through the audience, its sound—pleasant, intelligent, kind, with tinges of both humor and authority—put everyone at ease, as if they'd forgotten the sticky spring weather.

Some reporters who interviewed William Key tended to depict his accent in the stereotypical Southern black dialect exaggerated by minstrel shows. But, in fact, aside from a Tennessee country cadence, Doc Key's articulate use of the English language was finely cultivated from years of public speaking. That may have surprised Princess Alice, though she, of all people, should have known better than to believe everything she read in the papers.

As he prepared the audience for Jim's entrance, Key must have felt kindly toward Alice Roosevelt, given his esteem for her father. Dr. Key's friends at some of the humane societies were not happy with the hunting enthusiast of a President, despite his much publicized 1902 refusal to shoot a bear cub on a hunting trip and despite the "Teddy bear" craze that followed and had yet to abate. The President had benefited from the ingenuity of a shopkeeper-turned-manufacturer named Morris Michton, who saw the news item as a marketing opportunity. His wife made the first prototype, which sold after five minutes in his front window, followed by a deluge of orders. Michton made a mint, and the stuffed toy bears would keep Teddy's namesake for posterity.

William Key had other reasons to see Roosevelt as a man of character. Three years before, Theodore Roosevelt had invited Booker T.

Washington to dinner and had become the first president in American history to meet with a Negro leader in the White House, making Washington the first African-American so honored. The historical gesture was meaningful not only because Dr. Key was a personal friend of Mr. Washington's; Bill Key also admired the President for doing what was only right because he recognized Roosevelt's courage in being willing to incur the political wrath of many Southern states. The vitriolic condemnations followed swiftly, including some southerners' blasts terming the dinner a "crime equal to treason," with newspapers proclaiming that no true son or daughter of the South be allowed to accept invitations to the White House.

The backlash had stung Alice too. The year before, when she visited New Orleans, public sentiment against her father prevented her from being invited to the Mardi Gras Ball. At the time and throughout her life, she remained an outspoken advocate for civil rights.

While Dr. Key was obviously pleased to have the President's daughter and her distinguished escort in seats of honor for the show, Beautiful Jim Key—upon his theatrical entrance—was apparently indifferent. He glanced not at the front private boxes, where dignitaries typically sat, but all the way to the back, like a politician letting the folks in the rear seats know he was one of them. A *down-to-earth* famous horse. Or perhaps it was his way of checking to make sure there were no empty seats. Doc Key had admitted to reporters that Jim performed better for larger crowds and actually turned in halfhearted efforts when the applause was not to his liking.

After finding this crowd to his liking, Beautiful Jim Key turned his head from side to side, showing his best profile—the left one and the right one—milking the moment.

The Arabian-Hambletonian mahogany bay, standing at sixteen hands high, bore the traits of his ancestors with distinction—from his sleek, sinewy lines to the grace with which he moved, to his curly black mane and long, ropey black tail that nearly touched the ground. With splashes of white here and there, in a star on his forehead, on a blaze down his nose, in a half stocking on a foreleg and one full stocking on a hind leg, he actually looked like the equine blue-blood Messenger—foundation sire to lineages both Thoroughbred and Standardbred, and Jim's great-great-great-great-grandsire. Much was often made of Jim's wide-set eyes—said to be a measure of intelligence, an Arabian trait—but it was his constantly moving, tapered ears that were most distinctive, as he listened to the roaring applause with the delight of a connoisseur, one ear actively wagging in order to catch every ripple of the sound waves that surrounded him.

Throughout Jim's opening demonstrations, expressions of incredulity fluttered through the crowd. Many were keeping a close watch on Dr. Key, trying to discover any secret signals that he might be sending Jim, even as all the questions came, in no order or prior planning, from audience members. Off to the side of the stage, Dr. Key had his back to Jim, both of his hands inert, one holding a riding crop as he prompted individuals in the crowd to stand and move into the spelling exercises by asking Beautiful Jim Key to spell their given names.

With each request, Jim trotted to a rack holding cards of all the letters of the alphabet, out of order, and selected letters, one by one, with his mouth, carrying them individually to an adjacent rack—like a long music stand—with a thin nickel rail that let him slide the cards into slots. The more ordinary names were easy for him: *"M-A-R-Y," "T-H-O-M-A-S," "G-E-O-R-G-E."*

"Can he spell Alice Roosevelt?" shouted a man in the back.

"Well, Jim?" asked Dr. Key.

With a bent shrug of his front legs, Jim Key bowed his head up and down. Kid's stuff. He'd been reading and spelling the President's name for the last three years. Then he curled back his lips, showing clenched teeth in the form of the grin he practiced when grabbing coins in his teeth. A gasp shot through the crowd. It was the famous Teddy Roosevelt grin.

Doc Key shook his head. Even he was amazed. "Grin, Jim"—he beamed proudly at his protégé—"grin!"

Alice bubbled with laughter. With a flirtatious flick of his tail, Jim looked at her out of the corner of his eye, and for a moment the two celebrities connected on a visceral level, sensing a shared history. Both Jim Key and Alice Roosevelt had lost mothers early in life, both had once been given up for crippled, causing Jim to almost die and Alice to spend her childhood in metal leg braces. With the knack that certain horses have for picking up on the energies of certain personalities, Jim zoned in on her survival skill, her scathing wit, and instinctually knew that his great reward would be if he could get her to laugh again. Dutifully he headed to the rack, drew each letter without hesitation and placed the cards quickly—*A-L-I-C-E*, then a space, *R-O-O-S-E-V-E-L . . .* but just before he placed the letter *T* into position, another voice from the crowd cried, "Nicholas Longworth!"

The wagging ear caught the word, and Jim, as though he understood and had planned the joke he was about to make, shrugged his forelegs once more, placed the *T,* and spelled out the congressman's last name, adding it to the same rack, making it read "Alice Roosevelt Longworth."

The crowd erupted into laughter and cheers, none more enthusiastically than the guest of honor and her escort. Skeptical reporters, on the constant lookout for chicanery, were momentarily stunned. Over the next week, however, pens scrawled and presses rolled as the incident went the rounds of the nation.

With all his intellectual talents, it appeared that Beautiful Jim Key was also prescient. Two years later, on February 17, 1906, in an elegant ceremony for one thousand in the East Room of the White House, Alice Roosevelt married Nicholas Longworth. The society pages covered the event from every angle, making much of the fact that it had been thirty-two years since a presidential daughter had married in the White House, the last being Nellie Grant. To make sure she didn't abide too much by convention, Alice made even more headlines when she insisted on borrowing a sword from one of her father's guards in order to cut the wedding cake.

I t took a horse with a sense of humor to convince a generation of its human responsibility to care for animals, proving our interconnectedness by demonstrating his capability of thoughts and feelings as complex as our own. Given the underlying prehistory, that seems fitting, because once before, six thousand years ago, when Beautiful Jim Key's ancestors stood on the brink of extinction, the human race—fulfilling our own quest for survival—had rescued and domesticated the equine species. In return, horses have existed to serve humankind, as our primary mode of transportation (up until the last hundred years), as beasts of burden in our work, as soldiers in our wars. The current equine population, an estimated sixty-five million horses around the world, serve now at our pleasure. For that pleasure, for their noble majesty, for their six thousand years of service, we owe them an everlasting debt.

Evolutionary theorists have said that horses defy all principles of adaptation that stem from the theory of the survival of the fittest. The species, they say, has not needed to become fitter but has remained almost unchanged throughout the millennia, as close to perfection as any species can be. They are magical, supernatural creatures by virtue of the fact that when, by all the force of the universe, they should have perished, somehow they didn't.

The same journey into life happened for a horse from Tennessee in the spring of 1889.

PART

ONE

of the

HISTORY

2

Inauspicious Beginnings

A number of years ago, amidst the Nesaen pastures of Persia, the great Sheik Ahemid, a powerful ruler . . . ruled in love and firmness. . . . For there was in his dowar . . . the fair Lauretta, with a lineage carefully kept on tablets of ivory that reached back to the broods of Pharaoh, comrades, friends of the tented tribes whom long association, love and kindness had nearly brought up to their own plane, and when to their animal instincts had been added wits and a reasoning sense, they feel and know all of ambition, love and hate.

—ALBERT R. ROGERS,
"Beautiful Jim Key: How He Was Educated," first edition, 1897

August 7, 1897. Nashville, Tennessee.
The train depot on the corner of Church and Walnut.

ALBERT ROGERS WAS LATE. He hoped his two new business partners, Dr. William Key and his uncanny horse Jim, wouldn't mind. Taking care of last-minute arrangements for their trip to New York and for the press party he was hosting a week later on Saturday, August 14, he had struck upon an idea he was sure could make their fortunes.

It was to be a pamphlet, a quality brochure, perhaps a short biography of the horse and a little on his enigmatic trainer. Since he had only a week to conduct interviews, write, and publish the booklet, Rogers had already made notes for the preface, asking in writing: "How was Jim Key taught? How did his teacher, Dr. Key, come to notice the extra intelligence this horse possessed? What breed is he?

And a dozen similar questions are asked so often, that the writer has tried to give in the following pages, the answers to them all."

The moment he began the interview process, en route to New York, he seized on the romantic story of Jim Key's parentage, which was exactly what he needed to facilitate the horse's entrée into high society. That was, in part, what he had said he could help make happen when he convinced Dr. Key to let him be their promoter.

At age eight, Jim was not yet a star. Even though he was a veteran performer of medicine shows and county fairs, he had only just that summer made his debut as an "educated" horse at the Tennessee Centennial Exposition, basically as a novelty attraction within a larger exhibit. Rogers had discovered him there, only days before the three embarked on this train ride and grand experiment to make kindness to animals a household ideal. With no small effort, he had managed to persuade Doc Key not only that Jim was ready for the big time but also that he, Albert R. Rogers, was the man who could get him there.

At the train depot, William Key had been unruffled by Albert's tardiness and instead went about reassuring Jim—who wasn't the least bit fond of train rides, especially long ones—that the adventure ahead would be well worth the trouble. Moving with the energy and gait of a man much younger than his sixty-four years, the Doc proceeded next to lead Jim toward the foot of the ramp to the Nashville, Chattanooga & St. Louis Railways private boxcar that Rogers had secured for him.

Now reassuring the Doc that he would be just fine, Jim wore an expression that would become familiar in the press, his nostrils flaring with an aristocratic sniff of disdain—as if bored already with the fuss. Then Jim Key flashed a toothy, aw-shucks grin that, with a knowing twinkle in his eye, made him look like a country boy punch-drunk on his good luck to have been marked by stardom.

In moments, eighteen-year-old Stanley Davis, Jim's valet and groom, appeared on the platform, having stowed the steamer trunks and large crates that held the props used in their demonstrations. Like Jim and Doc Key, Stanley—the younger brother of Lucinda Davis Key, the Doctor's third wife, recently deceased, as well as being the younger brother of Maggie Davis (later to become William Key's fourth wife)—had been born and raised in Shelbyville, the seat of Bedford County in the heart of Middle Tennessee that was about sixty miles south of Nashville. Unlike Jim and the Doc, Stanley had never been out of state, and he was having a hard time concealing his excitement and his nervousness. Dr. Key had arranged for Albert Rogers to hire Stanley for their trip up north not because of their family ties but because his brother-in-law would be an asset in their work. Stanley was likeable and good-looking—with his warm, curious countenance, cream-and-coffee coloring, and thick, shiny black hair—all pluses when it came to dealing with the public. He also happened to have a gift for tending horses and other animals, traits that showed he had the makings of a first-rate veterinarian. While Bill Key had received no formal veterinary training, he was determined that Stanley attend veterinary college and become licensed as soon as their traveling days with Jim were over. It is doubtful that either knew how long those days were to be.

In contrast, Albert Rogers—hurrying through the torrents of travelers onto the overcrowded platform, waving an apology and a greeting to Dr. Key—may have had a keener sense of the distance they were about to go. Only a man of such convictions could have persuaded Key to enter into a partnership in the first place.

Bill Key no doubt had misgivings about throwing in his lot with a fellow he had just met. But there was something about A. R. Rogers he liked, something about the intensity of the man thirty years his junior that he found refreshing. The redheaded, bearded, stylishly coiffed and attired Rogers may have come from a world of privilege, but there was about his soulful, saucerlike eyes the look of a man who longed for more than the comfort and status of wealth. Key sensed that Rogers fancied himself as a showman in the mold of P. T. Barnum who, though he had died in 1891, still hovered as the most dominant force in American entertainment. But for some reason, maybe because Rogers was self-conscious in front of crowds, or because he lacked the requisite skills to be a performer himself, he had opted for the role of a behind-the-scenes impresario—destined to live out his dreams vicariously.

There was something else. Rogers had prominent ears. They were not the small, pinned-back type that horses interpreted as a threat or posture of anger in their own species. That may or may not have had anything to do with why Jim had taken to Albert Rogers right away, but Doc Key saw that Jim's instincts were to trust the stranger.

For as much as Bill and Jim were able to intuit about Rogers, their new promoter was still mystified by them. And that was a problem he hoped his interview for this promotional pamphlet might address. He had to come up with a way to entice the leadership from New York's prestigious ASPCA to attend his private press party, and a way to overcome the question he anticipated hearing—*just who is this "Dr." William Key?*

That was why, when he heard the tale of Bill Key's pure Arabian, Lauretta "Queen of Horses," he pounced on it and decided to make it the centerpiece of his publicity push. Was it true? Doc Key insisted it was. Then again, he quickly learned that Key was an artful storyteller, an occultist, a die-hard capitalist, a voracious reader (with interests that included the Bible, veterinary medicine, politics, the history and struggle of African-Americans, and strange news items dealing with outer space), and was, in Bill Key's own estimation, the best poker player south of the Mason-Dixon.

Rogers had to have known that promoting the story as fact, if it was fabricated, could undermine Jim's credibility. On the other hand, Albert Rogers was a romantic—a man born to wealth who didn't need to cavort with the masses but who sought on many levels to be one of them—and he chose to believe Doc Key's account mainly because it moved him. What was clearly evident in the telling was that Key, the son of a slave woman and a white father he never identified, had in the spring of 1889 anticipated the birth of his Arabian's foal as if he was awaiting a Second Coming.

Doc Key by that year was already fifty-six years old and recently wed to Lucinda Davis, the third of what would be four wives, with no children of his own. He had presided over hundreds of foalings, several from mares and stallions he owned. But this colt or filly was going to be something more special than any of them, having, after all, the finest pedigree in the nation. All the omens that spring were favorable.

William Key set stock in signs. Key explained to Rogers that black folk called it "mother wit," a kind of earthy second sight, an inherited knowingness. His ability to observe and interpret signs had helped him survive terrible times and prosper, allowing him to heal animals and humans, figuring out their ailments and devising homemade remedies that cured about anything. Despite the fact that he was self-taught, by the early 1880s his renown as a medical practitioner and expert in animal sciences had well earned him the appellation of "doctor."

His success came also because he understood the laws of supply and demand, and many times throughout his life he had faced down death by letting it be known that he had the ability to fix whatever demanded fixing. Cavalry horses shot or maimed, wild colts in need of taming, mules gone lame, milk cows turned dry, hens refusing to lay, wagon wheels to repair, saddles and harnesses to be restored. He had remedies for other human wants and needs: his own country cooking, rooms to rent, a hand of cards, and races to wager on.

Though Rogers obviously recognized that Key was an unusual man, he couldn't yet have known the extent of his success—that the kindly Doctor had created something of a small kingdom for himself, at various points owning and operating a veterinary hospital, a hotel, a restaurant, a blacksmith and wagon wheel shop, and his own racetrack. But Key couldn't restrain his pride in admitting that one of the different businesses that occupied him had boomed. "I had a liniment which I called 'Keystone Liniment,'" he told Rogers, almost casually, "and everybody wanted it, so that started me in the medicine business. I used to travel around the country with a minstrel band to attract a crowd, and then sell my medicine."

Rogers saw the approach as further evidence of Key's ingenuity. In this heyday of the patent medicine era, the highways and byways of much of the country were littered with all classes of medicine men selling their miraculous concoctions that promised everything from a cure for the common cold to life everlasting—boasting ingredients that came anywhere from the salt of the Dead Sea to the planet Mars. There were the usual scoundrels selling snake oil and the big-budget productions pushing famous labels like Kickapoo (products sold in elaborate Indian medicine shows starring Kickapoo tribal members, including a salve and a sagwa, or tonic, the precursor to the Joy Juice cola that had future comic book fame) and Carter's Little Liver Pills. But every now and then a product with actual therapeutic properties came along. One of them was Keystone Liniment, used internally and externally, for such horse and mule afflictions as joint spasms, cuts, splints, swelling, cholera, saddle sore, lameness, bots, colic, and their various corresponding human maladies. Breaking into the exclusive ranks of top-selling patent medicines, however, required not only a credible medical expert, but also a brilliant pitchman, as well as a riveting form of entertainment to draw an audience.

Cutting down on expenses, Doc Key did most of that himself, playing three roles: formulator, pitchman, and medical expert. Since he traveled with a group of black minstrels (typically banjo, bones, mouth organ, and sometimes fiddle), he had the advantage of employing friends and relatives, and he benefited because crowds were starting to prefer authentic Negro music to the minstrel tunes borrowed by whites in blackface.

Whatever his secret was, with repeat business and word of mouth, Key hit a gold mine, which kept him busy filling mail orders when he wasn't on the road. Keystone Liniment may not have been as big a name as Jack Daniel's—which was distilled and bottled in Lynchburg, Tennessee, not far from Shelbyville—but the low cost of production and the high demand made it hugely profitable. Just how profitable, Rogers wouldn't know until later, when he was shocked to learn that Bill Key was worth more than $100,000 (a multimillionaire by twenty-first-century standards). And that was *before* he went into the practice of teaching horses to spell.

Rogers made the initial decision to make little mention of Key's wealth in his publicity materials, choosing instead to promote Jim's costar by focusing on the less threatening image of a kindly, older, colored country doctor—the Uncle Tom figure from page and stage who was more popular than ever as the turn of the century approached. Initially, Dr. William Key went along with the portrayal, just in time for the New York press to be charmed by "Uncle" Bill's quaint colored country expressions.

Despite its patronizing ring (more pronounced in later generations), calling a man or woman of color "Uncle" or "Aunt" was long assumed by Southern whites to be a term of affection and familiarity. Then again, Doc Key would have agreed with the delegates to the 1865 State Convention of the Colored People of Tennessee when they complained about the demeaning ways that both former slaves and freeborn were addressed. One of the more famous complaints arose when a delegate had been asked by a white man who passed him on the street, "Well, Uncle, how are you getting along?" The delegate feigned surprise: "I was glad to know that I had a white nephew."

At the same time, as a poker player Doc Key knew it could be advantageous to presume upon the prejudices of others, in other words, not to show one's hand. This had been his secret, he told Rogers, in finding and buying the Arabian mare.

Around 1885, after getting a healthy start in the medicine business, Key and his group were out on the road when they met a man who knew of a circus that had become stranded near Tupelo, Mississippi. In order to raise money to get home, the circus owners were selling out, including their stock of horses.

The Doc was mighty interested, he recalled, but not sure if the risk of heading down that way, either alone or with his minstrels, would be worth it.

Risk? Rogers didn't yet understand the kind of peril that such a trip might entail for a black person, although over the years that he and Key worked together, Rogers came to witness many indignities of the color bar that his partner faced—from the different train compartments they were sometimes forced to occupy, to the hotels that prohibited Key from entering, to the rules of theatres and concert halls that permitted the Doc to perform onstage but which only allowed Negroes as audience members on certain days or in certain sections. Rogers hurt for the injustices, and later devised ingenious ways to break down some of the barriers. But no matter how much he sympathized, he couldn't change the color of his skin, and it would have been hard to relate to all the considerations Key must have had while traveling among the many worlds he inhabited.

Rerouting to Tupelo to inspect what was left of a small circus was not only inconvenient but it was, after all, Mississippi. There, as in other areas of the South (including pockets in Tennessee), in the 1880s lynchings were on the rise. The tide of justice that had helped Lincoln to free the slaves and had moved toward full and equal rights had turned back. Not only was the federal government unable to stop vigilantes and lynch mobs and the spread of groups like the Ku Klux Klan, but now there was also a trend moving south and north toward institutionalizing racism.

Doc Key's survival instincts warned him not to travel unfamiliar roads into Mississippi. Then again, he smelled a good deal—something he could rarely pass up—so he proceeded on down to Tupelo cautiously, keeping his troupe nearby but not with him, as he made sure he didn't arrive looking too much like a duded-up somebody. He went ready to play poker, prepared to look and sound as raggedy and illiterate as he could pull off.

When he came along the rutted road outside the stables where the sale was taking place, Key recalled to Rogers, he was struck by the sight of a gray mare standing in the field, like a sculpted though weathered marble statue, as if she'd been waiting for him for a long, long time. He read the signs: she was probably younger than she looked, underfed, badly abused. But despite the injuries that slowed her down, as she cantered curiously alongside his carriage with a fluidity that conjured images of desert sands, he could have begun to guess that the gray mare was a true Arabian and that she must have once been extraordinary.

Bill Key didn't elaborate to Rogers as to what kind of ruse he used with the owners of the circus, except to say that he first picked out a string of other horses to buy, before asking if the gray mare was for sale. Masking their amusement, the sellers brought her into the stables so he could have a closer look.

Since the time of the Prophet Mohammed, the laws of Islam restricted the sale of prized horses, so most pure Arabians in Europe or America were considered either stolen, illegally sold, or the descendants of either. Females were called Daughters of the Wind, because of their exceptional speed. Arabians were the progenitors of the English Thoroughbreds, horses originally bred primarily for racing. But Arabian blood was valued for other traits of equal or greater importance than speed: intelligence and a familial connection to human beings, even what some called a humanlike morality.

Arabians had another telltale trait that Doc Key easily spotted —jet-black skin showing through underneath a thinning iron gray coat, a genetic gift of equine sunscreen. The other signs were there—the wise eyes low and widely spaced, their color deep and dark, the small perky ears that pointed inward, and the distinctive shape of the head, tapered, with a prominent brow, chiseled cheekbones, flat nostrils—natural traits without embellishment said to make the Arabian an essential drinker of air, a breathing machine destined for speed.

These were the features of the gray mare inspected by Doc Key. Because of what he judged to have been years of mistreatment, she appeared to be in her midtwenties, not long from death. Once Key got a look at her teeth, however, pretending to be an amateur, he saw she was probably ten or twelve years younger.

Bill Key offered forty dollars for the old mare, a price high enough for the sellers not to bother hiding their laughter. But once Key and his troupe had finished hitching up the horses, Lauretta among them, and were back on the road to Tennessee, they were the ones having the bigger laugh. For forty dollars, Doc Key had just bought a horse that had once fetched $50,000.

L auretta's history, compiled by Rogers and Key, centered on a shady figure by the name of Jack Randall, a light-haired, blue-eyed Englishman, known to have traveled to Persia in the late 1870s, who arrived in the many-tented domain of the powerful Sheik Ahemid, bearing a gift of holy Arabic tablets of unknown origin. The charming Randall was welcomed by the sheik and treated roy-ally to a series of nightly feasts, earning the trust and generosity of his host through his flattering "tongue of oil." The sheik—his guard down—soon began to boast about his four priceless horses, the Kingly Four. There were three stallions, Philis, Ectes, and Ranus, and a mare, Lauretta.

Sheik Ahemid told the Englishman of their illustrious history, how they were the four remaining descendants of the horses who had lived in the time of the great pharaohs, that their names were inscribed on ivory tablets, and that none was more prized than she, Lauretta Queen of Horses.

Key and Rogers knew well that Arabian mares were valued over the stallions—indeed, that Prophet Mohammed had decreed, "Give the preference to mares; their belly is a treasure and their back a seat of honor." As the Islamic saying had it, "The greatest blessing is an intelligent woman, or a prolific mare." The superior ride and comfort of the female Arabian was so seductive, some even said the ease of her gait could render her rider effeminate.

Jack Randall, according to the Key/Rogers account, told Ahemid that he worked for a great sheik in far-off England, whose name was P. T. Barnum, that he had enormous power and wealth, and would pay an unprecedented price to purchase Lauretta—her weight in gold and one thousand horses.

"Sell Lauretta, my Queen? Sell the Mother of all Horses, to whom a million Allahs are said?" the sheik allegedly thundered. He would first pluck out his own eyes. So enraged was Ahemid that he ended the feast and sent the Englishman back to his tent, still not suspecting what the stranger might do.

In a frothy, almost cinematic piece of prose, Rogers and Key described Randall's daring predawn theft of the mare, detailing how he stole from his tent, gliding into the semidarkness under a starlit sky, creeping past the sleeping guards into the tent of the Kingly Four. "'Twas a moment that made his hair turn gray, but there at the very place stood Lauretta, her trappings on a post near her. No hesitation now; 'twas a lifetime in the minute it took to sling a bridle on her noble head and lead her out. Cautiously, with silent tread, in the sand he led her, and then bounding on her back glided as if she had wings, out in the desert."

Once the theft was discovered, Ahemid and hundreds of horsemen gave chase into the desert, but the shifting sands, blown by the wind, had hidden Lauretta's tracks.

While the sheik was reportedly overwhelmed by anger and grief, the whole of Arabia was outraged, and suspicion soon turned against him. The sheik's boasting was at fault, said some. Others believed he had secretly sold her to Jack Randall for some portion of the $50,000 that P. T. Barnum was said to have paid for her.

A short time later, when a gray Arabian began to appear as a main attraction in Barnum's European shows, the semifictionalized controversy turned into a real-life scandal. In the British Parliament, a lord lamented to the London press over the exploitation of the horse that was "drawing such crowds at the circus because she was known as the Queen of Arabian Horses, causing no end of annoyance by the fanatics of Arabia . . . all because of one gray mare." He called it tragic that Lauretta, the once proud queen of the desert, was now the "slave of a circus owner, though the greatest in the land, to be exhibited to the tens of thousands of the curious."

Key figured that the worst of her mistreatment began once the controversy died down and the crowds stopped caring about the stolen, royal horse. No longer a spectacle of intrigue, Lauretta was sold to a lesser circus, brought to America, and taught the typical circus tricks, through the typical means that were all too familiar to Doc Key. Some methods were violent, others more insidious like the common practice (considered less extreme) of using pins and sharp tacks, pricking the horse's head to teach her to nod yes, pricking her shoulder to teach her to nod no, pricking her leg so many times to get her to kick the dirt to tell her age, later using the whip to remind her of the pinpricks, then eventually using signals to remind her of the lashes.

Doc Key calculated she had been with at least three circuses before he found her in Tupelo, and he believed that besides the cruelty of her training she had also been broken down by neglect. Even though Key was well known in Tennessee and in other Southern states for his skill in rehabilitating sick horses, almost no one had any hope for anything more than a minor, superficial improvement for Lauretta.

Using his own cures, Dr. Key tended to her continuously, spending hours every day rubbing her down with his homemade liniments, feeding her his remedies, talking gently and kindly to her. After almost a year, she revived. She was as beautiful as he could have imagined she once was, though she would never again be as strong as was her heritage to be. But her spirit was back.

Because Lauretta had become so attached to the Doc, he couldn't bring himself to leave her at home when he was traveling and began to use her case in his medicine shows as proof of the healing properties of Keystone Liniment. Before long, he told Rogers, she showed an interest in performing and started to do some of her circus tricks to entertain the crowds. But instead of being pricked and whipped, she was rewarded with apples and sugar. Bill Key explained to Albert Rogers, "The whip makes horses stubborn and they obey through fear and they can't be trusted. Kindness, kindness, and more kindness, that's the way."

Rogers was curious. What about horses who weren't naturally of a superior intelligence?

The Doc said, "Give me any horse of average intelligence and I will train him."

Did that mean he could also teach any horse of average intelligence to read, spell, and solve mathematical problems?

Much to Rogers's surprise, Doc Key asserted that with patience and kindness, he could. He added, "I would rather have him four years old, providing he had not been abused. It is like teaching a blind child to read. You have got to find out where the power is and cultivate the senses."

Key had not advanced to teaching human academic subjects to Lauretta, but in recalling her with profound affection, he told Rogers, "She was the smartest horse I had ever seen."

William Key shared the view that when an Arabian mare had proven herself to have superior strength, courage, and humanlike understanding, it was in her very nature to pass on those exceptional traits to her offspring. For this reason, despite her age and her earlier injuries, he was absolutely intent on breeding her, certain that under his care she could be the dam of a true champion. And so, like any protective, doting father, he set out to find just the right match for her. Only the finest bred horse in America would do.

* * *

"All men are equal on the turf and under it" was a saying whose meaning would not have been lost on William Key. As a metaphor that had wound its way through time and place, it described the gamut of fortunes found and lost at the racetrack, and the diversity among kings and commoners whose passions have shaped the sport of horseracing and the breeding of champion horses.

Doc Key was also aware that in a geological fluke of equality, the actual turf of Kentucky's inner bluegrass region—with its calcium-enriched, limestone-laden soil responsible for the blue hue of the grass eaten by grazing horses whose bones became stronger and more resilient in the process—recurred almost identically some three hundred miles south in Middle Tennessee's central basin. These two veins of prime horse country in both states likewise shared the same gentle, rolling hills, a forgiving landscape that resulted from the millennia of limestone erosion. Breeders believed this kind of topography to be more conducive for exercising young equine athletes than rockier, steeper terrain. Some even observed that the gentle, rolling gait of horses raised in the two localities had developed naturally in response to the rise and fall of the earth beneath their hooves, much like the lilting Southern accents of the two regions, which contrasted with the roller-coaster accents of their mountain neighbors, or with the heavy, imperious tones of the deeper South.

Bill Key's backyard of Bedford County boasted other natural advantages for bringing up horses, claiming its own network of rivers and creeks that curled in and around the farmland, flowing down from higher rims, feeding the soil and making the pastures that much more lush. In a whim of nature's overachievement, the earth surrounding Shelbyville was doubly blessed by not one but two varieties of limestone—the white rock variety and that of sandstone, also known as fire rock. This combination, which provided such an ideal foundation for raising horses, also gave Doc Key the natural ingredients he used in making his horse and human liniment, a formula he kept secret but whose name, Key*stone*, hinted at its essence—pulverized bedrock. Mixed with oil, it could be absorbed by tissues; diluted by water, it made a tonic for drinking or a tincture to be applied to wounds.

Kentucky sires still had leading status, but rather than having to travel there to find a promising match for Lauretta, Doc Key felt he had plenty of options in his home state. From early on, after Andrew Jackson founded Nashville's Clover Bottom racetrack and spent many fortunes importing the best breeders, trainers, and jockeys to Tennessee, the Volunteer State had been recognized for promoting superiority of equine bloodlines, a fact acknowledged in the 1830s by Kentucky breeder Lewis Sanders, who went so far as to say that Tennessee had more and better blood than his own state.

Famous horses who bore that out were legends such as the acclaimed broodmare Madame Tonson, her son Monsieur Tonson, who became the top American stallion in 1834, Tennessee Oscar (who never lost a race and never paid a forfeit, said to have never been pushed to top speed by any competitor, having, in his second start, walked over), prolific sires Leviathan and Glencoe—whose lineages both ran to Petyona, the top money winner of the pre–Civil War era. Then there were champions being turned out with regularity at Belle Meade Plantation in Nashville, which by the 1880s had steadily acquired a position as the leading stud farm in Tennessee. The philosophy employed at Belle Meade, under the stewardship of head hostler Robert Green, also a former slave and revered horseman, was that winning bloodlines were more productive than the overuse of horses who had themselves been exhausted at the track.

Such thinking made Belle Meade the home of Iroquois, the first American-bred stallion to win the English Derby, and brought nineteen-year-old English import Bonnie Scotland to Tennessee, where he spent the next eight years fathering formidable racehorses, none more famous than Luke Blackburn. Known as the most muscular horse ever seen on American turf, so powerful that jockeys complained they couldn't walk after trying to hold him back, Luke Blackburn spent his season at age three by winning twenty-two of twenty-four starts.

Luke Blackburn had recently begun his stud career at Belle Meade just at the time that Dr. Key went out to find Lauretta's ideal mate. As a Thoroughbred, Luke Blackburn had bloodlines that couldn't have been more ideal. Not only was he a son of Bonnie Scotland, his dam was Nevada, sired by Lexington—the horse considered the leading American sire of the century. A mating between Lauretta and Luke Blackburn would have been easy to arrange, especially because Bill Key was a friend and contemporary of "Uncle" Bob Green at Belle Meade.

Convenient though that might have been, William Key wasn't looking for a Thoroughbred. The Doc had turned his attention to the Standardbred turf heroes, the trotters and pacers of harness racing who had, for the time being, surpassed Thoroughbred stars in terms of popularity and prestige. Traditional running races were regarded by increasingly sophisticated crowds as too primitive or lacking the skill that the demands of trotting and pacing required. Moreover, with scandals and infighting between turf owners and lawmakers plaguing the Thoroughbred racing world, some of the more famous running racetracks had changed to become Standardbred courses.

The Standard, a record of two minutes and thirty seconds (2:30) or better for a time trial of trotting a mile (with the proviso that "a record to wagon of 2:35 or better shall be regarded as equal to a 2:30 record"), was declared and published in 1879 as an admission to registration in the National Association of Trotting-Horse Breeders (later changed to the United States Trotters Association). The Standard for pacers required a mile to be paced in 2:25 or under.

Elements of harness racing had been in existence for thousands of years. The trotting gait had been described as early as four centuries B.C. by the Greek military officer Xenophon, a visionary horse gentler in the mode of Dr. William Key. He described the trotting gait as distinct from the walk and the gallop in its unbroken pattern, by which the front left leg moves at the same time as the right hind leg, the two strides alternating diagonally. In pacing, also recognized by the Greeks, the elegant, faster lateral gait required the horse to move his right front leg at the same time as his right hind leg, distinguished by a gliding side-to-side motion.

When William Key decided to establish Keystone Driving Park, a half-mile harness racing course on Key's Lane, just off the heavily traveled Shelbyville and Murfreesboro Turnpike, not far from his veterinary hospital, he may have been influenced in his choice by John H. Wallace. The editor of *Wallace's Monthly*—published between 1875 and 1893—Wallace wrote about a range of turf topics, promoting the prestige of Standardbred racing, and created *Wallace's Year Book*, a Standardbred registry.

Doc Key had an audacious plan up his sleeve. Instead of scouring the country for just the right pedigreed trotter or pacer to sire Lauretta's colt or filly, he imagined that he could use Keystone Driving Park to lure some promising Standardbred blood to his neck of the woods. The line he was most interested in was the Hambletonian. At the time, the Hambletonian was a relatively new breed, later viewed as progenitor of almost 99 percent of latter-day harness racers, the very cornerstone of the Standardbred. But in 1887 when William Key opened his track, what interested him most was the Hambletonian story. It was a saga of an American original who had sprung from modest means to become practically the most fashionable horse of the day. A truly modern horse.

Rogers, a marketing man, knew only that the Hambletonian was an elite name, but he had to be reminded by Dr. Key that the story centered on the faith and foresight of an elderly stable hand named William Rysdyk up in Sugar Loaf, New York, who tended to the birth of an unpromising foal born to the aging, injured dam known as the Charles Kent Mare (of Norfolk Trotter descent) after she had been bred to a questionable stallion named Abdallah.

Reputed to be ugly and mean, Abdallah was redeemed by the fact that he was the grandson of Messenger, one of the most illustrious horses in breeding history. An imported English Thoroughbred, Messenger had sprung from the bloodline of the Darley Arabian, a stallion brought to the British Isles in the early 1700s that went on to be seen as one of the most influential progenitors of English Thoroughbreds. In an uncanny similarity to William Key's account of the theft of Lauretta from Arabia, the history of the Darley Arabian had it that Thomas Darley may have stolen the impressive stallion from a Bedouin sheik in Syria. Through the importation of Messenger in 1788, the Darley Arabian's blood came to the American shores, where, instead of furthering the English Thoroughbred line, a new breed emerged. After the spring of 1801, during which Messenger stood at service in the stables of Anthony Dobbin's Stagecoach Inn of Goshen, New York, a batch of foals began to exhibit a similarly distinctive gait, described as a slinging walk that when sped up produced a masterly trotting gait. After a few more generations were foaled, Messenger and his progeny had brought renown to Goshen as the Cradle of the Trotter. The Standardbred line had been born.

Even with Abdallah's pedigree, when the Charles Kent Mare gave birth to her foal in 1849, his owner didn't see enough to like about him and accepted old Rysdyk's offer to purchase the dam and her colt for $125. Registered as Hambletonian (10)—registries like Wallace's typically assigned numbers to resolve confusion over names being reused for often unrelated horses—the ugly duckling of a colt began to transform under the care given him at Rysdyk's stable in Chester, New York, near Goshen. With a muscular behind pitched higher than his shoulders (later dubbed a "trotting pitch"), the dashing mahogany bay had the ideal anatomy for racing under harness. At age two, before he had even proven himself on the turf, Hambletonian began his stud career, covering four mares. When he went on to win decisively in a series of blistering match races and time trials, Rysdyk's Hambletonian, as he was also known, trotted his way into celebrity status. He more than lived up to his reputation as a sire of speed, raising his stud fee to as high as $500 and repaying his devoted owner's investment many times over. By the time of Hambletonian's death at age twenty-seven in 1876, he had sired a trotting dynasty that began with an astounding 1,331 foals. Among his immediate offspring, four sons in particular—George Wilkes, Dictator, Happy Medium, and Electioneer—furthered the Hambletonian lineage to such an extent that it came to obscure other trotting bloodlines in future Standardbred stock.

Was it audacious in 1887 for William Key to believe that his own aging, injured Arabian mare could be bred to a blue-blooded

Hambletonian, perhaps for his own crossbred foal to launch a new equine dynasty? To many it was the height of audacity. But from what Albert Rogers was learning about Key early on, that wasn't going to stop him.

The morning of Saturday, June 18, 1887, had dawned in Shelbyville like most Middle Tennessee mornings that follow the weeks of spring rains—humid, sunny, and abrasively hot in the season's run-up to summer. These were the kind of weekend days when everyone tended to slow down and take life a little easier, to tend, when possible, to avoid the everyday annoyances and excitements. But weather notwithstanding, an unavoidable atmosphere of excitement percolated throughout the homes of many leading citizens of Shelbyville, Bell Buckle, Wartrace, Flat Creek, and other satellite villages of the area.

The day promised to be one in an ongoing series of Saturday-morning races at Keystone Driving Park out on Key's Lane, open to the public, with a specially invited cadre of Bedford County officials and business leaders. Having served as grand marshal for the livestock divisions for various county fairs, Dr. William Key had set out to create the same festive atmosphere at his own racetrack, hoping to attract owners of well-bred horses from around the county.

By midmorning a large, eager crowd, including a young reporter from the *Shelbyville Gazette,* had gathered in time for the exercises to be opened with a dramatic pacing race, in which even Shelbyville mayor W. G. Hight had entered one of his best pacers but lost to a plucky bay owned by businessman Sam Thompson of Flat Creek. The friendly competition didn't raise blood pressure too badly, but the next few races did, especially the highlight of the morning, a harness race between Mr. T. C. Buchanan's trotter, Muggins, and Keystone, the favorite, a handsome trotter belonging to Mrs. Sally Whiteside, whom she apparently named for Dr. Key. The two contenders, "both fine ones and fast steppers," noted the *Gazette* article, got off to an explosive start. The crowd immediately went silent, everyone holding their breath as they watched each trotter maintain an impressively fast pace, holding neck and neck for the first half mile. On the second half mile, the spectators exhaled collectively as Muggins faltered down the stretch, and amid chaotic applause, the spirited contest was won by Keystone.

Doc Key didn't spot the Hambletonian he was looking for that Saturday, but he was encouraged by the democratic scene of his own making. It was an uncommon mix of class and race, a grouping of former slave owners and former slaves, former Confederate soldiers and former Union soldiers, and just as complicated an assortment of current political opposites. But the old and deep wounds that remained were not in evidence that Saturday, and no one seemed to think it surprising that an ex-slave was the owner of so impressive a driving park and so comfortable a house cloistered under the trees beyond the track. There was no mention of color in the *Gazette*'s lengthy coverage of the event, although it was clear that the reporter was awestruck when Dr. Key invited him up to his house, where "a bountiful repast of substantials had been prepared under the shade of the trees and proceeded at once to refresh the inner man."

By midday, the sun's rays had become oppressive, and the crowd, visibly pleased with the morning's entertainment, quickly dispersed. Among the last to leave was the reporter, who profusely hailed Dr. Key as extremely courteous and attentive to the wants of all his guests.

When the article ran five days later, it ended with an added note from the paper's editors, acknowledging William Key: "The doctor is doing everything he can to bring the stock of our county to the front and we are glad to learn that he is meeting with much success. We are glad to chronicle these friendly meetings as they all tend towards the development and improvement of Bedford County's horse flesh."

In later years when the history of the origin of the Tennessee Walking Horse would be tied to Bedford County and to this particular time period toward the end of the nineteenth century, Dr. William Key's early contribution, which the *Gazette* had then described, would have been forgotten.

But what he did get for his efforts was exactly what he was looking for: the perfect match for Lauretta. The stallion, auspiciously named Tennessee Volunteer, was a great-grandson of Rysdyk's Hambletonian. In the spring of 1888, Doc Key took Lauretta Queen of

Horses the ten miles to the Bell Buckle livery stable—where Tennessee Volunteer was said to be standing at stud for the season—so she could have a look at her prospective beau.

Though Tennessee Volunteer's track record didn't show up in Wallace's registry, Bill Key assured Albert Rogers he had seen the Hambletonian race.

How fast was he? Rogers wanted to know.

"Well," said Key, putting it simply, "he couldn't be beat."

But it was Tennessee Volunteer's pedigree that really interested Key. Early in the prolific career of Hambletonian (10), he had sired the excellent trotter Volunteer (55)—who held a pre-Standard record of 2:37 while hitched to a wagon. In turn Volunteer sired Kentucky Volunteer (2784), foaled in 1874 and bred by a John S. Briggs of Cincinnati, Ohio. Kentucky Volunteer went on to sire Tennessee Volunteer, ownership unknown.

Even though Albert Rogers grew up in Cincinnati and may have been acquainted with the Briggs family, upon hearing this history he became fixated on the idea that Jim Key was "bred in Old Kentucky." Not so. The confusion about the Ohio-bred Kentucky Volunteer was that he took his name partly from his dam, Kentucky Girl. She too was not necessarily Kentucky bred, although, along with her sire, Blue Bull, she did come from a winning bloodline noted for fast pacers and may have won races there.

Rogers and Key missed the irony of the fact that Jim Key was most likely conceived in Bell Buckle, a burgeoning academic enclave set in the wooded rolling hills and a place so picturesque and serene it had been chosen in 1870 by William R. Webb for the location of a boys' private college preparatory boarding school. Old Sawney, as Webb was known, believed that by fostering character as well as a devotion to learning, Webb School's students would go on to excel at higher levels of education and in life. His philosophy would be borne out, making Webb School, later a coeducational institution, the most prestigious college preparatory high school in the South, producing over the decades to come an impressive ten Rhodes Scholars and three governors of different states, including three-term Tennessee governor Prentice Cooper, a native of Shelbyville. Old Sawney's presence would linger long past his life, forever freezing the look and feel of the town in the time of the 1880s—when Webb's original classroom building was built.

If Doc Key had been paying attention to the signs, he might have interpreted the significance of Jim's conception in Bell Buckle as an indication that Jim was destined to become a horse of higher learning.

But for once, the Doc misread the signs. At least that was his conclusion for nearly a year following the birth of Lauretta's foal.

May 1889, foaling time in Bedford County, was marked by the kind of raucous explosion of nature that the season was known for: the air, warm, thick and wet, pungent with the smell of regeneration, its moistness a match for the black rich earth long fed by the Duck River, which had lured the early settlers of Shelbyville to its banks.

The profusion of color and fragrance, everything growing and living and being born, in so extravagant a manner as to be downright dizzying, conspired to create signs that could have seemed to the expectant doctor like a welcome celebration for the foal.

"Knowing he was the finest bred horse in the country, I was very anxious to see what he would turn out," Doc Key told Rogers, recalling his ambitious visions of owning a famous, noble racehorse. "I had some very fine Bible names picked out for him."

And why not? Rogers was shocked to hear the Doc say that the foal he had planned to name for a revered prophet or disciple "pretty damn near broke my heart."

The foaling apparently proceeded normally, starting with the incomparable, overpowering smell of equine amniotic fluid, which summoned the Doc and his stable hands to Lauretta's stall at night—often a dam's instinctual time for avoiding predators by giving birth under the blanket of darkness. Lauretta frantically paced, then lay down, her whinnying crescendoing with the night-splitting universal cry of a female in hard labor while Key coaxed her with his indecipherable, whispered words—a self-created language based on the practices of his African and Cherokee ancestors. As the foal emerged in its white sack, he was there to help the weakened Lauretta by tenderly clearing the white cloak off the foal.

In answer to his prayers, he at first rejoiced in seeing that the foal was a male. As close to a son of his own as he would have in this life.

But as he continued to examine the colt, Bill Key saw that he was as misshapen and bony as any sickly foal could be.

Neither Lauretta nor the foal improved over the next twenty-four hours. The dam, in fact, was to deteriorate dramatically over the next eight months, the ordeal of procreation having depleted whatever reserve of health Doc Key had helped her regain before breeding her. From the beginning of the colt's life, it was obvious that his dam's ability to care for him and guide him into his journey as a young equine was to be impaired. His first efforts to stand and walk were not unlike most foals'—with bent, splayed legs teetering up only to slide down, then hunkering up and flailing into an attempt at balance, only to wobble from side to side, making scant progress at forward motion.

That was normal, sometimes for the first hours or day of life, even for a day or two longer, before most foals—some with maternal nudging—find the natural dance of movement that is part of their genetic gift, and are soon galloping with finesse. But after weeks, Lauretta's colt could barely walk or run.

The Doc kept hoping he'd improve as the days went by. "For almost a year I had no hope for him. He was the most spindled, shank-legged animal I ever did see." His coat was a dingy, tufted brown—not even a hint of dark bay—and he appeared to be in a pain so severe from an unidentifiable infection or injury that the grooms working for Doc Key begged him to shoot the foal and put him out of his misery.

"I made up my mind to kill him," Key said to Rogers, a statement made for the sake of his dramatic narrative, since it was impossible for anyone who knew Bill Key just in passing to imagine him committing such an act, even if committed in mercy. Despite his supposed intention, he focused his energies instead almost exclusively on saving Lauretta's life and easing her colt's ailments, hoping and praying that Keystone Liniment and his other remedies would provide the solution. Doc Key was sure the foal wasn't going to make it, but not giving up, as he confirmed to Rogers, "I took mighty fine care of him."

Yet his disappointment was so pronounced that instead of the biblical name he had planned to bestow on the stallion that he had once imagined being immortalized on the turf, he refused to give the misfit the name he'd chosen. "It would have been blasphemy."

Searching for a name that would fit, after watching the colt attempt to walk, he had an encounter with a Mr. Jim Hunter, a bow-legged, no-account drunk who wandered by his stables on occasion. "If this raggle-taggle, trashy man had attempted to walk through a wheat field, he would have ruined it."

As though to mock his own audacity, perhaps having in his own mind, as Tennesseans like to say, "gotten above his raisin'," Bill Key named his raggle-taggle horse Jim. But just in case Jim understood and took it as a lack of kindness, he gave the unpromising young Arabian-Hambletonian his own last name.

Jim Key was a member of Bill's family now, but still a long ways from being beautiful.

3

The Human Who Could Talk Horse

Horses are herd animals, and so are we. Both species survive in groups, keenly attuned to the gestures of dominance and submission in play around us. We both bluff, exaggerate, ignore; maintain alliances, betray loyalties, reward courage, seek affection; we annoy one another out of boredom; we mock our betters; we respond to flattery; we punish and humiliate those we can, and with those we can't we cultivate appearances. We try to get along. We know the real thing when we see it.

—KEVIN CONLEY,
Stud: Adventures in Breeding

HISTORY REPEATS ITSELF. Patterns of repetition occur not only throughout collective history, but across the individual histories of those who belong to different collectives.

On August 9, 1897, when the train transporting Albert Rogers, William Key, Jim Key, and company pulled into New York City, they still had more to learn about one another. But what they had now discovered was a piece of shared history, a pattern of experience in each of their disparate lives that was the same. They had intuitively found a common bond that is the root of communication among beings born to dissimilar cultures, which in their case was the sense that each in his own way was born somewhat strange. Each in his own way did not belong entirely to the herd from which he sprang; each in his own way—by choice or force or necessity—came to live for a time among other herds. Each learned to speak other languages, bridging communication gaps between class, culture, race, gender, and specie.

Jim Key in his first half year of life didn't just look and walk strangely, his behavior was also to become even stranger. At first Doc Key—so consumed by the daily decline of Lauretta Queen of Horses and with nursing Jim through his early ailments—barely noticed the colt's unusual preoccupations. Nor was he conscious of the fact that during the time he spent rubbing his liniment onto Jim's nubby coat, over underdeveloped muscles and twisted tendons, massaging and relaxing the colt's crooked, spindly bones with his human hands, he had created a primal connection—a form of language in itself. In the process Jim seemed to first understand that Doc Key was worried about him, that he was sick and likely to die. And then out of the unspoken but palpable human expressions of concern a message from man to horse came through: *I want you to get better.*

Just as many a champion racehorse has been urged to accomplish athletic feats beyond known limits, Jim strove to do the impossible—to live, even when the Doc had pretty much given up on him and when stable hands were telling their distraught employer to kill the colt and save him from a more painful death. By the force of his own will to please Doc Key, Jim succeeded in living, transmitting the message back: *I will get better soon, honest.*

William Key recognized that message, but what he missed was the way that Jim was watching him, as if learning the practical means for getting better.

Jim watched Doc Key open and shut the gate to his stall. He watched the retrieval of vials, bottles, papers, books, and instruments from the black medical bag, noticing how the Doc examined labels on the objects containing the medicines, and he saw that the lines and shapes on the labels were different. Jim paid close watch to the frequency with which the Doc referred to one booklet in particular ("Bell's Handbook to Veterinary Homeopathy," Bell's Homeopathic Pharmacy, New York, 1885) and how some form of communication conveyed by those lines on the paper caused Doc Key's face to alter—from puzzlement to assuredness, or from mild consternation to dread.

Jim watched Doc Key in his interactions with other horses in the stable and with the various dogs, cats, chickens, goats, pigs, sheep, and other barnyard creatures that gravitated to the veterinarian's side, as well as the Doc's interactions with the other humans. Jim watched and he listened, concluding early on that William Key was the head of the herd, a benevolent ruler who was good and kind, though sometimes stern. Jim recognized his own name and understood that the other herd members—whether animal or human— each had a different name. Jim watched and listened, and not only did he sense that the differently named members of the herd looked and acted differently from one another, but he also grasped that each was capable of many different emotions, many of which were spurred by the behavior of other members of the herd.

As he was led out in Doc Key's attempt to exercise him each morning, the weakling colt who wobbled from side to side on knotty, spindly legs seemed to sense from the mix of the other species that to them he was strange, even to be scorned. An unsightly nuisance. He may have perceived that he was in danger, threatened by the others who—sensing his fear—would fight him, hurt him, take his food or his place in the herd, or worse. Without the strength to put up a fight, Jim inadvertently cultivated the survival skill of using humor to distract potential bullies and snobs, thus becoming the barnyard jester. Without being taught, the still sickly Jim had found his usefulness as a source of amusement. Comic relief. In time, it became apparent to William Key that the lame wobble was no longer physiological; Jim was feigning it for the human laughter and the animal attention and distraction that the funny walk brought him.

Even before Doc Key came to that conclusion, he started to spot the watchful way Jim followed him in his rounds of the stables, sometimes wobbling behind him as the Doc trekked up to his house after a long day. After leaving Jim out to graze in the pasture on a summer afternoon, Doc Key returned to his yard and began playing fetch with one of his dogs. "Sit," he told the dog as the canine happily obeyed.

"Good dog," said Doc Key, rewarding him with a generous scratching and massage around his furry head and ears. The Doc continued through a series of physical and verbal commands for routine behaviors, adding his own murmuring in a language that, though unintelligible to other humans, contained the commonly recognized commands: "stay"; "lie down"; "roll over." Each effort, successful or not, was followed by ample praise and encouragement.

Doc Key must have thought it somewhat odd when he turned back to the fence and saw that Jim had stretched his head over the rails with his eyes fixed on the dog, as if studying the behaviors that went with the commands.

The Doc forgot about the incident entirely until the following winter, when, just days after Lauretta's ill health had finally taken her life, something happened to bring the memory into the moment. If the disappointment of Jim's birth had broken William Key's heart, as he'd told Rogers, the death of his treasured pure Arabian gray mare nearly killed him. He was inconsolable. For the first few days, his wife and the Keystone stable hands attended to Jim and the other horses while the Doc kept to himself. When he returned to his regular rounds, the others seemed to know to keep their distance. That is, except for Jim Key, who refused to leave Doc Key's side, kicking at his stall gate when he was led back in, neighing and blowing foam from his lips until the Doc reluctantly let him out again, put a blanket over Jim, and allowed the colt to wobble out into the cold air.

Doc Key was looking away in a far-off direction, most likely at the spiny filigree of bare winter trees clinging to a nearby rocky ridge, when he felt Jim nudging his elbow. He turned his eyes back to the colt. In Jim's mouth was the stick that William Key and his dog had used for playing fetch months before. Jim pushed it toward the Doc's hand and waited. Doc Key understood. He threw the stick, and Jim launched into a doglike run, moving faster than the Doc had ever seen him move. When he returned, stick in his mouth, he placed it back in Doc Key's hand, then lowered his head, bobbing it to indicate he wanted his reward of praise and scratching around his ears.

That's when the first glimmer of Jim's strange intelligence had flickered through. Dr. Key explained to Rogers, "He was a knowing colt, I tell you. He showed me that he could fetch, and proceeded to try to do the other tricks that the dog could do. And so I taught him. He learned to sit, play dead, roll over, those kinds of things."

When that same evening arrived, instead of allowing himself to be led back toward the stables, Jim stood his ground, shank-legged and all, immobile, unwilling to budge. The enticement of a sugar cube or two produced no reaction other than a nostril snort. Not that Jim had ever responded to treats of sugar before. Doc Key cajoled him in a good-humored, schoolmarmish voice, telling the mulish colt he was welcome to remain outside in the cold and wet for the rest of the night. Then the Doc hurried up to his house, where Lucinda was already lighting the gas lamps and fanning the flames in the fireplace, her husband's supper warm and waiting on the potbellied stove.

As soon as William Key reached for the door, he felt Jim's breath on his shoulder. He tried to step inside and turned to the colt to coax him back to the stable, but Jim again stood his ground, clearly intending to follow the Doc into the house.

The episode, recalled by Bill Key for Albert Rogers, was not what the promoter had expected to hear. Instead of commencing his human education as a humanlike horse, it was apparent that Jim Key had crossed the threshold into his life among humans as a would-be favored pet dog, with canine aspirations.

Albert Rogers no doubt made sure he had heard correctly what Dr. William Key had told him. Did Jim actually live inside the Key household?

Doc Key confirmed that impression, saying, "He just lived and slept in my house and followed me around like a dog. Pretty soon he began to pick at me, trying to imitate me." Key explained, "He was inclined to be busy all the time and was not satisfied to be idle. He wanted to know what everything was and I commenced to teach him simple things." Jim learned to identify everyday household items. In return for rewards of stroking, praise, and pieces of apple—which became his favorite treat—he would fetch anything Doc Key might request.

Secure in his role as an indoor colt and member of the Key household, Jim then started to become more independent, exploring on his own. "One of the first unusual things he learned," Doc Key remembered with a chuckle, "and I didn't teach him either, was to unfasten the gate and let himself out on the road."

The scenes repeated themselves: the ungainly colt wobbling along the road on his own as a throng of Doc Key's grooms ran after him, each blaming the other for leaving the gate unfastened, and the befuddled face of Doc Key after refastening the gate himself and departing by buggy for his veterinary office on North Main Street (also known as the Shelbyville and Murfreesboro Turnpike), discovering moments later that Jim was following not far behind him.

As a yearling, Jim Key at last no longer weaved and teetered with his every step. Dr. Key admitted his own surprise, describing how

Jim finally managed to shirk the different illnesses that had plagued him his first year while, sure enough, his crooked legs straightened out and his proportions began to conform into the regal lines of both his Arabian and Hambletonian ancestries. Pampered with a diet of only the best oats and hay, drinking the purified mineral water that was used in formulating Keystone tonics and liniments, sleeping indoors in a warm room in the Doc's house on a bed made of fresh, clean straw piled high, over which blankets were laid, Jim metamorphosed. No longer the ugly shank-legged colt, by the summer of 1890 his spindly long-legged frame turned muscular and robust as his tufted, dingy-colored, sparse coat grew glossy and sleek, deepening into the rich, mahogany bay color for which he would one day be known as beautiful.

Despite his physical transformation, Jim nonetheless continued to be a quirky character. For one thing, Jim was house-trained, which certainly impressed Albert Rogers. It seemed Jim had become as discreet as any gentleman as a result of spending a critical period of his development watching human members of the Key household exit their home and make their way to the privy out back, as well as paying attention to the toilet habits of what he may have assumed were his fellow canines who lived in the house.

Jim's early lessons to seek privacy and the out-of-doors for his bathroom needs served him throughout his career, later causing a couple of reporters to note that in all his years performing in public—including some of the most famous halls in America—he was never known to once have an accident or even a gastric faux pas.

Jim Key's precocious sense of hygiene notwithstanding, his rapid growth eventually had him unintentionally breaking through floorboards and collapsing doorjambs, which meant he had to be relegated back to the barn.

Jim put up such an unbearable ruckus when he discovered that he was expected to sleep alone in his stall at night that Dr. Key eventually had to bring a cot out to the barn and sleep at Jim's side, thinking he would only do so for a night or two, just until the orphaned horse got used to sleeping out there on his own.

From that first night forward, this was how the two slept, virtually 365 nights a year, every year for the remainder of their lives. Only when Dr. Key was called away on an urgent professional matter or when Jim traveled separately from him, were they apart at bedtime, and in those instances one of Jim's trusted attendants would take Bill Key's place in a nearby cot at night.

Future generations of his in-laws speculated that the reason William Key produced no heirs over the course of four marriages had less to do with any sexual or physiological impairment on his part, and more to do with the constancy of his attention to the animals he tended. His previous wives may have lost children in childbirth, while his third and fourth wives spent periods of time away at educational institutions. Early in Jim's life, Lucinda Davis Key, Bill's third wife, was commuting to Howard University in Washington, D.C., where she received her medical degree before returning home as one of the first licensed black female doctors to practice in Tennessee.

The Doc told Albert Rogers that when Lucinda came home to find out that her husband had taken up residence in the barn, she could only laugh at his devotion to Jim.

To be still closer, the Doc moved a large desk into a corner of the stable to serve as his office so that Jim could watch him as he did his daily bookkeeping work. Carefully writing in his clean, swirling script in a bound accounting ledger, he kept track of his Keystone and veterinary businesses, and other financial activities. Perhaps in the course of simply making conversation he may have explained to Jim what he was doing, what the numbers meant, and why it was important to be mindful of figures and money. To demonstrate, the Doc held up different coins, teaching Jim the difference between pennies, nickels, dimes, quarters, and silver dollars. A game evolved. Whenever Jim correctly identified the coin that Doc Key requested him to select, he was rewarded with a whole apple.

On a subsequent afternoon when Jim was out grazing, the Doc devised a plan to maintain a large supply of apples by hiding them in a deep desk drawer. As the drawer tended to become stuck in the damp, he tied a length of string to its handle, which would give him easier access. After leaving to take care of other concerns that day, Doc Key returned to find the drawer empty. Lucinda assured him she had not been in the stables, which prompted him to guess, "Must be one of the boys about the place."

The next day he put some more apples in the drawer, and they too disappeared. After refilling the drawer that afternoon and announcing that he was leaving, he pretended to depart from the property, returning covertly to watch through a window. Some minutes later he observed Jim Key blithely amble back into the barn alone. As though checking to make sure he wasn't being observed, Jim's ears rotated separately, searching for clues of sound, while his nose quivered as he tried to pick up any telltale smells. Satisfied that he wasn't being watched, Jim veered toward the desk, pulled the drawer open by tugging on the string, held tightly between his teeth, and then buried his head in the drawer, voraciously devouring every last apple, before nudging the drawer shut by leaning into it with the weight of his flank. Jim turned and strolled back out of the stable, not bothering to conceal the look of self-congratulation that would mark him in years to come.

The Doc was less concerned with Jim's thievery than he was proud of his mimicry, and he praised Jim for learning to open and close a desk drawer through imitation, although he had to explain that he had no apples to offer as a reward. Instead he reached into the pocket of his suit jacket and plucked out a couple of sugar cubes, which, as usual, his discerning young horse took in his mouth and spat to the ground. Doc Key laughed exuberantly, reward enough it seemed for Jim.

That was when, William Key told Albert Rogers, he began to think that Jim might be a natural performer like his dam, and he started coming up with some novel ideas for entertaining bits that Jim could learn to perform in his medicine show.

Rogers wanted to know if that was the turning point when Dr. Key recognized Jim's "extra" intelligence. Not exactly, said Dr. Key. By now he readily saw that Jim had a certain alert and quick mind, watching and imitating as he did. But it was actually Lucinda who first came to the conclusion that Jim was even smarter than they realized. She announced the news—with the startled, serious expression she often wore—as she came running out of the stable just as Doc Key was returning from town.

"Doctor, Doctor!" Lucinda Davis Key called to her husband, beckoning him. "The horse can say yes!"

William Key remembered the event sentimentally. He related to Albert Rogers that during the initial time period when he had begun training his fledgling equine performer, "My wife used to tell me to let the horse alone and come out of the stable. She knew that I'd go crazy over Jim. But it came around that Lucinda got very fond of Jim and was soon very much attached to him. That day she happened to go into the stable while eating an apple, and she said, 'Jim, do you want a piece of apple?' He bowed his head up and down. The next thing I heard was her calling for me that Jim could say yes."

Doc Key went in and asked Jim the same question, but the young bay stallion just stared down his nose at the Doc. Lucinda tried again, and Jim didn't respond either, blinking back at the two of them, as though they were both awfully strange humans to be asking him something so obvious.

"Well," Key continued, "I did what I'd done before, went out and came around to watch from where Jim couldn't see me and saw him 'say yes' for my wife. From that day she fell in love with him and would always reward him with apples whenever he would do what she asked of him."

Eventually, Lucinda was able to convince Jim to say yes to Doc Key, who soon taught Jim to also say no by swaying his head from side to side. In this fashion, a new learning game was invented for teaching Jim to identify primary colors. If the Doc held up cloth that was yellow and asked Jim, "Is this the color red?" his earnest student could choose to bow yes or sway no. There was a right or wrong answer, Jim learned, and the right answer would earn him a reward. But he was given a choice to answer correctly or not. There were other kinds of questions, however, that Jim came to understand had answers that were not necessarily right or wrong. Did he want a bite of apple? Did he want some sugar? Would he like to go out and run in the pasture? Would he like to be ridden to town by saddle? Or be hitched to a buggy? It turned out that Jim, like many horses, had preferences and opinions, not just as to what he ate or what color blanket he liked best or how he passed the day, but also his own ideas about different individuals' personalities, about human actions, even about events of the times and of the past.

Did Jim want to hear a Bible passage? Would Jim like to see the battlefields where Rebels and Yankees, human and equine, fought and died? Did Jim approve of Republican President Benjamin Harrison (who in 1888 had lost the popular vote but won the electoral majority, a concept then too sophisticated for Jim)? Was Jim a Republican? No? A Democrat? Yes?

But Abraham Lincoln was a Republican! (As was William Key.) Fine, Jim, if you want to be a Democrat, that's your choice. (That

Jim wasn't eligible to vote and that Dr. Key had only limited voting rights and was concerned that his fellow citizens of color were being barred from those rights didn't seem to keep the two from having political affiliations.)

Unlike many horses, Jim was being taught that he was entitled to have his own likes and dislikes and, even more uniquely, how to communicate those feelings. And so, rather than teaching him to respond affirmatively or negatively to rote questions, William Key bestowed upon Jim Key a gift that had been denied him in his own childhood and youth, a power and purpose of biblical proportions: free will.

What Albert Rogers construed from these stories was that the controversial art of horse whispering, made famous in the later 1800s by names like Busbey, Offutt, and Rarey, was as Dr. Key described it, both a dance and a dialogue.

In the twentieth century, the legendary Monty Roberts, the definitive horse whisperer, actually went on to codify the language that came from this choreography that equines used with one another, which was similar to Dr. Key's methods. The positioning of his body in relation to the horse or mule was critical, as was the importance of turning his back to the equine, or at an angle, so as to invite, rather than force, the horse to follow him.

The "Dialogue Between Man and Horse" comprising these physical gestures was described by Denton Offutt to his horse-training students in a well-circulated pamphlet of the late nineteenth century:

Man: I wish to put my hands on your face, and come near you.
Horse: If so, you must let me see that you will not hurt me, nor will have anything about you that will, nor anything that smells badly. I am a stranger to you; all that will offend any of the five senses, I will guard against, and those five senses must have proof that you will not hurt me, before I will allow them to be on me.
Man: I wish to put my hands all over you.
Horse: This you may do by commencing at the face. Commence rubbing on the face and repeat it; then pass on down the neck, first as slight as possible, and as I become used to it, rub the harder. Remember always to rub the way the hair lies smooth.

My tail is, when I play, to be held up high; and as my pride and beauty, you must be careful in handling it. But after you raise it, be sure to repeat it, and raise it and put it down several times, until it goes up quietly. It becomes habituated by use.

Man: Then the more I rub you, and repeat it, the quieter you get?

Horse: It is so in all beasts.

Doc Key took these principles a step further, whispering his wordless sounds of encouragement as his body language asked the questions. *How do you want me to teach you?* He knew to let the horse do most of the talking.

As he took these notes for his pamphlet, Albert Rogers was clearly ambivalent about portraying Dr. Key as a horse whisperer—generally considered at the time to be suspect. Rogers also believed that the Doc's various incantations and occultist habits might not appeal to the officers at the New York–based ASPCA or to the planners of the American Institute Fair at Madison Square Garden—where he was hoping to book Jim next as part of his Northern debut. The question recurred: *Just who was this "Dr." William Key?*

Albert Rogers was still hard-pressed to answer that question himself.

D oc Key said very little about his early life which began in Winchester, Tennessee, in 1833. He was born a slave, he stated plainly, and took the name of his master, John W. Key, of Shelbyville. When Rogers later asked about his unusual generosity toward John W. Key and his family, William Key only shrugged and said, "I was one of those fortunate men who had a kind master."

Bill's special status in the Key household might have suggested that John W. Key was William Key's white father. Although they were blood related, the more probable connection was that master and slave were first cousins, evidenced by deeds, wills, and court documents, most of which were to be lost during four separate destructions of the Bedford County courthouse.

Amid the clues that remained, William Key had made his inauspicious entrance onto the pages of documented history at the age of five years old, as an entry of property belonging to Captain John Key of Winchester, Tennessee, an uncle of John W. Key of Shelbyville. In this document, Captain Key's last will and testament, his list of slaves included nine adults and eight children. Among them was six-year-old Nancy, who was William's sister; their mother, Caroline; and Caroline's brother Jack. It was from Caroline, a cook and a medicine woman who was probably of a mixed Cherokee and African background, that Bill first learned how to find and distill roots and herbs into life-saving concoctions, and how to cook so masterfully that his talent would one day save him from the gallows. From his uncle Jack, a blacksmith and tanner, Bill learned early how to shoe and outfit horses as well as other survival skills that ensured he would not be sent out to the fields.

When Captain Key died, unmarried and without heirs, his will stipulated that Jack, Nancy, and her children be deeded to his nephew, John W. Key. The slaveholding Keys had strict family agreements that property—slaves included—stay in the family, except when necessity forced the selling of property, in which case the revenue had to be used to take care of the extended family members. In this group of Keys, originally from Albemarle, Virginia, there was a focal point for this policy: Strother Key.

Captain Key's brother and John W. Key's father, Strother was the family scourge. As a boy of five arriving in a strange household on a different farm, Bill soon figured out that his fate was tied to that of the tragic Strother. The polite version of how John W. Key's father had become permanently helpless and deranged was that after proudly serving as a mounted gunman in the War of 1812, he had reenlisted and had been mysteriously injured.

The real story was that his incapacity was due to profligate living—drinking, gaming, and womanizing—so intolerable that his wife, Margaret, divorced him, complaining that when they married he was possessed of respectable property but had gambled everything away. Rather than shouldering his debt and letting it drain the fortune she brought to the marriage, she asked the court to grant her the divorce so that she could live "as a feme solo." Margaret C. Graham Key was granted her petition, excluding her the right to remarry, but she and the rest of the family had to make sure Strother was clothed and fed, and not causing himself or others grave harm. Before young Bill's arrival, problems with Strother had been getting worse, but the family noticed immediately that the boy had a calming, sobering influence on the old man, instantly endearing Bill to the Old Missus Margaret, to Marster John and his wife, Missus Martha.

Everyone was taken with the small, charismatic child, with his piercing gaze and an almost magical presence of being. Rogers wrote in his brief "Sketch of Dr. Wm. Key's Life" that "in his early years he had a great fondness for the animals. Ever kind to them, and many a poor dog or a worried cat was he the defender of on the old plantation."

"My entry into the barnyard," Doc Key told Rogers, "was the signal for a general commotion. All the animals, big and small, recognized me as a friend." He had a special connection to horses, his gentle and intimate manner producing such a calming effect on wild colts and balking, kicking mules that he was soon being sent into a pen or pasture by himself to tame and train them, working his magic. That's what was suspected by others in the black community, Key recalled, who believed he was bewitching them.

Word began to seep out that up at the Key place there was an extraordinary child who could talk horse.

"They tell stories about me when I was six years old," the Doc remembered. "I had a rooster and a yellow dog that could do wonderful things."

One of those who grew up to tell stories of that time—and who became mayor of Nashville—was a boy named Richard Houston Dudley, around the same age as Bill. The well-to-do Dudley family lived four miles from John W. Key's tanyard. At first, Marster Dudley was there to gawk in amazement at the tricks performed by the yellow dog and the rooster. But before long, Richard treated Bill less as a source of entertainment and more as a playmate, while Bill replaced deference with familiarity. The two became fast friends, with a bond that lasted until old age.

John W. Key was a kind, well-liked, well-intentioned man who had been saddled with responsibilities for which he was never suited. A series of lawsuits and debts testified to his dubious business judgment, while an emphasis on education in his household suggested that instead of owning livestock for tanning and making his living as a merchant, John would have preferred the life of a scholar. But his father's problems prevented him from following that path. Instead he educated himself and eagerly encouraged a love of book learning in Bill, tutoring him in every academic subject that time allowed. While John schooled Bill in reading, writing, mathematics, and science, Martha supplemented those lessons by teaching him such gentlemanly skills as presentation, elocution, and etiquette.

A daughter of a wealthy Nashville family, Martha Minter Key was among that growing number of Southern wives who convened in sewing circles and afternoon teas to voice candid opposition to slave owning. In covert rebellion, it was women leading the charge to teach slaves to read and write, despite laws in most slave states against doing so.

At the age of nine, Bill may not have known that in some places John and Martha would be at risk of breaking the law for endowing him with the power of literacy, places where the punishment ran from fines to imprisonment and worse. Some localities saw teaching slaves to read and write as a crime equivalent to distributing abolitionist material to incite rebellion, which was a hanging crime.

There were stories of benevolent rural masters who sent the children of their slaves to Free Negro schools in Nashville and were appalled when they returned with foolish ideas of liberty in their heads, refusing to work in any capacity and running off, sometimes forging their own passes. They were resented by their fellow slaves, so it was claimed, who described them as "dangerous niggers."

Even so, with the exception of Memphis, where the education of Negroes was illegal, in most of the state the practice was so widespread that Englishman James Sterling, writing about the condition of slaves in America, observed that in Tennessee he heard none of the "nigger gibberish" noted elsewhere and that, for the most part, the African-Americans he met in the border state "seem to speak better, or at least more agreeably to an English ear, than the whites."

Negro literacy thrived not only in the John W. Key household but also in much of Shelbyville, which had a strong contingency of those who supported black education and emancipation.

Known for its three distinct geographic regions—the mountains of East Tennessee, the low hills of Middle Tennessee, and the flats of West Tennessee—the Volunteer State had fostered what were generally three corresponding sets of beliefs and practices regarding slavery, shaped by the distinct terrain of each given region and its respective agricultural and economic activities. Because farmland in East Tennessee was less suitable for tilling on a large scale, a lower demand for slave labor was one factor that led to a social environment in which antislavery and later pro-Union sentiment flourished. The opposite held true in West Tennessee, where there was a predominance of the so-called slave crops (or, in the more genteel phrase, "money crops")—cotton and tobacco—as there was the defense of slavery as a necessary evil. Middle Tennessee was the proverbial and literal middle ground, where proponents and opponents of slavery lived in proximity. Since many farmers of the hillier areas had smaller farms that combined livestock herding and less labor intensive crops such as corn, many didn't own slaves—and those who did, like John W. Key, had fewer than ten slaves—and both groups tended not to be apologists for slavery. Yet it was also in Middle Tennessee's fertile valleys that some of the state's most expansive improved acreage could be found, where slave ownership and its staunchest defenders were likewise concentrated.

These diverging attitudes based on regional and economic differences were difficult for Dr. Key to explain to Albert Rogers, a Northerner born after the Civil War, who actually promoted at expositions a popular attraction known as the Old Plantation, which reinforced the myth of the earlier, simpler days of antebellum grandeur.

The Doc didn't try to explain how those stereotypes were wrong or how slavery in Tennessee was manifest in every extreme, from its most abhorrent to most lenient, the institution having been contentious even before Tennessee became a state in 1796. Over time, the net impact of these disparate beliefs about persons of color—slave or free—gave blacks something of a dual status. Before the 1830s, there were more antislavery groups in Tennessee than in any of the other slave states combined. Within a decade, the pendulum had swung the other way, and by 1837 there was not one abolitionist society in the whole state. Contradictory laws permitted both the legal emancipation of a slave by a master but also the capture and sale back into slavery of free Negroes. While a person of color accused of a crime had the right to a trial, a right of personhood, by civil law, all slaves, William Key included, were chattel: not entitled to legally own property, deprived of the right of suffrage and even civil marriage, subject to the control of a master—to be worked without cease, to be confined in movement and travel, to be humiliated, beaten, starved, raped, to be sold to the highest bidder, and ultimately to be killed.

This was the reality nine-year-old Bill understood, making him painfully aware that even with a kind master and mistress, and even with his favored status, his future and the futures of his loved ones remained tenuous at best. If Strother died and Bill wasn't needed to look after him, he feared the Old Missus would force John to lease or sell him. Or if John's financial straits worsened, then it could lead to the same result.

There was another concern. At the tanyard, he increasingly heard the inquiries and comments about himself—spoken in front of him as if he were foreign or deaf—not just from masters and their overseers but also from other Negroes. He could do tricks and should be taken and put on show, said some. He was spoilt by his master, a few said. True, he had a way with horses and livestock, but he belonged in the stables as a groom or out in the pasture and should not be allowed to come and go as he pleased. Although John W. Key made it known that Bill was not for sale at any price, he was offered escalating amounts to purchase the mulatto slave child who could do magic (some slaves called it voodoo, or its variation, hoodoo). With his talents, however derived, to tame wild beasts and cure sicknesses, and with his educated speech and manners, he could be a fine houseboy up in Nashville.

There were one or two attempts to try to buy Bill in order to teach him his place, including that of a certain slave driver who worked as a local overseer of a large plantation, and who was reputed to administer cruel and unusual torment to slaves. "That man was my worst enemy," he told Rogers, never naming him.

The overseer had complained to John before about Bill's insolence and demanded that the boy be whipped. When John refused, the overseer began taunting Bill at every occasion, threatening to wrest him away from the Keys.

Finally one evening, as Bill sat next to John in the wagon while driving home with the sun going down into the green grassy cleavage of the Tennessee hills, he extracted a promise from John never to sell him to that slave driver's boss.

John made that promise, reassuring Bill that day would never come. Still, he wondered if Bill might not prefer living in a grand plantation with a rich master instead of with a struggling tanner and hill farmer. That would be fine living, John W. Key proposed. Another reality for any slave was that your status could be determined not only by your position within your master's domain, but just as much by the status of your master. At the tanyard, Bill had heard the way ornately uniformed Negro manservants belonging to the more prosperous owners liked to ridicule lower-class slaves in their burlap breeches and makeshift shoes. "Don't mind them darkeys," they'd say when Bill went to help with their similarly mistreated mules, "they belong to po' white trash."

After Bill assured John that he cared nothing about being the slave of the richest man in Tennessee, his cousin acknowledged that Bill was a member of his family. John promised again: no one will take you away from us without your consent.

As Bill predicted, that certain slave driver soon showed up at the tanyard, bringing his boss with him. The two came ready to pay enough cash to clear John's considerable debts in return for the purchase of William. After a stammer or too, John gave the plantation owner a firm no.

Relieved beyond words, young Bill had no time to thank John before he saw the furious slave driver make a beeline toward him. Seething, the slave driver swore at Bill in a hoarse whisper, saying, "Boy, one day I'm gonna get you and lick the blood out of you!"

Those were the exact words that Dr. Key recalled to Albert Rogers, hinting that later such an occurrence nearly transpired.

From then on, Bill Key believed he owed a debt of gratitude to John Key for keeping his promise and standing up to the overseer and his boss. But other circumstances arose that John couldn't so easily unravel. John and Martha's family was growing with the arrival of two sons, Merit and Alexander, and more children on the way. With money becoming more and more scarce, the Old Missus insisted that the slaves be sold or leased out. Up until now, the care Bill gave old Strother had deterred Margaret Key from demanding that John do it. That was why, in 1842, when Strother suddenly died, Bill knew his days there were numbered. Worse, John had become ensnared in legal problems, somehow involving Martha's brother, Jeptha Minter, ostensibly for loans he had failed to repay.

A settlement was reached that turned the ownership of Bill, his sister Nancy, his mother, Caroline, and his uncle Jack over to Jeptha, allowing him to lease their services out as he so deemed. Being an unusual individual, young Bill Key responded unusually to the next ten years of being sent to work at a range of different plantations and businesses. Turning adversity into opportunity, he managed to use this passage of his enslavement as a way to elevate his reputation across the state as a doctor for both horses and humans.

Something fundamental changed in his sense of self, a shift that Rogers grasped as a clue to understanding just who Dr. William Key was. From then on, contrary to outward conditions, Bill vowed to have no masters other than God and himself, and whether his legal status was made free or not, he would become free in his mind and come to be responsible for whatever good or evil befell him.

On August 27, 1852, in Shelbyville's town square on the steps of the Bedford County courthouse, nineteen-year-old William Key held an emotional reunion with John and Martha Key, after some legal and financial wrangling that morning in the Chancery Court with Jeptha Minter.

Much had changed. Now known in some circles as Young Doc Key, Bill not only had grown into a man but also had seen enough of the state beyond Bedford County to become a much different person. Those were the years in which his horse-training talents had sent him to places like Belle Meade Plantation, and where, at such locations, he met famous black horsemen and jockeys, fellow slaves who also lived in dual worlds. He learned from them and their lore, adding to his knowledge of magic making and omen reading as well. Whether he believed in luck or not, he hedged his bets and came away with a lifelong fondness for the use of the rabbit's foot.

He wasn't alone. One of humankind's oldest symbols of fertility and prosperity, the rabbit's foot had visited a myriad of cultures, dating back to as early as 600 B.C. It had now made its way into nineteenth-century America—mainly in the South, in African-American culture of the day, and definitely into the belief systems of those whose fortunes could rise or fall at horse races.

Young Doc Key had also met individuals in the Negro community who shared with him the navigational secrets of what became known later as the Underground Railroad, including knowledge about routes and safe houses he later used. Some of the men and women he met between 1843 and 1852 were associated with Reverend Jermaine Loguen, originally from Tennessee, and with Harriet

Tubman and Frederick Douglass. He also related to Rogers that as a slave belonging to Jeptha Minter but entrusted to travel extensively either on his own or under a "loose rein," he was permitted to provide free doctoring for slaves—pulling teeth, setting bones, delivering babies. Stories about his kind generosity and miraculous healing abilities spread across the state.

William saw the extremes of living conditions for those he tended—from palatial Thoroughbred stables to the unprotected, foul-smelling draft horse pens, from lush grazing fields to the chicken-scratch dirt of poor barnyards, from the fine homes of rich slaveholders to the comfortable if cramped quarters for the more fortunate and better fed Negro house servants, to the unsanitary, overcrowded, unventilated, leaky-roofed slave huts where field hands were confined. He had to have been struck by the similarities between the treatment of horses and other animal property and that of fellow slaves. He had to have nurtured some slow, seething anger when he saw the worst of the worst—a labor force fed only enough so as not to die, but not enough to live, with rages of small-pox, measles, whooping cough, cholera, pleurisy, and other diseases proliferating. Surely he had to swallow hard and look away when owners complained of the economic loss that would result from the death of a slave, as if they were talking about a good working mule or a milk cow. But instead of saying a word, he went to work, patiently expressing his gratitude for being able to be of help, quietly making suggestions that were almost always effective.

The fact that his veterinary and medical expertise was self-taught didn't lessen his value. At the time, there were plenty of self-taught physicians, white and black. And as it happened, Negro practitioners, male and female, were suspected by many of being superior doctors—with their body of handed-down medical knowledge that included such advanced treatments as a smallpox cure and a derivative of the African midwives' practice of performing caesarean section. When it came to a choice between the typical white practitioners—like the barber who bled patients or the old wives and druggists who prescribed potions that regularly ended more lives than they saved—or a doctor of color, the latter was often preferred.

William's travels had brought him back to Shelbyville, and he had seen John Key and his family in passing and had seen the town changing. At last, he was glad to be legally back with the Keys, and happy to be back in Shelbyville. Southern Railway had come through, laying tracks through the center of town and building a depot that appeared to be bursting at its seams. The square too was alive with commerce: wagons and buggies unhitched and amassed everywhere, as horses were led in weary groups into a central livery stable while humans sought the shade of building overhangs and the poplars and elms that surrounded the courthouse.

To William's surprise, Old Missus Margaret had apparently felt remorse about separating William from the family, so she helped arrange for his return. Now that Martha's brother owned a piece of property next to the Keys, William didn't have to go far to see his mother, sister, and uncle. And, as if no time had passed, he was embraced by the John W. Key household, human and nonhuman, and encouraged to pick up his studies where he had left off.

Dr. Key told Albert Rogers that his "Young Marsters," eleven-year-old Merit and nine-year-old Alexander, helped tutor him so he could make up for lost time.

Legally, William belonged to John W. Key, but at this time period he was able to start keeping portions of the revenue he helped generate. John realized that William's fastidiousness about his time and money actually helped his own bottom line. Everyone prospered.

"I was sent for," the Doc told Rogers, "by neighbors from miles around. If a wild colt was to be broken, I took the frightened colt and kept him with me at my marster's farm. In a week's time, I returned the same colt ready to ride or drive."

His technique? Always the same: "Kindness and patience." It was that simple to him. Young Doc Key continued to take special pride in his expertise with kicking and balking mules, and he was also called upon to reform vicious dogs. For him there was no end to the wondrous results of a gentle touch.

That he earned and saved money during the last decade of slavery was borne out by friendships he was making in the white community—with businessmen, bankers, and lawyers who may have used his services and paid him, or lost a hand of cards to him—and with one lawyer in particular, who served as a personal banker for the Young Doc. The lawyer's name was William H. Wisener, an outspoken Whig who advocated for immediate and full emancipation. And

Wisener wasn't afraid to say so either, blasting his abolitionist opinions in the headlines of the leading Shelbyville newspaper that he bought in the 1850s, much to the consternation of local Democrats, who didn't so much want to preserve slavery as they were angered by anyone with the gall to take the side of interfering Northerners.

But many area residents found slave-holding increasingly distasteful and agreed with Wisener. By 1860 Bedford County's total number of slave holders was on the decrease. In a county population of over 13,000 whites, only 980 were slaveholders; of the 275,000 slaves in Tennessee, 6,744 were enslaved in Bedford County, putting the county at fifteenth in the state in number of slaves. Thirty percent of the slave holders owned either one or two slaves, while most of the remaining owners still held fewer than ten slaves, and there were no longer any slave holders in Bedford County with one hundred or more slaves.

One factor in Shelbyville's trend away from slave-holding was that its economy was becoming based more on commerce and industry, and less immediately on agriculture. Bedford County's hardworking populace, especially in Shelbyville, was also highly literate. If there was a community ripe for electing to banish slavery, it would have been Shelbyville.

But even as Dr. Key described to Rogers how tolerant most folks in his hometown were, he couldn't deny that by 1860 the tensions and divisions across Tennessee were beginning to mirror those that were fracturing the rest of the nation. The river town of Shelbyville, like the rest of the border state of Tennessee, was about to become trapped in the crossfire between the North—with its edge in developing industrial superiority—and the South, where its economic power stemmed from an agrarian system that harnessed the toil of four million slaves, valued then at three billion dollars (more than three trillion dollars in the twenty-first century).

A witness to every side of the conflict, Young Doc Key was there when the fissures gave way in Shelbyville—where the vote on Tennessee's secession was virtually decided, shaping the fate of the rest of the Volunteer State and, ultimately, the nation.

Before Albert Rogers heard those stories, he interrupted the interview to catch up on his notes and begin designing the look of his pamphlet.

Starting with the cover, he placed an earlier photograph of Jim Key in the middle of the page. Then, along the top border, Rogers wrote out a question: *How was he taught?*

Along the bottom border, he answered it: *He Was Taught by Kindness.*

4

War Stories

By late Spring of 1861 only the formalities were needed to place Tennessee in a state of war. The difficult ... part had already been accomplished by the politicians. Like expert harpists they had strummed the emotions of the people ... who stood in town squares and heard the politicians extol the virtues of the South.... Political rallies took on the appearance of religious revivals ... after which "men of courage and patriotism" were invited to come forth ... to protect southern property and the honor of southern womanhood.

—BOB WOMACK,
Call Forth the Mighty Men

August 10, 1897.
The Rogers home, 75 Maiden Lane. New York City.

THE REMAINDER OF THE INTERVIEW for the pamphlet took place in Albert's stables behind his stylish townhome, where, the night before, his wife, Clara, and their three young sons had excitedly welcomed the Tennesseans to New York.

The following day Rogers resumed his questions on the subject of Jim's education, returning to the point at which Doc Key had first come to believe that he was an unusually smart horse. As his exchange with the Doc proceeded, there was something unnerving to Rogers about the presence of the tall bay, who seemed to be following the interview closely, even nodding yes to agree with points, at other moments nickering for dramatic emphasis.

Rogers finally commented about it. Was he imagining things, or was Jim following the conversation?

Bill Key almost laughed. "Of course, Jim understands what one is saying."

Astonishing, Rogers said, then turned to Jim Key and told him how magnificent and brilliant he was. Unmistakably, Jim Key nodded in agreement and preened for his admirer.

"You see," said Dr. Key, "when he is praised his head goes up so as to say, 'What horse is as smart as I?'"

Rogers had a twinge of suspicion. Maybe this was all part of their act, a trick.

Dr. Key sensed the skepticism and spoke to it, matter-of-factly, explaining that he and Jim had established their connection as a powerful open channel of communication. "I believe he knows every word I say to him, and sometimes it seems to me that all I've got to do is to think a thing and he knows it."

Was it, then, some strange symbiosis or hypnosis? Rogers had to ask, knowing that reporters at the press party would be watching Jim and Dr. Key closely, looking for familiar tricks and signals, anything that hinted at fraud, including mind control.

"Some say it's hypnotism and that kind of thing—but I don't know anything about that." The Doc was diffident, adding as an afterthought, "But I do know Jim knows and does what I ask him to do."

This was also how Jim Key so easily mastered bits for the medicine show. Initially, the Doc hadn't planned on putting him to work. But since the two were inseparable, it had been only natural that the year-and-a-half-old Arabian-Hambletonian had wanted to get in on the act. Not unlike his dam.

By the 1890s, with the patent medicine era thundering toward its peak and a crowded marketplace creating increasingly tougher competition, the marketing challenge for every medicine vendor was how to provide innovative, spectacular crowd-drawing entertainment. The medicine man of the 1890s, unlike the pitchman of old, needed to be a theatrical producer. For quack and genuine healer alike, what was needed was a gimmick.

Doc Key paid attention to what others were doing, learning from those he met on the road, and those he heard about. He heard about a New York street merchant down on Wall Street who had a poker-playing pig that stood with his hooves propped up on a card table, ready to take all comers. One well-known dark-cloaked vendor gathered a crowd by calling out, "You are dying, Sir! And you, Madam!" mesmerizing his audience with scare tactics until he finally had them, proclaiming, "You are all dying, and you think there is no way to avoid it! But there is, and that is why I am here!" Then he would introduce his lifesaving wares and sell them in splendid quantities.

One highly successful medicine man had perfected the trick of setting out a length of rope, a skull, and a Bible, and spending as much as an hour arranging and rearranging the objects. The moment he was satisfied with the density of the crowd surrounding him, he would turn and smile and pitch his products, never once referring to the rope, skull, or Bible. Others promised drawings for free merchandise at the end of the presentation or gave bonus gifts with purchases. Some vendors set up tents for visits with "doctors" who pulled teeth and diagnosed symptoms for fees, in addition to prescribing and selling their own remedies.

One of the most effective forms of patent medicine promotion was live testimonials by previously satisfied customers. And who better to illustrate the wonders of Keystone Liniment than Jim Key? The Keystone show combined crowd-drawing methods, starting with Doc Key cordoning off a sizable area and then stringing up the hundreds of rabbit feet he had collected, many from Civil War battlefields. As a small handful of the curious gathered, the Keystone minstrel players used their upbeat tunes to pull a larger audience, moving next into rolling rhythms and pleasing harmonies to set the stage for the kindly, confident Dr. Key to begin his lecture. But just as he began to introduce the marvels of Keystone Liniment, Jim interrupted, scampering up to him, doglike, a stick in his mouth.

The bit had the Doc apologizing to the crowd, turning to the gangly, growing young horse to reprimand him, but ever so kindly.

> Dr. Key: "I'm talkin' to the folks now, Jim. Be patient 'til I'm done and I'll be mighty glad to play fetch with you later."
> Jim Key: (To irrepressible audience laughter and applause.) Shaking his head, he puts the stick in the Doc's hand, gets him to throw it, fetches it, then obediently sits, lies down, and rolls over on command.

With the crowd continuing to grow, Dr. Key followed this up by explaining that Jim was still somewhat confused, ever since he was born an ugly duckling horse too crippled to stand but who had been saved by the very liniment that the lucky folks were about to have a chance to buy. Taking out a bottle, he demonstrated its uses and gave Jim a rapid rubdown. Suddenly, the hound imitator transformed into a regal, young equine prince trotting elegantly in a circle for all to see, eliciting cheers of delight.

Jim Key was a born actor. Dr. Key recalled to Rogers that as Jim embellished upon his performing role, his willingness to learn new bits led them to adapt the act. "After a while I taught him to give symptoms of bots and colic," said the Doc, describing how through rewards Jim learned to evoke the subtly different ailments. Colic came in two forms, spasmodic or flatulent, and was known, when left untreated, to become a potentially fatal inflammation of the bowels. Jim soon mastered the ability, by mimicking Dr. Key, to suddenly appear to be seized with pain, moving about in a restless, uneasy manner until, out of apparent frustration, he began to strike his belly with his hind foot. As the veterinary surgeon diagnosed his disorder to the crowd, Jim became increasingly distressed, perspiring heavily, and finally he heaved himself onto the ground, rolled onto his back while madly striking his hooves in the air. Just when it looked as if the horse was beyond hope, Dr. Key would give him a drink of his tonic, and Jim would miraculously recover from his symptoms.

Bots, the larva of the gadfly, also caused intestinal irritation when lodged in the stomach, as well as causing sore throats or nasal congestion when deposited in those mucus membranes. Jim learned to pretend to have the strange array of symptoms associated with bots—everything from turning up his upper lip, to pawing and pacing, from craning to look at his side, to giving the appearance of becoming instantly weak and fatigued. Here too, just as the otherwise handsome, tall bay stallion began to stagger to the ground, Dr. Key would bring out both his tonic and his liniment, recommending a course of treatment that used both. No Shakespearean actor in a death scene coming back to life for his curtain call could have outdone Jim Key's onstage transformation. Needless to say, the Keystone products often sold out before the troupe could make it back to Shelbyville for more stock.

After that, Key said, "Jim learned to make believe he was lame and act as though he were suffering with other kinds of troubles, the general symptoms of which he would reproduce."

Since Jim had been such a quick study as a performer in the medicine show, Rogers assumed that learning to read and spell came to him rapidly as well.

Not at all, Dr. Key admitted. At first, the process was slow and unpromising. "The hardest thing I had to teach him was to learn how to eat sugar."

Really? Rogers looked surprised. Jim Key, listening, gave a small neigh of amusement.

"Yes, sir," recalled the Doc, "I tried every way, and had it tied to the bridle, but Jim would always spit it out. One day I saw him eating apples in the orchard and I got the idea that if I put a piece of sugar in the apple he would eat it. I fixed an apple and then watched Jim. When he picked it up and munched it, I thought he would go crazy with satisfaction and delight."

Doc Key tried again to feed Jim the sugar by itself. No success. For the next six months, the Doc experimented with different techniques. "If I covered the apple with sugar, he would eat both with great relish," he remembered. "So I gradually reduced the quantity of apple over the sugar, and then he would have a piece of apple laid over the piece of sugar in my hand, and when he would reach for the apple he would get the sugar. In this way he learned that sugar was sugar and apple was apple." By that time, Jim loved both rewards equally.

Albert Rogers had to ask, "Why were you so intent on having him learn to like sugar?"

William Key probably milked this moment and gave Rogers a sideways glance, as if to suggest that the answer was obvious. After all, how else was he going to teach Jim the alphabet?

This was the story Rogers had been waiting for. How had that come about?

Dr. Key had no story to tell. He simply had gotten it into his head that his eager, able performing equine could be trained to recognize and select the letter *A* from a grouping of other letters. "When I began I had in my mind only to teach Jim to pick out the letter *A*. I got some cards with the letter *A* on them, and put sugar on those cards."

Albert now understood. "You had to teach him to eat the sugar first and this was after Jim had grown to have a passion for sugar?"

"Which he has never lost," the Doc echoed. "I held the card up and would say, '*A, A, A.*' And while I was doing this I would let nobody in the stable, and I would keep him away from other horses. I said *A* a good many times, and Jim used up many cards, as he would lick the cards so much."

Realizing he had sent Jim the wrong message—that letters of the alphabet were edible—Dr. Key adapted his methodology. Instead of paper cards, he used pieces of tin with the letter *A* painted on them, sprinkled with sugar, and mixed in with pieces of tin that had other letters painted on them without sugar. "It took months and months, a half year, before I was satisfied that he would know the letter *A* when he would see it. Then, I thought that if Jim could only be made to bring the card to me I would have just what I wanted. I at once began to train him for this end." For this process, the Doc put a piece of an apple in a handkerchief and taught Jim to bring it in his mouth to him, giving the handkerchief to Dr. Key and receiving the apple as his reward. "I soon had him tugging at the card with the *A* on it and then bringing it to me."

Further questions led Albert Rogers to see that the lessons for learning the letter *A* occupied hours of the day, requiring extraordinary patience. What, then, had possessed Key to continue with other letters? Why wasn't he satisfied?

"Of course, I thought I had my fortune made when one day I happened to think if the horse knew *A* when he saw it he could be taught the entire alphabet, and in this I was right."

From the answers to these questions, Rogers put to rest his concern that skeptics would be suspicious of a man and a horse whose act grew out of a medicine show background. In his way of thinking, having two seasoned salesmen would be an asset for the humane movement, not a deterrent. The plan was simple: Bill and Jim would draw the crowds and then, instead of selling a product, sell an idea, albeit the socially challenging idea that all cruelty toward animals was abhorrent and unacceptable.

Rogers also felt that the story of how Jim learned the alphabet was simple and logical enough and would sway at least some cynics. But there was one other thorny area of questioning that had to do with how Northerners might feel about a slave who had chosen to align himself not with the Yankees but with the Confederate States of America. The answers that followed were not simple and had nothing to do with logic.

On June 12, 1861, Young Doc Key, age twenty-eight, made haste to Camp Trousdale in Sumner County, three counties north of Bedford, with the intention of preventing twenty-year-old Merit and eighteen-year-old Alexander from enlisting to fight for the Southern cause. Too late. On June 11, the two sons of John W. Key had been mustered into service with the Eighteenth Tennessee Infantry Regiment, Company F, under Captain Benjamin F. Webb. Dubbed the Festerville Guards, the unit was made up of men from Bedford and Rutherford counties organized earlier in the week in Bell Buckle and in Murfreesboro under General Palmer.

How had it happened? What speech in which town square or which neighbor had goaded the two boys, peace-loving scholars that they were, to take up arms against the Union?

Madness. For six months the divided house of Tennessee had refrained from secession. "When the War clouds began to gather," Key recalled, the signs were mixed, boding both that the impossible could never happen and that it was inevitable. Lincoln—vowing not to end slavery where it existed, but only to arrest its spread—had instantly become the mortal enemy of every slave state. The first to secede was South Carolina, in December 1860, then within a month Mississippi seceded, followed by Florida, Alabama, Georgia, and Louisiana.

Would Tennessee become the seventh state to secede? The question was put to a vote on February 9, 1861. Predictably, the majority of East Tennesseans voted emphatically against secession, while most West Tennesseans voted to leave the Union. The decision came down to Middle Tennessee, and the winning margin was helped in Bedford County where the count was 1,656 to 828, two to one against secession.

But despite the "no" vote in February, with Tennessee's strategic importance, too much was at stake to too many forces to allow her to be left on the sidelines. Pressure mounted from within and without.

Texas seceded in March, and then, on April 12, the president of the fledgling Confederacy, Jefferson Davis, ordered a preemptive strike on Fort Sumter, which gave the South an almost bloodless victory. The sole casualty was a horse, whose death unceremoniously marked the first of an estimated one and a half million horses and mules that would be killed or wounded in battle and the resultant marauding, or would die from starvation and disease over the course of the next four years.

With the slaying of a single horse in its opening battle, so began the bloodiest war in American history.

For many wavering Northerners, the assault on Fort Sumter was cause enough to put aside ideological differences over slavery and states' rights, and to take up arms. But for many Southerners, Lincoln's subsequent call for 75,000 troops from each state in the Union had a similarly galvanizing effect, setting into motion like dominos a string of three more secessions: Virginia, Arkansas, and North Carolina.

In Shelbyville, Young Doc Key could feel the pendulum swing of local sentiments shift as mercurially as a wave of bad weather. Again, on June 8, the question was put to the Tennessee voters. For weeks the matter had been pushed back to the polls by the slave-holding class and the politicians. Bill Key knew that not many of those who wanted the war would actually serve. It was going to be mostly the poor and middle-class soldiers—few of them slave holders—who were going to fight and die in the widening conflict.

That was one point made by Parson William G. Brownlow, the fiery antisecessionist from East Tennessee, who raced across the state to bring his message to the Shelbyville public square, where he boomed it from the steps of the courthouse. A favorite of the ladies for his passionate oratory, Brownlow preached loyalty to God and nation, begging the end of slavery's abomination. Heckled by a man who accused him of abetting the Yankee devil to defile Southern women, he thundered back, "I am an unconditional Union man and advocate the preservation of the Union at the expense of all other considerations!" as the women waved their handkerchiefs in support.

Young Doc Key's friend, lawyer, and state legislator William H. Wisener also took to the steps of the courthouse to beg business owners to think about how their stores and wares would be co-opted by the demands of the Confederate government. Likewise taking a stand against secession was the prosperous Lewis Tillman. Though he was a slave holder, Tillman believed the city had too much to lose and little to gain from leaving the Union. But for many area farmers, Brownlow, Wisener, and Tillman were unconvincing. These Bedford countians were much more moved by the stirring military airs played by the staunch "secesh" advocates. In contrast to the gloomy Unionists, many Southerners were practically giddy with the "glorious future" promised by Jefferson Davis, as if to remain with the Union would be to miss out on the festivities. To them, the reality of bloodshed was remote, especially if the noble Volunteer State was willing to take the battle north to the enemy where Southern fire in the belly would vanquish foes of the South in short shrift. In ninety days, the maximum amount of time most reasonable Southern strategists believed the war would take to win, life would return to normal, the better for all not to live under the yoke of Lincoln.

From the back of the gathering, Young Doc Key heard all this through the loud hum of the crowd, like a mill wheel powered by Southern bravado, churning its grist into fear and loathing. Mothers recounted their children's nightmares of being stolen from their beds by invading Yankees, of their husbands and sons murdered; fathers, husbands, sons, and brothers readied themselves to do their duty. Those who disagreed began to hold their tongues.

Hardly mentioned was either the right to own slaves or the wrong of owning slaves, in part because slavery was not the main fuel that drove Tennessee's economic engine, and partly because Lincoln himself, still almost two years away from declaring an end to slavery, denied that it was the central issue of the dispute. And yet it was a blaring subtext, the only one, igniting throughout the political and regional strata the tinderbox it had always been.

Around the periphery of Shelbyville's town square, standing in the back of the crowds—tending to horses and buggies or other tasks, ignored as though invisible—were representatives of Bedford County's nearly seven thousand Negroes, fifty-two of whom were free. Blacks were a full third of the total population of the county, but no one spoke for them. Without words, William Key knew many of them shared the same fears and hopes. In a war, life could only be harder for black people. But, despite Lincoln's haltering steps to be the deliverer whom history demanded he be, freedom was coming, war or not.

The Tennessee ballot on June 8, 1861, asked voters two questions, to vote for or against "separation" (whether or not to secede) and to vote for or against "representation" (whether or not to join with the Confederacy). In most counties where the vote was against secession, it was also against joining the rebellion; most who voted for secession also voted to join the Rebels. But in Bedford County a strange thing happened. In a reversal of the numbers from February, the count was 1,544 for secession and 727 against. But on the question of representation, 1,544 voted against joining the Confederacy, and 737 voted in favor. What the net result of the vote really showed was that residents of Bedford County had a profound desire for neutrality. For this, the Middle Tennessee haven would be alternately rewarded and punished, almost continually occupied by all manner of invading armies.

Despite divisions, by day's end Tennessee became the ninth and last state to secede from the Union and join the Confederacy. East Tennessee remained a Union stronghold while Middle Tennessee and West Tennessee, with some exceptions, stayed true to the Southern cause. Bedford County continued to be split, contributing troops to twenty-three Confederate units, while also sending soldiers into twelve Federal units. The Volunteer State's war of neighbor against neighbor and brother against brother had begun.

Three days later William Key arrived, one day late, at Camp Trousdale. He found Merit and Alexander, already looking hungry, worn, and somewhat bewildered as to how they had been recruited. Being not far from the Kentucky border, Young Doc Key realized that he was closer to freedom than he had ever been before. He could take the Keys' horse; he would go with their blessings. But instead he chose to stay and follow John W. Key's two sons.

Rogers didn't understand.

Bill Key explained it simply. "I loved my young marsters. I was afraid they would get killed or not have anything to eat, so I went with them." His choice had as much to do with his stubbornness as with his humanity.

This put a different twist on his partisanship, making the answer to the question a more complicated one. Yes, he had been with the

Rebels, Key told Rogers, but he had also helped the Yankees, served as a guide on the Underground Railroad, acted as a medic and surgeon for soldiers and horses from the gray and the blue, operated as a spy, military strategist, architect, diplomat, thief, and hero. To survive and to ensure the survival of the Key boys, he had stubbornly decided he would need to belong to every side, and to none.

Through the summer and into the fall of 1861 the early Confederate victories had kept spirits high in Company F. Then ninety days passed and the war was not finished. Winter set in, bringing storms that overshadowed memories of celebratory parades and political bravado. In January 1862, the rain turned to sleet and snow as Captain Webb and his unit slogged west through mud toward Dover, Tennessee, just below the Kentucky border.

It was here at Fort Donelson that Company F prepared to face its first battle. Bill had been relieved when, thanks to their reading and writing abilities, Merit and Alexander had been selected for communications duty, mainly for protecting important papers and sending dispatches. Bill hoped these responsibilities would keep them off the front lines as much as possible. The way things were shaping up at Fort Donelson, however, that didn't look likely.

Ulysses S. Grant, now launching his campaign into Tennessee, had easily taken nearby Fort Henry and was now headed for Fort Donelson. Less of a fortress and more of a stockade, Donelson covered fifteen acres that overlooked the one-hundred-foot bluff above the west bank of the Cumberland River. With a garrison of 15,000 troops, a dozen heavy guns arrayed to meet Grant's gunboats, and three miles of trenches along the river, the strategic advantage appeared to belong to the Confederates, despite their being outnumbered by Grant's 27,000 troops. But the Young Doc saw two glaring problems. The first had to do with disagreements among the generals—Floyd, Pillow, and Buckner. The second and biggest problem he saw was that their focus was on defending the fort from the boats, without any planning being given to defending against a siege by land. In a worst-case scenario, even if the assault by water was stopped, Grant's attack by land could still trap and pin the Confederates against the river. Off the front lines or not, the Key boys would be captured.

With the Battle of Fort Donelson ranking as the tenth most costly engagement of the war—resulting in more than 19,000 casualties, 80 percent Confederate—Bill Key's strategic assessment turned out to be correct. There had been bizarre shifts in the weather—from being so unseasonably warm one day that many of the Northern boys threw off their coats, to a sudden bout of freezing rain and heavy snow the next day, to a wind so bitter later that a dying Yankee crept into the Rebel rifle pits to warm himself by their campfire, where his enemies shared their ration of coffee with him before he died.

Like the weather, the battle's momentum shifted radically, first favoring the Southerners when the brunt of the assault came from the gunboats. From close range, the cannonballs overarched and missed their targets while the Rebel big guns pummeled and overpowered the boats. But as Bill predicted, when breastworks were being hastily built along the water's edge, few were erected to stave off the land assault that came after all. Ultimately the victory went to the North, providing the occasion upon which Grant refused any special terms except unconditional surrender.

From this battle, the initials "U. S." of Grant's name came to be known henceforth as "Unconditional Surrender." A year earlier Grant, a washed-up military man, had been a clerk in a harness maker's shop; now he had given the North its first meaningful victory of the war. The Battle of Fort Donelson would eventually not be ranked as a major battle. In fact, when Albert Rogers described it in the pamphlet, he mistakenly referred to it as Fort "Donaldson." But many historians would also argue that the loss was catastrophic for the South. With it, the Union had corralled Kentucky and had made the breach into Tennessee—up two of its rivers no less. For those on both sides who had never seen combat before, though there were worse images to come, nothing would ever be as haunting as the sight of the bodies in blood-soaked gray and blue that littered the icy snow, the faces of the dead said to be literally frozen, with eyes and mouths gaping wide.

Fewer historians preserved a fascinating piece of history about the Battle of Fort Donelson, which began before the shooting started as Bill Key, accidental military strategist, set about to assess the gaps in the line of defense while also making mental notes for any possible escape routes. A noncombatant, he then looked for a spot to build some sort of fortification to hide himself.

"Yes, sir," Key told Rogers, "that became the famous fort that the soldiers called Fort Bill."

Fort Bill? Albert was dubious until this story was confirmed to him later by Nashville's Mayor Richard Houston Dudley, Bill's childhood friend. The lives of many of Bedford County's sons were saved there.

"It was only a small place dug in the ground and covered with logs to keep the bullets out," Doc Key told Rogers. He was able to stay out of the line of fire, as did Merit, Alexander, and several of the other Festerville Guards, once he was able to coax them in with him. Initially, when he tried to wave them in to take shelter, the soldiers refused. But the carnage soon changed their minds.

"When Fort Donelson was captured in the night," Doc Key went on, "I stole out and found a place unguarded and took my young masters out, with important papers, and we escaped."

As the three forged on foot through ice-encrusted streams and into gullies of waist-deep mud, they made their way south and caught up with Lieutenant Colonel Nathan Bedford Forrest. The brash cavalryman had been at Fort Donelson and had been furious when his superiors chose to surrender. Ironically, Nathan Bedford Forrest, a native of Bedford County, from which he took his middle name, had scouted the same gaps in the Union line that Bill Key had found. When Forrest argued for retreat, he was allowed to lead out a column of 700 men, through the same route that the Young Doc had navigated, only an hour or so afterward.

Nathan Bedford Forrest had been one of the richest, most notorious slave traders in Tennessee. Now on his way to becoming a general, he was also earning a reputation as one of the most brilliant cavalry officers of the Confederacy. Forrest was said to be two men: a kind, soft-spoken gentleman away from the battlefield who, at the flip of a switch, could be transformed into war mode and the embodiment of a fighting machine. His own mother described him as having, while a child, a terror-inducing voice when angered. Yet under stress, he had a decision-making ability that was uncannily prophetic, his own form of mother wit. But brilliant as he was, it turned out that Nathan Bedford Forrest was nearly illiterate. Bill Key knew this and didn't hesitate to inform him that Merit and Alexander were at college level in book learning. When Forrest found out that Alexander had been able to withhold important papers from the enemy at Fort Donelson, he made A. W. Key an officer, assigning both Key sons to jobs as scouts and guides.

Shelbyville historians later boasted that William Key served as caretaker for Forrest's own horse, while the Young Doc was also allowed to be an unofficial guide along with the Keys. He earned enough favor with General Forrest that he was given a pass to go home. For a man of color to possess such a piece of Confederate paper was highly unusual.

Without being found out, the Young Doc exploited this gift by spending the next period of the war assisting fugitive slaves through the lines, a job that enabled him to go home to Shelbyville and discover why it had come to be called Little Boston.

———

L ike Bill Key, the folks back home were doing what they could to survive and get along, both with their occupiers and one another. John and Martha Key described how feelings that had once been only friendly disputes between neighbors were now growing more acrimonious by the day.

After the defeat at Fort Donelson, Confederate troops were temporarily stationed in Shelbyville under the command of General Hardee, which coincided with widespread foraging of farms and the disappearance of 30,000 head of hogs and many numbers of beeves. John's tanyard had been heavily looted, and though some merchants were paid for the stocks and goods taken, the Confederate paper money was as yet of little value.

With resentment against the Rebels percolating, Shelbyville got an added shot of antisecessionist venom when Parson Brownlow was brought through as a Confederate prisoner, causing an uproar among the ladies in town. Before he could cause too much trouble, the Confederates pulled out in time for the arrival of incoming Yankees, led by the Fourth Ohio Cavalry. The reception was so warm for the Northerners that *Harper's Weekly* soon ran a sketch of "Shelbyville, the only Union town in Tennessee." The accompanying article proclaimed, "The names of such men as Wisener . . . and others deserve to be perpetual in history for their unyielding fidelity to the great republic."

Not everyone shared pride in the new nickname "Little Boston." Nor did all the citizens of Shelbyville prefer occupation by Yankees any more than by Rebels, especially when food supplies ran short and the Northern boys helped themselves to livestock and grain stores. For his part, the Young Doc got on splendidly with many of the Union officers he met during his sporadic visits home, sometimes helping some of the Yankee boys through the lines. He figured his help would be remembered, and the fact that he was protecting Confederate sons of Shelbyville wouldn't be held against him. But he was soon to be wrong about that.

At the end of March, when William had been away from the front for almost two months without word from Merit and Alexander, a grave foreboding came over him. Inquiries brought back information that they were with General Forrest heading toward Pittsburgh Landing, in southwest Tennessee, not far from the Mississippi state line. The Young Doc rode there at top speed, not sure what he'd find.

Confederate Tennessean John Gumm crawled to shelter in the waning hours of the battle fought on April 6 and 7, 1862, and scribbled in his diary:

> I have learned the name of the Battel ground they call it Shi-
> loah . . . it was . . . the greatest Battel in modern history . . . its
> duration and Bravery never his bin Surpassed Either in ancient
> or modern history . . . it was one Continel Charge. . . . Bombs and
> Grape Shot fell as thick as hair and Minnie Balls whising round
> my Years like Bombel Bees.

In a battle named for the whitewashed, log-built Shiloh (from the Hebrew word for "place of peace") Church, which stood amid peach trees west of the death pond or "blood pond," where the water turned red from the bodies piled one on top of the other, the strong advantage began with the 45,000 Confederate troops throughout the first day. The weather had been springlike and gentle, as a breeze rustled the peach blossoms and sent them fluttering down on top of the fallen. But a rainstorm that night and then rein-forcements on the second day of fighting (which gave the Union as many as 65,000 troops) saw a momentum shift—enough to force the Rebels to retreat toward Corinth, Mississippi, and to give Gen-eral Grant the muted victory. Between both sides, 3,000 were dead and another 20,000 wounded, more casualties than in all previous American battles.

In this hell William Key found Alexander and Merit with General Forrest, whose mission it was to protect the retreating Confederate infantry from pursuit by the Union cavalry.

As he had before, the Young Doc tried to convince the two Key boys to follow him to safer ground, but only Merit, with the excuse of guarding papers, was in a position to find cover in a clearing called Fallen Timbers. With a thunderous shaking of the ground came the approach of the Fourth Illinois Cavalry, and Forrest lifted his saber to give the order to take the fight to the enemy, gallop-ing like a cannon shot toward the incoming riders. Alexander Key, as part of the rearguard, readied his rifle and started off on foot. William looked after him miserably, here in the shadow of Shiloh. Certain that John W. Key's secondborn son would die if he didn't do anything, Bill pulled out his trusty pistol and aimed it straight for the midcalf of Alexander's leg.

Just before the Doc pulled the trigger, Officer Alexander Key whirled around and stopped him, cautioning, "I'm keeping a close watch on you, Bill. You were going to shoot me, weren't you?"

Grumbling, Bill admitted that he was, but only so they wouldn't have to fight anymore. Alexander hesitated helplessly, then followed the last of Forrest's men off after their leader. Alexander returned to the camp intact, but General Forrest was badly wounded when, after riding into the midst of Union cavalrymen who surrounded his horse, which began to rear and turn, cries of "shoot him" brought a rifle so close to him that it grazed his jacket as its bullet ripped into his hip and lodged in his lower spine. History marked that shot as the last one fired at the Battle of Shiloh.

William Key swore that nothing he would live to see could ever match the bloody nightmare at Pittsburgh Landing. But eight months later, he found himself yet again on the sidelines of a bat-tle that did. From December 31 of that year until January 2, 1863, at the outskirts of Murfreesboro along Stones River, about thirty miles north of Shelbyville, Doc Key witnessed his third and final large-scale battle that proportionally incurred more casualties on both sides than at Shiloh, leaving almost one-third of the total of 75,000 who fought either killed or wounded. The battle had pitted Confederate general Braxton Bragg against General William Rosecrans and should have been won by the Rebels after Bragg forced the Yankees into considerable retreat. But at the Nashville Pike the theretofore overly cautious Rosecrans rallied his Union troops and held the line, ultimately forcing Bragg into retreat.

Stones River was not viewed as so decisive a battle as others in Tennessee, but in a winter following numerous setbacks for the Union, their victory at Murfreesboro was another important turning point.

The end of the battle coincided with news that on January 1, 1863, Lincoln had issued the Emancipation Proclamation, freeing the slaves. The great, long promised day of jubilee had come at last, except that free status meant little in the seceded states. Yet Bill knew now that the North would win, and that the colored regiments authorized by Emancipation would be the reason why. He was having an increasingly difficult time helping the Confederacy even indirectly, knowing the price to be paid for its victory was to be the loss of freedom. Or as he told the Union soldiers when they captured him and he tried to explain why he had switched affiliations: "I was tired of the Rebels and I wanted to be free."

Unfortunately, his reputation had preceded him, or someone back in Shelbyville had it in for him. The pro-Union sentiment there had become less pronounced by now, for a variety of reasons. The plight of Union spy James J. Andrews and his Union rangers—who hatched a plot in Shelbyville to commandeer "The General," a prized Southern steam engine, only to be hung shortly after the plan's failure—may have had a sobering effect on outward demonstrations by the Little Bostonians. Soon after, Confederate cavalryman John Hunt Morgan came through the area, retaliating against Union sympathizers. There were extensive reports of houses and farms being burned, stores looted, horses and Negroes abducted and assaulted.

The Key family matriarch, Margaret Graham Key, died during this period of the war. It may have been of interest to the Young Doc that in a report of this time a Yankee soldier described an eighty-year-old woman named "Mrs. Graham" strangely reminiscent of the Old Missus. This energetic elderly woman climbed up on a pedestal and, with her own bare hands, tore the flag of the Confederacy down from a post in the town square, raving that her husband had fought for the Stars and Stripes and had given his life to his country. The account certainly matched the family myth of Strother Key. She had family members, Mrs. Graham said, who had been dragged from their home and had been shot for favoring the Union.

The reality was that divided alliances had given way to mob rule that operated differently from hill to hill. The county began to breed guerrillas, thieves, and home guards of many persuasions. Boys were leaving their units and coming home shoeless and starving, only to be shot as deserters. Neighbors pointed fingers at other neighbors; family members turned in other family members. Suspicion and fear spread. No one was safe.

Starting at this period more than 22,000 Negroes from Tennessee, a tenth of the total number of African-Americans to be mustered into Union service, began to pour North to take up arms or to join local colored units being organized. One of the few guides able to navigate the routes leading out of Bedford County for them was William Key, and in the beginning of 1863 he was doing so with increasing regularity. That was when he ran into some trouble with his Union contacts.

In February, he related to Rogers, "I undertook to get another darkey through the lines but was caught by the guard, the Sixth Indiana Regiment, and accused of being a spy."

The Indianans were willing to accept his explanation that he was finished with the Rebs. But one of their officers became wary. He remembered hearing something, maybe from one of the Ohio officers who had been in Shelbyville, about a mulatto horse surgeon associated with the detested Nathan Bedford Forrest. The Ohioans were summoned, took one look at William Key, and began to smirk. Doc Key recognized them, he told Rogers, as "Union men that lived at my home."

"That's him," said one of them to the Indiana officers, "the worst Rebel in the South."

Doc Key's justification of being compelled to serve his master's young sons didn't wash with the Yanks. They decided he was a dangerous prisoner and clamped him in jail somewhere between Murfreesboro and Nashville under the command of General James Scott Negley, with the plan to hold him there until they caught Officer Alexander W. Key, another presumed spy, and then hang them together.

"I staid in that prison six weeks," the Doc recalled. At that point he overheard some grousing from his guards about the demands being put on them by General Negley. A reputed taskmaster, he had ordered his men to find him a decent cook.

The Young Doc beckoned a guard with whom he was on friendly terms. "They call me the best cook in Tennessee," he whispered. "If you don't believe me, ask anyone from my home." A Shelbyville Confederate prisoner was located and when asked he ventured, "Best cook in Tennessee? Bill's the best cook in the *country*."

General Negley, accompanied by Captain Allen Prather, came to interview Bill.

"Negley and Capt. Prather both wanted me," Key told Rogers. "I liked the looks of Capt. Prather, and I knew he was a great poker player." With a bit of hedging, the Doc was able to have Negley order his temporary release into the custody of Captain Prather, for whom he would serve as cook, with the implicit understanding that the general be invited to dine regularly.

Key may have waited a day or two before offhandedly mentioning to Prather, after cleaning up from the evening meal, that he sure would love to play some cards.

"You any good?"

"Never found a man could beat me."

This was enough to pique Prather's interest, and he was eager to discover how much of a bluff that had been.

Albert Rogers understood Dr. Key never lost at cards, having, as Key had told him, an occult ability to know what cards his opponent held in his hands at any time. So how did this work out?

William Key was happy to report, "In six weeks I owned everything Capt. Prather had; he owed me over a thousand dollars. He gave me a pass to go home for the debt."

During these weeks and months Shelbyville had its own jailed spy, a Major Pauline Cushman, an actress turned Federal secret agent who was caught attempting to smuggle Confederate papers out of town and sentenced to hang by General Bragg, whose troops were having an extended stay in Bedford County.

Fending off the winter's cold, hunger, illness, and lice, Rebel soldiers were ordered by Bragg to be respectful of the occupied townspeople, with instructions, for example, not to enter a store unless invited in. This led to some goodwill between the townspeople and Rebels, despite some resentment after the courthouse was badly burnt when the Rebel high command took up residence in it, allegedly from an accidental fire caused by Confederate soldiers just trying to warm up.

During the six months that followed, while Major Cushman's execution was continuously postponed due to her illness and fatigue, with the excuse that she was not well enough to walk to the gallows, Bragg played a cat-and-mouse game with Rosecrans that finally erupted in June 1863 at the Battle of Hoover's Gap.

Of the near constant skirmishing that took place in and around Bedford County, the Battle of Hoover's Gap was the largest battle to occur in the area. Rosecrans won it by bluffing and starting his approach from a different direction and then turning at the last minute to the less reinforced position, taking Bragg by surprise. Occupation of Shelbyville traded hands yet again, leaving Pauline Cushman to be liberated by Federal authorities as the Union took control once more and loyalists crept back out of hiding.

The Battle of Hoover's Gap and the hasty evacuation of Shelbyville had a different significance for Young Doc Key. It seemed that in their hurry to get supplies safely out of town, a handful of Bragg's officers had forgotten the stash of Confederate money they had left hidden under the floorboards of a certain store run by a known Union man. Attempts by any one of them to return to retrieve the money would be disastrous. But there was one person, they decided, who could do the job and get away with it.

When the officers first informed the Doc that they wanted him to retrieve the money, he was shocked by the amount: $500,000. Their proposition was that he would be given $100,000 in return for getting through the Union lines, going to the store, finding the money, and bringing it back to them.

Dr. Key admitted to Rogers, "I didn't like this job, but there was so much money in it that one night I stole out by the camp."

Bill's strategy had been to wait behind the store until its early opening. If he could get in and out without running into anyone who recognized him, he was sure it would be easy to have a friendly conversation with the storekeepers and distract them long enough to get the money before slipping away and back past the camp.

He made it past the camp without a problem, but on his way into the store, the first person he encountered, and the last person he ever hoped to see, was the one he had described to Rogers before as his worst enemy. He was that certain slave driver who had tried unsuccessfully to buy young Bill Key and had sworn one day to get him and lick the blood out of him, a memory that made the Young Doc whirl around and attempt to run—straight into a group of Union soldiers. Though the slave driver had no allegiance to the Yankees, he insisted that the mulatto horse doctor was a convicted Rebel spy who had escaped once from their jail, and he demanded that Bill be walked across the square, clapped into prison, and hung before daylight the next day.

"Well," Dr. Key said to Rogers, "they would have, if not for W. H. Wisener, the lawyer who knew me and knew that I had money." For the one thousand dollars that Wisener knew Doc Key had in his shoe, he promised to get him off.

"My case was put off time and time again by this lawyer," Dr. Key recalled, "until one day the inspector said he wanted a good white-washer. I told him that was my regular business, and that my brushes were at a certain store in town. He sent me there with a guard. I went behind the counter and pulled off the sole of my shoe and gave the money to the lady who run the store, and she gave it to Wisener." Then, in a feint to go collect his brushes, he went to find the elusive 500,000 Confederate dollars. Someone had beaten him to it.

William Key was disgusted. If Wisener didn't manage to have his case dismissed, or if he wasn't able to escape his sentence while whitewashing, he was going to be hung for no crime at all.

Albert Rogers was eager to know what strings the lawyer pulled or what Houdini-like escape Doc Key masterminded next. Neither was responsible, as it turned out. "The next day the Rebels raided the town and captured the place and I was let go."

Rogers assumed he had to have been grateful for that bit of providence.

Yes, Dr. Key agreed, except for the fact that after his lawyer was locked up, his own money was gone too.

The Confederate raid that rescued Doc Key from the gallows the second time was followed by a brief stint of Rebel control. That soon yielded again to the Yankees as Shelbyville became a Union garrison town for General William Tecumseh Sherman, subject to intermittent skirmishing, ongoing attacks by guerrillas, home guards, and bushwhackers, and general lawlessness.

When Sherman began cutting a swath of devastation across the South in his March to the Sea, some Tennesseans believed he spared much of the Volunteer State from greater destruction on account of the pockets of support for the Union he had observed in places like Shelbyville. Others simply felt that there was nothing left to destroy.

Such was the scene of death and ruin that met William Key when he returned Merit and Alexander, alive, to their parents. A few weeks before their return, the surrender of General Robert E. Lee to General Ulysses S. Grant at the Appomattox Courthouse in Virginia had ended the Civil War. Five days after Lee's surrender, while attending a play with his wife, President Lincoln was assassinated by John Wilkes Booth. As cataclysmically as it began, so it concluded.

The world changed, as though altered on its axis. Three million Americans fought, 600,000 died, while many times more were left disabled, homeless, widowed, orphaned, sick, and impoverished. And four million Americans who had been slaves were free. Of those former slaves, 275,000 had been from Tennessee. She had been the last state to leave the Union, and the state that, with the exception of Virginia, had been scarred by more destruction than any other state in the nation, and so plummeted from former economic stature. But Tennessee was to be the first Confederate state to return to the Union.

Racism would find some of its greatest foes on Tennessee's home soil, but also its greatest perpetuators—including the KKK, which was founded in Pulaski, Tennessee, the same year as the war ended. On the other hand, only a month after Lee's surrender, black and white activists opened schools for African-Americans across the state. In May 1865, a Texan Confederate soldier named Samuel Foster was heading home through Greenville, Tennessee, and he marveled in his diary that he had that day seen Negro children going to school. He stopped a little girl "about 12 years old dressed neat and clean," and asked her to show him what she was studying. "I opened the Grammar and the middle of the book and asked her a few questions—which she answered readily and correctly. Same with her Geography and Arithmetic. I was never more surprised in my life!"

The power of education was radically made evident to Foster by a radical change in his thinking:

> It seems curious that mens minds can change so sudden, from opinions of life long, to new ones a week old. I mean that men who have not only been taught from their infancy that the institution of slavery was right; but men who actually owned and held slaves up to this time,—have now changed in their opinions regarding slavery ... to see that for man to have property in man was wrong, and that ... "all men are, and of right ought to be free" has a meaning different from the definition they had been taught from infancy up. .... These ideas come from not the Yanks or northern people but come from reflection, and reasoning among ourselves.

The famous and not-so-famous individuals whose journeys had intersected Bill Key's, if only peripherally, met varied fortunes. Grant became the only general of the Civil War to accept the surrender of three separate armies after three major battles and, of course, went on to be elected to two terms as President of the United States. Parson Brownlow's fiery antisecessionism didn't hurt him at the ballot box, and he became governor of Tennessee in the years immediately following the war and later a United States senator. Major Pauline Cushman enjoyed celebrity status for a while but eventually fell from the public eye and died penniless. Shelbyville Unionist Lewis Tillman became an advocate for Negro suffrage and went on to serve as a U.S. congressman. W. H. Wisener prospered in business, but his radical Republicanism in his fight for racial equality proved unpopular during the turbulent Reconstruction era. David

Key, a first cousin of John W. Key, made a name for himself when, in 1877, he was appointed postmaster general of the United States under President Rutherford Hayes.

Though William Key didn't boast to Rogers how he had helped John and Martha, the story was subsequently recounted by Nashville mayor Richard Dudley, Bill's childhood friend. The mayor noted that Dr. Key had remained with John's sons for the duration of the hostilities and that "upon their return found the tanyard and every- thing else belonging to the family destroyed." An invalid by this time, John W. Key lived long enough to see his boys come home. Unable to pay the heavy mortgage hanging over his property, he tried to raise the money by selling a large portion of it to his nephew, J. M. Minter, along with the last of his livestock: one bay mare and colt, and six hogs.

But the money didn't cover their debt, and when John died shortly thereafter, Martha could do nothing about the $5,000 still owing for the mortgage. Mayor Dudley recalled that it was Bill who went to work to raise the capital, paying off the note and tearing it up when he was through. Apparently the Doc had accumulated some substantial poker winnings after spending much of the last year and a half up north. Descendants of townspeople and relatives confirmed they had heard accounts that Dr. William Key not only paid off the mortgage but also supported Martha and her offspring for the remainder of her days, paying for her kids' education and starting them in business. Some claimed that Bill even paid for Merit and Alexander to attend Harvard, partly as a vicarious expe- rience he would have prized for himself, and partly because that would have been the education that John would have most wanted to provide for them.

Many of the Doc's friends of color went north during and after the war. He had thought about joining them and had apparently been on trips to look for a place to settle. His idea was to open a hospital for horses and mules wounded in combat, something he assumed might be better received in Northern cities—where the first themes of the humane movement were now being sounded. But by September 1865, he changed his mind about leaving, bought his first piece of Bedford County property—spending $650 for two and a half acres bordering North Main Street, also known as the

Shelbyville and Murfreesboro Turnpike—where he established his horse hospital and veterinarian office.

Within five years Doc Key was known as one of the more prosperous, prominent men in town. He had received the blessing of reuniting with his mother, Caroline, with whom he had stayed in close contact in earlier years, though he lost her soon afterward, much to his sorrow. Free to legally marry, Bill wasted no time making his longtime sweetheart, Lucy Davidson, his wife. Similarly, his sister Nancy got married right after the war was over, becoming Mrs. Henry McClain.

The fact that Bill and Lucy had no children was probably for the better, considering that the household couldn't have accommodated one more individual, what with Lucy's mother, Arabella, living there, along with Bill's uncle Jack, various nieces and nephews, stable hands, and with the Doctor's nonhuman patients staying over more often than not. Before long, Doc Key built a second home on his property for the overflow.

In short order, William expanded his operations to include a blacksmith shop next to his horse hospital, then opened up a wagon wheel and harness-making business at a separate location. With these revenues he raised the capital to manufacture Keystone Liniment on a scale large enough to market it through his traveling medicine shows across the South. In turn, Dr. Key's restaurant, hotel, and racetrack were enterprises launched with profits from the liniment sales.

A quintessential entrepreneur, Bill Key had mastered the ability to parlay one success into the next one. His gambler's sensibilities guided him to take calculated risks and to know how to fold when he was losing. A scrupulous businessman who took goods in place of money when poorer folks couldn't afford to pay in cash, he had also learned, from John W. Key's excessive borrowing and loaning, to avoid both. Friends and relatives told stories about what a hardcore capitalist he was. A sister-in-law later claimed, "He would walk a mile to collect a nickel."

Rogers asked if gambling had continued to help fuel Dr. Key's financial success after the war.

"When I ran my restaurant," the Doc admitted, "I won a peck of onions from a farmer I beat playing poker." Although the farmer made threatening remarks, Bill didn't see cause for worry. But he was wrong. "Sure enough, the farmer had me arrested and fined forty-five dollars. That slowed down my gambling." Dr. Key grinned cryptically, letting Rogers come to his own conclusions.

Most of the black citizens who stayed in Shelbyville after the war, like Dr. Key, had a pronounced entrepreneurial determination that was all the more remarkable, considering the problems of a backlash against freed Negroes that increased during Reconstruction. The Freedmen's Bureau assessment was that although former Unionists and former Confederates generally approved of black schools, whites were united in bitter opposition "to any action looking to what they are pleased to call equality."

Bill Key managed to stay above the fray, maintaining warm personal and business relationships across color and class lines. Even so, he was very much rooted in the black community. He was inducted as a member of the Colored Masons not long after lodges were chartered in Tennessee, and he belonged to an African-American Episcopalian congregation.

It was not surprising to the much younger Rogers that a man who had lived so many lifetimes had also suffered his share of setbacks and losses. He had been crushed by the death of his mother-in-law, Arabella Davidson, in 1882, followed three years later by the death of his wife, Lucy, to whom he had been married almost seventeen years. When asked what he wanted inscribed on Lucy's gravestone, William could hardly speak and mumbled the reply that eventually read: "She was but words are wanting to say what think, what a wife should be, she was that." Less than two months later, his sister died. Nancy McLain's headstone was inscribed: "Erected in token of love and affection by her brother William Key."

The Doc remarried, making Hattie Davidson (Lucy's younger sister) his second wife. Known for her cheerful temperament and exceptional singing voice, Hattie brightened Bill's home and stables with her presence. But less than two years after their wedding, sudden illness took Hattie's life. Brokenhearted, the Doc swore never to marry again. Family and friends attempted to change his mind. No one had any luck until his friend George Davis, a much respected area blacksmith and father of eleven younger Davises, encouraged Bill to consider his eldest daughter as a prospect. Twenty-seven-year-old Lucinda Davis was a beauty *and* a scholar, who refused to marry anyone until she found a way to attend medical school at Howard University. Such stubbornness would have scared off most men. But William Key was not most men. In fact, he leapt at the opportunity to sponsor Lucinda's education. She was not only a strikingly handsome woman, but she also had a curiosity and boundless energy that made the Doc, at age fifty-five, feel like a young man again. Besides that, after the two were married in April 1888, she went on to tolerate and then encourage her husband's unconventional tutelage of Jim Key.

In his stables at 75 Maiden Lane, Albert Rogers concluded the interview for the morning. He had covered the Doc's extraordinary war stories as well as his extraordinary creation of a life after the Civil War. These notes also detailed the extraordinary manner in which Jim Key had honed his performing talents in the medicine-show business and had then learned to recognize the letters of the human alphabet.

Oddly, the more Rogers learned about man and horse, the more mystified he was by them. He remained incredulous that Bill Key had spent seven years creating a daily classroom for Jim, even when they were out traveling, just to be sure his smart horse didn't miss out on his education, as the trainer slowly and deliberately taught his equine student to recognize all his letters and his printed numbers from 1 to 30. Only someone as stubborn as Dr. William Key could have had such patience.

The Doc shrugged. Maybe. But once he had finished teaching the basics, he said, "From that time on my work was comparatively easy." Soon Jim Key could demonstrate an ability to add and subtract, and in reading he showed that he could successfully select words and names that the Doc printed on cardboard. Dr. Key then started him on spelling (using a system of phonics), along with lessons in multiplication, division, writing, and the Bible.

Rogers observed the small, well-worn Bible that William Key kept close at hand. Was Jim receiving religious instruction? The Doc explained, "We're studying the places and quotations where the horse is mentioned in the Bible, for horses were mighty prominent animals then." On a scrap of brown paper he had transcribed in pencil a question-and-answer session with his horse:

Jim, how many times do words *boy* and *girl* appear in the Bible?

Answer: One time.

Where?

Answer: Job, 3rd chapter, 3rd verse.

In contrast, so far they had counted fifty-four biblical passages with allusions to horses. Doc Key related that he was going to teach Jim to cite chapter and verse upon hearing the quotations spoken aloud.

Albert Rogers, still not ready to shake his amazement, left the dutiful scholar and his kindly professor to carry on. Their stories had given him much to write in his pamphlet and much to think about. As he contemplated how a former slave and a once crippled colt had come so far, it occurred to him now that the survival of the fittest was strangely less relevant than the survival of the smartest.

5

Higher Calling

The educated horse, Jim Key, will be privately exhibited at
Field's stables, 156 E. Twenty-fifth Street, New York, to-day, by
R.R. [sic] Rogers. The horse reads, writes and spells, tells various
pieces of money without error and makes change.

—THE BROOKLYN EAGLE, "SPORTING NEWS,"
Wednesday, August 18, 1897

DURING THE REMAINING DAYS before Jim's debut in New York,
Albert Rogers worked feverishly to complete his pamphlet that
trumpeted "He Was Taught by Kindness," while also hustling about
town to talk up the exhibition of the uncanny horse such as none of
his circle had ever seen before.

But interest was lackluster. Sophisticated Manhattanites tended
to view entertainment involving exotic or circus animals as lowbrow;
the curiosity market for more mainstream New Yorkers had been
overly saturated by the recent spate of World's Fair animal extravaganzas and in earlier decades when P. T. Barnum had kept his
American Museum in lower Manhattan chock-full of dangerous and
unusual creatures. The press was cagey, wary of promoting another
hoax, for which newspapers like William Randolph Hearst's *Journal*
were being criticized in this nascent era of yellow journalism.

Rogers was dismayed to hear from the officers of the ASPCA that
they wouldn't be attending the showing. He was just as stymied by
the leadership of the American Institute Fair, which was set to open
in a month for the fall season at Madison Square Garden. If only he
could entice those individuals to come and see Jim with their own

eyes, he was sure that the Institute Fair planners would be thrilled to book Jim and Dr. Key for the two-month event and that the ASPCA would kneel at his feet for the opportunity to sponsor the perfect candidate for an organizational mascot. So why weren't they interested?

Rogers seemed to be unaware of the long-standing distrust between the humane movement and promoters of live animal acts, dating back at least as early as 1867, when a scathing exchange of letters between P. T. Barnum and Henry Bergh was published by the New York *World*. As the founder and president of the humane society, Bergh was famous for using the press to bring attention to animal mistreatment—such as the merciless beatings of streetcar horses committed by unsupervised teamsters—and then pursuing remedies in the law. But when he took on P. T. Barnum to complain about the American Museum's feeding live rabbits to its boa constrictor as cruelty being masked as public entertainment, the effort backfired.

Ridiculous, claimed Barnum, calling Bergh the laughingstock of every naturalist in Christendom. Everyone knew that reptiles naturally ate their food alive. Barnum denied Bergh's suggestion that if a boa was hungry enough he would eat a cooked rabbit and enclosed a letter to that point from renowned Harvard professor Louis Agassiz. Not immune to controversy, his work in the classification of species having been used to uphold slavery, Agassiz boldly took Barnum's view: "I do not know of any way to induce snakes to eat their food otherwise than in their natural state: that is alive." From the same authority who used the code word *philanthropists* when referring to abolitionists came a further jab at the elitist sensibilities of the ASPCA: "I do not think the most active member of the society would object to eating lobster salad because the lobster was boiled alive, or refuse roasted oysters because they were cooked alive, or raw oysters because they must be swallowed alive."

Henry Bergh roared back at Barnum and Agassiz, suggesting that they were in favor of animal cruelty. But it was P. T. Barnum who had the last word after a campaign of character assassination against Bergh whose behavior, he charged, betrayed "low breeding and a surplus of self-conceit." Though Barnum won in the short run, Bergh was vindicated a year later when fire shut down the American Museum, killing dozens of the exotic animals and reviving public criticism of the wealthiest "professional liar on earth." Three years later when Barnum took his new show on the road—a menagerie with barking Alaskan sea lions and Italian goats performing stunts atop rare Arabian purebreds all the while bounding over spears thrown by genuine Fijian cannibals—once again, voices of concern about animal and human exploitation were drowned out by the roar of the entertained crowd.

The sparring between Barnum and Bergh began a lasting wave of protests from many quarters against the circus maestro's mistreatment of animals; but it also firmly embedded the notion in popular consciousness that upper-class do-gooders like Bergh tended to be unreasonable to the point of absurdity. Though neither of these influential men remained alive in 1897, it was still the case, as Rogers ought to have known, that humane organizations were historically suspicious of any animal show or promotion.

Rogers decided on another angle. If the humane people weren't ready to see the wonder that had been accomplished by kindness and education, he would go the show business route and first establish a name for Jim Key with the public. This brought him to answer the universally thrilling question of just how the star was first discovered. To tell that story properly, Rogers realized he had to include some background on himself. After all, he needed a ready answer in the event that exhibitors received his press materials and wanted to know—*just who is this Albert R. Rogers?*

The Rogers family of Cincinnati, Ohio, were blue bloods every which way. Albert's grandfather, Hiram Rogers, descendant of the Connecticut founding family of the Rogers lineage, had made his fortune in the railroad industry, and with his wife, Cordelia—from an old Kentucky family—had planted their dynasty in southern Ohio. In Cincinnati, their enterprising son Hiram Draper Rogers rose to higher stature by expanding the family business to include the manufacture and wholesale of railroad supplies, and by marrying Rhode Islander Mercy Adelia Reynolds, a direct descendant of Samuel Gorton—a founding father of Rhode Island as well as a founding champion of American religious freedom, with his followers known as the Gortonites.

The Rogers men clearly had a propensity for marrying strong, influential women, evidenced by the male tradition of listing property in their wives' names, and by the way the women shaped the Rogers family values. Mercy Rogers was the prime example, a woman who had inherited an independent, rebellious streak and a love for animals that she passed on to her firstborn son, Albert Reynolds Rogers, who was born on March 28, 1864.

The eldest of five children, Albert was undoubtedly expected to one day take over the family business, and by the age of sixteen he was already working full-time as chief clerk at the main store in Cincinnati. But early on it was clear that the prospect of spending the rest of his days in the manufacturing and wholesale of railroad supplies would kill him. His interests were elsewhere, somewhere in the realm of providing entertainment to the masses.

Rogers was a young man of many contradictions. He was practical and idealistic, flexible yet stubborn. He could be outgoing and shy, diplomatic and willful, sensitive and aloof, verbose and terse. In the same way that Jim Key had not been able to become one of his herd, and that Dr. Key never quite belonged to one group or another, Rogers found himself feeling more at home when he was away from home, lost in the company of strangers. His favorite place to be was when he found sanctuary in the dark under the big tent or at the opera house, waiting for the show to begin. He loved mingling with the carnival crowds at fairs, riding the rides, exploring the attractions, listening to barkers compete for his attention.

Soon he became sure his destiny lay in that direction, but when he tried his hand at promoting a few fair rides, nothing quite hit. Yet despite his failure, he learned the ropes, allowing him to use his naturally likeable personality to make contacts in several new arenas. Rogers found that marketing in show business wasn't so different from marketing in the railroad supply business. What he really needed was a great product—a star attraction—to market.

In the mid-1880s, Albert's family relocated to New York, where Hiram had established Rogers Manifold and Carbon Paper Company several years earlier. As was the fashion for those who could afford it, Hiram and Mercy purchased both the 75 Maiden Lane townhome—with close proximity to the company's offices on Wall Street—and "Glenmere," a majestic country estate in the exclusive Montrose Park section of South Orange, New Jersey. Albert became the chief officer of the company, with Hiram taking the subordinate position of treasurer.

A. R. Rogers much preferred the daily workings of the carbon paper and printing business to that of the railroad supply business. His vision was to apply what he learned from circus barkers to the principles of marketing copying paper and typewriters.

In the patent medicine world, the pitchmen were originally distinguished as either high or low, depending on whether they hawked their wares from a high platform (back of a wagon or stage) or whether they set up on the street, displaying their goods on "low" three-legged stands. Similarly the amusement front talkers used verbal come-ons that could be termed as being hard sell or soft sell. Borrowing from high and low, hard and soft, Rogers sought ways to translate this range of seductions onto the printed page, playing with different fonts and colors in his materials, which boasted visually interesting letterheads and logos, artfully worded promotional language and product endorsements.

A late bloomer at twenty-four, Rogers seemed to have found his calling and took this, in 1888, as the right time to marry Miss Clara Bloss of Beaver Dam, Wisconsin, a daughter of upstanding New York parentage. The newlyweds gladly took up residence in the Maiden Lane townhome—which remained for some time in Mercy's name until it was deeded to Clara—and the couple went on to have three sons, Clarence, Newell, and Archibald.

In his press materials, Rogers described himself as a "New York industrialist." But as his family could attest, he was still in the process of finding himself. His greater interest was definitely in the amusement field, something that in the last few years was beginning to pan out with some modest investments in a couple of rides and attractions. He also had developed new ambitions to become a philanthropist. His wife and his mother may have suggested that he direct his energies toward the humane movement. In Clara's social sphere, a new topic of interest, especially in women's reading circles, was the sharing of touching and illustrative animal stories that advocated protection of God's most unprotected creatures from cruelty and neglect. For her part, Mercy believed that while it was often the values and ideas of women that ultimately changed social consciousness, men were nonetheless needed for leadership roles in organizations.

Duly inspired, Albert sought and was eventually given an introduction to Ida Sheehan, a New York society pillar and humane
society grande dame. On May 23, 1896, he wrote her a heartfelt
note, describing his desire to help raise funds and awareness for her
important cause, and received her reply four days later in which she
thanked him for his kindly interest. Ida Sheehan wrote:

I am a great lover of all animals, and, do what I can for their
protection, in an effort to lighten the burden of the noble, much
abused servant of mankind—the poor horse. I came to the conclusion that if the horses of the city were ever to receive better
treatment, a kindly feeling of appreciation of their faithfulness
and worth must be instilled in the hearts of the drivers by some
substantial suggestions; hence my idea of presenting annually a
gold medal to the most humane driver coming under my personal
observations.

The "Ida" medal, she went on to say, had thus been instituted. With
an invitation to call her on that Monday next, she concluded:

I am always happy to greet those whose heart goes out to God's
helpless, speechless creatures—the poor suffering animals. Wishing
you every success and blessing in your noble work, believe me.

The meeting proved to be cordial and illuminating. Albert was
apparently surprised to learn how disconnected the many humane
organizations were from one another. Moreover, he now saw that
despite the charity of certain wealthy contributors, most groups
were either underfunded or mismanaged their funds, and as a result
were ineffective in their work. There was another problem, he felt,
which was the humane groups' stigma of elitism. He believed that if
he could only help the ASPCA and fellow organizations find a way
to connect to the masses, then their toughest challenges—money
and image—would be overcome.

Rogers had a brainstorm to create a linkage between his promotional enterprises and his charitable aspirations. Once his amusements investments began to pay off, he was certain to accomplish
that goal. Finally it looked as if two of his attractions had that potential. One was a ride called Shoot the Chutes. The other was the Old

Plantation, an increasingly popular exhibit that simulated antebellum life and traveled complete with movable cotton fields, full-scale Colonial plantation homes, and authentic slave cabins.

Infectiously enthusiastic as he could be, Rogers convinced other investors that the steep costs of transporting, installing, and running these attractions would be negligible when compared with the profits to be made in the plethora of local, state, national, and international fairs. When income didn't quickly exceed expenses, he assured others and himself that the next big fair would definitely allow profits to materialize. That's what he claimed when the next big fair was being held in Nashville, Tennessee.

After booking his concessions there at the last minute, Albert felt very strongly that his fortune in the promotional arena was going to turn on the Tennessee Centennial and International Exposition. He had no idea how dramatically it would.

The circumstances that led Dr. Key to feature Jim Key in his professional debut at the Tennessee Centennial were much different. But Bill was likewise influenced by a woman, his wife, Lucinda Davis Key, M.D.

In 1894, Lucinda had received her medical degree from Howard University and returned for good to Tennessee to establish her medical practice, as intended, in Chattanooga. From the moment she opened her doors, Dr. Lucinda Key was kept overwhelmingly busy ministering to Negro patients who came seeking her services from miles away in every direction. Dr. William Key worried about his wife becoming ill from exhaustion or exposure to contagious diseases. Whenever he could he traveled with her to Chattanooga, bringing Jim along with them, of course, whether by carriage or locomotive.

During these trips, he told Rogers, "Jim and I gave free exhibitions in the street and after the exhibitions I would sell my liniment to the crowd."

Toward the end of a demonstration one afternoon, Jim surprised him with a piece of improvisation right at the moment when Doc Key typically prepared to introduce his medicines with his speech about "good for man or beast." Just then a man in the crowd called out, "How much you want for the horse?"

Dr. Key paused and puzzled over the question. "Well, Jim," he asked at last, "how much should I sell you for?"

Jim Key snorted in surprise. His expression was almost mocking: *Sell me? You'd never sell ME.*

"Now, Jim"—Doc Key played along, putting on his countrified airs—"you is a fine, healthy horse, and can fetch a fair price." He turned to the crowd and began to entertain offers, encouraging his handsome bay stallion to parade back and forth to show potential buyers his elegant gait.

As if resigned to his misfortune, Jim inched tentatively forward and began a resentful but obedient stroll. Ascending dollar amounts were called out from the crowd, starting at ten and rapidly reaching five hundred.

"Sold!" The Doc beckoned the gentleman with the highest bid toward the staging area to pay up. Suddenly, with all the melodrama of a dying opera diva, Jim Key crumpled to the ground. Desperately the bay tried to hunker up and then wobbled from side to side before collapsing pathetically again.

Dr. William Key masked his smile. Jim was pretending to go lame, the same trick he often performed but now in a new context.

The crowd, not sure if this was part of the act or not, held its collective breath. With a wink, the Doc turned his back to Jim and in a pronounced stage whisper declared the sale off, at which point a gleeful Jim Key bounded to his feet and pranced back and forth in emphatic relief.

Laughter rang through the streets of Chattanooga. This was to become a feature of Jim's performances from then on.

In telling this anecdote to Rogers, Doc Key remarked that Jim's stint in the medicine show circuit gave him a steadily increasing value. "At three years old, I couldn't have gotten fifty dollars for the horse, but at five years old he was worth five hundred." Not long before Jim turned eight, the Doc received his first of many offers of $10,000 for his unusually gifted stallion.

The occasion was at the Chattanooga train depot, where Dr. Key was approached on the platform by a stranger he ascertained to be a "circus man."

"I hear you got a horse who can do anything," the man ventured.

"That's right, sire," Doc Key answered deferentially, as was his professional habit. "Jim can do almost anything."

"I'll give you ten thousand dollars for him if he can take a silver dollar out of the bottom of a bucket of water without drinking any of the water."

William had never thought of that trick and had never heard of any horse performing it, especially because it required a trainer to convey to a horse the need to submerge his head underwater and hold his breath while opening his mouth. Pretty much impossible. But instead of saying so, he confidently insisted he could teach Jim to do it. The man agreed to return in a few weeks and see if he had bought himself a new horse or not, and then boarded the outbound train, never to be heard from again.

Dr. Key admitted to Albert Rogers that he had no intention of selling Jim, but in the weeks that followed he couldn't get the challenge out of his mind. "I laid awake nights thinking how I was going to teach Jim how to take out that dollar without drinking the water. Finally, I got an idea." Much in the way he obsessed over teaching Jim the alphabet, he devised a method for training that began with sugar, plus a silver dollar and a new pail. "The dollar I covered with sugar and dropped into the empty pail. Jim licked all the sugar off the dollar and brought it to me in his teeth to put more sugar on it. It only took a few days to teach him that he'd get sugar when he brought me the dollar. Then I began to cover the dollar with water, and he picked out the dollar just the same."

When the depth of the water started to intimidate Jim, Doc Key changed the game by putting an apple in the pail. Day by day, he increased the depth of the water and decreased the size of the apple, then substituted small items. Eventually he had Jim submerging his head in the pail of water and drawing out the silver dollar with his teeth—without drinking a drop of water. The circus man never materialized again, but ironically the stunt he had scripted for Bill and Jim Key—which with the use of a glass barrel would be a mainstay of their repertoire—was to become the single most heralded feat that Jim ever performed, over and above his often inexplicable mastery of human intellectual skills.

Jim's psychic abilities were also cultivated in the course of his travels. Dr. Key had by now accumulated more than five thousand rabbit's feet, most of them, he confirmed to Rogers, he had personally collected from Civil War battlefields, the majority of them from Chickamauga, the last battle he witnessed. In a battlefield where almost 35,000 soldiers lay wounded and dead, the Doc presumably took the feet from the thousands of rabbit casualties—before they could be appropriated by starving soldiers for stew. There were other, supposedly luckier methods of capturing rabbits that required killing them at midnight under a full moon, which apparently William Key disdained. When asked about his practice of stringing them up for demonstrations, he insisted that they helped to clear and comfort his mind, as well as Jim's. To prove it, he told the story about one journey to Virginia when Jim's clairvoyance was put to the test with impressive results.

The crowd had thinned after Dr. Key finished his liniment sales, and as he began to pack away his bottles, while Jim held court with straggling admirers, an "old ex-slave lady" introduced herself. Ancient but with a sparkle in her eye, she whispered to Doc Key that a relative died before telling her where he or she had left buried treasure—money and jewelry hidden in a pot. She knew generally where the land was but had no idea where exactly to dig. Could the horse help her find the treasure?

Doc Key vowed that Jim's dam, Lauretta Queen of Horses, had helped someone else find buried money and that his smart stallion could do it too. Through a series of questions he asked the old woman, he had Jim lead the two of them to the very spot where the pot was indeed buried. Key told Rogers, "The ex-slave gave me half the treasure, and the pot too."

This was not a story that Rogers necessarily wanted promoted to the skeptical New York press. Personally, he wasn't wild about the rabbit's feet either. Doc Key couldn't understand such concerns. For the generations who had any direct or inherited memories of the Civil War, spiritualism and belief in the possibility of communicating with the dead were survival skills. Besides, as far as Dr. Key was concerned, the public mind could always use healthy doses of mystery and magic. He knew this for a fact from the many daily newspapers he read that advertised three times as many faith healers and occultists as they did licensed medical doctors.

Rogers's real concern with the rabbit's feet, however, was that they would upset the Ida Sheehans of the world. The Doc recognized this as a potential problem but noted that it was better to be lucky than too careful.

At what point, then, did Jim Key leave behind the world of liniment sales and step into his career as an educated horse?

That had begun to happen, said Dr. Key, around 1896, when he decided to retire from the patent medicine business, except for the occasional mail order. At the age of sixty-three, he was a very wealthy man and could afford to slow down a bit, perhaps even to move to Chattanooga, where he had bought a large piece of property, to be closer to his wife's work there. But his instincts had told him that he had important work before him. What exactly, he wasn't sure.

Dr. Lucinda Key saw a path that her husband hadn't yet considered. From the moment when she and Jim had connected after her discovery that he could say yes to her offer of an apple, she came to feel that the horse's unusual gifts could be put to use for a higher calling. Her idea was vague, perhaps that Jim Key could serve as an ambassador in the cause of the advancement of people of color, or to encourage education, or simply to demonstrate to all the power of patience and kindness.

As a matter of fact, that was the role that Jim had already begun to carve out for himself in his appearances alongside the Doc at numerous county fairs cropping up across the South. At these fairs, Dr. Key's services were in high demand in advisory and ministerial roles, whether as livestock and agricultural director, or as a judge in competitions, or sometimes as grand marshal of parades and races. In and around Shelbyville, Jim Key was already a hometown star.

Doc Key had seen the local Bedford County fair develop from its first annual event in 1857 to forty years later, where locals considered it the biggest event of the year, and he served in a directorial position of honor. A precursor to the annual Tennessee Walking Horse Celebration, which would come into being in 1939, the Bedford County fair of the 1890s boasted a quarter-mile racetrack, a promenade, and an exhibit hall with bounty on display and for sale—crafts and handiwork, produce, canned goods, and the latest in home and farm machinery. The superlative Bedford County taffy was a perennial best seller, and refreshment vendors typically ran out of food before the fair was over. Awards were given in multiple agricultural categories and age groups, with prizes that included everything from a pair of registered Berkshire pigs (awarded to the owner of the best animal on four feet) to a set of fine lace curtains (for the best lady rider).

Traditionally the last day of the fair was reserved for the presentation of awards and for elected officials and politicians to take to the judge's platform in the center of the racetrack. In this context, Dr. Key found a ripe opportunity to demonstrate Jim's latest academic achievements and, in the process, for them to serve as self-appointed ambassadors of civility. This was where Jim Key first began to give demonstrations of his ability to read and spell short, common words. Along with the letters and numbers on cards that Doc Key put on display, he also had a handful of last names on longer cards that included notable Bedford countians, the President of the United States (then Democrat Grover Cleveland), the Democratic presidential candidate William Jennings Bryan, and his Republican rival, William McKinley.

Much to the entertainment and surprise of the crowd, Jim correctly selected the corresponding card for every name of every local official announced that day. As a final bit, Dr. Key and Jim reenacted their original debate over politics, in which William Key identified himself as a Republican and Jim Key adamantly proclaimed himself a Democrat, whinnying in support of Bryan.

This was a bold move on Doc Key's part, since the majority of the hundreds of fairgoers in the crowd that day were fervent Democrats. A smattering of Republican handkerchiefs waved in support of the Doc's admission, but others did not reveal their alliance to the party then associated with the North, with big business, and with "what they were pleased to call" equality for Negroes. Jim Key, Southern horse that he was, became the crowd favorite.

Variations of this bit took place at many fairs across Tennessee, where Dr. Key and Jim held demonstrations in the spring and summer of 1896. Most county officials assumed that Jim would be a featured act at the Tennessee Centennial and International Exposition that was scheduled to open in Nashville in the fall of 1896. Whether or not Nashville—or any Southern city, for that matter—could pull off a major world's fair was still in question. Three years earlier Chicago had hosted the World Columbian Exposition of 1893, the most ambitious grand-scale world's fair ever mounted, against which every subsequent international exhibition struggled to compete, including Atlanta's 1895 Cotton States and International Exposition. Now Nashville was daring to host a world's fair to celebrate one hundred years of Tennessee's statehood and to promote itself as the capital of the new South. Most of Bedford County took it for granted that the planners would want to feature a horse as marvelous as Jim Key. But when the Doc wrote to inquire about being booked, he received no response whatsoever.

Bill and Lucinda were aware that although Jim had numerous admirers across the state, there were two significant challenges that needed to be overcome. The first, of course, was that it may have sounded absurd to the planners that a horse could spell, read, figure, and handle money. The more insidious problem was the issue of William Key's color.

It wasn't that the planners were against having African-Americans participate as exhibitors. To the contrary, the organizers and underwriters of the Tennessee Centennial were determined not to incur the kind of trouble that the Chicago World's Fair had seen, when Negroes were left out of the planning process, or the criticism that the Atlanta Exposition received after its planners promised to be more inclusive but fell short. But the lack of response suggested that the officials didn't regard Dr. Key as being representative of the Negro community. He was not a man of the cloth, not a trained doctor, not affiliated with any Negro educational institutions, and spoke for no established groups. Though his stirring success story was impressive, he was possibly not seen as the portrait the planners wanted to present of the "advancing Afro-American" of Tennessee. Perhaps he was too light-skinned, too wealthy, too independent.

Not to be discouraged, he decided to take Jim up to Nashville and meet with the officials in person and then see what they had to say. After a short demonstration, the planners agreed that he was extraordinary but felt the act bordered on being a sideshow. Where would Jim fit in?

By summer 1896, Doc Key realized the Centennial planners were distracted by bigger problems. With the mammoth undertaking of a world's fair in Nashville only a month away from opening, construction of the exhibition halls had fallen drastically behind schedule, and several buildings had barely broken ground. Worse, funding sources, local and federal, had been exhausted. The embarrassment wasn't what the region needed.

The Doc understood that the Tennessee Centennial Exposition was either going to be postponed or scrapped, depending on whether or not other funding could be found. Chicago's Columbian Exposition—originally scheduled for 1892 to mark the four hundredth anniversary of Columbus's voyage—had been postponed to the following year and was no less legitimate for the delay, as proven when twenty-seven million Americans, or almost half the nation's population, attended the fair. Then again, other world's fair celebrations had been canceled or scaled back when their undertakings proved too mighty.

On August 20, 1896, Dr. Key also had larger concerns on his mind when he returned from being away and was met by the shock of his lifetime. Lucinda was sick in bed at her father's house, close to death. William tended to her every way he knew how, boiling his roots and herbs, chanting and praying, drawing from every ancient and modern medical secret he had read about or been given. But when at last Lucinda's breath became labored, Bill knew that they needed to have a final conversation. He asked what she would have him do to help her go peacefully to the next world.

She spoke of others. Take care of my parents, she asked, make them comfortable in old age. Lucinda asked that her siblings be helped to receive the education she had been so fortunate to receive. That included her younger sister Maggie, a widow and schoolteacher. On her deathbed, Lucinda planted the seeds for Dr. Key to consider marrying Maggie. Lucinda didn't want to be worrying about him in the by-and-by and knew he needed a woman to be there when he came back from traveling. Against his protests, she laid out her vision, assuring him that a new life was beginning that would take him and Jim to distant places and greater heights than he could even imagine. And finally, she exacted a final promise that her husband not give up on entering Jim in the Tennessee Centennial.

As Lucinda started to slip into her final sleep, Bill called her back, asking out loud what she wished him to do, not for others, but for herself. She answered serenely in words William Key chose to have inscribed on her gravestone: "Whatever happens to me, my dear, it is well with my soul."

Six days later the *Shelbyville Gazette* noted in a brief announcement that her passing had taken place on August 21, 1896: "Mrs.

Lucinda Key, wife of Dr. William Key, died at the home of her father, George Davis (colored) last week and buried Saturday."

I n the Northern and Southern celestial hemispheres all the planets aligned for the success of the postponed Tennessee Centennial and International Exposition when it was rescheduled to run May 1 through October 31, 1897. From this, Jim Key was about to get his proverbial big break, thanks ultimately to the ambitions of the Louisville and Nashville Railroad. In fact, but for aims of the L&N that had little to do with underwriting a world's fair, the exposition in Nashville wouldn't have taken place.

On March 13, 1897, Dr. William Key stood on the stage of the exposition's only completed full-scale auditorium, in an assembly of Centennial dignitaries, marveling at the determination of Director-General Eugene Castner Lewis to bring to fruition what others swore was a doomed affair. Lewis had brokered a politically risky deal with the New York–owned L&N and their Southern subsidiary, the Nashville, Chattanooga & St. Louis Railroad (the NC&St.L), whose president, John W. Thomas, was also the president of the Centennial. In return for the L&N gaining the right to monopolize the tracks in and out of Nashville at the lavish new train station that they were already planning to fund, the railway company was given the privilege of paying for the costs of the unfinished Exposition.

To the chagrin of many who knew that locally owned rail companies would be ousted by the locomotive giant, L&N saw their advantage and accepted the deal. With Northern money and a mandate to improve the railroad's public relations image across the South, more pressure was put on the planners to show the world that the Tennessee Centennial was worth attending. It had to deliver crowd-pleasing elements that fairgoers had come to expect from the Chicago and Atlanta expositions, but it had to have a pull of its own—a distinction that was of its place and that embodied the optimistic, expansive spirit of the times.

At a committee planning meeting, E. C. Lewis had a brainstorm for what could provide the fair with its unifying theme and major landmark, which was much needed, given the array of architectural schemes. "About the center," Lewis proposed, speaking of the mid-point of the two hundred acres of land—previously known as West Side Park, a harness racing track—"on an elevation . . . I want to put a reproduction of the Parthenon in actual size, line for line, and call it the Fine Arts Building."

The rest of his fellow committee members were stunned into silence, with one exception, a gentleman who simply murmured, "I'll be damned."

Lewis and Thomas built on the vision of the Parthenon, promoting Nashville as the "Athens of the South" and strewing likenesses of the goddess Athena and her Olympian relatives into statuary, fountains, bridges, and cornices across the exposition grounds. The Centennial's definitive poster showed an Athenian "Lady Tennessee" as she rose up "out of the ashes of the War between the States and the Reconstruction period, leading the New South into the next century."

To validate their claims, the planning committee members chose to make the presence and participation of African-Americans a top priority. They put significant resources toward erecting a Negro Building and creating a departmental committee composed of the most respected Tennesseans of color. This was the capacity in which Dr. William Key was invited to participate in the Centennial and to attend the March ceremony that marked the laying of the cornerstone of the Negro Building.

Together with such revered individuals as the Reverend R. B. Vanderfil, Bishop M. P. Saltier, and Dr. W. A. Hadley, among a dozen others, William Key had been asked to preside on the Executive Committee of the Negro Department, and also to serve as chairman of the Livestock Committee, the only member of the Executive Committee to have a dual role. It gave him immense joy to reunite with colleagues and friends and to share the first sight of what would be a strikingly elegant, expansive three-story building. Designed in the style of the Spanish Renaissance, to be finished in white staff, the building was to have an interior capacity to include eighty-five exhibits and to accommodate a rooftop restaurant pavilion with lofty vistas.

The speeches by Centennial officials to an auditorium full of an astounding ten thousand spectators, mostly African-American, were incredibly rousing, but none more so than a piece of oratorical sleight of hand delivered by Professor William H. Council, former slave and founding president of the Agricultural and Mechanical College for Negroes in Normal, Alabama. For ten spellbinding minutes, Professor Council gave a speech so majestically eloquent that few detected his departure from the Booker T. Washington's Atlanta Compromise of "separate but equal" and his rebuke to those who referred to racial concerns as the "Negro problem."

Professor Council first acknowledged, "These occasions mark the evolution of Southern thought and industry, and the result of the *self-directed* energy of the Negro." Finished with stereotypes and backlash, he then thundered, "Here on this spot the world may see the other side of the Negro life than 'Sam Johnson, the chicken thief.' Here it may see the beautiful buds of Negro handicraft, Negro art, science, literature, invention. Here the world may see the hitherfore giant energies of a mighty people waking into a conscious activity."

Dr. Key was among those applauding madly and then listening breathlessly when Council added, "I challenge the annals of man to present so beautiful a spectacle."

Professor Council praised Nashville and Tennessee for the opportunities to put on display what "we have accomplished in our three hundred years struggle . . . right here in the Egypt of our bondage," continuing to assert that "only as we recede from Appomattox . . . only as memories of former hates shall have drowned in the Red Sea of brotherly love, and the good things we have done for each other come like angels in conscious view, will the old master and the old slave know what helps they have been to each other. We must love. We can not afford to hate."

But what of the Negro problem? Council challenged it, pointing out, "There still remains the Caucasian problem. In view of what the Negro has done for this country, in view of what the white man has done for the Negro, will the white man continue and enlarge the work of encouragement in the struggling race; or will he use the shotgun instead of the Holy Bible; the bloody knife instead of the spelling-book?" In the speaker's opinion economic equality was paramount, not only to elevate the person of color, but also to elevate tolerance and to "make the South a new earth."

What Council said about tolerance and forgiveness between former slaves and masters resonated with Dr. Key, as did Council's emphasis on black education. Indeed, he was so impressed with Professor Council that after the speech was over, he introduced himself and began the process that would enroll Maggie Davis at A&M in Normal, Alabama. But the words that most moved him came at the end, when Council spoke of the hope for the next generation:

> Teach the Negro boy the sacredness of human life; teach him that man must be as precious in the sight of man as he is in the sight of God. Teach him that the transmission of a disregard for the law is the transmission of the spirit of the mob, the spirit of riot, the spirit of hate. . . . Teach him that he belongs to a glorious race, which stands before God with its hands unstained in human blood. Teach him to honor and revere this record. . . . Teach him that it is better to be persecuted than to persecute. . . . Teach him that the man who hates him on account of his color is far beneath him, but the man who hates his condition and strives to lift him up may be his superior. . . . Teach him that man, that race, is superior which does superior things to lift mankind to superior conditions.

Except for the fact that Jim Key was not able to witness the speeches and the dedication ceremony that followed, the events of March 13, 1897, had given Dr. Key one of the most gratifying days of his life.

Albert Rogers had meant to visit the Negro Building on plenty of occasions, including the March dedication ceremony, but other preoccupations intervened. Much of his time was spent installing the Old Plantation as part of the Agricultural Building's exhibit and Shoot the Chutes in the amusement area known as Vanity Fair.

When the Exposition opened on May 1, 1897, the *Nashville American* depicted Vanity Fair's vibrant atmosphere by writing, "Here are gathered together from the far corners of the earth people representing nearly every race and nationality who with their continuous babel of unknown languages and their queer and quaint costumes present a Kaleidoscope panorama ever intensely interesting to the Centennial visitor."

Rogers felt instantly at home. By summer's end he had been so industrious that he became the booking agent for an additional handful of concessions such as the Mirror Maze (a fun house that evolved into a staple of carnivals and amusement parks) and the Edison Mirage, a popular attraction that offered choices of four different motion pictures in its Electric Scenic Theatre, which sat the audience on a revolving disc as it turned around a series of screens. All of a sudden, A. R. Rogers had attained a first-rate reputation as a promoter. In this short time, he proved to have a knack for handling the intricate logistics of transporting and installing attractions, and he seemed to have an arsenal of innovative techniques for generating publicity and revenue for the concessions he represented.

The Chutes—an early hybrid of roller coaster and water slide—sent boats on tracks shooting down from a high, steep incline and plunging into the lake below, splashing plumes of spray onto the crowds gathered around the water's edge. Rogers cleverly positioned the Chutes at the highest point of the Exposition and only charged a ten-cent admission, thus outselling the ride's biggest competition, the Giant Seesaw—a steel latticed seesaw developed by a Nashville company that had cages carrying groups of riders on each end rising at full tilt to 208 feet in the air.

Shooting the Chutes had the advantage of being less frightening for most ages and it rarely experienced any operational problems, except for an incident that involved a woman politely said to be quite stout. When her boat hit the water, its impact—amplified by her girth—forced the bottom of the boat to fall out. Thrashing and screaming that she could not swim, the woman suddenly stopped her hysteria after discovering that the lake was only thirty inches deep. She pulled herself erect, came to her feet, calmly smoothed out her very wet attire, and with as much dignity as she could muster, walked to the platform at the water's edge and was helped to dry land.

Albert Rogers teased the press with the story, successfully increasing admissions sold for the Chutes. He may have done the same to help promote an exhibit of the birthplace cabins of two famous Kentuckians, Abraham Lincoln, President of the Union, and Jefferson Davis, President of the Confederacy. A rumor spread that somehow the logs from the disassembled cabins had been mixed up during shipment, an apparent scandal that only caused more fairgoers to visit the attraction.

Besides tending to his many responsibilities, whenever Albert attempted to visit other destinations at the Centennial (except for stopping over to the Old Plantation to admire his thriving cotton patch), it seemed that the Vanity Fair had so much else to occupy and entertain his free hours. There were the gondolas to be ridden, a flight up in the sky for several hundred feet in Barnard's Airship, the nearly naked belly-dancing coochee-coochee girls of the Streets of Cairo, Italian immersion at the Blue Grotto (modeled after the Isle of Capri), rides on camels named Alibaba and Yankee Doodle, sword-playing tumblers, clowns on stilts, magicians, the Cuban and Chinese villages, the Moorish Palace, the Café of Night and Morning, inspired by Dante's *Inferno* (where restaurant tables were made from coffins), and food and drink to be sampled from a dozen different ethnic cuisines.

Doc Key looked forward to visiting Vanity Fair but was likewise occupied by his official duties at the Negro Building and with the increasing number of daily shows that he and Jim Key were offering there. By early June, much of Shelbyville—traveling by rail, buggy, on horses and mules—had come up at least once to visit their hometown stars and enjoy the Centennial. For many Bedford countians, it was the most memorable experience of their lives, endowing them with the treasure of stories and souvenirs they passed down to their descendants. For these families, Jim Key became synonymous with the 1897 Nashville World's Fair.

The tall, dark, handsome, educated bay—on exhibit at the Negro Building—was apparently the draw that brought in a crush of crowds who wouldn't have otherwise come into the Negro Building. The Centennial's *Official History* later asserted that "Dr. Key's educated horse, 'Jim', whose wonderful intelligence greatly amused and interested thousands of visitors to the Exposition," was in fact a leading draw of the entire Centennial.

As Lucinda Key had predicted, William and Jim had risen to a higher calling, first by advancing interest in the accomplishments of African-Americans. Now Doc Key wasted no opportunity to incorporate his humane themes into their demonstrations, always pointing to the use of kindness and patience as his educational secret.

Though the Centennial planners were profoundly pleased with the success of the Negro Department, when the Committee of Arrangements undertook to create an itinerary for the visit of President William McKinley on June 11 and 12, they did not put the Negro Building on his official schedule. It was left as a question mark for the end of the second day, scheduling and interest pending.

The planning for McKinley's presence in Nashville had ruffled feathers on both sides of the Mason-Dixon, primarily because the President had declined to preside over the May 1 Opening Day ceremonies in Tennessee. This was despite numerous written invitations and urgings and a committee of leading Tennesseans who traveled to Washington to meet with President McKinley in person. The envoys were politely turned down with the excuse that the President could not cancel previous engagements. Much of Nashville bristled at the slight but by Opening Day had only words of praise for the President for performing the now standard ritual of holding a White House ceremony. There he pressed a button that sent an electrical relay through Virginia into North Carolina and across Tennessee to Nashville, triggering the works of a cannon that fired a signal that unleashed the engines and opened the gates to the Exposition.

There was a feeling in some Nashville circles that a Southern-hosted world's fair had not earned the full endorsement of the Ohio-born McKinley—who had, after all, fought as a major for the Union during the Civil War, before serving as an Ohio Republican congressman for fourteen years in the House of Representatives and a term as governor of Ohio. Then another date was proposed by Asa Bushnell, the man who had succeeded McKinley as Ohio's governor, that the President visit Nashville on June 11 for the celebration of Ohio Day and that June 12 be assigned as Cincinnati Day, in order that two full days of events could be scheduled.

Once it was announced that President and Mrs. McKinley had accepted the invitation, the Centennial planners threw off their prior disenchantment and began preparations in earnest. The authors of the *Official History* recorded the city's buzz of excitement, which built for weeks in anticipation of the President's arrival, "not alone because of his high office but also out of regard for his distinguished abilities and his untarnished personal character." Political and geographic differences notwithstanding, the South—with Nashville as its designated representative—was eager to take William McKinley into her bosom. Compared with the elitist ranks growing up North, said area journalists, McKinley was personified by quiet dignity and a friendly manner and was, in sum, an accomplished, noble, yet still typical American.

William McKinley, Tennesseans concluded, was a regular guy. With his commoner's fleshy features, finished by a manly cleft chin, and heavy knit eyebrows, he even looked like a regular guy. Better still, in the opinion of most Southerners, he was a gentleman in view of his devotion to the First Lady. Ida McKinley was a lovely but frail china doll who suffered horribly from fainting spells and crippling attacks. Nonetheless, she was rarely absent from her husband's side at important White House events—often seated in a chair for receiving lines and usually holding a nosegay to hide her trembling hands.

To show Nashville's gratitude to her and the President, tens of thousands of citizens poured into the streets for the procession to the Centennial on the morning of Friday, June 11.

Up until this date, the weather in Nashville had been custom-made for the World's Fair. Spring in Middle Tennessee bloomed with a lush excess of color in gardens, lawns, fields, rivers, and woods, setting off Nashville and the Centennial like jewels. Skies were so sunny and almost cloudlessly blue, with the usual humidity so low, that the chairs of the Committees of Arrangements and Receptions congratulated one another for weather that could not have been more ideal for the Centennial and the President's arrival. But in partisan fashion, by the dawn of that Friday, the mercury rebelled, sending the temperature spiking up to an intense level, the humidity wilting the landscape into an impressionistic steamy blur. In the plucky spirit of the Volunteer State, however, as the *Official History*'s authors observed, "Everyone appreciated this was beyond the control of the Committee of Arrangements, and the inevitable was therefore accepted with amiable resignation."

Traveling with a retinue of forty correspondents from every major newspaper in the country, the McKinleys' party had left Washington at noon on June 9 by special train over the Chesapeake & Ohio Railroad, accompanied as well by an entourage of cabinet members, Washington dignitaries, families, and staffs, and arrived in heat-laden Nashville on the L&N, pulling into the depot on time at 7:55 A.M. A receiving party of two hundred delivered the President and his companions to the regal Maxwell House. By ten o'clock, President McKinley was waiting in the elegant parlor of the Maxwell where he welcomed his cohonorees, Tennessee's governor Robert L. Taylor and Ohio's governor Asa Bushnell, along with a brigade of prominent Ohioans, among them the mayors of Cincinnati and Cleveland.

The procession of eighteen carriages and as many tallyhos for staffs and press—the President and Mrs. McKinley in the lead carriage—was thronged by ever more mounted police and military officers as it forged through Church Street to Vine and then moved onto Broad Street, past the Custom House out toward Vanderbilt University. On the streets a surging mass of humanity bestowed on President McKinley one continuous ovation.

At the Centennial grounds, the vast Exposition Auditorium was already filled to overflowing, and when the thousands inside heard the shots of the cannon announcing that the President had passed through the gates, they stood and roared their cheer of welcome, raising their fervor and volume as a waving President William McKinley strode down the aisles to the belfry chimes of "America." The jubilation was not marred by the absence of Mrs. McKinley—who had been escorted to private quarters to rest—since much of the public knew she was no doubt taxed by the heat, the excitement of the morning, and the exhaustion of her journey.

Toward the end of several speeches praising Nashville, Ohio senator W. T. Clarke declared that the Tennessee Centennial had surpassed every other world's fair to date. "Philadelphia, the pioneer of the exposition work," Clarke said of the 1876 World's Fair and true marker of one hundred years of nationhood, "did fairly well." He wasn't so kind about the 1893 Columbian Exposition, saying that "the World's Fair in Chicago, upon governmental crutches, stood nearly upright." The 1894 California Mid-Winter Exposition in San Francisco had been a good start for the West. "But Nashville indeed has done herself proud, and is the morning star, heralding the sunrise of a higher, better, and nobler civilization."

Senator Clarke bowed to his fellow Ohioans, to the President, to the three cabinet members, and to the numerous out-of-towners, commending all the cities of their origins before he went on to marvel at Nashville as a capital of learning,

> having the largest scholastic population in any city in the country; four female seminaries; three colleges for the education of the colored people, including Fisk University, the singers of which have established a worldwide reputation. Vanderbilt University, with

her endowment of over a million dollars, three medical schools, three schools of pharmacy, two law schools, three large dental schools, the largest in the United States, and a complete common system for white and black, with her population increasing in the last quarter of a century fifty percent.

The program in the Auditorium, which culminated with a short speech from President McKinley, Ohio's favorite son, offered a spontaneous highlight just after he was called to the platform when an outburst of applause came in response to the sudden appearance of Mrs. McKinley. On the arm of an official, the First Lady slowly made her way down the aisle toward the stage as row after row stood to applaud her presence. She wore her trademark smile, at once kind, brave, and sad, and accepted the audience's approval with a modest low tilt of her head. Her effort to participate in some degree in the formal exercises was overwhelmingly appreciated, since the public knew that Mrs. McKinley was not, as it was said, in the most robust of health. But the moment that truly electrified the Auditorium was the sight of the President abruptly leaving the speaker's platform and hurrying to meet his wife to help her to a seat on the stage. In that small, fine detail—so the Southern newspapers and the authors of the *Official History* acknowledged—McKinley revealed his true self, allowing "the real man" to show himself.

"Deeds of knightly chivalry we see only occasionally," recalled the *Official History*, "and then generally they appear in books. . . . It was not the ruler of a great nation performing a remarkable act that the audience on this occasion applauded, but the gentleman and the husband discharging a simple courtesy."

William McKinley proved once and for all, at least to every Southerner present, that he was one of them.

A lbert R. Rogers was unfortunately absent from the Exposition during the two special days celebrating his native state and his hometown. Rogers did, however, read and hear countless reports of the President's victorious visit. He heard McKinley's approving words that the Tennessee Centennial and International Exposition, "in fine, is a gem, and at night a perfect dream," inspired by the sight on the first evening of the electrical illumination of Centennial City, reputed to have outdone all previous expositions, as well as a pyrotechnic display that included a lifelike fireworks portrait of William McKinley emblazoned across the night sky.

Rogers heard that the receptions held at the Women's Building in honor of Mrs. McKinley were the crowning social events of the Centennial season, the "bewildering profusion" of floral arrangements notwithstanding. Other than the stifling heat on Friday and a smattering of humidity-driven rain on Saturday, the festivities planned for Ohio Day and Cincinnati Day surpassed every expectation.

From many quarters, Rogers kept hearing about President McKinley's fascination with a horse he had seen at the Negro Building, an "educated" horse named "Jim."

Though the possibility of a visit to the Negro Building had been left for late on Saturday, time permitting, the President insisted that it be scheduled as part of his general inspection of the grounds earlier in the day. The Committee of Arrangements should have known better, as McKinley was a fairly vocal proponent for the advancement and education of people of color. He was a professed admirer of Booker T. Washington, founding president of Tuskegee Normal and Industrial Institute in Alabama, established in 1881, and he, in fact, would a year later be the first U.S. president to visit Tuskegee.

Fortunately, in the expectation that the President would look favorably upon an impromptu visit, the Negro Department's Executive Committee was prepared, so that when he arrived midmorning—after stops at the buildings of Kentucky, Illinois, and New York—a huge, appreciative crowd awaited him and his entourage. The *Official History* observed that McKinley toured the entire contents of the Negro Building—its three tiers of over eighty-five exhibits swathed in the flags of the United States, Tennessee, and the lands of Africa—and that he showed exceptional "interest and surprise" in everything, including demonstrable delight in the several numbers sung by the Mozart Society of Fisk University. After Chief Richard Hill introduced each of the musical artists along with the members of the department's Executive Committee and the Negro Woman's Board, in a momentary hush, with all eyes focused on President McKinley, Hill said, "Mr. President, that God may bless you and yours is the wish of millions of black men and women in this country." No more passionate and sincere an ovation was ever delivered to him than the one that followed.

Then, having saved Jim Key for last, Chief Hill turned to Dr. Key to lead the President and his party toward seats in front of a railed-off platform that was preset with a chalkboard, steamer trunks, a shelf of mailboxes, a rolltop cabinet with alphabetized file drawers, Jim's spelling rack, and his folded screen displaying letters, numbers, and an assortment of names of the dignitaries present. President McKinley and some of his cabinet members were apparently puzzled by the bewildering profusion of the five thousand rabbit's feet that were festooned over the stage. Dr. Key explained—"gravely" noted one of the Northern correspondents—that these were all left hind feet of graveyard rabbits, caught at midnight at the dark of the moon, many from battlefields and burial places of the Civil War. Jim relied on them, he added, to concentrate.

With that, the Doc gave the signal, and a magnificently groomed Jim Key entered from a side door and was escorted onto his platform by Stanley Davis. Lean and strapping, his coat brushed to a silken shimmer, his black ropey mane and tail both tied in ribbons of red, white, and blue, Jim strolled past the President of the United States with a demure nod, and then seemed almost to smile in a self-congratulatory way, as if he had long expected to entertain royalty and was happy to finally get the show under way. But in contrast to Jim's equine composure, and Dr. Key's grand, stately calm, a bout of incredible nervousness had struck seventeen-year-old Stanley, obviously having something to do with being in the presence of President McKinley himself, plus three cabinet members and a former postmaster general, along with Nashville's Mayor McCarthy and more than forty newspaper correspondents. Among others.

From the time that his sister had died, less than a year before, Stanley had worked for his brother-in-law as Jim's groom. Dr. Key, in his capacity as head of the Negro Department's Livestock Committee, had also put him to work in helping to oversee the well-being of animals entered in the various competitions and races held throughout the course of the Exposition. The Doc had already begun making inquiries of new contacts about where to send Stanley for veterinarian studies and had learned of Collins College for Veterinary Surgery in Nashville, the place where Stanley later attended.

Luckily no one seemed to notice Stanley's state of awestruck immobility as Dr. William Key took his place downstage, facing the audience with his back to Jim, his short riding crop held motionless in one hand throughout. Dr. Key introduced himself and gave a brief background on his educated stallion, sired by Tennessee Volunteer, a Hambletonian, and whose dam was Lauretta Queen of Horses, a pure Arabian that had once belonged to P. T. Barnum. Before beginning a demonstration of the results of patient, kind, intensive education, Dr. Key explained that his Southern-bred horse was a gentleman who could not start without first greeting the ladies present. Since Mrs. McKinley and many of the women traveling with the presidential party were still at a breakfast in the Women's Building, the ladies in the audience were either from the Negro Women's Board, from Fisk's Mozart Society, or there as newspaper correspondents. With a gallant bend of the knee and a slow bob of his head, Jim bowed individually to each female he spotted, waiting afterward for a surge of applause. Upon hearing one round of clapping, he found another lady in his sight lines, then bowed again. And again, and again. It became evident that Jim Key was quite taken with one of the ladies in particular, apparently not one of the younger or prettier women, but a rather matronly correspondent to whom he bowed several more times. Smiles, laughter, and applause rippled through the crowd as Doc Key, wearing his poker face, discreetly urged Jim to get on with his performance.

The program followed the standard format of this time period, starting with Dr. Key's polite request that Jim go to the steamer trunk to his left, remove the brass bell, ring it, and replace it, and then to remove a silver bell and ring that. To demonstrate that Jim had not rehearsed a set order, Dr. Key invited a volunteer from the audience to request that he take out and ring either bell. With his ears rotating and twitching to capture each infinitesimal sound wave, Jim, a good schoolboy, promptly and correctly responded to a series of requests for the two bells.

The President was said to be utterly transfixed throughout the demonstration, which continued to be performed in response to random questions from the audience. Bringing letters to his spelling rack, Jim spelled a couple of first names of cabinet members with no problems, and then, after a volunteer came up to the alphabet rack and rearranged the order of the remaining letters, he was asked to spell his own name in full—*J-I-M K-E-Y*—which he did successfully after a thorough search of the rack. Next was a learning exercise in the operation of a post office, Dr. Key explained (with apologies for its simplicity to the former postmaster general). A gentleman in the group was prompted to direct Jim to go to one of the mailboxes of his choosing and retrieve a letter from it. The name on the envelope was read aloud by Dr. Key, and Jim was told to take it to the cabinet and file it under the proper letter of the alphabet.

Without hesitation Jim went to the cabinet, letter in mouth, pulled out a slide at the bottom with his nose, placed the letter on it, raised the rolling cover of the cabinet also with his nose, and opened the correct drawer with his teeth, put the letter into it, and then pushed the drawer closed. Jim repeated this task several times at the instruction of different audience members, removing different letters from different boxes and filing them in the correct mail drawers without error.

For arithmetic problems suggested from the crowd, Jim added, subtracted, multiplied, and divided with only a few mistakes, as long as sums did not exceed the numeral 30. He could figure 17 divided by 4, for example, by picking out the number 4 and responding to the question of how much was left over by striking the ground once with his front hoof. But he was stumped when it came to the question of 17 minus 18, negative numbers having not yet been covered in his curriculum. Jim didn't bother trying to look for a number to select but instead shook his head no at Dr. Key, twisting his mouth and squinting his eyes to suggest that someone was trying to trick him.

Jim appeared to be relieved when math questions gave way to playing cashier, a game that involved selecting the correct coins for hypothetical amounts of change as suggested by audience members. He was even more pleased at a prompt from Dr. Key to "write" his name, *Jim*, on the chalkboard. A skill he had only recently learned, Jim did it by holding a small eraser in his mouth and moving it in the pattern of the script letters on a chalkboard covered with chalk dust. Doc Key had taught him the pattern by forming it first on the chalkboard with sugar water and training Jim to lick it off with a swirling motion of his tongue and head. Bit by bit, he diminished the amount of sugar until Jim understood that he would be rewarded with it after he performed the writing motion. Bill had been working on ways to teach Jim to manipulate a piece of chalk in his mouth so he could actually write letters on the chalkboard, but so far the chalk pieces kept breaking off, not to mention that Jim was none too fond of the taste.

The President and his entourage had their breath taken away by Jim's feat of retrieving a silver dollar from the bottom of a glass barrel full of water and laughed to the point of tears at the bit at the end when the big bay feigned lameness in response to hearing that he was to be sold. But the showstopper, as might have been predicted, was when Jim Key acknowledged President McKinley. The moment followed a challenge to Jim to go to his folding screen and select the cards on which were printed the names of the President's cabinet members—Secretary of State SHERMAN, Secretary of War ALGER, and Secretary of Agriculture WILSON. Even after an audience member had rearranged the order of the display, Jim successfully chose the name of each cabinet member as announced. Apparently two names were left on the screen—McCARTHY (the mayor of Nashville) and McKINLEY. Dr. Key said, "There are two remaining names on the board. One of them is the name of our fine Mayor, and the other is the name of our great United States President. Jim, please bring me the card that has the President's name on it."

Naturally, Jim Key was quite familiar with the name of the President of the United States. Not at all thrown by its similarity to the mayor's name, he speedily delivered the card to the Doc. Then Dr. Key asked, "Jim, can you show me where President McKinley sits today?"

Jim turned directly to the President, for the first time in the performance, and bowed slowly and respectfully.

Governor Taylor, sitting by the President, paved the way for the bit he knew, announcing loudly, "Jim Key is a good Democratic horse."

"Ho, ho," President McKinley was heard to laugh. "I will change his political views before I leave. Jim," he asked, "now, aren't you a good Republican?"

Jim swayed his head from side to side, as firmly to the negative as if he wasn't responding to the chief executive of the United States, a good Republican.

Respectfully, Dr. Key turned toward McKinley and assured him, "I vote Republican, sir, and voted for you." The President accepted this news graciously. Dr. Key went on, "Jim voted for you too, right Jim?"

Jim Key repeated his earlier "no" response.

McKinley chuckled, echoed by giggles and guffaws that fluttered through the gallery. The Doc appeared to be embarrassed and twisted his questions to convince Jim to pretend to have voted for McKinley, but nothing worked. They went through the routine, Bill and Jim milking it for all it was worth as they got down to debating the horse's politics. Was he a populist? No! A socialist? No! So, was he a Democrat, after all? Why, yes, but, of course! A "silver Democrat" in point of fact. The mention of replacing the gold standard with silver that had been William Jenning Bryan's unsuccessful platform when running against McKinley caused Jim to nicker outright, snorting and blowing foam from his lips.

The President and the rest of the audience exploded into applause and uproarious belly laughter that reverberated through the exhibit space and filled up the three tiers of the Negro Building.

Two days later, in New York, Albert Rogers read the story originally from the *Nashville Sun*, reprinted in a New York newspaper—which he cut out and put into his files. A Tennessee correspondent had submitted the piece from Nashville, on Sunday, June 13, 1897, writing, "Of the many points of interest visited by President McKinley, none seemed to interest him as much as his visit to 'Jim Key.'" Albert Rogers was surprised to read that the horse had become, in the words of the Nashville reporter, "the greatest attraction at our exposition." He was also very intrigued by the following excerpt from the article:

After the exhibition was over the President seemed loath to leave and after patting the horse and shaking hands with the Doctor, he said, "This is certainly the most astonishing and entertaining exhibition I have ever witnessed. It is indeed a grand object lesson of what kindness and patience will accomplish."

Within the week, Rogers returned to Nashville. With the growing number of attractions he was now booking in fairs around the country, he had many items to handle. But a singleness of purpose drove him. He had to own that horse.

D iffering accounts emerged over the years as to the details of the actual agreement made between Albert Rogers and William Key.
Some oral renditions passed along by folks in Shelbyville were in keeping with a version submitted for publication to the *Shelbyville Gazette* on October 13, 1945. The article's author had been a boy of nine or ten in 1897 but clearly recalled:

> It was during the Tennessee Centennial and Jim Key, the cele-
> brated educated horse, owned and developed after seven years
> intensive training by Dr. William Key, the personal cook and
> caretaker of the horse for Nathan Bedford Forrest in the Civil
> War. Well, he was in Nashville exhibiting Jim Key at his first
> prominent exhibition in the Centennial and the news came over
> the wires—yes, we had some kind of telephone or telegraph wires
> then—that Jim Key had been sold to Mr. Albert Rogers, a capital-
> ist of Orange, New Jersey, and a Vice President of the Ameri-
> can Humane Society for a large sum. Variously estimated from
> $10,000 to $100,000. At least the former price is a safe bet for
> soon thereafter Dr. Key gave my father $10,000 to purchase the
> Johnson Ryal's farm on the Tullahoma Pike. Anyway, the little
> berg of Shelbyville was all excited on this memorable day at the
> big sale and most of all that Dr. Key, who had spent seven years
> in extensive training for his education program would part with
> Jim but later we learned that Jim was to remain in possession
> of Dr. Key as long as either lived, and that a good salary usu-
> ally referred to as $125.00 per month was to be given the Dr. for
> attending him.

A second version, passed down through oral accounts from Dr. Key's family members, was much more likely. In this telling, Rog-ers went to see Jim at the Negro Building and had to push his way through a crush of spectators that encircled Jim's platform. The instant he laid eyes on Jim and then turned to survey the astonished crowd reaction, he decided, then and there, to make an offer to buy the act, on the spot, for a hefty cash price. But the purchase didn't proceed as planned.

When the dapper Rogers approached Dr. Key, after the lines to meet Jim had at last dwindled and the young groom had led the big, smart horse out to where he was stabled, Rogers committed a bit of a faux pas by asking, "Who trained this horse?"

Obviously, Albert Rogers had assumed that Bill was a hire, a sideshow performer or stage persona cast by the act's promoter to personify the kind of wise, old, kindly black man, such as were often sought in the South for tending to horses. This made sense to Rogers because he knew, after all, that the managers of the Old Plantation exhibit hired Negroes to play the roles of slaves. Besides, a trainer with the gifts to train such a horse would have to be one of the most famous animal experts in the world.

Patiently and kindly, the Doc assured Mr. Rogers that he was, in fact, Jim's trainer.

Oh? Well, then. Albert dug himself a deeper hole, asking who, in fact, owned the horse?

If he had insulted William Key, the older man didn't let on. Patiently and kindly, the Doc assured Mr. Rogers that Jim was indeed his horse.

Now aware that he was losing ground, Albert Rogers tried one last question, asking who promoted the act.

Doc Key paused and thought for a moment. The Doc supposed he was their promoter, but that was more when they were in the patent medicine business; admittedly, he was not an expert promoter in the area of expositions and such.

Albert R. Rogers had found an opening. With a doff of his hat, he presented his card, pitched himself as a promoter and booking agent for some of the top attractions in the country, and presumably rattled off impressive fees that his acts commanded. He figured Jim Key, properly promoted, could equal or surpass his most profitable attractions, earning weekly amounts of as much as $500, even $1,000.

Dr. Key laughed. He knew Rogers had to be blowing smoke. But then again, he liked the sound of that kind of profit.

Rogers then made his proposal. He would buy Jim Key for $10,000 and, if Dr. Key stayed on, he would pay him a percentage of the gate as salary. Bill Key, poker faced, rejected the amount out of hand, explaining that he had turned down higher offers. Albert then raised the amount, first doubling it, then tripling, continuing until he stopped at $100,000. The Doc savored each increasing offer before declining it, but this last one—the estimated value of his estate at the time, the sum material attainment of sixty-four years of life—made him stop and think hard. He must have considered that his relationship with Jim Key was not rooted in ownership. He rarely, if ever, used the word *owner* in reference to himself and his role in the care and training of animals—equine, canine, or other—who were part of his household and stables. Bill spoke of himself as Jim's teacher, companion, mentor, and confidant. He no more owned Jim Key than Jim Key owned him. But perhaps his reluctance to sell Jim, no matter the price, may have been rooted in his understandable aversion to the concept and practice of humans owning and selling other humans; the master-slave paradigm was much too close for comfort to the manner in which many people treated their horses. Then again, he was not being asked to part with Jim, except on paper, and in return would receive $100,000 and a percentage of the money this Rogers fellow seemed certain they would rake in. A man had to be very proud or very foolish to say no.

And yet, as the story went, Bill Key turned down all that money. Rogers couldn't believe it. That's when he offered a compromise. What if he gave Dr. Key $10,000 cash up front for the exclusive rights to promote Jim Key on a percentage basis. The Doc mulled the amount over. Getting desperate, Rogers added that in addition to that he would pay Dr. Key a salary, plus expenses.

The Doc warned Rogers that Jim had expensive tastes. The hay and grain had to be specially ordered to make sure it was free of impurities. Plus, from early colthood Jim Key had only been given the purest drawn spring water to drink, and he also required the services of at least one full-time groom. Moreover, he told Rogers, "Jim has got to have a private car for long distances. He's a light sleeper anyhow and when the train gets moving, he has to stand up the rest of the way. He just refuses to lie down." Jim was very sensitive, he went on, to the constant jarring and bumping of all the stops and starts.

Rogers suggested, "For long distances, I would be glad to arrange a stopover at a halfway point so he could enjoy the comforts of a local stable, and get the rest he requires." A little too eagerly, trying to close the deal, he summed up his offer—ten thousand dollars cash up front, a split of the gate, plus salary and expenses for the doctor, his groom, and for Jim.

Dr. William Key liked this offer and he liked Albert's enthusiasm. As much as he was skittish about a business partnership with anyone, let alone the young redheaded white man he had only just met, he realized that Rogers was exactly what he and Jim needed to navigate their way onto the national scene. But again he hesitated, not wanting to be rushed into a decision. "Let me think about it," he said at last, not seeing the hurry.

Rogers panicked. If they waited, he was sure that Key would either talk himself out of joining forces with him, or that someone else would come up with a better offer. He had to create a sense of urgency and some form of enticement that Bill Key couldn't refuse. In that moment, Albert R. Rogers had the brainstorm that would seal the deal and transform their destinies. It involved telling something of a lie, albeit motivated for philanthropic reasons. Rogers quickly explained to Dr. Key that there was, as it so happened, no time to wait, that he was tasked with filling a lucrative spot at the American Institute Fair within the month. If Key was interested, they would have to leave in only days for New York. But there was more to his hurry than just financial interests, Mr. Rogers insisted. As a matter of fact it was a cause very close to his heart. He wanted the opportunity to present Jim Key as a "grand object lesson of what kindness and patience can accomplish"—to quote the President of the United States—to the ruling powers of the ASPCA, with whom he was closely associated.

A light filled Bill's probing eyes. Seeing it, Rogers went further, proposing that a percentage of earnings from Jim's performances go to the ASPCA to be used to promote the organization's concerns on a nationwide and even international basis, perhaps to establish needed rescue shelters, animal hospitals, horse ambulances, and to encourage the organization of more branch societies.

Doc Key was sold. Even if he guessed that Albert Rogers had overstated his connections, he was so impressed by the younger man's salesmanship—and it took one to know one—that he accepted in full the terms of the deal.

A mix of these versions found their way into different press accounts. In Albert's promotional pamphlet, he may have originally described the $10,000 as a payment of good faith for the right to exhibit Jim. But he ran into problems when trying to solicit interest from exposition managements. He found that whenever he referred to Jim as his own amazing, educated horse that he had just purchased at the Centennial, curiosity was much more piqued.

Dr. Key appeared to recognize that Rogers, as a white upper-class Northerner, could provide access to him and Jim Key that they couldn't have otherwise obtained. He also seemed to initially accept the public relations story that Rogers included in his promotional materials about his ownership of Jim.

After an almost sleepless night of preparations at his New York townhome at 75 Maiden Lane, Albert Rogers woke early on Saturday, August 14, and beheld the first draft of the PR pamphlet, including his version of how he had discovered the horse:

> While at the Nashville Exposition, Mr. A. R. Rogers, a businessman of New York, saw for the first time this marvelous, intelligent animal. Being very greatly interested in humane societies, and a great lover of horses in particular, he purchased from Dr. Key for $10,000 this beautiful animal, but Dr. Key put in the contract a clause to the effect: "I am always to be Jim Key's groom and teacher," for he would not part with his pet. So North went Jim and Dr. Key.

All that the two men and the horse knew of each other they had learned in the eight days that had transpired since their departure from Nashville on August 7 and Jim's New York debut that Saturday at Field's Stables. Doc Key and Jim may have been provincial Tennesseans, but they might have guessed that the size of the gathering wouldn't give them the sort of splash in the New York press that Rogers had promised. However, they may not have been aware—as the small crowd was led through the chilly downpour into the large, well-appointed stable where the performance was to be staged— that there were no representatives from the American Institute Fair. They may not have known that neither was there anyone present from the ASPCA.

What was evident was that the rainstorm had deterred many from attending and that several ladies were so mortified by having to traipse through the mud and muck into the stable that they did not stay for the demonstration. Since Doc Key had warned Albert that Jim was known to turn in halfhearted efforts when audiences were small or not overly enthusiastic, the promoter most likely didn't tell them that reporters from the *Journal* and the *World* had failed to show. And yet, Jim comported himself as brilliantly as he had for the presidential entourage, rising to the challenge of dazzling the little group that clustered about his platform amid the smell of wet hay and the drumming sound of a late-summer rain on the stable's roof.

Rogers watched with sinking spirits, not defeated, but facing the fact that this act was not going to be as easy to promote as he had imagined. Nonetheless, he smiled and thanked his guests for coming out in the inclement weather, mentally making plans to hold another private showing on the following Wednesday, August 18, and perhaps to debut the act in Cincinnati—where the public was less jaded than in New York. As his friends and colleagues dispersed, he may have been surprised to see Dr. Key in conversation with a couple of young men scribbling notes on writing pads while a third gentleman, a sketch artist, was finishing off a drawing of Jim in his most glamorous pose.

Miraculously, it turned out that two newspapers—not wanting to be out-scooped—had sent their most junior correspondents. Fledglings or not, both reporters wrote with such enthusiasm that the following day, the Sunday *New York Sun* included a mention of the showing and the Sunday *Herald* ran a half-page article on Jim along with a collage of small drawings of him performing his extraordinary feats.

Rogers could never be sure what magical spell Dr. William Key had employed to suggest to each of the writers that the horse be billed with a new name, but somehow both the *Herald* and the *Sun* unwittingly included it. It had a ring to it, Rogers had to admit, a grandeur suited to the one-time ugly duckling of a horse whose career as a celebrated, educated Arabian-Hambletonian had now begun. Prominently displayed in both newspapers in captions over the articles was: "BEAUTIFUL Jim Key."

PART

TWO

of the

HISTORY

6

Key, Key, and Rogers

> Progress in humane feelings is hard to discern during the decades
> when 25,000 streetcar horses died annually. Poverty and frus-
> tration in human society multiplied animal suffering . . . with
> penalties frequent and jobs scarce, little compassion remained
> in the weary driver of a dray or streetcar for the feelings of a
> horse that was not even his. So human dilemmas triggered
> many instances of cruelty. Neither the moral nor the emotional
> aspect of the helplessness of animals appeared to have touched
> the public mind.
>
> —GERALD CARSON,
> *Men, Beasts, and Gods: A History of Cruelty*
> *and Kindness to Animals*

IN THE EXCLUSIVE VILLAGE OF SOUTH ORANGE, in the Montrose Park neighborhood of New Jersey, there were larger estates
than Glenmere, on more expansive pieces of property—with owners whose names suggested they were among the very richest of
New York's elite families, all staking out their country retreats in
the manner of English nobility. There were Mandevilles, Meekers,
Babsons, Pages, and Firths; the estates of James T. Woodhouse and
William Redmond covered as much land as many of the other lots
put together, while investors like I. M. Freeman and John T. Lord
owned several small noncontiguous tracts. Compared with some
of the imposing mansions and grounds in the Village, the estate
belonging to Mercy Adelia Rogers and her husband, Hiram, could
have almost been considered modest. But because of its certain dis-

tinguishing characteristics, an invitation to Glenmere was coveted in any season in society circles from all of the Oranges.

For one thing, it was only one of two named estates in the whole of the private enclave off of Montrose Road, the other being Wood-house's dominion known as Hillside. For another, Glenmere had been designed as a kind of enchanting inn—probably so that Mercy and Hiram could depend on frequent visits from their two sons and three daughters and their grandchildren. Modeled after the fanciful French palace at Fontainebleau, it was sometimes mistakenly called by that name, even though Mercy and Hiram would be quick to point out that their home was but a cottage in comparison to the sixteenth-century castle once belonging to a de Medici. Glenmere's location on Ridgewood Road was also prime real estate, bordered by a flowing brook that ran along its one side, and was one lot away from a riding ring, a quarter-mile track.

At first, it hardly occurred to A. R. Rogers that Glenmere could be an ideal launching place for Beautiful Jim Key. After the gatherings at Field's Stables, he was sure that with the "crisp" New York notices, they would be flooded with requests for engagements at exhibitions in large halls. When that didn't happen immediately, he sent out a new press release that included President McKinley's quote from the Tennessee Centennial exhibit, along with the *New York Sun*'s assessment that "such a performance as Beautiful Jim Key goes through with has never been equaled by any horse in this vicinity," and, of course, the *Herald*'s sensational review: "Almost all things seem possible to Beautiful Jim Key, except the power of speech. So perfectly is this wonderful horse trained that the trainer does not touch him with hand or whip."

A trickle of interest began to flow. On Thursday, August 19, a telegram was sent to Albert at Maiden Lane from a J. L. Fynes, the assistant general manager of B. F. Keith's Amusements Enterprises—which was the entity that booked theatrical entertainments for Keith's New Theatre of Boston, Keith's Opera House of Providence, Keith's Bijou of Philadelphia, and Keith's Union Theatre of New York. The letterhead was cause for Albert's heart to pound—this being just the echelon he sought for Jim—but the telegram made no promises. "Dear Sir," Fynes wrote, "If you care to have the horse go through his performance on our stage next Thursday A.M. at

10:30, I shall be pleased to witness same, and will then see whether I can place him."

Beautiful Jim Key's first real New York audition seemed not to go well. A big problem was the lack of response—positive or negative—that Jim received from the three or so theatre men in attendance; they simply had never seen anything like the act before and didn't know how to react. But as disappointing as the B. F. Keith rejection was in the short term—and Albert had delayed their trip to Cincinnati because of the audition—it set into motion the collaboration that needed to occur between Key, Key, and Rogers.

Dr. Key pointed out to Rogers that from his years in the patent medicine business he had learned that different kinds of audiences responded to different kinds of presentations. For the general public, a free-flowing, informal demonstration—such as he and Jim had done at the Centennial and for the press gatherings—worked fine. Doc may not have been a New York sophisticate, but he could obviously see that for the higher priced ticket these men who booked the fancy, big-city opera houses were looking for a real show, with real stage scenery, music, and lights, and if not a set script, then at least enough of a predictable structure that the folks knew when to applaud.

A play? Why hadn't Rogers thought of that? Already he had begun to harbor lofty ambitions for his promotional pamphlet, seeing his presentation of Jim's accidental journey toward higher education as an entrancing saga, all the more moving because it was true. Rogers believed "He Was Taught by Kindness" could touch a public nerve and even rival the manner in which the latest fictional works were captivating an increasingly literate populace. He couldn't help but think of that small paperbound booklet published in England twenty years earlier—a fictional "autobiography" of a horse by the name of Black Beauty, written by Anna Sewell.

Sewell's book by this time had sold in the vicinity of three million copies (selling ten times that many over the next century and a half). In spectacular fashion, the thin volume had opened the public mind to the importance of preventing cruelty to horses. Probably no book had so managed to become a tool of social change in the United States to such an extent, other than Harriet Beecher Stowe's antislavery novel, *Uncle Tom's Cabin*, first published in 1852, which had provided the abolition movement with one of its most power-ful, enduring voices.

Forty-five years later, the staged version of *Uncle Tom's Cabin* con-tinued to reign as the most popular drama in the country. There were so many traveling productions performing it on the repertory circuit (newly referred to as "the road") that "Tom" troupes were known to bump into one another in transit, one company barely pulling up stakes as the other was pulling into town.

If Rogers could envision his pamphlet as a great bestseller, he could just as easily see it being turned into a traveling or Broadway spectacle. A full-scale play that embodied themes of *Black Beauty* and *Uncle Tom's Cabin*? Why not?

On the train to Cincinnati, as Rogers and Doc Key started to write the dramatic piece, the former medicine showman was more of a realist, proposing that their first effort be on a more cost-efficient, modest scale. Rogers agreed, and the two proceeded together to map out the scenes for a two-act play, *The Scholar and a Model Office Boy*. Beautiful Jim Key was to star in the dual leading roles of the Scholar and the Office Boy, and Dr. William Key was to play the Professor in the first act and the Employer in the second act. But no amount of enticement or cajoling could convince Stanley Davis to play the role of Jim's Valet in the school setting and the role of the Chief Clerk in the office setting. An actor would have to be found, suggested Rogers; preferably a classically trained Negro actor, sug-gested Key.

As the details were debated and while Rogers dispatched tele-grams ordering the construction of a twenty-foot stage and a custom-designed blue-and-white-striped tent to seat five hundred, a new set of obstacles awaited them in Ohio. Albert had been so sure that after his New York disappointments over the lack of interest from the ASPCA and the American Institute Fair, his hometown would provide a welcoming haven in which to debut not only the differ-ent versions of the act they were now developing but also to do so under the auspices of a local humane organization. Unfortunately, the Ohio Humane Society, while interested, couldn't commit to sponsorship, its board of directors being concerned that the costs would exceed any profits they might generate.

Although Beautiful Jim Key made several new fans from a press gathering that Rogers hosted, no inquiries about hiring him followed. But Albert's uncle, Professor C. C. Long, principal of the Eighth Street District School, smitten with Jim and profoundly impressed by Dr. Key, had a startling idea. Wouldn't it be marvelous, he proposed, if all the students at his school could witness one of Beautiful Jim Key's performances?

Better still, Rogers added, why not make performances available to every young student in the city? He could see it then: entire school systems of every major city in America closed in honor of officially decreed Beautiful Jim Key Days. In his imagination, Rogers visualized Jim being presented with keys to those cities, along with medals, awards, and commendations.

Those visions were soon mocked. At a meeting with the municipal school board that his uncle quickly arranged, Albert Rogers and Dr. William Key described the value that a series of performances for students throughout Cincinnati would have on their understanding of the object lessons of kindness and patience. Noting the dubious expressions on the faces of the board members, Albert went further, offering to host the performances himself at no cost to the school board. If he hired the Auditorium, with its seating capacity of four thousand, Jim and Dr. Key would perform thirty-minute shows throughout the day, which ought to accommodate all the children of the city; if not, a second day of performances could be arranged.

"Absolutely not" was the unanimous response of the board.

"Why, sirs?" Rogers felt compelled to ask, nearly speechless.

"Because," retorted an indecorous board member with a chin thrust out toward Bill Key, "we can't close our schools for horse shows, or monkey shows."

Furious, Rogers later apologized to Dr. Key. Of course, the Doc had heard much worse in his lifetime, and he only encouraged his partner not to pay those comments any mind. The best way to counter stupidity and unkindness was to go the opposite direction and not give up.

Those thoughts and what seemed to be setbacks lit a fire in Rogers, and within a matter of days he was able to secure three excellent promotional opportunities, covering three different strategies. The first of these came during a meeting with the management of the Odeon Theatre. Promising them that his "remarkable new play" would make their stage the talk of the theatre world around the nation, Albert convinced the Odeon to engage the show at their earliest convenience. Almost too early, the managers promptly engaged the play to run for a week starting October 18, less than two months away.

Emboldened, Albert decided not to take the school board's no as definitive and went next to the Auditorium's manager, booking the huge hall for the three days following what he predicted would be a sold-out week at the Odeon.

Before leaving Cincinnati, a third opportunity that fell into their laps at the last minute was a charitable performance on behalf of the six hundred children of the House of Refuge, not precisely the foray into philanthropy that Rogers had been looking for, but an opening nonetheless. As much as A. R. Rogers professed to know and care about animals, and horses in particular, the marked sensitivity that Jim showed toward the orphans—as though he actually knew they had met with unfortunate circumstances in their lives through no faults of their own—struck him as uncanny. Again he wondered if through some hypnotic force Dr. Key was cuing Jim to perform differently for different audiences. The Doc would have scoffed and expressed his observation that animals were often more highly in tune with human feelings than were other humans. No matter how Jim accomplished it, from the start to the finish of his performance, Rogers witnessed a visible transformation on the part of the children.

A letter to that effect was delivered from the House of Refuge's president, Charles Thomas, as Albert prepared to depart for the train station. Thomas sent his thanks, with gratitude from the board of directors, for the gift Beautiful Jim Key had bestowed on the orphans. He noted, "If you could have heard not only their many expressions of delight during the performances and those given me privately afterward I know that you would have felt repaid for the ray of sunshine you have thrown into the lives of these homeless waifs." Rogers brought the letter at once to show to Doc Key and to Jim, showing the two the passage that described lessons the children had learned about the importance of humane practices toward animals. Since many of the House of Refuge's orphans would be placed in homes in the country, the lessons would have practical as well as moral benefits. "Several boys who have had the care of horses before coming to us," wrote Thomas, "said that they would never whip a horse again."

Just as exciting to Albert was the fact that the letter included their very first—and unsolicited—publishable endorsement: "The perfection to which you have brought the training of Jim Key is truly wonderful and surpasses anything of the kind that I have seen. I feel confident that he has not his equal in intelligence."

Within a week, they had received more than a hundred additional endorsements, thanks to a four-day engagement at the Waverly Park Fair in Newark, marking the end of summer and the New Jersey State Agricultural Fair. Mayor James H. Seymour of Newark, Elizabeth's mayor John C. Rankin, the officers and membership of the Women's Christian Temperance Union of New Jersey, and every possible other area civic leader wrote recommendations and signed petitions extolling the virtues of the "most highly educated horse in the world" (according to the *Newark Evening News* on September 9, 1897). *The Newark Daily Advertiser* claimed that a "more mystified and delighted audience never watched" a performer, human or otherwise, of Beautiful Jim Key's inexplicable talents. President W. L. Tomkins of the State Agricultural Society wrote that it was gratifying, "in these days of Houchee Couchee shows," to be called upon to attest to an attraction as meritorious as that of Jim Key. If only more trainers and promoters would spend more time developing such acts, he wished, than "the class which has been in vogue, and leads to the degradation of the human being."

Ironically, Rogers had first been hesitant about appearing at the fair, since the tent and the new stage weren't ready yet. The Doc apparently encouraged him to take the engagement. After all, he and Jim had been performing in county and state fairs for a few years and could employ the same format they had used with such success at the Tennessee Centennial. Dr. Key's instincts were correct as usual, and as early as September 1, while they were launching into Rogers's next strategy, the buzzing began. The *World* soon jumped on the Beautiful Jim Key bandwagon by featuring a half-page, illustrated article on him (Sunday, September 11, 1897) as Albert started fielding invitations, securing dates through much of the fall. They agreed to appear for the last five days of September at the Casino Hall Summit for the Trenton Interstate Fair, and continue on to Pennsylvania for an exposition during the first week of October (offered the top weekly fee so far of $500). That gave them only a week off before the debut of the play in Cincinnati on October 18.

The Danbury Fair in Connecticut loomed as a possibility for November, but before pursuing the engagement, Rogers sent one last inquiry—and a packet of press clippings and endorsements—to Mr. Allen Williams, press bureau chief of Madison Square Garden as well as a director on the Board of the American Institute Fair. Mr. Williams replied two days later, disappointing Rogers one last time. "The only trouble with having Jim Key at the American Institute Fair," the press bureau chief acknowledged, "is that they do not seem to want any such Show attraction, no matter how great its merit. I urged it upon them because I was wonderfully impressed with the performance which I witnessed at Newark." In fact, Albert's colleague volunteered to write an endorsement for the horse and a letter of introduction that could be used for press references. Once again, however, Williams delicately hinted that part of his board's objections had to do with Dr. Key's lack of established credentials. He went on to reiterate that "if this equine prodigy is managed by such a successful veteran as Major Pond, I think his owner should be a great financial winner."

Rogers took no personal offense from such attitudes, though they frustrated him. He recognized that Major J. P. Pond, the peerless lecture circuit promoter, had taken the value of the spoken word to unprecedented heights and had helped to build the fortunes of some of the most famous American thinkers of the age: names like Mark Twain, Henry Ward Beecher, Ralph Waldo Emerson, and Wendell Phillips, as well as emerging authorities such as Thompson Seton, a lecturer on the subject of wild animals. But even with Albert's own knack for hyperbole, he couldn't imagine convincing Major Pond that Dr. Key and his horse could be counted as masters of the spoken word. Although the man and the stallion were extraordinary in myriad ways, to suggest they were paragons of great American thinking was, believed Rogers, at least for the moment, overreaching.

It was true that Pond, who led a Wisconsin unit in the Civil War as captain and major, also managed musical entertainments, having conceived the idea of promoting military bands as concert attractions. He had managed the careers of many notable singers and musical novelties such as the boy violinist Florizel. Through the management of Gilbert and Sullivan, he had made himself a small mint by retaining rights to some of their operas—*Pirates of Penzance* for one. Upon further reflection, Rogers had to realize that if he wanted Major Pond to take over Beautiful Jim Key's management, it might not be a difficult proposition to interest the impresario. The real problem was that he could see himself being pushed out of the picture, a possibility he dreaded.

Rogers decided instead to be as Pond-like as he could in his own efforts to establish Dr. William Key's name and reputation on a broader public scale. He immediately revised the press materials—adding deliberate phrases such as "successful veteran horseman" and "renowned throughout the Southland"—that featured the Good Doctor's background more prominently. As a result the *Newark Evening News* wrote a follow-up story to an earlier one, declaring Beautiful Jim Key all the rage of the Waverly Fair with credit clearly due to Dr. Key. Drawing from Albert's research, the *News* became the first paper to write at length about the "venerable looking colored man" determining him to be a "character of the most unique order."

The stigmas of being described as a practitioner of voodoo and being known as a horse whisperer—or a dabbler in methodology thought by the better known equestrian authorities to be suspect—were offset by the reporter's series of questions to Dr. Key about his educational formula of kindness and patience.

"I made him understand that by learning promptly," the Doc told the *Newark Evening News,* "that he would earn a piece of lump sugar or some other dainty, while dullness meant no sugar and a good scolding."

A scolding? Did the trainer punish his horse with the whip? The reporter had to raise the question because of rampant abuse of circus and other performing animals.

"No, sir, I never used a whip in training Jim." Dr. William Key compared whipping animals to whipping children, saying that in either case, "The whip makes 'em stubborn and fearful." Trust was the firmament for education, he explained; fear destroyed trust.

With a few other press pieces positioning Bill Key as an expert in his field, it occurred to Rogers that if Dr. Key could win an endorsement from the Orange Driving and Riding Club—an almost unspeakably prestigious group of equestrian enthusiasts who had never hosted a horse show of any kind—then the Major Ponds of the world might help their cause, just to be associated with their caliber of excellence. But by what strategy could Albert, Bill, and Jim entice the impervious lions of the club to sponsor a couple of evenings at their unspeakably exclusive clubhouse?

The answer arrived at once: Glenmere. Why hadn't he thought of it before?

M uch later, Doc Key must have laughed when he read Albert's revision of the section in the promotional pamphlet on Jim's journey from home state star to national prominence: "So North went Jim and Dr. Key to Mr. Rogers' beautiful country home, 'Glenmere,' at South Orange, New Jersey, a suburb of New York, and here for two years Jim's education received its finishing touches before he was ever put on public exhibition."

Two years was obviously an exaggeration. The time spent in retreat at Glenmere was actually much closer to one week.

Nonetheless, by the evening of Tuesday, September 14, with Beautiful Jim Key's two-act play still in rehearsal, his general public presentation had been polished to a high sheen, losing some of its rustic county fair appeal and its patent medicine show elements, while several new elements had been added to reflect the astoundingly rapid advancement of Jim's educational level. He had seemingly jumped overnight from country elementary schoolboy to private high school student bound for college. Doc Key and Jim appeared very pleased as additions to sets and props arrived continuously, with new display and spelling racks, authentic post office–styled mail cabinets, Jim's own watch tower clock and mechanical calendar—of very fine design—an organ, a telephone, an electric cable car coin box, and, the coup de grace, a Beautiful Jim Key nickel-plated cash register, made just for him by the National Cash Register Company (a manufacturer out of Ohio), with leather tabs he could pull rather than having to press keys with his soon-to-be celebrated nose. Rogers had also ordered sets of oversize playing cards so that Jim could demonstrate his budding poker knowledge—Be careful, he cheats, Stanley Davis (who had been practicing with Jim) could have told Rogers and Key, but didn't—along with colored posters of the flags of different nations, which the Doc had been teaching Jim to identify.

The time spent in collaboration at Glenmere laid a needed foundation of trust between Dr. Key and Albert Rogers, a bond that was apparently made stronger by both Keys' instant fondness for the other Rogers family members. This included their English butler, Mr. Barton, and their Irish housekeeper, Mrs. Lowrey, along with the rest of the estate's employees who, Bill observed, were treated with respect and kindness, if not as equal family members. The Doc and Albert's father seemed not to have enough hours to discuss subjects of mutual interest—the news of the day, outer space, philosophy, business, and Hiram's health. Just two years younger than Doc Key, Hiram had a few ailments that bothered him, and he was clearly impressed by his sixty-four-year-old guest's youthful vigor. Key may have actually recommended his own Keystone tonic for the elder Rogers, or possibly treated the ailments with an herbal remedy and even an incantation or two. Whatever Dr. Key did was able to produce such a positive result for Hiram Draper Rogers that he continued from then on to confer with Key whenever medical worries arose.

Jim, always partial to the ladies, had Albert's mother, Mercy, and his three sisters—Alice, in her early thirties, Grace, age twenty-seven, and twenty-four-year-old Stella—fluttering in and out of the stables, catering to his every whim. At Maiden Lane, Dr. Key, Jim, and Stanley had already spent time getting to know Albert's wife, Clara, and her three boys, eight-year-old Clarence, six-year-old Newell, and the toddler Archibald. At Glenmere, Stanley found more opportunities to play with the boys—who enthusiastically showed him around the estate, with Archie, scrambling to keep up. Later Stanley reported to Albert that his youngest was quite a little athlete. Albert's sons sat in on Jim's lessons and enjoyed thinking up words and names for him to spell. He became very proficient at spelling C-L-A-R-E-N-C-E and N-E-W-E-L-L (even though the first time Jim tried he spelled it with only one L), but he had problems spelling the name of the youngest, which he insisted was A-R-C-H-E. The concept of the non-phonetic I-E seemed to amuse Beautiful Jim Key, and he was stuck on "Arche" from then on.

The suburban rumor mill of the Oranges chewed on the mysterious goings-on at Glenmere. When word spread that only a select group of prominent citizens had been invited to attend the Tuesday evening party, those left out pooh-poohed the horse's alleged abilities and raised questions of credibility. The mulatto trainer was a voodoo man, they had heard; the so-called Arabian-Hambletonian wasn't even a legitimate breed. And Albert Rogers, despite his parents' respectability, not only dabbled in dark arts of amusement promotion and publicity stunts, but also mingled far too openly with the lower classes. When the grumbling reached the editorial offices of the *Orange Chronicle,* a representative from the local newspaper called on Rogers to ask why he had not invited any of their correspondents to attend. This was a switch for A. R. Rogers, after having to twist the arms of reporters in New York to attend his gatherings, and he eagerly, albeit belatedly, extended an exclusive invitation to the *Chronicle* to cover the informal evening.

Even though the newspaper tried to send a cynic, from the moment his carriage turned up the long, elm-lined circular drive to Glenmere he fell at once under the same spell that the other guests experienced. The anticipation of witnessing the private exhibition of the "wonderful trained Southern horse that has created such a furor wherever shown," the correspondent reported, was almost equaled by the enjoyment of being greeted by the three lovely, charming Rogers sisters. Alice, Grace, and Stella, their husbands and children, along with Hiram and Mercy, hospitably showed guests around their Fountainebleau-esque home, and then led everyone along a path to the stables.

Intended to suggest that the group was entering a magical realm, huge Japanese lanterns lit the path from the main house, past the guest wing, through the trees that sheltered the round open-aired summer house, and back toward the stables and carriage house. Hosts and guests entered the main carriage room to find it transformed into a small theater space—prettily decorated with flags and bunting—while one half of the room was comfortably arranged with stable seats and the other half was railed off to designate the stage area. Jim's new display rack—"a large framework, on which in parallel rows were cards, with the letters of the alphabet on them, figures from 1 to 25 and a number of names of individuals"—covered much of the rear of the railed-off space. Jim's new set piece conveyed "an imitation of a post office, with boxes numbered from 1 to 30, in each of which was a letter."

As everyone took their seats, Albert and Stanley entered through the doorway from the horse stalls and sat down with the rest of the audience, followed next by Dr. Key and, at last, the star—who stepped carefully, almost shyly, as he was led to the stage. This was not what the *Orange Chronicle* reporter had expected. Perhaps local detractors were right to say that the fuss being made over the Southern horse was unfounded. Under the correspondent's objective scrutiny, the large dark bay horse at first sighting was far from noteworthy, except perhaps for his "remarkably bright and clear eye," which was evident as Jim turned to take in the audience. But was he beautiful? No, not to the man from the *Chronicle*, who stated that in appearance there was nothing unusual at all in the horse's makeup. He described Dr. William Key, Jim's trainer, in passing as "an old colored man." Despite the later explanation given for the efficacy of the rabbit's feet festooned over the enclosure, he seemed to find them to be rather off-putting.

And yet, no sooner had Dr. Key made a short introduction and asked Jim to bow to the ladies—which he did, of course, repeatedly and excessively, his shyness suddenly replaced by an equine expression of romantic ardor as he gazed with unapologetic longing at a giddy spinster—the applause and laughter that filled the carriage house made it very difficult for the reporter not to become as riveted as everyone else. He managed to suggest that some of the tricks, like Jim's shaking of his head no and bowing of his head for yes, might have been indicated by the position "in which the short whip was held by the trainer." But that was all the skepticism he could muster. For the rest, he wrote that Beautiful Jim Key's other feats defied explanation. In his estimation, proof that no deception was being used lay in the fact that almost all of the questions were posed to the educated horse by different audience members; the responses were clearly unrehearsed.

One of the first questions to Jim was to pick out the name of McKinley, which he did, not surprisingly, without hesitation. Then the name of New Jersey Governor Grigg, a guest of the evening, was called, and Jim trotted over to the card reading GRIGG and brought it to Dr. Key. The name of a former mayor, TRUMAN, was asked for when someone in the audience had to add, "the best Mayor Orange has ever had," and that card too Jim unerringly selected and took to the Doc. The next request was for the name of the current mayor, GILL, which Jim also had no trouble selecting. A voice from the back, possibly that of Albert Rogers, stirred up some fun, asking, "Is Mr. Gill a better mayor than Mr. Truman was?"

Jim took a beat, milking it so that both the former and current mayors could brace themselves, before nodding his head with an emphatic yes. Politically savvy as Jim was in certain circumstances, he might have understood that one ought always to advocate the current administration, if one wanted to succeed on a grassroots basis, or at least if one wanted to receive one's better share of sugar.

Jim was next asked to spell the name Gertrude and after that his own name, doing so as he had been taught by bringing the letters one by one from the rack and lining them up on his spelling stand. What astounded the audience was that while this required two *R*s and two *E*s, there was only one of each letter on the main rack; a secondary display of letters was on a smaller screen close to the front of the railed-off space. The *Orange Journal* reported that in each instance, "Jim hunted over the rack and not finding the letter there turned around and picked out the desired one from the supplementary list in front of the audience, all this with no apparent indication from his trainer as to what he should do, just the simple reminder of, 'Now, Jim, get an *E*', repeating the direction in exactly the same tone of voice and using the same words in the case of the *R*."

For the next exercise, Dr. Key announced, "Now, Jim, I want a letter from the post office." Jim turned toward the letter cabinet with the numbered pigeonhole mail slots and waited for someone in the audience to request a particular box number.

"Box 18," one of the guests volunteered.

Dr. Key made the request official, asking in a kindly though firm manner, "Bring me a letter from box 18."

Beautiful Jim Key did so, drawing the unmarked envelope out from the niche marked 18 with his teeth and walking it to his trainer, who slipped him just a taste of sugar as he opened the envelope. "This letter is addressed to Colonel Morrell," the Doc said, while a trill of laughter elapsed close to where Colonel Morrell was sitting. Doc Key placed it back in Jim's mouth, telling him, "Please file it in its proper place."

Strolling to a second cabinet, his rolltop mail center, Jim scanned the drawers until he saw the one marked *M*, pulled it open, and dropped the letter into it, then nudged it shut. He sauntered back to receive his next request before stopping, as though he had forgotten something. No, it was the audience who had forgotten to applaud! He did a slow take to the guests, which earned him the laughter and applause he wanted, along with unmasked expressions of awe.

The next letter, addressed to Miss Myrtie Peek, a noted horse-woman present for the gathering, provided more of a challenge, since the proper mail drawer was not labeled with the letter *P* but with *N–Q*. Jim scrutinized other drawers to make sure *P* hadn't been placed elsewhere and then turned to Dr. Key, stumped.

"*N, O, P, Q*, Jim," his teacher reminded him, and that was all Jim needed to deliver his letter to Miss Peek in the proper drawer.

The *Orange Chronicle* reporter, like the *Newark Evening News* writer who observed a similar challenge for Jim during the post office demonstration, may have used the fact that Jim did not execute each task perfectly as proof in his own mind that no fraud or contrivance was being employed. He became even more convinced that he was in the presence of true genius when Jim did his show-stopping retrieval of a silver dollar tossed into a glass jar full of water, and when he imperfectly "wrote" his name "with some wiggles" on the chalkboard, plunked out a few notes on his organ (music was not Jim's forte), performed his ever popular bit of feigning lameness in response to being sold, and acted out his newest roles as streetcar conductor and store cashier.

To operate his streetcar register, Jim was tasked with answering how many five-cent fares were represented by any coin named by ringing the trolley bell the correct number of times. Beautiful Jim Key's general store was a more elaborate affair. When a member of the audience decided to purchase any item, Dr. Key announced its price and asked how much money the "customer" was prepared to pay for it. Jim then pulled tabs on his customized National Cash Register to enter the purchase price, say, $2.37, by pulling the cent tab seven times, the dime tab three times, and the dollar tab two times. In this instance, a request was made for an item costing $3.46 and a $5 bill was offered. Dr. Key told Jim, "Go to the cash drawer and ring up a $3.46 sale and bring me back the change for a $5 bill." Jim efficiently did so, ringing up the correct amount and bringing back, piece by piece, four pennies, a fifty-cent piece, and a paper dollar.

Prices for the various items at Beautiful Jim Key's store might have been based on the going rate for dry goods at the well-known Bamberger's, "the always busy store" on Market Street in Newark, where a pair of men's imported black cotton socks sold for eighteen cents, ladies' cotton hose for twenty-five cents, a yard of fine silk lace for fifteen cents (Jim could figure the price of two yards), and a bed quilt was listed at $1.69. To deliver the thirty-one cents change, Jim was able to choose the three coins—a quarter, a nickel, and a penny—without verbal prodding, unless, of course, he brought the wrong change, as he did occasionally, and he would be given a second chance.

The select citizens of the Oranges rewarded Beautiful Jim Key, Dr. William Key, and Albert Reynolds Rogers with a standing ovation. During the walk back to the main house, where refreshments were served, a couple of directors from the Orange Riding and Driving Club proposed to Albert that he exhibit his horse at their clubhouse, even though such a show broke daringly with club tradition.

Rogers attempted to seem unsure as to whether Jim's schedule could accommodate their interest. But after giving it some thought, he confirmed that they would be available.

The whirlwind began. The clubhouse on Halstead Street sold out a total of four performances, which took place on Tuesday and Wednesday, September 21 and 22, with matinees at three-thirty in the afternoon and evening shows at eight-fifteen both nights; evening prices were fifty cents (including a good seat) and one dollar (front rows), while matinees were twenty-five cents for the balcony and back rows, fifty cents for down in front.

By the time his hired men had finished setting up the new tent and stage at the Casino Hall Summit on Thursday, September 23, for the Trenton Interstate Fair, Albert had in hand another stack of crisp press releases and effusive endorsements, including a testimonial from the Orange Riding and Driving Club's president Charles Hathaway, "and other prominent Orangeites," and a commendation from none other than Major Pond himself, "under whose management all the celebrated lectures and entertainment of the past twenty years have been given."

Pond's golden endorsement read: "I have been twice to see the wonderful performance of Beautiful Jim Key and it was hard to come away. His performance is almost human. Everybody will surely see this remarkable horse as soon as he is known."

Albert, Bill, and Jim hoped that he was right.

The New Jersey coronation continued at Trenton, where as many as five thousand spectators came to see Beautiful Jim Key with their own eyes. Area newspapers ran daily updates, sometimes with multiple articles in the same edition. Temporarily silencing the cynics, they depicted Jim as more beautiful than ever. The Trenton *Sunday Advertiser* proclaimed him the "handsomest and most intelligent horse ever seen upon any stage." A testimonial by editor Thomas Malone stated, "The person who misses seeing Beautiful Jim Key, the educated horse, whose blue-and-white-striped tent is located near the entrance to the fairgrounds, misses the best of the fair." The fair's promoters ran their own endorsement.

Besides the mounting numbers of testimonials, at the Interstate Fair—through no strategy of Albert's—Jim started to receive gifts and letters from admirers. Following a benefit performance for the student body of the New Jersey School for Deaf-Mutes, the children were asked to put in writing what they had been saying to each other in sign language, and several did so, addressing their letters to Beautiful Jim Key at Glenmere in South Orange, known by this juncture as the horse's own palatial estate—thus launching his collection of the hundreds of thousands of postcards and letters sent to him by youngsters that were to amass in one of his several monogrammed steamer trunks. Rogers couldn't refrain from including one letter in his press materials, identifying it as a "composition from an eight-year-old deaf and dumb scholar":

> *Dear Jim Key—You are a very wise horse. I am surprised that you can count, telephone, write, subtract and add better than other horses. I want to see you again. Do you know all deaf pupils? Do you like deaf or hearing people best? A man told you things through a telephone. I would like you to come to school. You can write a letter to me. I am amazed to see such a cunning animal. You must be very polite. Good-bye. Your loving friend, Jennie Cohen.*

Crates of apples and sugar began showing up at his stall, giving Stanley even more responsibilities for keeping track of Jim's things. The Doc and Rogers agreed that a second groom should be hired, along with a few more roadmen to help transport the tent, sets, and props. After this discussion, Rogers had to rush off to interview a line of waiting applicants for the job he'd listed the day before in the *Trenton Sunday Advertiser:* "WANTED—A good BARKER who has had experience. Apply early Monday at the Fair grounds, Beautiful Jim Key's Tent."

The next stop for the rising star was in western Pennsylvania in the town then known as Pittsburg. In 1890 an official decision by the United States Board on Geographic Names had abruptly snatched the *h* from Pittsburgh, along with all the *h*'s from cities across America whose names ended in *-burgh*. Later, in 1911, the same board reversed its decision by declaring its name: "Pittsburgh, a city in Pennsylvania (not Pittsburg)." Nonetheless, in the years that Beautiful Jim Key became a local folk hero to the city, as he would have asserted, its spelling was decidedly P-I-T-T-S-B-U-R-G.

In fact, the first week at the Pittsburg Exposition generated so much press that even with shows running on the hour from nine in the morning to nine at night, Jim's tent couldn't accommodate the crowds. On October 5, three days into the first week, the exposition management paid Rogers in full and implored him to extend the engagement for a second week. If he accepted, the West Pennsylvania Exposition Society would build a larger pavilion to house the Beautiful Jim Key exhibit and move it to a site more easily accessed than the tent had been, just to the left of the main entrance to the fairgrounds.

Albert brought the offer to the Doc. The problem was that if they stayed on at Pittsburg they would have only two days to travel to Cincinnati to open *The Scholar and a Model Office Boy*. Could they be ready? This was a close call.

Dr. Key felt that Will Griffin, a new member of their entourage, could help rehearse with Jim on the train, so they were probably going to be in fine shape—as long as their star could manage to get his beauty rest, no pun intended. That too would be Will's job. Raised in the North, Afro-American Will Griffin—a multilingual college graduate with classical stage training who also happened to have worked with horses before—had not only been cast in the play but had also come on board to serve as Jim's secondary groom and valet, officially as an assistant to the younger Stanley. Though they came from different worlds, Davis and Griffin made a friendly team, working together to groom Jim and tend to his various needs. But when Griffin placed a silver bell in the stall for Jim to ring whenever he needed something, Stanley put his foot down. Somebody had to try to keep the "Equine King"—as the papers had started calling Jim—from getting too big of a head.

But it was too late. A reporter for one of the Pittsburg newspapers had already leaked the story about Beautiful Jim Key's new attendant, writing that the educated horse "has the services of a groom who happens to be a college graduate and speaks six languages. When the horse needs the services of his valet he rings a bell the same as a man of wealth would do to summon his servant."

Rogers and the Doc agreed there was more to gain by doing the second week of the exposition and decided to stay on. In accepting the offer, Rogers did not ask for more than the $500 fee he had been paid for the first week, but only with two conditions—first, that the West Pennsylvania Exposition Society sign an endorsement testifying to the fact that "Beautiful Jim Key is the best draw we ever had; he is high priced but he is worth it," and second, that Jim Key be put on the same promotional bill as John Philip Sousa. The endorsement was not a problem, but the Society members balked at making the great and almighty Sousa share a bill with anyone, let alone a horse.

A. R. Rogers stood his ground, confidently assuring the exposition management that the March King would be an even greater draw with the Equine King on his figurative marquees. On this gamble for all concerned, flyers and ads were hurriedly made up:

THE LAST WEEK! A Fitting Finale to this Most Successful Season of The Great Pittsburg Exposition. Beyond Comparison the Greatest Musical Organization in the World, JOHN PHILIP SOUSA And His Band of Fifty Five Artists. Conductor—John Philip Sousa, THE MARCH KING. Mr. Arthur Pryor, the greatest living Trombone Soloist. Mr. Franz Hell, Fluegelhorn Soloist. Mr. Albert Bode, Cornet. Mr. Jean Moeresman, Saxophone. Every Resident of the Two Cities Should Hear SOUSA. And: *THE WONDERFUL EDUCATED HORSE. On account of the unprec-*

edented demand to witness the marvelous feats of BEAUTIFUL JIM KEY by those who were unable to attend the Exposition last week, the management have determined, not withstanding the great expense, to retain JIM KEY at the Exposition all of this week.

Not every Pittsburg Exposition director thought Jim was worth the expense, some complaining that he was an inflated "side show." Although Rogers was sure they would be proven wrong, he ran his own series of small ads in area newspapers with the adamant lead line: "Jim Key *Not* a Side Show." The numbers told that tale too, as an estimated 35,000 clamored to see Jim in the two-week period.

The staggering turnout quieted the naysayers. While John Philip Sousa may have been initially peeved about the attention given to a horse act, when Dr. William Key visited him to express his personal appreciation for the maestro's musical genius and to extend his personal invitation for the bandleader and band members to attend one of Jim's shows, Sousa accepted. Albert Rogers reserved seats for the conductor and his entourage in the front, where, his eyes brimming with tears, John Philip Sousa became a humble fan. Afterward, he went up to embrace Jim and to shake Dr. Key's hand, saying, as was extensively quoted, "I cannot refrain from expressing my admiration for the marvelous intelligence of Beautiful Jim Key. I consider him the most accomplished specimen of his kind I have ever seen." Rogers took this as an endorsement and added it to the press materials, inscribing the quote as FROM THE GREAT AND ONLY SOUSA.

Not every promotional ploy by Rogers met the approval of Key and Key. Since Rogers did not exactly own Jim—but it had been agreed that he could say so—the byplay in the press that was made of escalating offers to purchase Jim by outsiders may have chaffed at the Doc. In the private New York gatherings in August, Rogers had boasted that he had been given several offers of $10,000 for the educated horse but had turned them down, stipulating he wouldn't consider any amount under $25,000. In early September he told the Newark papers that despite many individuals' attempts to purchase Jim for $25,000, he would only entertain amounts of $40,000 or more. At Glenmere, the *Orange Chronicle* reported that he had turned down at least two offers for $50,000; and, in fact, Rogers now listed that as Beautiful Jim Key's value on the cover of his promotional pamphlets. In Pittsburg, a representative from Barnum & Bailey verified that he had tried to buy Jim for $60,000. Albert's youngest son, Archie, later recalled that it was Bailey himself who came to Glenmere with cash to pay in full.

Rogers predictably turned that down too, insisting that he considered $75,000 and upward the new going price, but he still managed to wrangle an endorsement from the Barnum & Bailey representative who told the *Pittsburg Commercial Gazette:* "This educated horse is undoubtedly the most intelligent horse in the world. We have never had any that could begin to do what he so easily does. Nor have I ever seen any such exhibition, though I have witnessed the performance of every trained horse on both continents."

Not every idea that Key and Key tried in their performances met with the approval of Rogers. One of the newer bits that had their show ending with a tableau of the Doctor setting up his cot next to Jim as the two pretended to go to sleep—their actual nightly routine—didn't go over well. Some said it was touching, but others thought it strange. They soon dropped the new bit.

Rogers seemed to enjoy the smattering of press who showed up at surprise hours, sometimes at Jim's stables, or early in the day when Beautiful Jim Key was known to be taken out on his long morning run, as though they were trying to catch him and the trainer off guard, in the act of putting together their trickery. Rogers knew they would find nothing. But with a trail of suspicious fellows lurking about, Bill and Jim became less amused. Normally, it was the Doc's habit to let reporters interview Jim out of his presence, with Stanley or Will standing nearby, to prove that he wasn't signaling his horse to respond in any particular way to their questions. He told them in advance to make sure that they stuck an apple or two and maybe some sugar in their pockets—to play a game of hide-and-seek with Jim—or else he'd have nothing to say to them. Once after he returned to find that the reporter couldn't get Jim to spell his name at his spelling stand, it turned out that it was because after a thorough search of the reporter, the petulant bay hadn't found a thing. As the story went, Doc Key asked, "Well, how was it?" to which Jim did begin to spell, lining up the letters *"F-R-U-I-T-L-E-S-S."*

Only once did Dr. Key come close to losing his patience with a reporter who seemed hell-bent on exposing him as a quack, accusing him of making up the tale about Jim finding the buried treasure for the ex-slave lady. In other accounts, this reporter pointed out, Dr. Key had said that it was Jim's dam, Lauretta, who had the telepathic powers and had found the pot. Some newspapers had stated the treasure was worth $1,000; others said $4,500. So what other tall tale was the "doctor" telling?

Playing dumb, William Key smiled and said nothing.

The reporter continued, "Now, Dr., what about your claim that you personally collected most of the rabbit's feet yourself at Chickamauga?"

Doc Key shrugged. What about it?

"Well, it's generally believed that to have any efficacy a rabbit's foot must be got at a graveyard at midnight by a cross-eyed nigger and you're not cross-eyed and the Chickamauga battlefield is not a graveyard."

"Oh yes it is a graveyard," Bill Key countered sharply. "There are thousands of bodies buried there, and it doesn't make any difference about a nigger being cross-eyed." With a searing look at the reporter, he added calmly, "Any good nigger can collect the feet and they will have full power."

With fame came higher scrutiny, distortions of the facts, and outright fabrications, as a mythologizing process began. The press started to describe Beautiful Jim Key with the romantic phrase "he was bred in Old Kentucky," and that stuck, even though it had never been claimed, but may have spun from the fact that his Hambletonian grandsire was Ohio-bred Kentucky Volunteer. Some newspapers mixed up the political persuasions of Bill and Jim, sometimes on purpose, depending on the leanings of their readership.

Like all stars, Jim and his associates also suffered a loss of privacy, experienced early on the last day of the Pittsburg Exposition, when Jim and company were mobbed as they attempted to board the train for Cincinnati. This could have caused Rogers—typically late—to almost miss the train, but as he rushed up, he had a new letter for Doc Key to see. Just received from Jas. Heekin of the Jas. Heekin Company—makers of "celebrated Cincinnati high-grade roasted coffee"—the letter of introduction requested his business colleagues to receive A. R. Rogers and to let them know that any courtesies extended to Albert and his fellows would be most appreciated.

The letter helped, and so did the advance press, evidently, as another crowd was waiting for the train in Cincinnati. Amid these signs of Jim's increasing celebrity status, the Odeon Theatre managers excitedly informed them that the coming week's run of *The Scholar and a Model Office Boy* was close to being sold out in advance.

With the opening of the play, Rogers used the occasion of a debut in his hometown—where Jim was being given the fawning reception that he'd anticipated on his previous visit—to begin to earn back his investment and, with the additional 25,000 or so admissions sold for the subsequent run at the Auditorium, then some. A century later, the merchandising concepts of A. R. Rogers might seem commonplace, but in his era, and given the range of venues in which he was promoting a most unusual act, they were truly brilliant, truly ahead of his time. In the printed programs handed out at the Odeon, at the very spot on the page where the act break was marked and intermission implied (during which, since the Doc wanted music, the Orchestral Regina Music Box, furnished by the Rudolph Wurlitzer Company, was played), theatergoers could also discover:

> Those who desire a large and very handsome photograph of Beautiful Jim Key, to show to their friends, can purchase the same in the lobby. There are five different views, Filing Letters, Writing, Reading, Spelling and Counting, Using the Cash Register and Taking the Silver Dollar from the bottom of the Glass Bucket of Water. Price, 25 cents each.

For prices ranging from $5 for private boxes, which sat six, orchestra seating for fifty cents, and balcony seats at twenty-five cents, twelve thousand Cincinnati theatergoers fell in love with the almost human horse. Will Griffin played his parts winningly too. But the truly brilliant star was Dr. William Key—whom Rogers had highlighted in the program as "the most successful trainer of horses ever known"—and whose dignified bearing and aura of kindness and intelligence captured the favor of audiences and critics alike.

Though the play itself was not necessarily a literary triumph, the run at the Odeon was a stunning success on several counts. The structural choices worked, making Act I ("Scene—School Room: The Audience are requested to ask the questions") the more informal, free-flowing demonstration, incorporating the easier exercises or those Jim had been performing the longest:

1. Jim's admiration of the ladies.
2. Jim opens school ringing brass bell and silver bell around the ring, tells time and reads the calendar for any date asked for.
3. Jim picks out any letter, playing card or number asked for.
4. He will spell any ordinary name requested by any one in the audience.
5. Jim brings various names from the rack at command.
6. His views on politics.
7. Jim shows his proficiency in figuring, adding, multiplying and subtracting in any numbers below 25.
8. He writes.
9. Jim plays the organ.

Act II ("Scene—The Office") had Dr. Key in the role of the Employer and W. G. Griffin in the role of the Chief Clerk, both guiding most of the questions (with some audience input), in a more scripted format, with Jim doing some of his harder or newer bits:

1. Jim goes to the post office.
2. Jim distinguishes various pieces of money from 1 cent to $20, ringing the amount on a street car register as correctly as the conductor.
3. Jim goes to a regular cash register with a five dollar bill, rings up any amount requested and brings back the correct change.
4. He will show how he rang up money in his cash box used at the Nashville Centennial.
5. He rings up the telephone.
6. Jim takes a silver dollar from a large glass bucket filled with water, without drinking a drop.
7. Jim distinguishes colors and flags, and tells how it is he is able to do these wonderful feats.
8. Jim offered for sale—not wanting to leave his owner he becomes lame—well again.
9. Jim says good-bye.

The reviews traveled quickly to other cities, spurring inquiries from theatres across the Northeast; some were reprinted elsewhere, like the article that ran in the Cincinnati *Commercial Gazette*, and also made the New York *Mail and Express*. The writer raved, "Speech alone is denied to Jim Key, the most intelligent horse that ever looked through a bridle or munched oats, but he makes himself as clearly understood as the most accomplished linguist. When it is said that speech is denied to Jim Key, audible speech only is meant." Critics who questioned his breeding had to hear him praised as that most "handsome bay, through whose veins flow the purest of Arabian and Hambletonian blood." The ever-simmering accusations that Key, Key, and Rogers were involved in a hoax were answered in reviews that read like full-page testimonials, including a list of signatures from representatives of Cincinnati's military, police, and courts in a declaration that read: "we the undersigned . . . take pleasure in testifying that Beautiful Jim Key does all that is claimed for him and that there is to the best of our belief no deception, but that the horse really seems to have very remarkable intelligence, and we cheerfully recommend this very interesting, astonishing, and amusing entertainment."

W. L. Lykens, one of the most well-known theatrical booking agents in New York City, was inspired enough by the write-ups to make the trip to Cincinnati. Not at all disappointed, he went on record as saying, "In my province, I have handled many native and foreign attractions, I have seen the exploited novelties in this and other countries, but without solicitation and unhesitatingly I have the honor to say that the education of Beautiful Jim Key and the acts he performs are not short of marvelous."

Prior to their arrival in Ohio, Albert had received a cable from his uncle saying that the stodgy members of the school board were still opposed to the idea of shutting the schools down for a day-long series of children's shows at the Auditorium. That didn't change, even with reports that many schools in Pittsburg had directed their students to the Exposition, and as Jim's pending Odeon run had become the talk of the town. In Cincinnati, Albert responded by inviting every principal, teacher, and school board member to attend the Monday opening evening performance at the Odeon as his guest and by scheduling a special discounted children's matinee two days later. The invitation proposed: "If, after witnessing this performance, you agree with me that every child should witness it, and you would care to announce it to them, I would appreciate it. This special School Children's Matinee will not be advertised."

When news followed that a crush of thousands of Cincinnati children flooded the streets surrounding the theatre and had reached near riot levels on Wednesday evening—after it became clear that the Odeon could seat only the earliest arrivals—the school board held an emergency meeting and approved closing down the schools for the day on Monday, October 25, so that every student in the city be given the chance to witness Beautiful Jim Key's grand "object lesson of what can be accomplished through kindness and patience." The board voted unanimously to reject Rogers's offer that the shows at the Auditorium be free to the students, resolving instead to charge an admission of ten cents each—except to those who couldn't afford it—the logic being, as one board member quipped, "A free show does not impress the mind of a child."

While the only coverage that Cincinnati newspapers had allotted Jim back in August had been one brisk blurb about his benefit performance for the House of Refuge, by now he was their darling. The Cincinnati *Commercial Tribune* went so far as to offer "Twenty-five Dollars in prizes to the scholars of the public Schools for the best composition on Beautiful Jim Key. The best compositions to be published from day to day."

If Bill Key harbored any reservations about some of Albert's marketing tactics—and he did—he recognized that what the promoter had accomplished with the Cincinnati school board was a monumental coup, a turning point in a journey he was beginning to see as reaching far beyond anything he had dreamt back in Tennessee when waiting for his future turf champion to be foaled. From here on out, almost every city where they performed would be able to follow the model established in Cincinnati; indeed the former skeptics on the school board signed a testimonial, touting their own leadership in the cause of humane education.

Albert Rogers likewise understood that his aims notwithstanding, the heroes of their ambitious venture were the horse and the man from Shelbyville, Tennessee, who in three short months, in spite of some obstacles, had begun to capture the attention and hearts of the public—young and old, male and female, rich and poor, educated and not. The much more difficult challenge that lay ahead, however, was to capture the public mind, and to change attitudes and behavior toward animals.

The turn from the nineteenth century to the twentieth was a cacophonous time in America. It was literally loud and noisy, with the roar of industry and the crash of conflicting concerns about a host of old and new issues. For any activist, it was not the most opportune moment in history to launch a movement, let alone breathe a second wind into a cause that seemed to have had its day, or to help unify its well-meaning but disorganized proponents.

The problem wasn't just that the greater volume of protest was about humankind's cruelty to other humans—with prominent voices speaking out against America's growing imperialism and increasingly violent racism toward blacks, Native Americans, and immigrants, as well as women's inequality, and the battle heating up over workers' rights—but that the prospect of a rapidly transforming world made it that much harder to craft a resonant message to last beyond a season.

Perhaps at no other time in the country's history had so many radical changes taken place, on every plane of existence, so suddenly, with technologies, social structures, values, and belief systems loudly clashing and clanging up against one another. In just a handful of decades the agrarian base of commerce had been toppled by the industrial revolution. Inventions that could not have been imagined in the early 1800s were by late century exploding into reality almost daily. In the decade between 1896 and 1906 alone, human ingenuity created everything from Jell-O (gelatin dessert, 1897) to the engine-powered airplane (1903), as well as:

radio (1896)
electric stove (1896)
aspirin (1897)
telephone with answering machine (1898)
anesthesia (1898)
flashlight, battery-operated portable (1899)
tape recorder (1899)
wireless telephone (1899)

radio telephone (1900)
zeppelin blimp (1900)
electric vacuum cleaner (1901)
electric typewriter (1901)
air-conditioning (1902)
crayons (1903)
electrocardiogram (1903)
silicone (1904)
animation of motion pictures (1906)
radio amplifier (1906)

Although travel by rail and by horse for most Americans would continue to be the main modes of transportation for a few more decades, by the turn of the century a number of automobiles were increasingly spotted on city streets and country roadways. In 1908, Henry Ford's assembly line would ring in the era of mass production, making the horseless carriage affordable to the booming middle class, as the numbers of cars on the road multiplied exponentially. Electric cablecars were appearing in many cities, eliminating the use of horse-drawn trolley cars and saving those horses from abuse, but those equine servants still pulling individual carriages were still exposed to dangerous conditions. In most urban areas, where immigrants were now flocking in ever greater numbers, bursting already crowded lower-income neighborhoods at their seams, the challenge of crossing the street was as much of a life-and-death proposition as it had been in 1866 when Henry Bergh founded the ASPCA.

By the mid-nineteenth century, like several larger cities, New York City was inhabited by teeming masses of homeless nonhuman species: pigs, hogs, goats, dogs, cats, ducks, geese, various and sundry rodents and birds, donkeys, horses, cows, sheep, and other livestock abandoned or escaped from the numerous pens kept near shanties and Central Park squatter houses, or from the many slaughterhouses, despite efforts to keep the meat-packing industry near the city's more remote addresses. After a visit to New York, Charles Dickens wrote friends about his attempt to cross lower Broadway, warning them about the estimated ten thousand hogs roaming freely about town. "Take care of the pigs," he noted, "a select party of half a dozen gentleman hogs have just now turned the corner."

In the 1860s, as many as one million nonhumans called New York City their home, not including insects. Despite laws that had been passed both to prevent cruelty and to cope with the overwhelming noise, sanitation, and health problems, enforcement seemed impossible.

Henry Bergh, son of a prosperous shipbuilder and upper-class scion, decided to challenge the status quo. After a visit to England, where he was inspired by the work of the Royal Society for Prevention of Cruelty to Animals, he brought the movement to the United States officially in 1866. Bergh had some advantages, not the least of which was his wealthy circle of friends, who were keen to participate in some form of philanthropy and helped to fund his activities. His timing was also such that with the end of the Civil War and the cause of ending slavery no longer the focus of forward thinkers, abolitionists and humanitarians of the day turned their already stirred energies to consider the plight of their animal brothers and sisters. To Bergh's disadvantage, even though he named his organization the American Society for the Prevention of Cruelty to Animals, with the ambition that it have a national reach, the structure of local, county, and state jurisdictions fairly limited his authority to the city. Nonetheless, the tall, thin-faced elegant gentleman with the droopy mustache—known as Don Quixote of Manhattan—spurred the establishment of SPCAs in localities across the country.

Bergh successfully lobbied for the passage of a law that made it illegal in the state of New York to inflict *unjustifiable* harm on any animal, by intentional violence or by neglect, whether it was a teamster brutally whipping a horse, a private citizen abandoning a sick or dying horse, a rag boy kicking and throttling the enslaved dog that pulled his overloaded rag cart, beef importers who stacked bound live calves in piles on the docks, businesses that transported cattle in suffocating death cars, or butchers who bled live cows for eight hours to make for a whiter veal. One of the secrets for Henry Bergh's 90 percent success rate in the cases that he and the ASPCA brought to court was the logical argument he presented time and again that cruelty to America's eighty-five million nonhuman individuals came at an oppressive cost, financial and societal, to humankind. Cruelty to livestock, for example, destroyed dairy products; unsanitary horse stables and neglected equines spawned diseases that assumed epidemic proportions. At one point, as many as 70 percent of working horses in the city came down with a deadly respiratory disease that brought the transportation systems to a standstill, forcing New Yorkers to travel on foot on already dangerously overcrowded streets and sidewalks.

A tireless crusader, Henry Bergh was not afraid to take on high-society sportsmen who engaged in live pigeon shoots, or the gambling clubs that gathered to bet on a fight to the death between a bulldog and a black bear, or the Bowery Boys, who for entertainment set terriers on rats in gaming pits, or any of the other cockfights, dogfights, or instances of animal exploitation that he could uncover. He also became a newspaper regular, sometimes as the object of satiric renderings, but always punching back with vivid and heart-wrenching descriptions of animal cruelty that bent the sensibilities of the public toward his cause. Although he had tussled with Professor Louis Agassiz over feeding live rodents and rabbits to the boa constrictor at P. T. Barnum's museum, Bergh earned the assistance of Agassiz in another campaign, albeit an unsuccessful one. This was Bergh's attempt to halt the torture of imported green turtles used for the delicate flavor of turtle soup. They were brought in alive and made to lay on their backs for weeks without food, strung together through hand-punctured holes in their flippers. Agassiz confirmed that the turtles could feel the pain and deprivation, but it was not enough to stop this practice.

P. T. Barnum, that great impresario and master of humbuggery, took Henry Bergh's constant criticism on the chin. The two adversaries eventually gained a mutual respect. In one instance, Bergh defended Barnum from another group's attack on his allegedly inhumane elephant-training practices. Barnum replied by contributing handsomely to the ASPCA as well as to the SPCA in Bridgeport, Connecticut, where he resided in his later years. Upon his death in 1891, he left money to Bridgeport to erect a monument to none other than Henry Bergh.

Those newspapers and critics charging that the leaders of the various fledgling humane organizations were misanthropes who cared more about animals than about humans were silenced for the moment when Bergh became involved in exposing a horrific case of child exploitation. With published artist's renderings of the girl known as "Little Mary Ellen"—emaciated, in rags, with bruises and scars as evidence of chronic beatings—the public became enraged. Henry Bergh seized on the opportunity to send his message that all cruelty ought to be intolerable, thus extending the work of the humane movement to include the protection of children, as well as animals. He also helped to establish a new organization specifically devoted to protecting minors from abuse, the New York Society for the Prevention of Cruelty to Children. Though not the first child welfare group to be founded, it was one of the more powerful to date.

After Henry Bergh died in 1888, even though the animal welfare movement continued to grow as more and more local organizations cropped up in towns and regions across the country, the loss of one of its guiding lights certainly diminished the energy that had brought the issue of cruelty to animals to national prominence. Several factors, which Albert Rogers was just beginning to grasp in November 1897, hindered the efforts of other humane groups from rekindling that energy. Because most of the organizers of the charitable organizations were wealthy, there was a sense that animal protection was a luxury to be enjoyed mainly by the upper classes. There was also scrutiny of some founders of these groups as to their true motivations, with more than a few being accused of self-serving intentions, perhaps for financial or political gains, or just for the aggrandizement of their egos. Most problematic, as much then as later, were the conflicting messages, priorities, and approaches of the different groups. Infighting resulted over the most thorny of questions, such as the pros and cons of animal testing for medical research and especially live vivisection; the debate between activists for the humane treatment of animals waiting to be eaten or killed for their fur and skin and total vegetarianism; and the argument over whether or not the movement should embrace those who didn't believe nonhuman species were entitled to civil rights but generally loved and cared for their companion animals.

So the question that became clear to Key, Key, and Rogers was not only how to find the right group or groups with which to align, but more important, what message they wanted to send into this noisy, message-crowded place in time. Was it simply what President McKinley had said, that Jim Key served as a grand object lesson of what could be accomplished through kindness and patience? Or was it something more?

As Rogers reviewed everything Dr. Key had said about the manner in which a horse of above-average intelligence had been educated, he recalled how the Doc believed that Jim understood everything his teacher said to him. Bill Key's attitude seemed to be that every species had its own way of experiencing feeling and thought, along with its own form of language. In the Doc's view, the only barrier between humans and nonhumans was this language gap, one that he and Jim had bridged together. Doc Key could understand and communicate in Jim's language—which is what the term *horse whisperer* had come to mean—while the Arabian-Hambletonian could understand and communicate in his teacher's language. The message in that, Albert Rogers concluded, was living proof to the world that animals were sentient creatures, capable of feeling and thought different from but akin to our own, which was why kindness and patience toward our nonhuman relatives was important, urgently so.

Upon the return of Beautiful Jim Key and his entourage to Glenmere from Ohio, Albert presented his idea for moving forward with the newly focused humane message, which received complete approval from Key and Key.

There was, however, a problem. The Tennesseans needed to return to Shelbyville, if not for the remainder of the winter, then for as long as could be agreed upon. Apparently when Bill, Jim, and Albert had formed their partnership, they had not discussed a timetable. Rogers argued strenuously against doing anything to interrupt their incredible momentum, but Dr. Key insisted that Jim was homesick and needed to see the hills of Bedford County. Besides, the demanding hours that Jim was working, in addition to traveling among different winter climates, could pose a health risk to their star. That was all the Doc had to say to remind Rogers that it would be self-defeating to exploit one animal in the name of preventing the exploitation of others. Resolving to use his time productively, Rogers agreed that they would resume their adventure in March. From then on, he offered, they would try to exhibit only during the warmer months.

Shortly before Dr. Key, Stanley, and Jim were scheduled to depart Glenmere to return to Tennessee, Rogers was contacted by E. J.

Nugent, a popular vaudevillian, who wanted to bring *The Scholar and a Model Office Boy* to Broadway during the week before Christmas; producer R. M. Gulick was backing a bill of novelty and comedy at the Star Theatre and suggested Beautiful Jim Key as a headliner. Before turning down the offer, Rogers took it to the Doc, who was keen to do it, even though it was not, they each understood, a stepping-stone into the more serious New York humane circles.

Still, Dr. Key contended, providing amusement and laughter was one of the most effective ways of opening minds. Not to mention that being able to brag that he'd taken a step or two across the Broadway boards would make for fine conversation back in Tennessee. He came up with a compromise. He, Jim, and Stanley would leave as planned for Shelbyville but return to New York after two weeks and remain through the end of December, then go back home for January and February. He would be willing to do that, Doc Key said, if Rogers would be willing for a production of *The Scholar and a Model Office Boy* to be held at the Opera House in Shelbyville, Tennessee.

The plan was mutually approved, and as soon as the Tennesseeans had left, Rogers hurried back to the city to begin writing a blizzard of letters to every humane group that he could, giving himself until the end of the year to obtain sponsorship from an influential organization.

As he typed away, compulsively using the carbon paper that he had in nearly limitless supply, thanks to the family business, letters of endorsement from Jim's new fans in Cincinnati began to arrive by the bundles, like birds migrating en masse to 75 Maiden Lane. Clara and the boys helped Albert to organize and open the letters, but soon, as correspondence began to pile up in the appearance of snowdrifts around the study and elsewhere, a post office box was obtained. One of the letters, as it turned out, was a testimonial Rogers had requested when he was in Cincinnati. It was a kind letter of endorsement from the Ohio Humane Society, applauding Beautiful Jim Key and his trainer, along with a request to sponsor a benefit upon their next visit to Cincinnati. Perfect.

Albert Rogers wrote one last time to the officers of the ASPCA. Not hearing back, he procured a letter of introduction from his uncle Mr. L. R. Rogers, a businessman like Hiram, who was friendly with one of the ASPCA board directors, Mr. Frank Connelly. With the letter in hand, Rogers went to call on Connelly at his townhome on

106th Street. This he did not once but several times, being politely turned away in each instance, until on November 23, when he sent a letter that took a different tack, simply inviting Connelly to come and see his horse, Beautiful Jim Key, just returned to the city:

> I give a private matinee for my friends and some of the press boys at the stables 155 East 25th Street at two o'clock Wednesday. If you find it convenient to come I would be very glad to have you do so, and when you do please introduce yourself to me. . . . I want to have your wife come down and see it, but the stables is not a very pleasant place to bring ladies.

In the meantime, Albert wrote to the presidents of the American Humane Society, based in New York, and the American Humane Association, based in Boston, telling both of them that before he accepted the sponsorship of the ASPCA, he wanted to offer that opportunity to their respective organizations. He invited John Haynes of the AHS to attend a Saturday private showing that was being given for "a few of my little friends" and promised that Haynes would not be disappointed. Besides, confessed Rogers, "I brought him to New York practically for the purpose of exhibiting him to you."

Since he had gone that far, he also added that the competing Boston group was very interested in a sponsorship role, but he wanted, before accepting, to make sure that Haynes, "of all men," met Beautiful Jim Key for himself. Rogers had not, of course, heard anything tangible from the American Humane Association, but he had a unique strategy for appealing to George Angell, president of that group. Knowing that the animal welfare pioneer was interested in the potential of education as a means of promoting humane values, Rogers highlighted the educational opportunities that an educated horse might offer to the movement:

> As the superintendent of the Ohio Humane Society said ". . . years of teaching in the schools with stories would never . . . leave as deep an impression upon a child's memory as will one hour in watching an animal who really thinks." . . . What I hold more interesting to myself, as one who is deeply interested in the children, the compositions that the children write in the schools after seeing the horse, in which as they often tersely put it "that now

as they have seen a horse that really reads and writes and seems to know everything they will always be kinder to them."

Perhaps Albert's most persuasive line in his letter to George Angell was one he had borrowed pretty much verbatim from Dr. Key: "I have always argued that if a mule in a cornfield can be taught what 'gee' and 'haw' means, that with patience and time that any animal can be taught a great deal more."

Unfortunately, the Ohio Humane group's testimonial line that played down the impact of stories upon children's humane education may have struck the wrong chord with Angell. Obviously, Rogers knew much more about Henry Bergh and the ASPCA than about George Thorndike Angell and the American Humane Association, except that it was an offshoot of the Massachusetts SPCA, which Angell had founded, and that a new organizational wing had been launched that was known as the American Humane Education Society. If Albert had been better informed about the amazing Mr. Angell, he would have most likely traveled at once to Boston and not left without meeting the seventy-four-year-old philanthropist. If Dr. Key had been consulted, he would have advised Rogers to forget the other groups and to pursue only George Angell.

What made the self-made man of means from Massachusetts such a good match for Key and Key was that like the two Tennesseans, he did understand the power of story, having had a fascinating one of his own. The poor son of a Southbridge Baptist minister who had died young, George T. Angell had been raised briefly by his widowed mother, a schoolteacher, and then went to live with different relatives, mainly in rural settings. Throughout his youth he was exposed to many different kinds of animals to whom he had a close affinity. He witnessed both extremes of kindness and cruelty. As a child he was said to have drafted a will, long before SPCAs had come to America or he had taken up the cause, leaving his then imaginary estate for the care of uncared-for animals.

After putting himself through college and law school, he went on to a stellar legal career that made him wealthy enough to retire in 1868, at age forty-five, on Washington's birthday to be precise, the same day he attended an event that changed his destiny and that of the humane movement. It was a forty-mile, harness trotting race between Empire State and Ivanhoe—for a purse of $1,000—from

Brighton, a suburb of Boston, to Worcester, over rough wintry terrain, with each horse drawing two men at speeds as high as fifteen miles per hour. Ivanhoe was of known Hambletonian descent, while the unregistered Empire State probably was Hambletonian as well. Both Empire State, who was declared the winner, and Ivanhoe died by the race's end. They had literally been raced to death.

Angell's letter the following day in the *Boston Daily Advertiser* expressed his outrage. Something had to be done to stop cruelty to animals in the Boston area, he stated, an effort already admirably begun in New York. "I for one," he pledged, "am ready to contribute both time and money and if there is any society or person in Boston with whom I can unite, or who will unite with me in this matter, I shall be glad personally or by letter to be informed."

An outpouring of interest and money followed, allowing Angell to launch the Massachusetts SPCA with upward of 1,700 members, some of them from the oldest and most affluent Boston families, others from reigning literary and philosophical circles. Many early activists, whom George Angell credited with providing the spirit to the MSPCA as well as to the American Humane Association (formed in 1877 as a federation of all local humane groups across the country), were women. One of them was the woman he soon married, a widow named Eliza Martin, and another powerhouse was Mrs. Emily W. Appleton. As the wife of Nathan Appleton, a successful manufacturer, Emily contributed so significantly to the organization that many questioned why she didn't have a board position. But in the Victorian era, Angell later explained, that would have been seen as exploiting "a lady's name." And still, as the MSPCA took on many of the same ills being battled by Bergh and his associates, the former lawyer—and former law partner of the ardent antislavery activist Samuel E. Sewell—was not afraid to share the spotlight with the many celebrated names that joined in his mission. Angell used the courts and the press to sway public opinion, though not to the same extent as did Bergh and the ASPCA. Instead Angell found other ways to influence popular consciousness, sometimes more far-reaching ways.

George Angell saw the big picture, the connections between all forms of social injustice, and was an outspoken advocate for peace and crime prevention. After a visit to a Massachusetts prison and a survey of inmates, for example, he observed that the overwhelming majority of individuals who committed crimes in adulthood had never owned pets in their youth. This in turn reinforced his beliefs that in order to change the public mind and public behavior, humane education was necessary at an early age. To capture the imagination and passion of children, who would grow up to shape the values of their generation, he employed one of the most consciousness-changing and enduring books ever written. He had stumbled across it while in England—where he had come to lecture to the RSPCA—in the form of a short, paperbound manuscript that told the first-person story of a spirited horse who was subjected to a range of abuse sadly common to the times. It was, of course, Anna Sewell's *Black Beauty: Autobiography of a Horse*, which Albert Rogers had in mind when he fantasized about the impact that his pamphlet could have. Published in England in 1877, only a year before the author's death, it provided one of its most resonant lines as a touchstone for George Angell: "If we see cruelty or wrong that we have the power to stop, and do nothing, we make ourselves sharers in the guilt."

In England, Sewell's work had a widespread impact, calling into question many abusive practices, including the use of the checkrein and the docking of horses' tails, while fueling the reach of the RSPCA. In her story, Sewell dramatized the harm caused by the use of the checkrein or bearing rein—the short strap running from the bit to the harness that was tightened to prevent the horse from lowering the head, thus appearing fashionably lifted. She also bemoaned the practice of docking horses' tails, another conceit of fashion, used to make the tail stand up as though to appear in the style of a military epaulet, but causing physical agony, humiliation, and discomfort to horses and depriving them of their defense to ward off flies.

Angell was the first to see *Black Beauty* as the "*Uncle Tom's Cabin* of the horse" and rushed to have 100,000 copies published at his own expense for free distribution to any individual involved in working with horses. The American Humane Education Society then issued the first edition of the book in America, selling 226,000 copies in less than two years. Though this was only a fraction of the estimated thirty million copies it went on to sell in various incarnations, Angell had turned Anna Sewell's *Black Beauty* into a classic. He followed suit in the early 1890s with a similarly conceived book about the sufferings and spirit of a dog named *Beautiful Joe,* which had been written by Canadian author Margaret Marshall Saunders.

Understanding the power of written stories, Angell also grasped the value of celebrity and invited the likes of Henry Wadsworth Longfellow to deliver a line of poetry or two to swooning members at organizational meetings, and he profiled leading thinkers such as Dr. Oliver Wendell Holmes and Daniel Webster in the Education Society's publication *Our Dumb Animals.* Dedicated "to speak for those who cannot speak for themselves," the magazine was the first of its kind and went on to have international circulation that included distribution in schools across America.

A pragmatic idealist, as well as being a tall, handsome, articulate, socially gregarious and charismatic presence, George Angell used equal measures of humor and toughness to keep the three branches of his organization running smoothly. But in these later years of the 1890s, with the humane movement spreading yet fracturing, gaining steam on local levels but dissipating as a collective, there seemed to be some rumblings of discontent among his various board members. Maybe some believed he was too old to lead the cause; others might have been jockeying to take over his leadership role. The internal political climate, whether Albert Rogers had any sense of it or not, complicated his efforts to bring Jim to the attention of the organization.

Waiting for replies from one and all, he composed in a swirling, romantic font a two-page cover letter to accompany his three months' accumulation of "newspaper clippings and testimonials regarding Beautiful Jim Key, The Educated Horse, valued at $50,000." Emblazoned on his letterhead was a warm and friendly sketch of Jim holding an envelope in his mouth with the return address, "Mr. A. R. Rogers, New York City, Box 2368." The second page was addressed "To Those Interested":

> We are now making dates for 1898, and to managers of Theatres, Fairs, Expositions, etc., who desire an attraction that is unique and which will draw large crowds, and one that at the same time will be high class. . . . Humane Societies, Ministers and the best people generally, will endorse this attraction. . . . Newspapers treat this marvelous exhibition very generously in their news columns. It is an attraction that advertises itself—for those who

see it, will tell others. Doubt and curiosity will lead many to witness that which seems so improbable.

In the weeks leading up to Jim's Broadway debut, the flood of requests to book the exhibit enabled Rogers and Doc Key to agree on a schedule for all of 1898, and some of the following year. Leaving no stone unturned, when the Tennesseans returned to New York, Rogers hosted yet another demonstration at Field's Stables, which was very well attended and attracted a good smattering of the press, including a reporter from the *New York Times*. The newspaper had recently been purchased by Adolph Ochs, a newspaperman and Jewish entrepreneur, from Chattanooga, Tennessee. In this era of yellow journalism, made-up news, and sensationalism, the *Times* was out to distinguish itself with the intent of publishing legitimate news. Its motto, "All the news that's fit to print," had been born.

Reeking with seriousness, the *New York Times* reporter stood apart from the other press fellows, as though not sure the demonstration merited an article. But the story that ran under the headline "Jim Key a Clever Horse" on December 1, 1897—after he watched Jim add and subtract numbers, spell words, and play cards "like a gambler"—documented his change of opinion.

At this demonstration, Rogers and Dr. Key took turns inviting questions. Rogers began the spelling exercises, asking a young gentleman, "What is your name, sir?" When the answer was given as Thomas, Rogers turned to Jim and gave him the request, "Now, Jim, spell *Thomas* for us."

The way that Beautiful Jim Key cavorted over to his letter rack, carefully picking out *T-H-O-M-A-S*, then going on to spell other words and names suggested at random, was interesting to the man from the *New York Times*. But it was Jim's knowledge of mathematics that made the serious journalist a true believer. When asked to add 9 and 16, Jim Key bobbed his head, appearing to add the numbers mentally, and then hurried over to select the card reading 24 from his numbers rack.

"Now, Jim!" Dr. Key murmured. The Doc's tone, the *Times* reporter later noted, was one a mother would use to calm a fretful child. For a moment, Jim Key contemplated the rack and then shook his mane, as if to say *silly, me!* and smugly pulled out the card reading 25. The *New York Times* article asserted: "His tutor did not appear to have any system of signals, nor to urge him in any set phrases."

Rogers was overjoyed by the boost in legitimacy that the story gave Beautiful Jim Key, although he didn't know what to make of its depiction of William Key. Some of it had come from the pamphlet, including the mention that as a "slave boy on a Southern plantation" Bill had the reputation of taming the most vicious mules and mollifying the ugliest tempered dogs. Rogers wasn't overly concerned by the article's mention that "by other Negroes" the Doc had been regarded as a "dabbler in the black art" and that "when he was of a mature age he was termed a 'voodoo man.'" He didn't especially mind that the reporter emphasized how all his life, William Key had "lugged around with him a host of talismans and potent charms." But he was surprised by the exaggerated manner of "quaint Plantation speech" that the reporter used to portray Dr. Key in suggesting that Jim's abilities were empowered by forces beyond mere training:

> "Thar's them rabbit foots," he said yesterday, pointing to what onlookers had mistaken for festoons and garlands of corncobs, "neber knew them ahr to deceive meh."

Rogers knew that Bill Key believed those words wholeheartedly, but he found it odd that Bill Key didn't want himself quoted with the less colloquial speech he typically used. That aside, Rogers was pleased to see a quote from his press release in the December 1 article stating that following the Broadway run, "Jim will shortly go to his new master's home at South Orange and rest his brain till early next year."

Despite the positive impact the news piece had on New York theatergoers, not one word came from any of the humane societies.

Rogers was forced to apologize to Dr. Key. In Nashville, when they had formed their partnership, based on the promise that a part of their proceeds go to benefit the animal welfare cause, he had exaggerated his connections to the ASPCA. Doc Key didn't appear to mind. But Rogers was no less frustrated. Without the stamp of approval from one of these national groups, the humane message would be diluted. An afterthought.

William Key merely encouraged Rogers, recommending one of his preferred words: "Patience." The Doctor was feeling lucky.

And, indeed, they were more than lucky, because before the curtain rose at the Star Theatre on the evening of December 20, 1897, they received a response from George Angell, letting them know he was very interested in meeting them and that they had matters of mutual interest to discuss.

It was as Key and Key had been trying to say to Rogers. The hard part was done. The gates had been opened. Now it was time to take the ride.

7

Service to Humanity

>⊷⊶⊙⊷⊶⊷

There are eleven million horses in the United States, and not one
man in a million who knows how to educate them in the highest
degree of usefulness. We say *educate;* for the horse is an animal of
high and spirited organization. . . . Primarily, the word educate
means to *lead out* or *lead up;* and it is by this process of *leading
out* and *leading up* . . . that a colt becomes a useful horse. Now,
teachers, like poets, are born, not made. Only a few are gifted
to see . . . through any form of highly organized life, discern
its capacities, note the interior tendencies . . . and discover the
method of developing the innate forces until they reach their
noblest expression. . . . The few who have this gift are teachers indeed, and, next to the mothers of the world, deserve the
world's applause as foremost among its benefactors.

—D. MAGNER,
Magner's Art of Taming and Educating Horses

>⊷⊶⊙⊷⊶⊷

October 26, 1901.
The Boston Food Fair.

DR. WILLIAM KEY HAD TO HAVE BEEN AMUSED by the sight of the
small brigade of somber gentlemen, many whiskered and bespec-
tacled, who filed into the front rows of the auditorium at Boston's
Mechanics Building. Glancing furtively around the cavernous hall
where there hovered the ghosts of the Mechanics Society's patron
saints, Paul Revere and Benjamin Franklin, they carried notebooks
and writing instruments which they began to use as soon as they
were seated. Some seemed to be sketching the stage and the props
on it; others made cursory notes of anything that, by the look of

their flared nostrils, might smell suspicious to them. The sight of the aerial display of five thousand dangling rabbit's feet appeared to confirm their worst expectations, as several nodded and pointed.

The Doc knew that this team of Harvard professors—leading names of academia from the fields of psychology, medicine, linguistics, and zoology—had come there under the supervision of Harvard president Charles Eliot. Probably the most influential individual in the field of American higher education, Eliot was a supporter of George Angell and one of Jim's more devoted admirers, and had no doubt arranged this examination of Jim and his teacher.

This was obviously a consequence of the rising swell of accusations that some forms of hoax or hypnosis, or both, were the only explanations for Jim's otherwise inexplicable abilities. But the ongoing bubble of controversy didn't bother Bill Key. He knew it was only one of the costs of fame. And, as the *Boston Globe* declared in advance of their appearance at the Boston Food Fair, Beautiful Jim Key and Dr. William Key were now both quite famous: "Horse, the pupil, and man, teacher, have been in nearly all the large cities of the country, and in many of them the schools have been dismissed for the day to permit the children to see a horse who can ring up a telephone as easily as he can trot a mile."

Dr. Key's celebrity status may have surprised Albert Rogers, especially after the early press coverage had so often described the trainer as "an old colored man" and Jim's "aging Negro valet" and after Rogers in their PR materials had first referred to him as a "faithful old Uncle Tom" (which led Southern newspapers like the *Atlanta Journal* to write about the Doctor, "Uncle Billy Key is one of the old time Southern negroes"). Even after Rogers had added notes in their pamphlet about Dr. Key's financial success in the patent medicine business and his unrivaled ability as a horse trainer, it was not until George Angell met the three of them and connected instantly with William Key that Albert recognized how the Doc was as much a star as Jim.

Angell and Key were kindred spirits. They were both getting on in years, George Angell almost eighty years old in 1901 and the Doc almost seventy. Despite their differences in color and height, they actually resembled each other. Both were lean, distinguished, typically dressed in simple but elegant attire. About each of their faces was an aura of kindness and intelligence, each with an intellectual openness and expressions that could alternate between lighthearted amusement and serious concern. When the two first met three and a half years earlier, Angell and Key discovered they had interests in common other than the humane cause and could discourse at length about such topics as the pros and cons of unregulated patent medicines, the influence of diet on health, about roots and herbs, about current events, the Bible, and even the oddities of talk that outer space travel would one day be possible. The former lawyer made a gift to the self-taught veterinarian of several copies of *Black Beauty* and *Beautiful Joe*, inscribing them to Dr. William Key and Beautiful Jim Key.

Doc Key was genuinely delighted and promised to read both aloud to Jim, presumably at bedtime before saying their prayers and good night.

From the start, Rogers recognized that though Angell appreciated the promoter's energy and ideas, and was immediately impressed with Jim Key, the reason that they received the full support of the officers and board of the American Humane Association was the impression that Dr. Key had made on the founder and president. Rogers now considered that he might not have had the level of resistance to "an animal act" from the other humane groups if he had thought to promote the visionary educator first, and then the horse second. Making up for lost time, he arranged for a photographic session to produce a publicity portrait of Dr. Key. Run in most of the newspapers and sold at exhibits, the photograph earned the trainer virtual overnight public recognition. At the same time, because of the almost eerie, mesmerizing look on William's face, rumors that he had to be a voodoo hypnotist became even more widespread.

The Doc took it all in stride. He had always been special, different, gifted, suspect. But that had never stopped him from challenging people's prejudices, and it wouldn't now. For his part, Beautiful Jim Key took to his stardom with what some described as a trademark modesty, an attitude of Aw shucks, spelling, figuring, reading? That ain't nothin'!

Would-be critics were nearly always caught off guard by Jim's onstage inventions. No matter how prepared they were to say that he was being cued by his trainer, they couldn't hold back the feeling of affection that his humanlike antics engendered in them, and that, by extension, made them feel that perhaps the goals of the humane movement were not so radical as all that. Jim's rehearsed bits, such as bowing to the ladies or his act of going lame and even his political routine, merely convinced cynics that he was a great thespian. Because they were baffled by the other feats that required elements of memory, critical thinking, and reasoning, many still distrusted what they saw with their own eyes, insisting that there was a trick. But the stunt of submerging his head underwater and removing the silver dollar without drinking a drop was not one of those inexplicable feats; it was very clearly the result of an incredible amount of patience and encouragement in a training regimen that transcended the language barrier between teacher and student. If reporters managed to sit through the whole show as nonbelievers, they were won over by the silver dollar showstopper almost every time.

One such detractor was present at a Cincinnati performance of the *The Scholar and a Model Office Boy*, in which it was customary after the dutiful office boy had retrieved the silver dollar and returned it to the Employer that his boss would say, "Jim, your mouth is all wet. The customers will laugh at you. Go and get a towel in your trunk and I'll wipe your mouth for you," and to the amusement of all, Jim would go to one of his steamer trunks, nudge open the lid with his nose, and then pick up the towel in his teeth. Jim's next rehearsed bit was to neatly fold the towel on a table and replace it in the trunk before closing the lid. At this particular performance, when Jim opened his trunk and removed the towel, he discovered that it was already soiled—obviously left there by mistake—and he immediately dropped the unclean towel on the floor, puckering his lips in disdain. From all accounts, his spontaneous reaction took the Doc and Will Griffin by surprise, challenging them both to keep a straight face.

Mrs. Long, a woman in the audience who had not until that moment been enthusiastic, was so impressed that a few days later she delivered to the star in person a half-dozen expensive fringed towels, each hand-embroidered with the name of Beautiful Jim Key.

In Philadelphia, where Jim was on exhibition for seven weeks for the 1900 Export Exposition, while he was preparing to give a demonstration to civic leaders, one of the city's most illustrious citizens was heard to grumble to Dr. Key that he thought the furor over the "educated" horse was ridiculous. He'd seen trick horses before, which he found to be embarrassing to the animals and to the humans involved. "What makes this horse so special?" he asked bluntly. "What can he do that I haven't seen before?"

"Well, sir," said Dr. Key without hesitation, "he can spell your name."

"Indeed? If he spells my name, I'll . . ." He paused, perhaps wondering if he really wanted to eat his hat or do some other outlandish act, instead offering, "I'll send him the finest blanket money can buy."

Jim sidled up, throwing a look to the Doc that the Equine King's grooms had seen him throw when reporters came back for interviews: oh, not *another* one?

Dr. Key asked the man to tell Jim his name, and to please speak slowly and clearly. The spelling of names was often where Jim made errors. Because the Doc had taught him to spell phonetically or to memorize the spelling of certain words and names, if Jim had never heard the word or name before, he was as capable as any student of making a mistake. Interestingly enough, this was how Bill Key spelled, inconsistently, although Jim, having had the tutelage of Stanley Davis and Will Griffin, could sometimes win in a spelling bee against his teacher.

"My name is Walton," the man said, looking somewhat awkward as he talked to the big bay. "F. M. Walton."

The name was either phonetically straightforward or one Dr. Key had practiced with Jim before, since they regularly had a list of names of prominent citizens in advance of arriving in new cities. In either case, Jim easily spelled and picked out the letters *W-A-L-T-O-N*, lining them up on his spelling rack.

The following week a horse blanket fit for a derby winner—with the name Jim Key worked into its design—was mailed to Albert Rogers with a note from Frederick Walton honoring "one of the most knowing horses in the world" *and* his trainer.

———⋆———

D r. Key's in-laws later recalled that both the man and his horse savored their successes, carefully collecting the gifts, trophies, awards, fan letters, and postcards they received, and taking crates of them home for safekeeping, whenever they could. It was said that nothing meant as much to either of them as the awards and honorary memberships they had begun to receive for their humane work.

While the early 1898 endorsement from George Angell and the network that formed the American Humane Association had dramatically opened numerous new doors for Key, Key, and Rogers, there truly could have been no greater boon to the organization or to the movement than Beautiful Jim and Dr. William Key. Within less than three years, almost 300,000 children signed the Jim Key Pledge: "I promise always to be kind to animals." Adult membership, predominantly female, exploded to as many as three million in the various Bands of Mercy, which came under the umbrella of Angell's American Humane Education Society. The idea for the Bands of Mercy had been borrowed from the RSPCA, a concept that basically allowed for the franchising of clubs or reading and social circles to discuss and embrace humane philosophies, often by sharing true or literary stories about animals.

The shift in public sentiment had begun. The movement had broken out of elite drawing rooms and had arrived at Main Street, thanks in large part to Jim Key; he had also broadened the focus of animal welfare to include not only protecting animals from cruel treatment but also celebrating the connection between humans and nonhumans through acts of kindness. The notion that animals could think, reason, and feel was no longer so radical.

But missionary work, like celebrity, could be exhausting, if the itineraries for the 1898–1901 seasons were any indication. Most of that second year had kept Jim Key and company in the North, starting with a return to New Jersey, with theater performances, humane benefits, and school events in Plainfield that made national headlines throughout the month of March that both praised and condemned the Equine Wonder.

There were already at least four different camps of those who seemed outraged by the growing prestige given an educated horse from Tennessee. These adversaries included those who believed the act was rigged or that Dr. Key was a hypnotist; those who thought Jim Key was a sideshow that belonged in the circus or strictly as children's entertainment; those who strenuously opposed the advancement of the humane cause and especially any Darwinian-type suggestion that we had more in common with our furry and feathered friends than we knew; and the most insidious of the lot, those who were threatened not by the prestige of a horse but by his Negro costar.

Taking the stance that all press was good press, Albert Rogers ignored the criticism and continued to gather testimonials and clippings, sending them out in thick, weighty packages. In one press release of this era, Albert announced that the Great and Only Bostock, the thirty-year-old Animal King who had been born in a circus caravan and had become a lion tamer at fourteen, had offered him $100,000 for Beautiful Jim Key, an amount rejected out of hand, with the claim he was worth twice that. The promotional pamphlet went into its third printing, declaring the Beautiful One to be valued at twice his former value or ten times his "purchase" price.

In the month of May, the show moved on to a stint at the Scenic Theatre in Atlantic City, across from Young's Pier, where everything that could go wrong did. First the rains came, blowing off the ocean in relentless slats across the boardwalk, shutting down all of the tented entertainment and throwing a wet chill into the stables and the theater. There was no local humane group sponsoring Jim and attendance was noticeably low, which didn't help the star's tendency to turn in a lackluster performance for smaller, less energized crowds. Many who did venture out in the stormy weather were holding press passes or were performers from the tented shows who had been given passes, and when the box office became very slow, Rogers turned it over to Stanley and his brother Sam (who was now traveling with Jim's troupe).

Rogers knew this had to be a temporary lull, but he was blue, as he admitted he could be at times, and after a telegram arrived for him at his hotel—its contents to remain undisclosed—he sent word to Dr. Key that he had been called away. This had happened before, when his father had taken ill, so the Doc was worried that the emergency had to do with Hiram. Evidently, A. R. Rogers now spent less time on the road, putting more responsibility on William Key, not only for stage and road management, but also for the money and the books. When later asked about this arrangement, with the inference that it would be tempting for any manager to skim from the pot, Albert Rogers vehemently asserted, "He is the most faithful man I ever met. I would trust Bill Key with my life." He also added the following paragraph to the promotional pamphlet:

Few men have seen as much varied life as has Dr. Key, and few men have done more good. It is said that the Doctor is worth close on to a hundred thousand dollars, but his love for Jim is so strong that he prefers to travel around with him rather than live in ease.

While it was the case that the Doc didn't need the "large salary" (Rogers did mention this point in his pamphlet), William Key was nonetheless extremely fastidious in checking Albert's bookkeeping and making sure that every cent owed him and his staff was paid in full and on time. When it came to addressing these matters, the Doc's tone, ironically, was somewhat scolding and schoolmarmish, though patient after a fashion, sort of the way he spoke to Jim when the horse wasn't putting forth his best effort.

Although the Doc wasn't upset with Rogers for the sudden departure, he did fear the worst and cabled him urgently at Glenmere to inquire if his father was all right. After a few days, Rogers sent a terse reply stating that Hiram was fine, but he was more concerned about how business was doing and how Jim was doing. Doc Key immediately wrote back in his sprightly, clean longhand:

Dear Sir
Everything is all right. Jim is well and doing his work O.K. Business is very dull on account of storms. We are playing hear the rest of this week and I am expecting to go home next Sunday morning if you are willing for me to go. I would like to hear from you in the mater at once so I may know what to do about getting ready. Please send me my check from Dr. Fields stable as soon as feasible. Have it handled with care. I would like to have it sent by express. In closed find statement of money I have received and spent for the month of April. I am very glad to hear that your father is better. I have been greaving over him as dead. As the porter of the hotel told me you had received a telegram of his death.
I remain very respectfully,
Wm. Key

After returning from an errand in the rain, Doc Key imagined he was about to confront his next cause for worry when one of the Davis brothers came to find him, asking him to hurry to Jim's stall. There was something he had to see. What was it? He would have to see for himself came the answer; there were no words to explain. Now in a full panic, the Doc raced back to the stables, obviously having come to the conclusion that Jim had hurt himself or become sick. He would have blamed himself and would have possibly recalled premonitions that the Atlantic City engagement boded poorly for the show. Why had he ignored instincts that had served him so well in the past?

It was bad enough that Jim Key couldn't go out for his morning run and that he had to be cooped up inside, without the usual distractions of reporters and admirers coming around. But what concerned Dr. Key was the homesickness he sometimes observed in Jim. Naturally, that was what *he* was feeling, and why he was anxious to get back to Shelbyville. Maybe the Doc had the blues too, brought on by the rain in Atlantic City, reinforcing the realization they were all starting to have that it could get awful lonely at the top.

It was good to have Stanley and Sam with him on this leg of their travels, even though it was their sister, Maggie, with whom he would have preferred to be spending time, if truth be told. As his late third wife had predicted, he did think about having a woman to keep him company, an attractive, kindhearted, intelligent woman no less, and spring in Bedford County was especially nice weather in which to go courting. He perhaps had expected that his interests in that direction were supposed to slow. But such was not the case. Maggie was still studying at the Agricultural and Mechanical College for Negroes in Normal, Alabama, as Dr. Key had arranged. When she was finished, however, he could see building a place on his new property and marrying Maggie. He looked forward to having Jim there too, since the increasingly valuable smart and handsome horse had pretty much missed breeding seasons, and it would be a joy to see him getting to be a horse for a few months.

These may have been the kinds of thoughts the Doc used to distract himself from imagining that the worst had happened to Jim Key.

At the stables, outside of the stall, a strange sight greeted Dr. Key. There in the middle, hopping around the hay and scrambling after a stick, much as he had done when he was a spindly legged ugly duckling of a colt, Jim was playing not *as* a dog, but *with* a dog. He was a small to middle-size, black-and-white wire-haired, scruffy mix of what looked like some terrier, some collie, and maybe schnauzer. He had just wandered in, one of the Davis brothers explained, who figured the dog was a stray trying to get out of the rain.

The moment that Jim lifted his head to acknowledge Doc Key, the dog began to bark in a very demanding manner: *Who are you and what do you want?*

That's what he had been doing to Stanley and Sam for the last hour, and he wouldn't let either of them come near Jim. The dog seemed to want to be Beautiful Jim Key's bodyguard. To prove it, the dog made a running leap onto Jim's back, much to the big bay's pleasure. Jim trotted back and forth as the dog squeezed his eyes into a pensive expression, as though he were meditating upon a subject of deep complexity.

Dr. Key communicated in like manner—as he knew how to do—his demeanor suggesting that any new friend of Jim's was a friend of his. He checked around with managers of the other acts then engaged in Atlantic City to see if anyone had lost a dog who could squint up his eyes and appear to contemplate important questions, but no one claimed him. At the end of the week, the dog they called Monk—either because of his thoughtful appearance or as a nickname, which was short for Monkey, in honor of his antics—left Atlantic City with the rest of the Tennesseeans. From then on, he was Jim's constant companion and guardian.

Monk never appeared onstage as part of Jim's act, but he received almost as much publicity as did the Celebrated Educated Arabian-Hambletonian, starting with an item that ran in Plainfield, New Jersey, where *The Scholar and a Model Office Boy* was to be presented for a week at the Stillman Music Hall:

> Jim Key . . . is in a box stall at Uncle Dan Roberts' stable where he is guarded by a dog. The dog stays on the horse's back all the time and carefully warns all persons away except the ones appointed to care for the horse, on penalty of being bitten.

Monk had a particular bias against reporters and would bark at any that tried to interview Jim unless they first made a to-do over him or if photographers were present. Monk loved to sit to have his picture taken, preferably by himself. Perhaps he had some vaudevillian training in his background because his routine was to strike a pose and then to bark as a signal to the photographer to take the shot. At night, he slept curled up on Jim's back and, as noted, spent the day happily perched there, alternately thinking deeply and enjoying the view. Of course, when it was time to put a saddle on Jim and ride him—whether it was Dr. Key (usually the one to take him out for a canter), Stanley, Sam, or occasionally Albert Rogers—Monk would begrudgingly leap down and allow his charge to be ridden.

Rogers was no doubt thrilled by the addition to Jim Key's entourage of the dog who had adopted a horse. He didn't offer any more of an explanation about whether or not it was his father's health that had called him away, or another business concern, or his own case of the blues. In any event, his high spirits were restored and he had returned bursting with new promotional ideas that included Monk when Beautiful Jim Key played Riverview Park in Baltimore.

Promoting Jim much like a political candidate, Rogers paraded his star and entourage through town, advertising showtimes on huge banners that draped Jim's customized open-air trolley car with his signature blue-and-white-striped canopy and a Hambletonian-size megaphone through which his barker cried out his approach. In a joint effort of a local humane group and the board of education, a series of spelling bees pitted fourth, fifth, and sixth graders against the educated horse with a prize of one dollar given to any human student who could win a round with Jim. The Equine King did lose now and then, mostly on difficult or longer words, but the headline grabber was when he won against a sixth-grade boy by spelling the word *P-H-Y-S-I-C-S*.

After an uneventful but restful trip home during the summer, Dr. Key, Jim, Monk, Stanley, and Sam traveled to Pennsylvania. In the Beautiful Jim Key advertising van, they were mobbed on the streets of Pittsburg and York, doubling the business they had done in Pennsylvania the year before. At the Pittsburg Exposition, fairgoers did not balk at the extra admission charged to enter Jim's pavilion, despite the fact that it hadn't cost them anything extra to see him at the last Exposition. For three weeks, the show, performed every half hour on the hour, took in over $1,500 per week, an impressive net of $1,000 per week when the weekly salary of $500 was deducted. This emboldened Albert Rogers to list their weekly fee at double what it had been, or to give venues the option of hiring them on a percentage, which soon led to increases of the average price of admissions from ten and fifteen cents to twenty-five and fifty. Allowances were made for special children's shows and humane benefits. Rogers and Dr. Key came up with a policy that in every city where they performed, free passes were to be granted to teachers, school administrators, and clergy, to any show or shows of their choice.

In a stroke of excellent timing, during the week of October 10, 1898, the annual convention of the American Humane Association was held in Pittsburg, an opportunity that allowed Dr. William Key and Beautiful Jim Key to present a special performance for delegates from around the country to witness the man and the horse that had won the endorsement of their president, George Angell. The reaction from the delegates was as if an equine angel had been sent to their cause straight from heaven.

Albert Rogers was deluged with even more requests, not only from regions in the Northeast but now from below the Mason-Dixon. Though he and Dr. Key had agreed not to take engagements in the winter months, neither could bring himself to turn down invitations from North Carolina and Georgia, where they were sorely needed to raise awareness and funds.

The fall engagement in Greensboro, North Carolina, met with enormous success, and some of Jim's most effusive write-ups. A reporter for the *Greensboro Record* posited that what he had witnessed Jim Key do—from correctly spelling the name Blackburn, to correctly answering questions out of order that included how many days in the week, the various months, the regular year and leap year, and performing his silver dollar trick twice—was proof that animals had minds; and if that was the case, animals were entitled to the rights of human beings, all in all, "a strong argument for the formation here of a society for the prevention of cruelty to animals."

A special series of performances of *The Scholar and a Model Office Boy* was held to benefit the local library fund with the intention, said the *Evening Telegram,* of purchasing books on humane subject matter in advance of starting a society. Performances at the Academy of Music were segregated: "Adults 25 cents, children ten cents. Colored people in their gallery 10 cents." A change of policy was instituted in which most subsequent engagements included special shows exclusively for Negro audiences that were advertised as being sponsored "at the request of Dr. William Key," offering all seats to any person of color at discounts.

Another barometer of the Southern climate at the time in North Carolina and South Carolina, where Jim performed in Columbia, was his billing as the Celebrated Democratic Educated Horse. In Greensboro it was noted, "Jim met President McKinley at the Nashville Exposition, but has never liked the President and is still a staunch democrat, though raised in a colored family."

Albert Rogers may have only then truly appreciated Dr. Key's brilliance in training Jim to "talk politics." Now he could also better understand why the Doc warned him about venturing too far off the beaten path when booking engagements in the South. Not that Negroes experienced prejudice and violence only in the Southern states or just outside of the bigger Southern cities. You had to be careful no matter where you went. Still, there was a sense of danger at the start of this foray into North Carolina.

Again the problems began with the weather. At a county fair in Raleigh, hurricane-force storms wracked the fairgrounds. With the winds starting up and the fair being shut down, Rogers sent Dr. Key, Jim, and Monk back to the stables and kept his roadmen, along with Stanley and Sam, to help him collapse the tent. They had barely done so when a full-scale hurricane bore down for the next six hours, requiring them to cling to the tent poles for dear life as they tried to save the tent and themselves from being swept away. Rogers made it back to the Carollton Hotel and fell into bed with a fever and nausea. The next week, when he had not yet recuperated, a distraught Dr. Key came to inform him that after a show Jim had cut his foot so severely that he wasn't sure he would walk again. But there was more. It seemed that Sam and Stanley had been kidnapped.

Without much more of an explanation, he insisted that he would handle the crises his way. In the meantime, he begged Rogers to consider leaving early, since a Yankee might not be safe in these parts traveling in the company of three Negroes with a $100,000 famous horse and only the horse's pet dog as protection.

Unable to gather his strength to leave, at any rate, Rogers described some of these events and others in a letter that he wrote to his friend Louise, a confidante:

rains last two weeks hurt business & we were in a great hurricane & nearly blown to pieces had to drop the tent and all hang on the poles all night while the wind hurled & the rain poured. Next experience a

drunken man got into my room & I pitched him out & then he tried to
shoot me. But I am still alive.

Came here in a special train . . . it looks like another rainy week. Jim
cut his foot badly & nearly killed himself last night—he is very lame &
I am greatly worried (if I ever worry) about him.

I have been very sick indigestion I guess—am staying at the Hotel
until I can get out—I send by same mail some cotton I picked for you
the other day & Enclosed find a photo of a friend you can always swear
by—I never meet any ladies—except dancing girls & these I just say
good morning to as they speak to me in the grounds—I hope you keep
well. I am feeling to miserable to write at length (if I ever do) Kind
regards to your good mother. Yours as ever, A. R. Rogers

After Albert tucked his sentimental cotton plant and photo of
himself into a Carrollton envelope, he had second thoughts about
mailing off his tale of woe and instead kept the letter folded away
behind his press materials. Doc Key sent word that the Davis brothers had been located and were returned unharmed. Dr. Key and
Albert Rogers expressly kept the episode out of print, not wanting
anyone else to get any ideas.

As to Jim's injury, no mention of it hit the papers either. Evidently Rogers took the public relations stance that celebrities, like
gods and goddesses of Mount Olympus, were immortal and therefore immune to illness and aging. In fact, he began around this time
to lie about Jim's age, keeping him at approximately eight years old
until reporters started doing the math, at which point Beautiful Jim
Key became permanently eleven years old. Rogers also started adding the line "he was bred in Old Kentucky" to his press releases,
simply because it had a ring to it, probably until Bill Key expressed
his disapproval. Why insult Tennessee? Besides, the truth was much
more interesting.

Under the Good Doctor's care, Jim's foot healed rapidly, leaving him with a bandage and a limp but able to perform at the
Piedmont Tobacco Fair in Winston and make his much-publicized
December debut in Atlanta. Here the humane group was a welcoming and eclectic group of clergy, Christian and Jewish, humanitar-

ians and literacy proponents, who actively embraced Beautiful Jim Key into the bosom of Dixie. For weeks before he arrived, the *Atlanta Constitution* had trumpeted his engagement, so that by the day his "royal procession" rolled into town in Jim's customized palace train car that advertised the dates and times of his performances, thousands reportedly came out to the train tracks, if only to say they had seen him pass by, while another several thousand flocked to Atlanta to see the show. The *Constitution* declared that "Jim Key the Fashion" was why so many theater parties were planning to attend his opening and subsequent shows, suggesting that as much attention was being showered on "the intelligent beast" as on an operatic star. The *Constitution*'s December 19, 1898, breathless review of opening night, written by the newspaper's editor, included a mention of the fact that when asked by a member of the audience Jim had spelled *C-O-N-S-T-I-T-U-T-I-O-N* "unerringly" (although he had remained motionless for a full minute to think it through first). Constitution!

The Atlanta Humane Society was applauded for the theatrical decor of the Hall at No. 80 Whitehall Street and the display window with its assortment of rosy apples surrounded by lumps of sugar and a printed message that read: "Beautiful Jim Key was taught by kindness, apples and sugar, and not by a whip."

The editor described Jim's physical appearance in fairly standard terms, noting the white star on his forehead, the white tip on his nose, white on a fore and a hind foot. Also: "He has a clean set of limbs, and no blemish. Jim's neck is finely arched; he has a powerful, fine eye, and sharp and small ears. He has the widest forehead of any horse, being thirteen inches from center to center of eyes." (This width was often given as evidence of the stallion's high IQ.) But the editor of the *Constitution* was fascinated by elements beyond the physical:

> *If there is aught of truth in gentle Buddha's teachings, the soul of a gentleman and scholar inhabits the Beautiful body of wonderful Jim Key—whom the Atlanta Humane Society has brought to Atlanta to demonstrate in brute creation's behalf that animals reason and think. . . . It will not be so very many cycles before that soul re-enters a human frame and adds another mighty figure to the book of time.*

As if the editor had experienced a spiritual awakening, he wrote that Jim Key was proof of a Divine Creator who could endow Jim Key with intelligence "equal to most children of its age," a Universal Mind who could similarly create a Michelangelo, Napoleon, or Shakespeare. He went on:

All of which Theosophists say goes to prove that Jim does possess a soul, and all of which materialistic scientists argue is convincing that a man no more has a soul than a brute; but the difference between the two is merely a difference of mentality, and Jim to them appears human, for they argue because his trainer, Dr. Key, by long association and persistent suggestions, "has ejected his own intelligence into Jim's long head."

First minds, now souls? In traditional circles, the suggestion that animals could possibly have souls was downright heresy. The old guard insisted that Man's Dominion over Nature was an absolute and unshakeable tenet of Existence. But with Jim Key now complicating the distinctions, others were starting to ask if instead of merely exploiting nature and its inhabitants to fulfill human desires and needs, wasn't a reverence for all creation just as much ordained?

In Nashville, another new humane group composed of ministers, rabbis, university officers, and prominent citizens said yes to that question and came together to find a way to welcome their native sons back to Tennessee in February 1899. In fits and starts a plan emerged that would soon have Beautiful Jim Key leaving a hoof print of sorts on the history of country music.

The Nashville Humane Society's timing was impeccable. Emboldened by Jim's success in Atlanta, a committee of influential Nashvillians—including J. K. Kirkland, the chancellor of Vanderbilt, and community leader Rabbi Isadore Lewinthal—proposed to the Reverend Sam P. Jones that they rent the Sam Jones Union Tabernacle for two days of performances, even though the magnificent barn-styled hall—with its curved tiers of wooden pews that could seat six thousand and with its unparalleled acoustics—had been expressly built for the purpose of saving souls, not for popular entertainment. This was a firmly held policy.

The benefactor of the Tabernacle, Captain Thomas Ryman, was a self-professed former sinner and operator of a riverboat gambling operation who, back in 1885, had gone to heckle Jones at a tent revival meeting where the reverend was preaching. In an effort to clean up Nashville's rowdy saloon-and-brothel-infested neighborhoods and riverfronts, Reverend Jones had targeted Ryman and fellow proprietors by demanding that they stop the sale of liquor in their establishments. No booze in saloons or gaming parlors? Who did Sam Jones think he was? But when Captain Ryman and an entourage walked into the tent revival meeting on May 10, 1885, ready to disrupt the event, he was shocked to hear Jones announce that the subject of his sermon was the importance and goodness of mothers. As it so happened, Thomas Ryman loved his dearest mama above anyone or anything; Reverend Jones knew that and had planned his sermon for effect. It worked, well beyond what the man of the cloth had wagered. Ryman was so possessed of the Spirit that he promised he would not only halt the sale of liquor on his boat but also build a church so that Reverend Jones would never have to preach in a tent again. Seven years later, Sam P. Jones held a revival in the completed Union Tabernacle and pledged to his friend Captain Ryman that the house of God would remain so, and would not be used or rented out for entertainment purposes.

By 1899, that policy had been bent only once, for a concert given by the Chicago Orchestra the year before, the logic for that being that the musical repertoire was religiously themed. In asking that the rules be amended again for a performance to benefit their work in animal protection, the Nashville Humane Society argued politely that the horse and his Negro teacher were, after all, missionaries doing God's work. The educational themes were also stressed, since the Tabernacle had been used in 1897 for graduation exercises for Meharry Medical College, an African-American institution. It was further pointed out that it had been used during the 1899 Tennessee Centennial for a gathering of the Confederate Veterans Association that had prompted the addition of the balcony commemorated as the Confederate Gallery. Jones and his board deliberated, many protesting that such a shift in policy could open the door to every sort of entertainment. What was next? Plays? Vaudevillians? Minstrels? Opera divas? Where would it end? There were those, however, who remembered that Jim Key and Dr. Key had been the talk of the town at the Centennial, winning praise from no less than the President of the United States. Meanwhile, the pragmatists reminded the board that the income from renting the Tabernacle for two days when it would normally be dormant could be put to good uses, which were, after all, God's uses. At last a decision was made to grant the request to the Humane Society for two days in the middle of the week, February 14 and 15.

The Nashville Humane Society went to work, arranging school closures and performances for entire student bodies from primary and secondary schools as well as college students, along with a special show for students from black schools and colleges. Mayor Richard Dudley helped the cause by contacting the local press. In failing health and about to leave town for warmer climates, Dudley regretted not appearing at the show but wanted his fair city to know the stories of Fort Bill and the mortgage that the Young Doc had paid off for the widow of John W. Key. The mayor told the *Nashville American*:

> "I regret very much that I cannot fill that engagement, but I have written to Governor McMillin, and asked him to take my place on the programme. . . . Outside of the good accomplished by the exhibition . . . a feeling of sentiment actuates me. You may not know it but William Key . . . and I were boys together in Bedford County."

After the reporter asked the mayor why he was so proud of "Old Bill Key," Dudley told of the deeds of his friend during the Civil War and went on to say that the Good Doctor was not satisfied with just tearing up the mortgage. "To help his old mistress he earned more money, educated her children and set them up in business." Dudley corrected the reporter, "That's Old Bill Key, now Dr. Wm. Key to you." The interview concluded, "So you can see why I feel kindly disposed toward William, and any enterprise with which he is connected. I hope the people of Nashville will give the performances the support which they richly deserve."

The *Nashville American* jumped on the promotional bandwagon with headlines such as "Chesterfield Among Horses Is Jim Key, the Wonderful Animal to be Exhibited Here: Has a Checkered Career. Began Life as a Scrub Colt and Is Now Doing Missionary Work for his Equine Brothers in Bondage."

Before the impact of the advance press could be gauged, a record-breaking freeze paralyzed Nashville and most of Middle Tennessee. The Nashville Humane Society board members were able to postpone the performances to the following week, but they were certain that the turnout would be significantly hurt by the change in dates. In desperation, the benefit committee wrote to Reverend Jones and asked, in the most complimentary way, if he wouldn't, with his grand powers of persuasion, preach to his Sunday following about the potential for spiritual improvement inherent in attending one of Beautiful Jim Key's performances. The Reverend Jones acquiesced, and all parties held their breath to see how many would come. To everyone's astonishment, despite the still freezing temperatures, 17,610 came out to wait in line to purchase tickets, not including the several thousands of students with reserved seats at special matinees.

Those who had predicted that Jim Key's appearance would set a dangerous precedent and open doors to other forms of entertainment turned out to be right. More touring symphonies soon came to the Tabernacle, followed by the staging of nonreligious operas, and the appearances of nonordained lecturers. The pattern continued after 1904—the death of Captain Ryman prompted Reverend Jones to rename his house of worship Ryman Auditorium—including sold-out performances by Sarah Bernhardt and Marian Anderson. After Sam P. Jones died in 1906, the antientertainment forces fell further by the wayside as the Ryman was visited by thespians of every stripe, by vaudevillians, magicians, comedians, dancers, minstrels, bands, lecturers, movie stars, musicians, and singers. It could be argued that entertainment without overt religious themes would have never been permitted at the Ryman had it not been for the precedent set by Jim Key. In no small credit to this history, in 1943 Ryman Auditorium became the official home of the Grand Ole Opry, also known as the Mother Church of Country Music. On the same stage where the Equine King had preached the gospel of kindness, came future legends that spanned the country and western spectrum, including that other King, Elvis Presley, who in 1954 blended music that was black and white, from the church and from the saloons, and shocked the Ryman to its core.

Nashville did not take to Presley at that time as fast as it had embraced Beautiful Jim Key in 1899. In competing rave reviews after the shows, the *Nashville American* and the *Nashville Banner* had a war of words over who had actually discovered Jim Key a year and a half earlier when he was only part of an exhibit at the Tennessee Centennial. Neither paper was responsible. It was, in fact, the *Nashville Sun* that first wrote about Jim and claimed he was the top draw of the Exposition.

Competitions arose among cities, states, fairs, humane societies, school systems, benefits, and box offices. Where were more seats sold? More money raised to rescue mistreated animals or investigate reports of cruelty to nonhumans, children, and the elderly? More testimonials? More publicity? More delightful and astonishing anecdotes about the most famous horse in America?

When the *Pittsburg Press* welcomed Jim back to their fair city's Exposition for a third season, the newspaper took one of Albert's earlier ideas and made a novel offer to the West Pennsylvania Humane Society to promote a fund drive to raise $400 for a much-needed horse ambulance. Contributors' names were publicized in the *Press* with amounts ranging from as high as $100 from presidents of prominent companies, down to donations of as low as $1 from a certain "Fido." With promotional help from Jim's live performances, the drive also got a huge boost from a half-page cartoon of a bespectacled Beautiful Jim Key, in his lounging attire, reading a copy of the newspaper. Plugging the Press Animal Ambulance Fund, its headline read "Pittsburg Needs an Animal Ambulance," and the caption for Jim's comment read "That's the best bit of news I've read in a long time!"

The drive raised $1,000, enough to buy a derrick to rescue animals who regularly fell into excavation areas, as well as what became known as the Jim Key Ambulance of Pittsburg.

Not to be outdone, the Women's Pennsylvania SPCA in Philadelphia, having heard about the 1897 Cincinnati newspaper-sponsored essay contest, decided to improve upon the concept and use the occasion of Jim's school performances at the Export Exposition on the Esplanade to sponsor a citywide composition contest on the topic "What Patience and Kindness Will Accomplish with Animals."

Every entrant received a large souvenir button with a picture of Jim and Dr. Key on it, as well as the name of the "Women's Penna SPCA," while medals in the shape of copper coins with Jim's likeness were awarded to the contest winners.

The frenzy to own one of those copper coins became a contagion that spread through Philadelphia, inspiring the Women's Society to mint Commemorative Beautiful Jim Key pennies for sale. They soon became collector's items across the state and the country, signifying the value of both humane beliefs and education.

Inadvertently, in these and other ways, the self-taught veterinarian and his horse spurred an ad hoc literacy movement, which in turn continued to sound the themes of the humane movement, and vice versa. Teachers and school administrators listened carefully to William Key, examining their own attitudes toward the discipline and instruction of young humans. How realistic was an approach of "kindness, kindness, and more kindness"? Many were willing to try to find out.

In Philadelphia, where on the dare of a student, Jim correctly spelled *P-E-N-N-S-Y-L-V-A-N-I-A*, and responded to another child's question of "how much is four times five, plus five, minus three?" by plucking up the card with the number 22 on it, one formerly skeptical reporter quipped, "What will he learn next, square roots?" Another less caustic Philadelphia reporter called him the "Equine Marvel of the Century" and the newly erected Beautiful Jim Key Palace on the Esplanade a shrine to humane education. This reviewer described the atmosphere at the start of the show as charged with excitement and applause:

> *. . . with all eyes centered on the beautiful horse as he comes on stage. A large bay, fully sixteen hands, with a head of exquisite turn, large eyes, soft as a deer's, half hidden by the dressed forelock and ears sharp pointed and well sloped forward, the nostrils open, the upper lip in motion. "Who are you?" he asks as plainly as man ever spoke. He is, indeed, entitled to his name, for every muscle of the rounded body, instinct with glorious life, is swelling and diminishing with his every graceful motion. As he advances upon the stage, he bows to the audience, with all the grace of a debutante, and stands waiting to respond to the questions that are so rapidly put to him.*

If kindness and patience could do that for a horse, what other applications could they have? More than one newspaper adopted the modern notion that perhaps "to spare the rod" would not spoil the child, or horse, or any other creature.

Because every performance continued to be different, flowing in an order based on the questions being asked, there were no pronounced differences between the presentations Dr. Key and Jim gave to younger audiences and those performed for adults. But in Philadelphia, as in every other city where schools were closed for half or whole holidays, local youth took a most proprietary stance toward the Equine Wonder, and they came in crushing armies to his shows. Wherever school matinees were held, police reinforcements were often called in to assist in what the "blue-coated" officers must have thought was akin to the "'Charge of the Light Brigade'—barring the shot and the shell" (so observed by a Minneapolis reporter) as fanatically enthusiastic children clamored to be let into the next show.

But as Dr. Key would have had occasion to recall at that 1901 Boston Food Fair appearance, as the ponderous Harvard professors got their examination under way, the claims that he used hypnosis were frequently leveled at him because children often exited Jim's shows in an almost serene state, as if the young audience was being mesmerized by trainer and horse.

In Plainfield, New Jersey, there had also been a reporter's suggestion that Doc Key might be leading Jim with tricks of his voice, clucks, or other coded vocal guides. But none could be discerned, and William Key's tone and cadence were admittedly conversational.

At the 1899 Export Exposition in Philadelphia, a man in the audience had stood up and questioned Dr. Key about his use of the short whip. It appeared that from time to time in the show the Doc would gently tap Jim with it, once, or maybe twice, but no particular scheme could be observed. William Key never explained the tapping. It might have been a secret signal, although how the code would have worked was just as much a mystery. It might have been a prod for Jim to focus on the task at hand and to let him know that it was not yet time for his reward. But rather than explaining the light tapping, Dr. Key offered not to use the riding crop at all during the performance. He put it backstage and returned, holding his arms at his sides without much movement.

For most of the rest of the show, Beautiful Jim Key was as much of an intellectual prodigy as ever until the show was interrupted, at precisely 3:42 P.M., by an earth-shuddering commotion that was accompanied by a monstrous shrieking of whistles. Much of the audience, thinking there was a fire, rushed to the doors. The mayhem so terrified Jim that he lunged straight for the floodlights and into the screaming audience.

"Jim!" William Key had been forced to bellow, stopping the stallion's stampede in his tracks, right at the last second, just before serious injury was inflicted.

The commotion was not caused by fire, but rather, the *Philadelphia Inquirer* reported the next day, an unscheduled departure of Admiral Dewey's locomotive on its way to Washington. Dewey had asked that he be routed close to the Exposition so he could see the "gaily decorated buildings" and be able to wave to cheering crowds as he passed by.

The incident was the example Dr. Key used from then on as to why he held the whip, in case of an emergency, and if he needed it to guide Jim out to safety.

On another tack, the Doctor countered skepticism by encouraging audience members to try to confuse Jim, whether by rearranging the letters, figures, cards, and words on his display screen, or by removing them. If a spectator asked, "Jim, go get the eight of clubs," and it wasn't there, Jim's usual response was to scan the screen a couple of times, just to make sure, and then to shake his head no, with one of his pseudo shrugs or even a put-on yawn to the Doc, as though they were having a private joke: *Amateurs!*

Sometimes Dr. Key liked to see what would happen if he challenged Jim onstage. At a theater in Syracuse, he asked his costar to bring him the six of hearts. When Jim brought it to him, the Doc stepped forward, his back to his horse, held up the card to the audience—to great applause—and then discreetly tore off a corner with two of the hearts from the card.

He turned back to his student. "Now, Jim, are you sure you brought me the six of hearts?"

Beautiful Jim Key moved his head up and down emphatically, then gazed out at the crowd, asking for affirmation. Amid a chorus of applause some voices warned Jim, "Check the card! Two hearts are missing!"

Acting confused, Dr. Key repeated, "You sure it was the six of hearts?" After Jim indicated yes once more, patiently, of course, because his trainer was getting up in years and it would be impolite to roll his eyes or act peevish, the Doc held out the card and asked, "Well, please count the number of hearts on this card."

Using his foot to strike the ground, he counted one, two, three, four hearts. What foul play was this? Dr. Key smiled, waiting for the audience to applaud him, but the Equine Marvel just then spotted the piece of the torn card on the ground with the two missing hearts. To laughter and a thunderous ovation, the man and the horse bowed modestly, proving their case, for the moment, that they couldn't trick each other, let alone the world.

S kepticism continued to grow proportionately to their success. But there was one place in all the nation where there was an entire city of true believers. Shelbyville, Tennessee. The suggestion to any of these citizens—or their descendants—that Dr. Key's methods were suspect or that Jim wasn't the most amazing horse who ever lived was to them an insult. Many in town had been up to the Tennessee Centennial to see Jim there, but almost nobody missed the grand event on January 27 and 28, when as had been agreed Albert Rogers brought a production of *The Scholar and a Model Office Boy* to the Shelbyville Opera House. The proceeds went to establish a Bedford County Humane Society that A. R. Rogers was on hand to help organize. The rallying cry of "Encore! Encore!" was enough to convince Dr. Key to return after their week in Nashville for two more nights in order to raise money for a humane society in Madison County over in West Tennessee.

The joy that Dr. William Key must have felt at these command engagements was probably rivaled only by Jim's pride. Three years back he was making political jokes at the county fair, and here he was, starring in his own play. Monk was obviously pleased just from the added attention. The engagement was likewise a celebration for the Davis family, who were able to witness the attention that Stanley and Sam received for being members of the troupe; not to mention that they were able to stay safely close to home. There was already talk around town about Stanley soon going off to Collins College for Veterinary Surgery in Nashville, which the Doc had recently arranged, and one day taking over Doc Key's veterinary business. The family was likewise happy that Maggie Davis was doing well in her studies in Alabama and that it looked as if there was a budding, long-distance romance brewing between her and Dr. Key, their thirty-three-year age difference not at all a hindrance.

It was, above all, the hometown crowd that experienced the biggest vicarious thrill for their conquering heroes. They could now certainly say they knew them when.

Less than two years earlier, most people in America had never heard of Shelbyville. But now, suddenly, with every article, booklet, or promotional piece put out about Beautiful Jim Key, the town was becoming as much of a household name as he was. As the family members of the next two generations of these firsthand eyewitnesses could testify, both the horse and the man defined and changed their lives; Bill and Jim Key were charmed, magical even, and made the city so as well.

As Bedford County breeders began to examine their horses for signs of the kind of extraordinary talent Jim had demonstrated, it was in this time frame that they started to notice that while there didn't seem to be anything out of the ordinary about their horses' intellectual abilities, there was in fact something distinctive about the local equine gait.

A mix of Narragansett and Canadian Pacers, Thoroughbred, American Saddlebred, horses of the Morgan strain, and, yes, Hambletonian blood (linking them to Beautiful Jim Key and his sire, Tennessee Volunteer) had coalesced into this emerging bloodline. These general utility horses that were sometimes called Nodding Horses, Tennessee Walkers, or Plantation Horses had a rolling, strolling walk that was smooth and courtly. Eventually, the three natural gaits observed came to be categorized as the flat-foot walk, the running walk, and the canter, each with enough lilt and rhythm so as to be dancelike but not so as to jostle a rider. The elegant nodding of the head resulted from the innate, unusual foot motion of these horses, as well as the undulating limberness of their backs. Another pervasive trait of this emerging breed was the Walkers' incredible relaxation, which allowed the top athletes to travel as fast as six miles an hour with the special pushing stride that the horses had developed in adapting to the rolling hills of Middle Tennessee. With the imminent arrival in nearby Wartrace of Allen-F-1, who had actually been bred in Old Kentucky, the Tennessee Walking Horse would soon be named, an equine dynasty that was to put Shelbyville and environs on the map as horse country forevermore.

During this stop in Shelbyville, Jim secured a major celebrity endorsement deal. The arrangement Dr. Key made was with the Robinson-McGill Mfg. Co., makers of "harness, saddles, collars, and strap goods," one of the oldest and most respected harness makers in Bedford County. For a premium, Robinson-McGill paid for the right to use Jim's name and likeness on all their advertisements and products, calling them the "Jim Key Brand," and the company also gave Doc Key salesman status, which provided him a significant commission on any orders he made while out of state when he was traveling. Albert Rogers was not involved in this merchandising opportunity, as it wasn't covered under his promotional agreement. Then again, when Rogers had arranged an endorsement fee from National Cash Register, maker of the customized cash box with leather tabs that Jim used in his shows, that had not been split with the Keys. Meanwhile, when he negotiated with NCR's competitor, Metropolitan Cash Register of New York, to use their nickel-plated Twentieth-Century Beautiful Jim Key cash register, at a sizable premium, that money was his. Rogers benefited from a similar arrangement with Amberg Imperial Letter Cabinet File.

This was another hazy area of the Key, Key, and Rogers partnership, like how to split proceeds from the hot-selling souvenir photographs, postcards, buttons, pamphlets, and other Jim Key paraphernalia. The Doc was becoming concerned that his percentage of those immense profits was too small, but he had not yet figured out a way to broach the topic with A. R. Rogers. Dr. Key had limitless respect and appreciation for Albert Rogers, knowing in the depths of his being that without him he could not have made the journey into the worlds that the promoter inhabited. But Key had survived by being smart, and he would not tolerate any whiff of an inequity or any possibility that he was being exploited.

There was another small problem. With the deluge of edible gifts—mainly sugar and apples—that Jim was receiving everywhere he went, he had begun to look a tad portly and didn't seem to have his normal verve on his morning runs. It was not something Dr. Key worried about, but when they played three weeks in New Orleans for the Horse Show and the Louisiana State Fair, the topic of Jim's added girth actually made the papers. Jim was, without question, the most illustrious equine there, standing out even more with the ubiquitous Monk on his back. Besides, the extra weight did little to change his handsome star presence, or so Albert Rogers pointed out in his latest edition of the increasingly read promotional pamphlet:

> Jim is a splendid saddle horse, and has led many big parades. His beautiful arched neck and the graceful curves of his body and long, sweeping tail, make a beautiful picture, as he keeps step to the music, though prancing and fairly dancing. At the New Orleans Horse Show, and many others where he has been on exhibition, he has taken all the blue ribbons in several classes.

Rogers didn't mention that when it was proposed that Jim participate in a one-mile trotting race, Doc Key, perhaps knowing better, couldn't say no. He had, after all, boasted more than once to reporters that the proud great-great-grandson of Rysdyk's Hambletonian could trot a mile under harness, if not at the two-and-a-half minute standard, then at least under the three-minute mark. Suffice to say, Beautiful Jim Key did not win the race and may have been rather embarrassed about it. The Doc shrugged it off, joking to the press that Jim's excess horseflesh was on account of the excess wine the pampered bay had been drinking.

Though Dr. Key devised a stricter diet and exercise regimen that Monk helped him monitor, Jim had his ways of sneaking treats. Coconspirators involved Stanley and Sam, as well as reporters, and Albert Rogers who could never refuse the lovable bay's soulful entreaties. Still, Rogers was quick to do some damage control about rumors that the star was spoiled or out of shape, writing in the pamphlet:

> *Either the Doctor, who trained him, or a groom is always by his side, and he could not be given more constant care and attention were he the fleetest racer in the world on the eve of the most important Derby of the turf. Even his grain and hay, though the choicest quality that can be*

bought, are examined very closely to see that no impurities are in them. His drinking water is not from the common hydrant, but is the purest spring water that can be had; often bottled water secured for him. . . . Every morning he has his gallop, and comes in reeking with perspiration to receive an hour's rubbing and combing until his coat fairly shines, and is then in fine condition for his daily work. . . . Never has been sick; always takes especial delight in his work.

Jim, Monk, Dr. Key, and Rogers were discovering, each to a different degree, that once you were famous, the public had a distinct sense of ownership about what you did or said, how you looked, and with whom you associated. Fans had a right to know everything, so it seemed, including one question that arose frequently: why had Dr. Key taught Jim to like sugar in the first place? Surely, he knew that so much sugar would be bad for Jim.

Nonsense, countered the Doc. Sugar was easier to use when training because it could be used in such small amounts, as compared with apples or apple pieces, which if eaten in too great a quantity could upset Jim's stomach. Moreover, he said, and Rogers quoted him in the promotional pamphlet, "Sugar I have always found good for animals."

The New Orleans performances produced a meaningful testimonial from Lew Parker, a manager of the St. Charles Theatre and Academy of Music, and a former contracting agent for Buffalo Bill's Wild West traveling show, who wrote to describe his early years traveling the world on the lookout for gifted equines. "In all my travels I saw all the trained horses. And I am free to say that Jim Key is the greatest of them. . . . I firmly believe Jim Key will live in history as the greatest horse ever exhibited."

Regardless of the obstacles, challenges, mishaps, and pitfalls of celebrity, Jim was the beneficiary of what seemed to be an unstoppable momentum, much like the champion racehorses he was being compared to. The numbers spoke for themselves:

- One week—Muncie Street Fair. $1,847 (1899)
- Seven weeks—Export Exposition, Philadelphia. 173,263 admissions; $20,612.00 (1900, similar to box office for 1899)
- Six weeks—Pittsburg Exposition $7,000 (1900, similar to box office for 1899)

⁕ March 17 to September 1, 1901—Young's Ocean Pier, Atlantic
City. "I have never had such a drawing card on my pier before;
during our large attendance at Easter time, over 80 percent of
the thousands who thronged my pier paid an extra admission
to see Jim Key." (John L. Young)

After their first engagement at Atlantic City, Rogers had not
been eager to return in 1901, even with the promise of headlining
a bill that included the likes of the incomparable palmist/astrolo-
ger team of Albert & Albert, the vaudevillians McMahen & King
("the funniest of all Black face Comedians"), the ever popular Colored Cake Walk dancers, The Gleckers ("baton manipulators"), the
Irish comedians Mike & Dennis, Albert C. Waltz, skater and cyclist
extraordinaire, a "light artist" and master of "clay modeling," and
Mademoiselle Dulce Durant, whose barefoot dancing was intoxicat-
ing. The summer at the New Jersey resort promised to be a profitable
one too, with crowds pouring down to the seashore in breathtaking
numbers.

But there was a conflicting venue that had much more potential
for reaching the masses. It was the Pan American World's Fair at Buffalo, set to run during the same months as the stint at Young's Ocean
Pier. William Key weighed in on the decision, expressing some sort
of bad premonition about Buffalo, sending a handwritten note to
Rogers with two question marks by the event: "Pan American ??"

The Doc may have further consulted with astrologers Albert &
Albert, to see what their predictions were for the world's fair. They
too, it seemed, saw a dark cloud over the enterprise. A. R. Rogers
complied with Doc Key's wishes and withdrew his application for
a Beautiful Jim Key concession at the fair, but he did not alter his
plans for some of the other attractions he continued to promote.

At first, with the staggering words of praise issuing forth out of
Buffalo, Rogers must have thought Dr. Key either overly supersti-
tious or simply wrong about whatever he had foreseen. At a cost
of ten million dollars, the planners had executed a miracle, said
papers across the country. In a daring departure from the uniform
white finish to most buildings used at most expositions—which had
been daring when it was first done to create the wonder of Chicago's
1893 White City for the Columbian World's Fair—the Pan American
planners had erected a Rainbow City by finishing exhibit halls in

shades of gold, green, red, and blue. The multicolored electrical night scene reportedly surpassed anything ever attempted, and the staging against the backdrop of Niagara Falls was exquisite.

But several things that could go wrong did. There was the typical lateness on the completion of the Exposition, leaving early visitors unimpressed. The Pan American theme to promote unity among nations of the Western Hemisphere was also a flop, especially with rising criticism of U.S. imperialism at the doorsteps of neighbors. Then there was the May 9, 1901, stock market collapse, the result of a panic that erupted when financial titans J. P. Morgan and E. H. Harriman battled it out for a takeover of Northern Pacific Railroad, plunging stock prices to near worthlessness. Though not the last Wall Street collapse ever to shake the nation, it was the first time in history that the market closed early, after investors' losses in the hundreds of millions. (The crash undoubtedly hurt the Rogers's family fortune, making Albert's income now necessary to support his loved ones, not just a hobby or, as he liked to say in the case of Jim, a philanthropic bet to see if he could prove to his friends that animals think and reason.) If the panic wasn't enough to plague the world's fair, the oppressive, unprecedented summer heat in Buffalo made more headlines than the exhibits. Then, in the fall, the weather finally cooperated with cool, glorious autumn days. But just when planners and investors hoped to recover from financial losses of more than $3 million and mushrooming lawsuits, tragedy struck on September 6, 1901, at the Pan American Exposition.

At a reception held in honor of President McKinley in the Temple of Music, a fairgoer named Leon Czolgosz, described as an unassuming man of average height dressed in a nondescript black suit, joined in a crowd of well-wishers to shake the President's hand. When he approached, at the range of two feet, Czolgosz raised his outstretched hand, which held a concealed revolver, and fired it twice, striking fifty-eight-year-old McKinley in the chest. One bullet became lodged in his breastbone and another in his stomach. As Secret Service men apprehended Czolgosz—an anarchist seeking to overthrow the government—McKinley's first concern was to admonish his aides to be gentle in telling his beloved and fragile Ida about the shooting. He also insisted that he was not seriously injured and asked that his assailant not be harmed, even as lynch mobs thirty thousand strong began to assemble.

Eight days later, William McKinley died in Buffalo, and Theodore Roosevelt, age forty-two, located in the middle of the night on a manly adventure off on some mountaintop and escorted at top speed to Buffalo, was sworn in as the youngest man ever to serve as president of the United States.

It was only one month after ascending to the presidency that Roosevelt hosted Booker T. Washington at the White House, a controversial yet courageous act that definitely earned him the admiration of Dr. William Key. Arriving jim Boston two weeks after that historic occasion, Dr. Key told reporters that Jim had always been a Democrat but had switched his party affiliation. Beautiful Jim Key was so upset by the news that one of his first famous fans had been assassinated that he decided to support McKinley's party in his memory. The horse also liked Roosevelt, a friend to the Negro people, and because the new President had spoken out against docking the tails of horses. As far as other candidates for other offices, it seemed that Jim would make up his mind, depending on the individual, not the party.

The *Boston Globe* reporter couldn't prevent a mocking tone from entering the article, commenting after Dr. Key's statements that readers could decide for themselves "whether or not horses have minds." This dubious stance appeared motivated not so much by journalistic integrity as it was by Bostonian snobbery, or that's how it must have felt to Albert Rogers, who'd had little success until now booking Beautiful Jim Key for any major exhibits in Boston. The sophisticated New York City audiences were almost provincial when compared with the elitist tastes not just of the Brahmins but also of most every Bostonian he encountered. Even with vibrant letters of introduction from George Angell to exhibition planners and school board directors, Rogers could not seem to find an opening. It mattered not that *The Scholar and a Model Office Boy* at the Star Theatre on New York's Broadway had been reviewed as daring (the choice of a vaudeville context at a melodrama theatre was "out of the usual line") or that it was described as a tonic for the jaded playgoer. "It is worth going below Twenty-third Street just to see theatergoers laugh until the tears run down their cheeks," one New York critic promised. "The star of the show was a horse, 'Beautiful Jim Key.' His tricks were entertaining and he seemed to get as much fun out of his part as the audience did." Nor were theater owners in Boston swayed by the money the play had made in other cities.

In 1900, one area theater had been willing to do the play, provided there was a name change, since, heaven forbid, what producer of any taste would open a show that had been done last in—now, where was that place, Shelbyville? Rogers didn't argue, thinking that a name change wasn't such a terrible idea, and brought *The Horse of the Twentieth Century* to Boston for a short run that thrilled George Angell and his colleagues and made a lovely splash with the general public but still didn't pave the way for the kind of receptions that were being bestowed on Beautiful Jim Key everywhere else.

The Food Fair planners may have finally been influenced by news of an unprecedented decision that Angell announced in a letter to A. R. Rogers:

> *It gives me pleasure to inform you that at the annual convention of the American Humane Association recently held at Pittsburg, Pa., Beautiful Jim Key was elected an honorary member of the Association. I think this is the first instance on record of such an act on the part of our organization. It was an expression of our appreciation of the intelligence of the horse, the kindness of his trainer, and the generosity of his owner.*

No newspaper account or piece of correspondence could accurately convey the significance of this honor to Jim or Bill. The romantic Rogers couldn't resist having Jim "write" a letter to George Angell that described what it was like when Mr. Rogers read the news to a large auditorium full of children and he learned of his status as the first nonhuman to be elected to so august and important an organization, and he promised to serve faithfully on behalf of every species. Despite this overly cute conceit, the event marked an evolution in Jim's demeanor as a celebrity, as though he genuinely recognized he was now a diplomat for his kind and had to be on his very best behavior. He shirked off his former modest blush along with his extra pounds, carrying himself less like a first-run and more like an unbeatable champion.

More honorary memberships followed. Jim Key soon became the first nonhuman honorary member of Angell's other organizations, the Massachusetts SPCA, the American Humane Education Society, and the Parent American Band of Mercy. Not to be left out, a literacy group elected him as the first nonhuman honorary member of their Pen and Pencil Club.

Dr. William Key was next elected to all four branches of Angell's humane groups, and at last Albert Rogers, for his energy and innovation, was made a vice president of the Education Society. He sensed that there had been resistance to this symbolic gesture from some of the other officers. Nonetheless, now that he could legitimately call himself a philanthropist, he was determined to live up to the example of his greatest inspiration, George Angell. He was even inspired to look for property to buy in or around Boston, seemingly preferring the aristocratic social set there to the New York and New Jersey elite. One of his first acts as an officer was to form the Jim Key Band of Mercy with the outlandish promise to sign up one million or more children within five years (this number was in addition to the one million signers of the Jim Key Pledge card he had been collecting), and he devised a kind of pyramid scheme for enlisting membership, with himself, "Uncle Bert," as the presidential figurehead. Also as an honorary member of the Parent American Band of Mercy, he daringly told Angell that he would boost the three million adult members of the various bands to ten million within those same five years.

Angell laughingly encouraged him, believing that if anyone could do it, the persistent A. R. Rogers could. Albert became more relentless than ever, securing engagements for Jim for dates more than three years ahead, flooding the planning committees of the world's fairs in Charleston, South Carolina, and St. Louis, Missouri, with petitions for buildings. He promoted practically in his sleep, soliciting testimonials from animal experts such as Professor J. W. Gentry of the Gentry Dog and Pony Show ("Beautiful Jim Key stands without a compeer on earth, and I have seen them all"), and from James A. Cathcart, owner of the famed educated Bartholomew's Horses ("I have never seen a horse the equal of Jim Key"), as well as from the most respected animal trainer alive, Adam Forepaugh Jr., who quipped, "I revere Dr. Key."

Free passes to educators and booking agents were now a fixture everywhere Jim performed, as were Jim Key Pledge cards and application forms for establishing a Beautiful Jim Key Band of Mercy ("sign up ten other friends and have your names pasted on the great

Jim Key banner roll"). Albert's AHES vice presidency didn't diminish his zeal as a promoter as he sent out press releases with Jim's new honorary memberships listed, and with new potent catchphrases: "Refined. High class. Interesting." "In New Acts More Wonderful Than Ever." "Higher Educated." "The Society Pet and Children's Delight." "The Talk of Every City." "The Pride of the South." And not to be forgotten: "He Was Bred in Old Kentucky."

Out of all the honors, the most prestigious one that the AHA, the MSPCA, the AHES, and the Parent American Band of Mercy chose to bestow was to Dr. William Key, with its presentation set for November 1, 1901, of the Service to Humanity Award. George Angell insisted that in spite of a spell of ill health he himself be present to award the gold medal to his friend and colleague in a public ceremony. He had to witness the moment for himself when Dr. William Key received his due.

So with that event in the works, the planners of the Boston Food Fair realized that it really couldn't hurt to exhibit the horse. True, the horse had nothing to do with food, but neither did the musical entertainments that were scheduled to perform. There was also the thought that Beautiful Jim Key did have a certain fondness for the ladies, who came in determined hordes to this fair to enjoy both the bountiful food giveaways and the lectures on topics such as new salads or the latest ways to prepare stag. Once the Food Fair had booked Beautiful Jim Key, the Cambridge and the Boston school superintendents decided to schedule special school matinees for their students after all.

But honorary memberships and national celebrity notwithstanding, Bostonians continued to be coy, wanting to be wooed. Even though Jim's show was staged in the massive hall at the Mechanics Building, for the first and second weeks of the Food Fair he was listed at the bottom of the newspaper ads, as an afterthought. Day by day, however, his name started moving up in the ad, as word of mouth spread. By the third week he was at the midpoint of the bill, and by the fourth week he was second from the top. By the last week, he was the lead attraction, ahead even of the Royal Marine Band of Italy whose conductor, Signor Giorgio Minoliti, composed the music for "The Beautiful Jim Key Two-Step" and began selling the sheet music, soon a collector's item, wherever the Italian musicians appeared.

There was no question. Boston had fallen in love with Beautiful Jim Key. The standoffish *Globe* reporter who had mocked Jim's politics and the suggestion that he had a "mind" now wrote tearful testimonials, describing how the big bay could spell *"G-L-O-B-E,"* or how anyone could stand up and ask him anything. "Tell him to multiply 6 by 8 and divide by 12, and he brings you the right answer"—4—"on a card from the rack." Could he identify the name of the President? "He picks out the name Roosevelt." Operate a general store? Indeed, "he slams the drawer shut on the cash register with as much dash as a girl in a lunch room who has fingers." The *Globe* reporter had his suspicions banished with this incident:

A lady called for a letter from the alphabet and Jim fetched *E*. Dr. Key remonstrated and said, *D*. And the woman thereupon stated that she had called for *E* and that the horse had understood her correctly while the man had made a mistake.

Incredibly, the *Boston Globe* then proceeded to publish human-interest stories about average citizens around town committing humane acts, with headlines such as "Man Rescues a Cat from a Tree at Great Risk to Himself," as well as in-depth articles about Bostonian companion animals like Mrs. Dr. Thornton's "mascot" named Filipino (Pino for short), a mischievous and lovable Java monkey known for stopping by police headquarters and firehouses, and for joining the fellows in drinks and a smoke during off-hours.

Jim Key had started something rather remarkable. But infatuation was not enough for a true and lasting commitment from Boston, Massachusetts, unless there was a way to prove there was not one iota of deceit involved in Jim's exhibition. Hoaxes were very much in the news after the scandal at the Pan American World's Fair over the discovery that the lucrative exhibit of a ten-foot-four, 2,900-pound petrified Cardiff Giant once said to be the Eighth Wonder of the World was a fake.

That's when someone, most likely George Angell, proposed that Dr. Key and Jim be subjected to a rigorous examination by a delegation of Harvard's leading authorities. President Charles Eliot was present for the duration of the study but did not make any comments, asserting that he would defer to the professors in their findings. (Eliot's own testimonial later read: "It is really the most remarkable exhibition I have ever witnessed. I have seen him several times.")

And that was how Bill Key found himself very much entertained by all the fuss.

During the first show, the curious group had repressed the usual reactions, neither laughing nor indicating amazement. They watched, listened, asked questions of Jim in loud, professorial voices, and occasionally took measurements. In between the two shows, they buzzed around the stage in a cooperative hive, peeking under props and in drawers, searching through Dr. Key's clothing and conducting a very thorough examination of the Educated Arabian-Hambletonian. They asked the Doc all the usual questions, looking for his system, and honed in on the short whip. Without objection, Doc Key agreed not to use it for the second show.

They seemed to focus much more closely now on their various specialties. During questions related to spelling and reading, the linguist paid the most careful attention; when the questions were mathematically related, the math professor jotted down several notes. After the show concluded, they shook hands with Dr. Key, thanked him for his patience, bid adieu to Beautiful Jim Key, and left to confer with one another before making a pronouncement.

The following day, October 27, 1901, the *Boston Globe* ran only a short piece with the headline "Examined by Harvard College Professors":

A number of Professors from Harvard made a special trip to see Jim Key, the celebrated horse, yesterday, for the purpose of examining him from a psychological point of view, some persons having expressed the opinion that the animal is kept hypnotized.

Just what was the secret the finest minds in America had uncovered about Bill and Jim? Their determination was unanimous. There was no hoax. No hypnosis. Jim was not a freak of nature. He was naturally of a high intelligence, but not a genius. Their explanation for his mathematical wizardry and humanlike reasoning and abstractions was succinct: "After a stay through two performances, during which the Professors made a careful examination of Jim Key's mathematical ability, and interviewed Dr. Key, the horse's teacher, they came to the conclusion it is simply education."

B ill began to think that he and Jim needed to take some time off from the rattling pace they had been maintaining for nearly five years. Maybe permanently. At almost seventy years old, he had started to ask himself why shouldn't he retire. Especially after reaching the pinnacle of his life's achievement on the day when he accepted the Service to Humanity medal from George Angell in front of a Boston auditorium filled to overflowing. How could any attainment surpass that high point? To make it that much sweeter, two weeks prior to his award ceremony, in the embrace of Bostonians who knew the real thing when they saw it, Jim had been feted and presented with a similar award, the Living Example Award from the Parent American Band of Mercy. Beautiful Jim Key had become to the humane movement what Black Beauty had been only on paper as a fictitious standard-bearer, it was said, while a crossbred "scrub colt" had grown up to be an actual living example that animals could think and feel; proof of the power of kindness. Jim's medal was fittingly beautiful, but the Doc's Service to Humanity medal was a priceless treasure, a gold five-point star that hung from a gold bar inscribed with the credos of the sponsoring organizations: "Glory to God, Peace on Earth, Kindness to All Harmless Living Creatures," dated November 1, 1901, to Dr. William Key by the Parent American Band of Mercy and the Massachusetts SPCA.

In December, Jim and Dr. Key were featured in their first of three appearances in *Our Dumb Animals,* which Albert Rogers was quick to promote as the publication of the American Humane Education Society with its motto of "Kindness, Justice and Mercy to Every Living Creature." As Uncle Bert, Rogers plugged the article in his next newsletter:

> This paper should be read by every lover of animals. It is the
> most quoted from paper in the country—full of crisp up-to-date
> facts, full of interesting information in the humane cause. Edited
> personally by Mr. Angell, whose terse signed notes are always
> to the point, and famous the world over. They are little acorns

from which great oaks have grown and will grow. Mr. George T. Angell, of Boston, is the great Apostle of Humanity toward the Birds of the Air and All Animals, and without question has done more to educate the masses to consideration and kindness towards animals than any one else. He is one of God's own noblemen, whom all love and revere for his unselfish devotion to the Humane Cause.

Dr. Key knew that George Angell had made sure that the magazine's staff, in their offices in Boston's Goddard Building at 19 Milk Street, wrote and placed the story in a way that acknowledged him and Jim, yet also promoted their mutual cause. On what better note to take their bow, the Doc couldn't imagine.

Whether or not William Key saw himself as lucky, he knew to count his blessings and knew that he had also worked for those blessings. He had shared his wealth, had repaid debts of kindness, and had lived an honorable life, bringing honor to his family and community. He had used his gifts well, had reaped what he had sowed, and recognized that there were responsibilities that came along with the privileged position in which he moved, as a traveler between different worlds. It might have been a long time since he had officially gambled, but deep down in him there was probably a feeling of not wanting to tempt fate any longer.

This would have been his mother wit talking. There were signs. He could probably feel, when he was able to stand still, that the winds were changing again, the shifting ground underneath his feet signified harder times ahead. Maybe he foresaw the coming world wars, the rise of the machines, the great struggle to come for civil rights, but in any event he somehow perceived that this window of consciousness that had opened wide to value kindness and goodness was going to be closing soon. He and Beautiful Jim Key had come along in the right way at the right time for the humane movement. But that time was fleeting. Why stay too long at the fair?

And there were other causes and concerns that needed aid in his later years. In the various black newspapers and journals that Dr. Key collected, there was an emerging divide that was troubling. There was the path of less resistance, the separate-but-equal approach of Booker T. Washington, whose focus on education at Tuskegee and formation of the National Negro Business League won approval from the Doctor. But there was also the recent voice of W. E. B. DuBois, the first African-American to receive a doctorate from Harvard, who wanted full equality, and who warned against the deepening color line, adding a sense of urgency to the need for leadership from the black upper class in helping develop political organizations and foster the economic empowerment for all people of color. William Key apparently believed both leaders were right, that education, education, education was the cornerstone of advancement on the one hand, but that a color-blind marketplace—such as he had created for himself—had to be actively, consciously cultivated, maybe even demanded. Those happened to be his values as a self-educated professional and as an entrepreneur, and what he hoped to convey to Negro audiences in whatever capacity he was able.

These were also his priorities for how he spread out his assets, spending generously when it came to assisting his relatives with their educational and business pursuits, and securing more property for himself. Besides the 240 acres that he wanted to develop, he owned the land and home near what had been Keystone Driving Park (soon to be turned over to the Davises) and his place on North Main Street, which had another house, stables, and offices for his veterinary businesses (eventually to be taken over by Dr. Stanley Davis), and he was also looking to purchase a house in town, closer to the train station and the courthouse square. The property he had in mind was on Bethany Lane, in one of the better neighborhoods in Shelbyville, with a graceful white Victorian home on it, a stables and corral out back, and plenty of pasture where Jim and Monk, and the other Key family horses and animals could graze and play. Now that Maggie had received her degree, he was ready to legalize their union and provide for her a comfortable life. Plus, he had never written a will, and that was another thing he ought to do. Not that he was slowing down much or was ever even tired after performing on his feet hour after hour. Maybe his Keystone tonic was a youth elixir after all. Then again, it was a wise man who knew that only this day was given and that tomorrow was never promised.

Perhaps he was not feeling as safe as he once had felt traveling among so many strangers, a symptom of fame and of not being able to be anonymous, as well as a symptom of the increase in racist attacks on people of color. When recent race riots exploded in New York, the white mobs went on a rampage, some with the express purpose of killing black celebrities and entertainers like Bob Cole and Bert Williams. To be an African-American of wealth and stature was threatening enough, but to be loved and admired by white audiences seemed to be a crime, especially when black male musicians and actors found favor with white female fans.

So though it was all very well for a famous big dark stallion to bow and make bedroom eyes at the white women in his audiences, if the venerable mulatto horse trainer ever tried it, he would have been killed, as they said, in a New York minute. Presumably, this was one of the reasons why William Key agreed for Albert Rogers to be presented as the owner of Beautiful Jim Key, so as not to be known as the owner of a horse now estimated to be worth upward of $200,000.

Fame aside, the Doc didn't have to know the statistics—that since 1893 up to this era, once a week, on average, two Negroes were lynched by mobs—to know that the brutal killings by hanging, mutilation, or being burned alive were not slowing down. The South was more dangerous than the North and West, but sometimes only by degree. Dr. Key, with his therapeutic orientation, needed to step back as a way of finding a prescription, or at least a perspective. Dr. W. E. B. DuBois wrote about a similar inner struggle of his divided self:

> It is a peculiar sensation, this double-consciousness, this sense of always looking at one's self through the eyes of others, of measuring one's soul by the tape of a world that looks on in amused contempt and pity. One ever feels his twoness,—an American, a Negro; two souls, two thoughts, two unreconciled strivings; two warring ideals in one dark body, whose dogged strength alone keeps it from being torn asunder.

Key needed to reconcile the duality that while he and many more in white America had flourished in recent years, too many African-Americans still struggled under the yoke of prejudice and cruelty. Of the ten million Negroes in the United States, nine million lived in the South, more and more separate, less and less equal. He wanted to do more to help, as he had done when he had visited North Carolina and made an ostensibly large contribution on behalf of the Women's Christian Temperance Union of North Carolina, an

African-American organization that "secured homes for the homeless" and had built a hospital as well as an orphanage in Charlotte.

One of the reasons it was becoming harder to include the humorous political debate with Jim in his act was that none of the political parties they mentioned any longer held the advancement of people of color as a part of their platforms. How could he and Jim joke about voting, when most black people were denied that right?

But his real reason for contemplating retirement was less about those or any personal trends, and more about Jim's well-being. He worried that the winter travel, in spite of the comforts provided to them, could be creating a time-lapse disaster. True, Jim hadn't come down with any illnesses from traveling, as of yet, but the Doctor believed that horses weren't designed to move so often from one extreme climate to another.

At the end of 1901, they departed in a November winter storm from Massachusetts, where the doting *Boston Traveler* reported, by the way, that A. R. Rogers said Jim was earning net 4 percent on a million dollars per year, and that he was sending Jim to balmy Charleston to their world's fair for the next three months, where, predicted the *Traveler,* "he is sure to be the main feature as he has been this past month," and where, if Charleston didn't yet have a humane society, they would soon after Jim got there.

The South Carolina Inter-State and West Indian Exposition was another financial disappointment to investors and another indication that the glut of big-scale fairs and expositions was beginning to erode the public appetite for them in general. But once again Beautiful Jim Key was a top draw, the proverbial horse who couldn't lose. He proved to be such a moneymaker and publicity success, he was declared the "Feature of the Midway," as his friends in Boston had predicted. Before long, Albert's fellow concessionaires hired him as a consultant to increase their business and then collectively elected him president of the Charleston Amusement Concessionaires Club. With his trademark spunk and ingenuity, A. R. Rogers launched a midway newspaper—for which he served as managing editor—to promote daily events and increase traffic to the various concessions.

By this point, Rogers had become a celebrity in his own right, sought after for his promotional expertise by peers like these in South Carolina, by fair organizers, creators of exhibits and rides, by other promoters, and even by entertainment trade papers such as *Billboard Magazine*. Nine months earlier, he was interviewed in that periodical about the new phenomenon of so-called electric parks, which were modest-size amusement parks set at the ends of trolley lines to make sure that American families had somewhere to go when they paid the full fare to take the trolley out of town. Rogers told the reporter, "Probably no amusement line has developed so rapidly the last three years as the street railway parks, or has any more profitable proposition been adopted." His "Advice to Street Railway Managers of Parks," as the column was entitled, was to capitalize on riders' idle time by publishing free newspapers like his *Street Railway Journal*, with paid advertising from park concessionaires. (The park phenomenon was not as long-lived as he predicted, however, once city dwellers began to make their treks to the suburbs to live.) Albert had raked in the bucks by publishing these railway journals, not just from charging the cost of the ads but also by including more Jim Key product endorsements.

Even though he represented many other successful attractions and was traveling less and less with Dr. Key, Jim, and Monk, the name of Beautiful Jim Key always appeared at the top of his letterhead and was always his most potent calling card. On one flyer of this era, in a fit of hubris by which he likened himself to Barnum, he did list himself above Jim's name, proclaiming: "ROGERS—A name that stands for all that is refined, high class and entertaining in the amusement world." But he must have reconsidered this approach, since he quickly dropped it, allowing his roster to do that pitch:

- **BEAUTIFUL JIM KEY,** The Greatest Drawing Card in America
- **Liquid Air Exhibitions**
- **Edison's Electrical Fairyland**
- **Sub-marine Tank Exhibition:** Deep Sea Diving in the Largest Tank in the World. A trip to the bottom of the sea. Divers at work raising sunken vessels, marine tableaux, etc.
- **The Novel Animated Picture Exhibitions**
- **Southern Life and Cotton Exhibition:** A reproduction of a Typical Southern Plantation with the Negroes gathering cotton in the fields, etc.
- **Barnard's Patented Giant Sea Wave**
- **Stella, Maid of the Moon:** The Beautiful Mysterious Floating Star

※ **Electrical Naval Battles:** Reproducing in miniature celebrated Naval Battles, with Guns and Mines Fired, Boats and Signals run, all by Electricity

※ **Am. Wild Game Park and Sportsman's Exposition:** A reproduction of a forest, with Live Buffalo, Moose, Caribou, Deer, Bears, etc., and an Indian Encampment with their Dances, Races, Games and Plays. Trappers, Guides, Log Houses, Canoe Races, Souvenirs, etc.

※ **Portable Electrical Prismatic Fountain:** with Fire and Serpentine Dances and Plastique Poses. "The Girl with the Robes of Fire."

※ **The Celestial Chinese Band and Festival Lanterns:** With Chinese Races and Games and wonderful Kite Flying Contests, with their Chinese Dragon and Centipede Kites 100 feet long, Mammoth Butterfly Kites ten feet high and other grotesque designs. Chinese singing and acting, Chinese Fireworks, Day and Night. In all, the most unique entertainment possible.

Less high class but more profitable, the amusement rides he brokered and leased for parks and fairs—updated versions of Shoot the Chutes and the Mirror Maze, along with roller coasters such as the Loop-the-Loop—were another avenue of income. In all his marketing efforts, Rogers continued to be as innovative and relentless as William had first known him to be.

Interestingly enough, since Jim had been rethinking his political views, he was no longer billed in the South as the Educated Democratic horse but instead as the Educated Southern horse. Dr. Key was undoubtedly upset that the Charleston Exposition had done much less than the Tennessee Centennial to involve people of color, both in planning and in attending the fair. Because of his concern, coupled with the influence of Albert Rogers, and the popularity of Beautiful Jim Key, it was agreed that New Year's Day, January 1, 1902, be celebrated as Negro Day. Special ten-cent discount coupons were issued that read:

This special ticket and 15 cents will admit the bearer to the astonishing performance of the Feature of the Midway, the Wonderful Educated Horse, BEAUTIFUL JIM KEY, Who can read, write, spell, count, figure, change money, tell time, play cards, etc. Taught by Dr. Wm. Key, the Most Successful Colored Trainer in the World. The One Show Everyone

Wants to See of ALL, Regular admission 25 cents. Don't lose this ticket. This ticket worth 10 cents. Good New Year's Day Only. Negro Day at the Exposition. This Special Price for Colored People Only, by Special Request of Dr. Wm. Key who wants all his colored friends in Charleston to see Jim.

New Year's Day 1902 had thus become another pinnacle, a day-long celebration with continuous performances in the Beautiful Jim Key Palace on the midway of the South Carolina Inter-State and West Indian Exposition. Fair planners were astonished to see how profitable the day had been and promptly opened admission to people of color; later it was believed that Negro fairgoers helped the Exposition from suffering worse losses. And it meant more to Dr. Key. On this New Year's Day in his personal history he was given a reprieve from the discomfort of being a Negro permitted to perform on stages of halls where other people of color weren't allowed to sit in the better seats or at all. But not only that: on this day he didn't have to hide or diminish who he was and what he had accomplished. His feeling was certainly akin to the sentiments expressed by Booker T. Washington in a speech—a copy of which Dr. Key came to own—to the almost all-white National Educational Association:

You may not know it, but my people are as proud of their racial identity as you are of yours, and in the degree that they become intelligent, social pride increases. I was never prouder of the fact that I am classed as Negro than I am today.

How did Jim, "who had been raised in a colored family," as the Southern newspapers had noted, feel about what this meant to the Doc? How much could he have understood, after all? What might Doc Key have explained to him? The only answer is that Beautiful Jim Key could unquestionably sense his teacher's unbridled happiness and pride, which in turn would have made Jim the happiest horse who ever lived.

Albert Rogers saw it. The secret of Beautiful Jim Key's extraordinary abilities was something more than "simply education." Yes, it was kindness and patience, together with the strange life among humans that Jim had lived early on and the inseparable nature of the relationship between horse and man. It was both more than all that, yet also more basic. It was love. The love between human and nonhuman was so powerful it had bridged the language divide, more similar to a father-son relationship than anything else Rogers could conjure. Jim was happy when Doc Key was happy. The secret was love.

At the end of January, this realization was with Albert Rogers when he, Key, and Key took a brief recess from Charleston to travel to the freezing North to do a benefit honoring George Angell in Providence, Rhode Island. The program proclaimed, "Kindness has accomplished what cruelty could not have," and further noted, "Affection toward an animal is never misplaced."

These deepening sensibilities inspired Rogers, a short while after their return to Charleston, to add a new line to the promotional pamphlet that was now in its seventh or eighth edition. Romantic though he was, he couldn't find a way to articulate what he now understood was really a great love story, saying instead very chattily: "One of the most interesting features of this marvelous performance is the affection displayed towards each other by the horse and his trainer."

In this edition he also included an interesting comment Dr. Key had made about the Bible studies he and Jim had been working on. They had found many more than the fifty-four biblical allusions to horses and donkeys that they had first counted but had stuck with learning those fifty-four. Jim had learned to recognize them when quoted aloud and to cite book, chapter, and verse from written cards placed on his screen. Dr. Key had only begun incorporating this skill into their shows and was also teaching Jim to spell the names of the prophets. Bill Key repeated what he had told Albert when they had started this process. "Jim likes to hear about horses in the Bible, for they were very prominent animals then."

Rogers couldn't have imagined a more prominent horse than Jim was in this time. He looked at the book names and chapter citations—Genesis 50, Exodus 14, Revelations 6, and so on, in no special order.

Dr. Key continued, "Jim likes the prophets. The prophets had visions of horses. John says he looked up and beheld a white horse in heaven, and what Jim wants to know is, if there are white horses in heaven, why can't a good bay horse go there also?"

A long silence naturally ensued. Albert had come to know William Key well, even with the formalities of their relationship, and he knew by now that this comment was both literal and metaphoric. What did he tell Jim? Rogers responded.

Doc Key had no ambivalence on this topic and assured Mr. Rogers that all horses go to heaven, good or not.

This set the mood for the Doctor to tell Albert that it was time for a break. By way of preamble, they discussed some of Doc Key's complaints, including the fact that since he did most of the selling of the souvenir items, he ought to be getting a bigger share of the profits, despite the cost of their production being on the promoter's shoulders. Rogers made some concessions, and they clarified some of the murkier areas of their arrangement, as well as how they could keep their humane work and merchandising activities going in the event that Jim had to suddenly retire.

This was a theoretical discussion until Dr. Key confessed what he hadn't really admitted to himself. Jim Key had woken up on a couple of mornings and had been unable to stand. A good guess was that he had a touch of rheumatism, and it could get worse. Much worse. But then the symptoms had vanished.

Understandably upset, Rogers proposed a way to continue the Jim Key Band of Mercy and the souvenir and pamphlet sales, without Jim having to perform. Rogers had recently purchased an especially smart pony named Dick who was being trained at Glenmere, as Doc Key knew. The hope was that Dick could eventually do shows and benefits too. The other hope, better yet, was that Dr. Key might feel differently in a month or two.

With that, the two men shook hands, and a few days later, Dr. Key, Jim, and Monk left Charleston for Shelbyville. After a month or so, as they all settled into a much slower pace, a letter arrived from Albert Rogers requesting that some of the equipment he had purchased or had made for the show be shipped to Glenmere. He wanted to know where the large megaphone was, and what the dimensions were for the display rack, as he was commissioning a new one for Dick.

William knew when he read Albert's letter that he was a man with a broken heart. The Doc had already shipped all those items some time before and had returned the megaphone just after that.

But Albert wasn't the only one who was suffering. For Jim and for Monk, the novelty of being back home and getting to play for hours, being free to live life as a normal horse and dog, not having to work or travel, seemed to be wearing off a little. There had been a few reporters for Monk to chase away, but no photographers. Jim got lots of visitors and fans stopping by, but that was a far cry from being onstage in front of thousands. Dr. Key figured this was to be expected, what a racehorse went through after an injury, or anyone with more time on their hands than they'd ever had before. He was still resolved that he had made the right decision. Writing A. R. Rogers, he reminded the promoter where to look for the items that he had previously returned and also went over the dimensions of the display screen. He continued:

> *The weather is very fine here most spring like. Jim is on blue grass every day for 4 or 5 hours & takes at least 4 or 5 hours to clean the mud & dust off that he rolls & tumbles in. Hoping you much success in your dates and to hear from you often. I remain yours truly, William Key*

Rogers wrote back to test the waters, wondering how he and Jim were feeling, and if there was the possibility of performing in the near future. Dr. Key wasted no time in replying:

> *I am in fine health—also Jim is in splendid condition, and good shape and ready to hit the road at any time.*

A month later, Beautiful Jim Key returned to public life, spending the spring and summer in Chicago—where he broke box office records at the amusement park housed in the White City that had been built for the 1893 World's Fair, even with its need for renovation—and enjoyed a picture-postcard-perfect autumn in Syracuse, New York, before wrapping up in October with the 1902 season of the Boston Mechanics Fair.

At a fee of $5,000, fifty percent of which was contributed to the MSPCA, Beautiful Jim Key spent just over a month solidifying his place in the hearts of Bostonians. The Massachusetts Charitable Mechanics Association wrote a testimonial declaring they had first believed the fee to be prohibitive until discovering that he was the best drawing card they had ever hired.

In Syracuse, after Jim had just finished as the star attraction at the Alhambra Pet and Horse Fair and was readying for a run of his play, a reporter for the *Post Standard* made it his life's purpose to find out what the Harvard professors had missed a year earlier. When he went to the luxurious, blanket-lined stall where the Marvel of the Century was being groomed, he faced down Monk, who barked out in no uncertain terms that no one was to disturb Jim during his toilet. When Dr. Key heard the commotion, he diplomatically intervened and led the reporter and Jim out and onto the Alhambra stage so that the famous horse could give a "private performance for the representative of the *Post Standard*."

In the hall where the stage was located, unfortunately, there was a window overlooking James Street that provided several distractions—horses and humans passing by—that were much more interesting to the pampered star than his "audience of one." Rather than chiding Jim, the Doc simply lowered the curtain on the window, at which point the handsome bay "reluctantly turned toward the auditorium and consented to show off."

Because of poor acoustics in the hall there was a vibration in the room that forced the reporter to lean forward and speak very distinctly. He began requesting letters and numbers to be brought forward, which Jim did with a "dead easy manner," and he then said, "Jim, spell *Post Standard*." Dr. Key stood aside, expressionless, the writer observed, while Jim directed a look at him that said: *I suppose you think you've got me, well, watch.*

The journalist until now had resisted Jim Key's charms. But the way he trotted back and forth, bringing forward the letters *P-O-S-T-S-T-A-N-D-A-R* and lining them up on his spelling rack, securing each card behind the nickel rail, until he was out of room and had to stand at the end, holding the *D* in his mouth, was too spontaneous, too inexplicable, and too wonderful to be disproved. Why bother?

From then on out, that was the attitude of most journalists. Beautiful Jim Key had other rivals and other hurdles to overcome, but skepticism hardly reared its head anymore. The *Post Standard* reporter conceded his own skepticism as Jim stood there grinning, the *D* in his teeth, with one of his shrugs and an expression that said *You see, I do read the papers.*

8

The Horse Who Could

> It is one of the supreme ironies of history that the Negro, whose folklore furnished the authentic core of popular culture in the United States and shaped its growth, should have had to fight against odds and obstacles to make his contribution to the performing arts and to express his talent. The vitality of the Negro's influence on American music, dance and drama has been irresistible, its impact profound and lasting.
>
> —ALLAN MORRISON,
> *"100 Years of Negro Entertainment," in* Anthology of the
> Afro-American in the Theatre: A Critical Approach

JUST AS EVERY IMPORTANT SOCIAL CAUSE can be greatly championed by a well-known celebrity, a well-articulated theme is almost mandatory for the success of any major social or civic event. This principal lesson was being learned at the turn of the century by planners of expositions on every level, from the annual county fair to the most ambitious world's fairs.

The Louisiana Purchase Exposition held in St. Louis in 1904, a centennial celebration of Thomas Jefferson's historic land acquisition for the United States, was a theme that worked. Elsewhere the American themes that centered on agriculture, trade, commerce, and technology were all well and good, but the winning themes were always those that remembered the glorious achievements of America's past and drew from them to create utopian landscapes of her future. These elements all came together magnificently in St. Louis.

There were the now customary problems, the scandals, corruption, financial mismanagement, and the proverbial delays that caused the World's Fair to open a year late, practically a tradition in this era. There was much criticism from a later, historical perspective that the Louisiana Purchase Exposition, like preceding world's fairs, reinforced negative racial and cultural stereotypes of American minorities and foreigners. On the other hand, with the fair's themes of progress and education, most of the news out of St. Louis at the time promised tolerance and inclusion.

Of course, for those who were comparing, it was hard for any world's fair to live up to the grandeur of Chicago, or to be anything but a lesser imitation. But St. Louis benefited somewhat from being a little less grand, perhaps a little more accessible to the average American, a little more affordable, and from factors simply of timing. Kicking off a new century, the 1904 World's Fair was carried forth in memories of most Americans alive at the time, finding its romantic theme of "meet me in St. Louis" echoed in the titles of books, songs, and movies. A toddler from Illinois who may have well been taken to the fair—which wasn't far from the small Missouri town where he and his family would soon move—was two-and-a-half-year-old Walt Disney, whose father, Elias, had worked on the construction of the Columbian Exposition. How much Walt consciously remembered from what he saw is questionable, although it is interesting to note that his "Carousel of Progress" exhibit—which he developed with General Electric for the 1964–65 New York World's Fair and later installed at Disneyland and Disney World—embodied the very themes launched at the St. Louis World's Fair. Indeed, the story that was staged for the Carousel exhibit was the journey of a middle-class, midwestern American family traveling through the twentieth century, experiencing all the new wonders of progress, starting with a scene in 1904 of the family just returning from the World's Fair. The lyrics of the theme song written by the Sherman brothers expressed the infectious optimism that the planners of the Louisiana Purchase Exposition had intended to convey: "There's a great big beautiful tomorrow, shining at the end of every day!"

Disney's theme parks, moreover, established in the mid- and late 1900s, were virtually permanent world's fairs that were not only built on the framework of past international expositions but, some might say, also improved upon to such an extent that the expanding Disney universe eventually made the modern-day world's fair obsolete. In any event, St. Louis helped blur the lines between amusement and education, so heavily drawn in the Victorian American consciousness, and it is possible that the birth of fantasy in popular culture which fueled Walt Disney and his generation took place at the Louisiana Purchase Exposition. The Pike also housed two exhibits that might have further influenced a very young Disney, two exhibits, as it happened, that were promoted by concessionaire A. R. Rogers. One was Albert's new attraction of animated motion pictures; these rustic cartoon movies still had lots of competition from the live-action movies that were only now starting to be made with story lines. But the other attraction, deemed the most lucrative concession on the Pike, was Beautiful Jim Key. Whether Walt Disney witnessed Jim perform or not, he would have certainly heard about him in his later childhood. Maybe it was coincidental or maybe not, but apparently at a young age Disney embraced humane values, taking to heart the messages that animals could think, feel, and communicate, as evidenced in the characters of Mickey Mouse, Donald Duck, and the rest of the nonhuman individuals who gave Walt Disney the stature of a modern-day Aesop. By the same token, while the humane movement informed Disney's values, it would likewise be indebted to the animator and storyteller for movies such as *Dumbo*, which exposed the exploitation of circus animals, and *Bambi*, a story that made the world look askance at game hunting as never before.

Cause and effect aside, the Louisiana Purchase Exposition seemed to coincide with the end of the institutional guilt Americans felt about taking pleasure in theatrical entertainment. For most of the nineteenth century, that guilt had been so pronounced everywhere, except for large cultural cities, that even the word *theatre* was shunned as connoting a place of ill repute, or a place where works of ill repute were performed by unrespectable individuals of ill repute. In most localities, the civic buildings constructed for any form of performing arts were therefore named with some variation of Academy of Music, or Music Hall, or Opera House. Instead of calling a play "a play," which sounded too entertaining, even in the case of a drama, dramatic works were referred to as "spectaculum vitae" and musical comedies were called "operas." Shakespeare's *Hamlet*, for example, bore the stigma of entertainment and was forcibly renamed in some productions *A Moral and Instructive Tale as Exemplified in the History of the Prince of Denmark.*

One development that seemed to inoculate provincial audiences from their entertainment guilt was the advent of melodrama. These stories, after all, had moral instruction to offer. So this disguised form of theatre could not be accused of being staged simply for shock value, even though melodramas had their greatest appeal with working-class audiences, who had little excitement in their own lives and were secretly thrilled to watch dire circumstances befall familiar stock characters—innocent and worldly, valiant and dastardly—that could conceivably also happen to them. Apparently, the dramatic talent of the performers was not a factor that affected the crowds' enjoyment. The biggest star on the circuit, Corse Payton, actually promoted himself as "America's Best Bad Actor" and was rewarded for it by being treated like royalty with gifts and letters from fans everywhere he went. Unlike the fancier-named types of shows, melodramas were less expensive to produce, in turn making ticket prices cheaper, down from a typical seat price of one dollar to thirty cents or less, with more money left over for aggressive advertising. For most of the touring and summer stock companies that were bringing what passed for theatre to the American heartland, melodrama paved the road, literally and proverbially.

The circus and the other traveling extravaganzas, in which animals and oddities often were the lead performers, were highly instrumental in sharpening the public's appetite for being delighted and awed. In this respect, animals have been regarded as the pioneers of American entertainment; from the days of the earliest settlers it was considered more acceptable to view nonhuman species onstage. At the circus one could also savor the experience of entering a huge tent and sitting under the big top in the dark, which in and of itself created a kind of covert act of pleasure. On the one hand, the world inside the tent was a neutral, guilt-free zone; on the other, the fact that everyone went to the circus did not make it the kind of respectable pursuit to be had in a Music Hall or Opera House.

Whereas Barnum and others attempted to lace elements of education through the circus entertainment to give it that respect, other tented gatherings, like the medicine and spiritualists' shows that were mainly to instruct and sell, offered just a small serving of entertainment on the side. At the turn of the century, the tent as a legitimate theatre was instituted by the leading actress and box office sensation of the day, Sarah Bernhardt, when she ran into problems trying to book a theatre in Texas and staged her productions in a custom-made tent (which she later donated to the victims of the 1906 San Francisco earthquake). In the meantime, the Chautauqua circuit—with its touring educational and cultural lecture series—made a huge splash with those still opposed to theatrical enterprises but hungry for spiritual and intellectual stimulation. So as not to be confused with the white tents of touring theatre troupes—which church officials would have banned—the Chautauqua organizers used brown tents to set them apart. No guilt was to be had in this brown-tented domain, where improvement of the body, mind, and spirit was the main subject matter.

Interestingly enough, the signature blue-and-white tent that had provided Beautiful Jim Key with his first stage had been a savvy move by Albert Rogers to make sure that the atmosphere surrounding Jim struck the right balance between being instructive and enjoyable. This was the same balance that the St. Louis Fair planners wanted for the exhibits on the Pike, where amusement was to be equally enjoyed and learned from, and where a belief in magic—if seeing was believing—was accepted. Ironically, in the fall of 1903, Albert Rogers was told that the St. Louis World's Fair was not interested in booking Jim for the Exposition. President David Francis had visited Jim at the Charleston World's Fair and made a verbal invitation to Albert to come to St. Louis. Two months before the fair, however, when he applied for a prime space, he was turned down flat. The problem was that the concession committee only wanted large exhibits on the Pike, saying expressly, there would be no "one horse show" at this world's fair. It was also, for lack of a better term, over-exposure. The St. Louis Fair planners argued that Beautiful Jim Key had already toured most of the country and that he wouldn't have any special allure on the Pike. Other concessionaires with expensive exhibits were threatening to pull out. The suggestion was that the popularity of the Celebrated Educated Arabian-Hambletonian had peaked and it was time to let other contenders for his throne be given a fair trial.

Albert fumed. In 1902, he had told reporters in Boston about the Jim Key pavilion that was to be built in St. Louis, asserting that the huge building would be erected in the shape of a "mastodon horse."

Rogers noted, "The halls and reception rooms will be placed in the other portions of the anatomy of the wooden animal. The building will also be equipped with elevators and will cost about $75,000."

Had he overreached? Not from his point of view. What the planners lacked, he believed, was a symbol. The Louisiana Purchase Exposition had an excellent theme but had not found the kind of distinguishing structure that the Eiffel Tower had been at the World's Fair in Paris or that the Ferris wheel had been in Chicago. Albert had hired a sketch artist to design a poster of the Beautiful Jim Key horse-shaped building as it towered over a world's fair in the background. The look was magical, fantastic, irresistible. But the planners were not interested. Perhaps he had overreached.

When the opening of the Exposition was postponed for a year, Albert tried again. He pushed the need for a symbol once more and why his vision was perfect for it, but the respective committees rejected him again. In the spirit of progress and education, and because St. Louis was also hosting the Olympic Games that summer, along with the first-ever sponsored International Peace Conference in Festival Hall, the one-hundred-foot-tall Louisiana Purchase Monument topped by a globe and a statue of the goddess of peace would serve as a symbol. Other fairs needed gimmicks; St. Louis did not. That was when Rogers was told that there were no plans for a Jim Key concession at all.

Rogers was mystified. He was convinced that the horse and the man from Tennessee not only had helped pioneer the humane movement but had, over the past seven years, in direct and indirect ways, changed the face of popular entertainment. It had actually amused him, not long after *The Scholar and a Model Office Boy* played a week on a lower Broadway vaudeville bill and began selling out special benefit productions across the country, that suddenly the big-budgeted theatrical productions began putting nonhuman cast members in their shows. Productions of *Uncle Tom's Cabin* added their own horses and real livestock—which were highlighted in their ads—not in background scenes but in newly created lead roles, and then began sponsoring the kind of composition contests that had brought in young audiences to Jim's shows. One Boston contest offered the prize of a Shetland pony for the winning composition on "The Lessons of Tom's Cabin." And as a result of their early successes with Dr. Key, a Negro, as part of an educational, entertaining show, in 1898 the first all-black musical comedies opened and ran to further success.

Jim's earning power by now was unparalleled. In early 1904, a syndicate offered Rogers $250,000 to purchase the same horse once dismissed as a sideshow. Albert pointed out that he could earn that in a few years' time and declared Jim to be worth $1,000,000. From then on, he was known as either the Million Dollar Equine or the Equine Millionaire. This, A. R. Rogers could argue, had ramifications for the value of racehorses, indirectly affecting the entire turf world, and all of show business for that matter.

Detractors were aghast. No longer focused on Jim being a hoax, the new line of attack was to say that there were better but less recognized educated horses. In 1903, Albert had been lured to Cooperstown, New York, to the annual county fair—known for raucous trotting and running races that were being overshadowed this year by automobile races—where a new "trained horse" category featured the Maguire Educated Horses. Mascot and Barney, two handsome white stallions, were billed as the "Greatest Pair of Educated Horses in America" who could "do everything but talk."

Albert saw them perform and thought their abilities were commonplace; he also had objections to the method of training that was used with them. He went away unimpressed.

Coincidentally, the educated horse destined to garner the most lasting international renown was starting to make the news in his native Germany. His name was Clever Hans, and his story had some curious parallels to Jim's. Kluger Hans, his German name, was five years old in 1900 when he was purchased by a retired schoolteacher named Wilhelm von Osten, who was expressly looking for a horse to educate. Herr von Osten had already tried to teach language and mathematics to a cat and a bear, without success, but he had a bit more luck with another horse, who learned how to distinguish left from right and how to count how many fingers were being held up in front of him. Within two years, Hans had mastered all that and much more. He could understand a decent amount of German, read common words, identify colors, count to thirty, and do simple arithmetic.

Like Dr. Key's slow, patient, encouraging method with Jim, the elderly von Osten worked with Hans on a constant basis for three years to develop a method of spelling and counting that involved the tapping of his hoof a certain number of times to correlate to each letter of the alphabet. But unlike the experience that Jim had obtained traveling with the Doc and his medicine show, Hans was not a performer in any sense and didn't come under the same public scrutiny as did the Arabian-Hambletonian. It wasn't until 1903 or later that witnesses started observing Hans in demonstrations and talking about him. Eventually, however, as word spread about the horse's developing math and reading talents, plus his knack for remembering birthdays of prominent citizens, Hans and his trainer had piqued so much interest that an intensive study was commissioned. Conducted by a panel of scientists, equine experts, and military officers, the quest was to find out whether Hans could actually reason and think, or if he was just doing tricks.

At first, the findings of the five-week study showed evidence of cognitive learning and thought processes. This horse could answer correctly when asked the square root of numbers by selecting from a list of answers drawn on a chalkboard. When shown a piece of paper for only one second with anywhere from nine to twelve dots, he could answer correctly how many dots had been shown to him. He even performed his various successful feats with blinders on, an attempt to make sure that Professor von Osten wasn't sending him visual clues. That is, concluded the study, as long as his trainer was standing nearby. The farther away from Hans he stood, the less likely the horse was to answer correctly. But even when von Osten was removed from the room, Hans still answered enough questions correctly that would have required mental processes other than rote memory. Not a genius, but very clever indeed. One of the scientists, Oskar Pfungst, then posited that Clever Hans could answer correctly as long as his questioner knew the right answer, that these answers were based on involuntary messages sent either from his trainer or any questioner. These messages could be as subtle as the tensing or relaxing of muscles, a minuscule change in posture or facial expression, or the quickening of breath and even heartbeat. "Tension signals." To prove it, Pfungst, his fellow testers, and Herr von Osten stood behind the chalkboard, and a questioner was brought in who did not know the answers to the questions. Hans proceeded to answer almost every question incorrectly.

Though a host of individuals and groups challenged the study, Clever Hans was doomed to become known as one of the most famous hoaxes in history. This was despite the fact that it was scientifically deemed an unintentional hoax. Nor did the recollection of posterity acknowledge that the system of communication through hoof tapping that Clever Hans mastered was itself rather remarkable. That he could read involuntary messages—described as a form of hypnosis—was also a mark of some sort of unusual cleverness. Instead, the equine once branded the most intelligent horse in the world was now branded a fake. The "Clever Hans" effect was a term psychologists later employed in reference to testing methods and the potential for questioners to influence the responses of subjects via subtle and involuntary messaging. Pretty much from then on, the controversial verdict unfortunately painted every other educated horse with the same discredited brush—as a hoax, a psychic, or the victim of skepticism.

Other famous smart horses of future generations were not given the full public hearing they probably deserved in the aftermath of Clever Hans. Earlier accounts of equines with humanlike intelligence were also written off, including the fascinating anecdotes of Morocco, a horse famous in Shakespeare's England who had some of Jim's talents for distinguishing different coins and a hat trick whereby he would fetch a hat or glove for any owner whose name was whispered in his ear. When Morocco was exhibited in Rome, he and his owner were suspected of being possessed by the devil and promptly burnt at the stake.

Even the heroic tales of the devotion and military brilliance of equine soldiers throughout the centuries were ascribed to animal instinct and servile fidelity, not to cognitive processes in any way related to human reasoning.

At the turn of the century, a time when there were more practicing clairvoyants than medical doctors advertised in most newspapers, a double standard was being applied in the analysis of trained animals. It was one thing for humans to be telepathic, but quite another for pets to be psychic. If it could be determined that hypnosis or thought transference was employed, then the idea of animal intelligence would be dismissed as a hoax.

From then on the debate over animal intelligence continued to be as much of a minefield as the debate over priorities in the area of animal rights. And Beautiful Jim Key deserves credit for stirring up the discussion. As a quote attributed to a turn-of-the-century issue of

Time magazine put it, "This wonderful horse has upset all theories that animals have only instinct, and do not think and reason."

Albert Rogers may not have understood something that Dr. Key would have easily recognized. Scientific skepticism was not the only cause for the need to reject theories that horses and other speechless nonhumans could think and reason. The true cause was fear, the same kind of deeply ingrained fear that made Charles Darwin's theories of evolution so terrifying to the nineteenth-century American public, and would continue to threaten generations to come. In fact, it was in Tennessee, not so far from Shelbyville, not so many years away, that the big legal fight over the teaching of evolution in the schools, known forever as the "monkey trials," would pit a schoolteacher against the Holy Bible and the wrath of the nation.

In the antebellum South a similar kind of fear had been used to justify slavery and brutality, as though the wrong of the institution was somehow mitigated by the belief that the black race was intellectually inferior. The terrifying proposition that people of color could have equal or superior intelligence was why black education and literacy posed such a threat long after slavery was abolished. Dr. Key had certainly known this when he and Jim traveled the South selling Keystone Liniment, when the point was to entertain and sell his products, not to promote the fact that he and his horse might just be more literate than most folks in the crowd. For the generations and classes who never learned to read and for those people who could not write their own names, fear more than anything else was the reason to dismiss the sight of a horse who could spell, do math, and draw his name in cursive on a chalkboard. Of course it was a trick, or voodoo, or the same funny stuff that horse in Germany was up to.

Albert Rogers and William Key knew little about Clever Hans, although Herr von Osten had undoubtedly heard and read about Jim, both through the German newspapers from Pittsburg and the international press coverage of world's fairs. These sources may have first prompted him to train Hans.

In the meantime, as insurance to distinguish Beautiful Jim Key from his competitors, Rogers continued to stress in his press materials that it was the audience members who asked the questions and that reporters were allowed to interview Jim alone. Just to assure the public that he wasn't in cahoots with the press, he went further, encouraging well-known, honorable citizens to visit Beautiful Jim Key without his trainer or grooms being present, and then to report their findings, positive or not. It was also at this time that instead of staying at inns and public stables when traveling, Jim and his entourage were typically invited to reside temporarily at the fine estates of some of these prominent types, many of whom were officers of humane societies or politicians, or both. Such stays were good both for publicity and for making sure that Dr. Key and the Davis brothers, if they were along, were not subjected to rude treatment based on color—which could happen in any hotel or stables, in any city.

In Detroit, Michigan, for example, the troupe stayed with Senator T. W. Palmer, president of Detroit's Humane Society, former president of the board of commissioners of the Chicago World's Fair, and one of the richest men in the state of Michigan. Senator Palmer reported that he went to see Jim in the stables and asked his human attendants to leave, agreeing to have Monk stand by:

> *I then asked him how much five times six less four was, and . . . he hunted out the figure twenty-six. No one knew what I was going to ask, nor I, myself, thirty seconds before I propounded the sum. If this was not done by logical process, how was it done? I am thoroughly convinced that the horse reasons. . . . Jim Key is doing a great work, not only for the children, but for all those who are not too old to learn.*

There were other anecdotes that boggled the mind for any explanation other than that Jim was listening and thinking, like the time he was playing store and a man in the audience asked the horse, "Can you change two bits?"

Beautiful Jim Key shook his head from side to side. He had no idea what that meant.

Doc Key allowed himself to translate. "He means a quarter, Jim."

A quarter? Oh, that was easy. Jim brought out the correct change without hesitation.

Perhaps if Jim's only claim to fame had been his intellect, his abilities could have been disputed with the argument of the Clever Hans effect. But Beautiful Jim Key was much more than a horse with or without provable cognitive talents. He was a celebrity, a thespian, a comedian, a standard-bearer, a hero. He was a horse with a rags-to-riches storied past. And he was the prodigy of Dr. William Key, whose own saga of overcoming the odds had caused a ripple effect on contemporary culture.

When the Doc began appearing on the most respectable stages of music halls and opera houses of the nation, he represented an anomaly, a cross between an authority and an entertainer who happened to be African-American. In that context, Dr. William Key, now known to hundreds of thousands, if not already a few million, white Americans, was probably regarded as one of the most famous Negroes of his day. This was in part by accident, not a goal to which he particularly aspired in his later years, but he was also the beneficiary of over a century of struggle by black leaders as orators and authority figures, and by black entertainers breaking down barriers in music, dance, comedy, and drama.

Doc Key knew there were only certain roles that black performers were typically allowed to play. Some of the blame for the exploitation of African-Americans onstage could be laid directly at the feet of P. T. Barnum, who had made his first fortune exhibiting sideshow Siamese twins, giants, dwarves, and so on, who were all black. Bill Key might have wondered at the irony that while it was common to ridicule and deride Negroes, more than a few white performers became famous by acting black. He'd seen that from the early days of minstrelsy, when white singers like Dan Emmett became rich by smearing their faces with burnt cork and appropriating black music. One of Emmett's signature songs, "Jump Jim Crow," was borrowed from another white minstrel in blackface who'd picked up the tune, lyrics, and dance steps from a slave boy who was singing it while dancing a jig on a street corner. Emmett's best known song, "Dixie," which became the anthem of the Confederacy, very ironically, was originally written by the songwriting and singing Snowden family, free Negroes who lived in the North. Even while black minstrel singers and comedians created their own troupes in the later decades of the 1800s, some continuing to use burnt cork and some getting rid of it—like the band that the Doc put together to help him sell Keystone Liniment—white performers continued to portray stock Negro characters either in blackface or without, well into the days of radio and early television.

After the staged version of *Uncle Tom's Cabin* was debuted in 1853, Negro singers and performers were cast only in chorus roles and sometimes forced to sing behind a scrim, while white actors in blackface were cast in the lead roles. That didn't change until 1877, when a white traveling *Tom* show became stranded in Kentucky without the white star and the producer had a brainstorm: why not have a real Negro play Uncle Tom? Black actor and musician Sam Lucas stepped into the role to such success that other productions soon began casting Negroes in the other lead roles too.

Daring African-American theatre companies devoted to the classics had been established in the early 1800s in New York and had inspired the likes of Ira Aldridge, the legendary Negro actor who became a star tragedian in England and throughout Europe, revered for his performances as Othello, as well as King Lear and Macbeth. And finally, at the turn of the century, musical comedies performed by all-black companies, written and composed by African-Americans, were coming into their heyday. Musical and theatrical greats like Bob Cole, Bert Williams, Will Marion Cook, and J. Rosamond Johnson collaborated with poets such as James Weldon Johnson and Paul Laurence Dunbar to create works that gained enormous popularity with white audiences. Like the self-deprecating songs and skits of black minstrelsy, some of the early black musical comedies, songs, and their stars (billing themselves as "Two Real Coons") were later accused of continuing to reinforce negative or exaggerated African-American stereotypes. Nonetheless, the productions employed growing numbers of black performers, no longer in blackface, and were responsible for first portraying ladies and gentlemen of color as beautiful and stylish, with all the social graces of their time.

African-American music, above all, had eroded the national resistance to having a good time. The seeded field of black traditions that turned into gospel, blues, jazz, rock and roll, and probably every popular musical form to grow out of the United States, had burst into bloom right at the time of the St. Louis World's Fair. It was known as ragtime. Though its syncopated rhythm had been imported from Africa, it was germinated in American soil and captured the feeling of the changing era more than any art form. Even before the Louisiana Purchase Exposition opened, everyone was asking whether there would be ragtime at the fair. John Philip Sousa, in a front-page *St. Louis Dispatch* story, "spoke enthusiastically of the prospects of ragtime programs." He did say, however, that no "bad ragtime" would be performed, noting, "good ragtime delights the heart and is the characteristic of the American people. There is bad classic music as well as bad ragtime but neither will be heard on the Exposition grounds."

With ragtime coming into its heyday, along with black entertainers and orators gaining mainstream followings, William Key was better able to attain the rapid acceptance he did in mostly all-white performance halls. On the other hand, he was not an actor, singer, or even a comedian, although he obviously used humor in his shows. Nor was he an authority in the same mold as the African-American leaders, ministers, and professionals who spoke in front of white audiences. He was, as usual, a hybrid, an interloper. Therefore, using common sense, or horse sense—the phrase every newspaper account of Jim had to throw in—Doc Key did his best to use his platform to promote his values of kindness and education, to entertain while he was at it, and, in his capacity as an accidental role model, to comport himself with a dignity that would positively reflect on fellow Negroes and himself.

Dr. Key and Jim Key were cultural icons. That's what Albert Rogers believed. So for the Louisiana Purchase Exposition to snub them was unacceptable. He had to do something. In November 1903, he plied the one connection he had refrained from pursuing all this time, a contact, "HDC," over at the *World*, Pulitzer's newspaper with tentacles that reached to St. Louis. A copy of the telegram HDC sent to St. Louis a few days later reached Rogers back in New York:

> *Dear Lincoln: This will introduce you to my particular friend, Mr. A. R. Rogers. Please do all you can to put him in touch with everybody he wants to know, that you know. Anything you do for him I will take as a personal favor. He has a big scheme on in connection with the Fair and may want to meet your friend Sexton.*

Albert's scheme resulted first in a new endorsement deal with the National Cash Register Company, the early sponsor that had been replaced by Metropolitan Cash Register. In return for leaving Metropolitan and its nickel-plated cash register that Jim had employed in his shows, Rogers agreed that the Equine Wonder would once again appear in NCR ads to promote its products and would welcome a new thousand-dollar gold-plated National Cash Register to use in his show. And there was something else. Albert Rogers convinced National Cash Register to pay for the construction of Jim's pavilion at the fair. Corporate sponsorship, why not?

There was another part to this scheme: a lengthy AP story was run at the end of November 1903 in countless newspapers and read by an estimated ten million readers about Beautiful Jim Key and the expectation that he would be at the World's Fair in St. Louis.

The concession was immediately granted.

M aggie Davis Key was thirty-nine years old when she made the trip to St. Louis, Missouri, traveling with her husband, Dr. William Key (sixty-six according to his publicist but actually seventy-one), along with Jim Key (either eleven or thirteen, depending on whom you asked, despite the fact he'd been foaled fifteen years earlier), his canine guardian Monk (age unknown), and Maggie's two brothers, twenty-five-year-old Dr. Stanley Davis and twenty-four-year-old Samuel Davis.

Dr. and Mrs. William Key had been married under a month, an event they had postponed a few times due to the Doctor's touring schedule, so in a way this was a kind of honeymoon. Maggie was a serene, handsome woman, with sculpted cheekbones, bronze coloring, and, like Stanley and Sam, other strong Native American traits. Possibly from that side of her heritage, she held to the belief that the camera could rob the soul and almost always refused to sit for photographs. Because the special passes issued for the World's Fair were designed as mock passports—with visas from the various buildings stamped on subsequent pages to show which lands had been visited—photographs were required, so Mrs. Maggie Key acquiesced to having her picture taken. For the wonders she was about to witness, she would never regret it.

Nor did Doc Key regret for a second his decision to come out of his brief retirement. The Louisiana Purchase Exposition was the real pinnacle of his adventures, never to be rivaled. And part of the reason for the sense of fulfillment this fair gave him undoubtedly was his ability to share it with Maggie. Quiet, private, studious, she was the perfect woman for him at this stage of his life, someone who ultimately preferred the slower pace of Bedford County, where they would return in the winter, possibly for good, yet who could also enjoy and appreciate being part of Jim's extraordinary ride.

Apparently, Jim Key was as fond of Maggie as he had been of her older sister, and he had his own way of communicating with the new Mrs. Key, which the Doc was glad to see. Not that he anticipated an imminent demise, but it was still reassuring to know that if the Lord took him before Jim went, Maggie would give good comfort to his dearest friend. Monk took an even more proprietary stance toward Mrs. Key than he did toward his equine charge. Besides keeping reporters and unauthorized individuals away from Jim, the black-and-white wiry-haired hound gave himself the added duties of protecting Maggie from photographers; they were then forced to take twice as many pictures of him.

The journey by train from Shelbyville to Nashville, where Jim's entourage transferred to a locomotive bound for St. Louis, allowed the travelers to explore the breathtaking new Union Station on Broad Street, which had opened in 1900. Built in the Romanesque style favored in earlier decades—a simple, imposing look founded in heavy, natural rock and masonry, with rounded arches throughout, all to exude a sense of grandeur and permanence—the station also boasted original, modern touches that Dr. and Mrs. Key marveled at. There was the statue of fleet-footed Mercury at the top of the tallest tower, an incomparable digital clock in the clock tower, and the two alligator pools at track level in which diminutive, reportedly well-treated alligators swam about and watched humans in their frenetic comings and goings. The true beauty was inside the station, where the ticket counters and waiting rooms were housed. Gilded murals of mythological figures (including scantily clad goddesses with faces superimposed to represent Miss Louisville and Miss Nashville in homage to the L&N) gave the four-story hall a golden glow that caused the multicolored mosaic marble floor to sparkle gloriously. It was undoubtedly as spectacular a piece of architecture as anything Dr. Key had seen in his worldly wanderings.

As they say in Tennessee and other parts, to have beheld the sights of the St. Louis World's Fair was to have lived and died and gone to heaven. Maggie certainly prized the memories and took them home with her, sharing them in detail with her sister-in-law, Essie Campbell Davis, Samuel's future wife. The Campbell dynasty of Bedford County was another entrepreneurial African-American lineage, and the Campbell-Davis match seemed to please everyone. The stories that Maggie told her sister-in-law were later passed on from Essie to a future generation of Davises and Campbells.

Maggie, like the almost twenty million other visitors to the Louisiana Purchase Exposition, witnessed an idealized preview of the century to come, with demonstrations of fantastic technologies and inventions that sooner or later would be common tools found in most American households. Appliances on exhibit were electric and steam heaters, copper boilers, knife sharpeners, candy machines, air conditioners, bread-making machines, electric and gas stoves, and electric dishwashers; also new were T-shirts, automatic player pianos, and, of course, ice cream cones and iced tea.

The St. Louis World's Fair marked a turning point in the recognition of the buying power of American women. Though women were still sixteen years away from winning the right to vote, the women's movement was gaining ground, evidenced even in the new fashions showing up at the fair. As corsets loosened and simpler, less-ornate dresses filled the racks, an entire gender must have breathed a collective sigh of relief, Maggie Davis Key among them, as did Clara Rogers.

Albert rarely brought his wife and three sons on his travels, but he knew that the world's fair would be something they would relish. Fifteen-year-old Clarence and thirteen-year-old Newell were put to work at the box office while eight-year-old Archie was looked after by his pal Stanley.

Opening Day, Saturday, April 30, 1904, brought in an estimated 200,000 visitors, breaking the attendance record of 186,672 set at the 1876 Philadelphia World's Fair for the greatest number of first-day admissions to any exposition. As the *St. Louis Dispatch* reported the next day with a blaring headline: "The Greatest of World's Fairs Impressively Opened." No one seemed to notice the haphazard choreography in which President Roosevelt turned the gold key in the White House that shot the electric current across the country before the oratory was finished, or that the flags unfurled at only half-mast, or that Director of Works Taylor stood up to speak with a hat too small for his head, since it belonged to fair president David Francis. The jubilance of the spectators and participants trumped all.

In a self-congratulatory stupor, the *Dispatch* ran a cartoon show-ing the different regional reactions to the fair. Beside a scowling man in a bowler the caption read "Chicago for once felt eclipsed," and next to an undecided upper-crust lady was "Cold, critical and from Boston. Of course." No less convinced was an old geezer whose description was simply "He's from Vermont," while a purse-lipped, top-hat-wearing gentleman had the caption "The New Yorker's eyes were opened." The man with the spectacles and fingers plugging his ears had a reaction that was "Too much for staid Philadelphia," and then there was the beaming fellow whose caption said simply "Just a native."

In addition to the Alice Roosevelt incident powering the gossip mill, Beautiful Jim Key made the newspaper coverage of Opening Day in two lead stories. The first was a feature on the five divisions of the Pike parade, in which he appeared, naturally, in the lead divi-sion. The second was a feature on the front page of the amusement section about the stampede of fairgoers on the Pike, even though it was far from completed:

> The street is roughly paved as yet, heavy hauling having worn great holes in the brick coating over a soft clay foundation, and flying paper and dust mingle with piles of timber and scaffold-ing to give the place an unfinished air. But not withstanding the debris . . . the Pike was literally jammed.

Most of the attractions that weren't completed yet gave free passes for Opening Day only, for a "taste of the good things to come," while it was noted that "Jim Key, the educated horse, was one of the few attractions ready for business."

The Silver Horseshoe Building on the Pike was a far cry from the horse-shaped extravaganza that Albert Rogers had previously envi-sioned, though it was appropriately fanciful and beckoning, with its western theme and portraits of Jim at a lectern and hovered over his National Cash Register. Instead of hiring a barker, Albert decided to bring on the famous clown Gordon Bunch to the Jim Key ensemble. Though not really needed to draw in crowds, he was an entertain-ing addition nonetheless. After all the trouble Rogers had faced in getting Jim booked at the fair, he took obvious glee in printing a midsummer edition of the Beautiful Jim Key promotional pamphlet that announced:

> The phenomenal success of Wonderful Jim Key at this exposition has been a surprise to all those who have builded [*sic*] the great shows of the Pike, many of which cost over $100,000. His beautiful theatre is crowded day and night, and though the price of admission was raised from 15 cents to 25 cents it made no difference. Jim Key is proving to be not only the most popular and best attended of all the attractions on the Pike, but will undoubtedly make the most money, net, of them all for his owner.

Albert was pushing. Why, Dr. Key probably didn't know. Maybe Albert himself didn't know. Then, again, his claim that Beautiful Jim Key was the most profitable concession at the St. Louis World's Fair was true. The cost of producing the one-horse and one-man show was negligible compared with what most concessionaires spent just to open their doors. Moreover, with Dr. William Key's consummate salesmanship, Beautiful Jim Key merchandise added to the profits, portions of which were donated to humane organizations. New souvenirs debuted at the fair, among them the Silver Horseshoe Building on the Pike's special edition postcards, gold Jim Key pinbacks, and miniature Jim Key National Cash Register replica banks that were all the rage. The old-fashioned large souvenir buttons with their "I have seen Beautiful Jim Key" message seemed a thing of the past.

The Exposition itself was fortunate to do a little better than break even. After its original bid of fifteen million dollars had tripled, its scope expanded to cover more than 1,200 acres, seventy-five miles of walkways, more than 1,500 buildings, and a network of roadway and waterway transportation. The Central Cascades cost one million dollars to create. The Palace of Fine Arts had a price tag many times that and was one of only two buildings to survive the Exposition. The most-talked-about exhibit of the entire fair was deemed to be the U.S. Government Building, memorable for its walk-through gargantuan-scale birdcage filled with every family of bird found in America; it too lived on after the fair.

Whatever was bothering Rogers didn't mar the feeling of triumph that Jim and Bill seemed to experience in what should have been their swan song. The Doc was not able to witness Booker T. Washington's address to the National Educational Association on Thursday, June 30, at 11 A.M., but afterward the two reconnected after having met on previous occasions. Washington gave Key the original copy of the speech, which began with thoughts similar to those the Doctor had been having:

> Every nation, race and each generation has its own special and peculiar problems. Each group of people in each period of its existence is likely to feel and argue that its difficulties are the most trying and serious. We often forget that if one generation could settle all the difficulties there would be little left for the succeeding one to do. For 250 years and more, one of the questions that has interested and permeated every section of American life has had to do with the presence and influence of the black people in America.

Maybe these words helped Dr. Key understand that though he could not cure all the ills of the world, he had played his part to fix some things. As the fair wound its way to its conclusion, he seemed to find the peace of mind that made him indicate he was now ready to go home with Maggie and say good-bye to public life. But was Jim ready to take his final bow?

The St. Louis World's Fair had brought the Equine Millionaire a relentless string of fans and famous friends, from encounters with his old costar John Philip Sousa to his celebrated encounter with Alice Roosevelt, along with Vice President Taft and his wife, cabinet members, multitudes of state governors, and foreign dignitaries. Beautiful Jim Key met them, spelled their names, answered their questions, approved or disapproved of their politics, and began predicting election outcomes. No account emerged over whether or not he met Helen Keller when she appeared at the World's Fair, but their proximity and presumed familiarity with each other suggests that a meeting would have been arranged. Their stories had overlapping messages. Both were born with something "wrong." Both had miracle-working teachers who employed kindness, love, patience, and ingenuity to unlock their innate intelligence.

As far as Albert Rogers was concerned, the Louisiana Purchase Exposition planners had been proven wrong. Beautiful Jim Key, besides making more money than any concession on the Pike, also showed that he could still capture headlines and the hearts of the multitudes. Rogers felt confident claiming that at least as many as five million fairgoers saw Beautiful Jim Key, or around a fourth of the total admissions sold to the fair. For seven months, with shows running from nine in the morning to ten at night, six days a week, the Marvel of the Twentieth Century never faltered, never tired. Rogers's numbers were not scientifically reached—and his book-keeping proved to be fuzzy—but what was certain was that the St. Louis World's Fair had solidified Jim's place in history as a celebrity, his education and humane work aside.

Yet just to make sure those contributions were not forgotten, Beautiful Jim Key was further immortalized in a children's book published in the fall of 1904. Entitled *Master St. Elmo: The Autobiography of a Celebrated Dog*, it was written by Caro Senour as "ghostwriter" for her educated, world-traveled English greyhound, who narrates a series of true-life adventures and epiphanies that culminate with a visit to the fair. Dedicating the book to Beautiful Jim Key, as well as its three final chapters, the dog-as-author confessed toward the end that he became concerned that if his starstruck mistress had remained at the World's Fair much longer, she would have either eloped with Jim or spent all her money attending his shows.

While his mistress took special delight in Jim's mathematical calculations, she was dewy-eyed over his recognition of biblical quotations and how easily he chose the correct card with the book and verse printed on it. Master St. Elmo also gave a rare description of Jim's use of his telephone, writing, "The telephone is on the wall, and he walks up to it, takes the handle in his mouth, and turns the handle around so that you can hear the bell ring, then he places his mouth to the mouth piece, and his master takes the receiver and holds it to his ear." Jim flapped his jaw and made chewing motions to simulate his phone chat until he heard the Doc say good-bye, his cue to hang up and mug to the audience.

Curiously enough, St. Elmo acknowledged that the special canine passport he received to enter the fairgrounds had been arranged by his cousin "Bert." There was no identification of this cousin as the same A. R. Rogers who published the excellent little booklet that St. Elmo and Senour plugged in the fall of 1904:

I hope that after readers have become acquainted with this wonder-ful horse, they will think of him always, and help all poor animals who are in need of homes and kind treatment, and above all report all cases which they may see of abuse of horses, either by whipping them or by making them draw overloaded wagons. And try to keep water in your yards for the dogs, cats, and birds, and do what you can to have watering-places for horses in the streets. . . . There is a little book of his life and how he was taught, which one can buy for fifteen cents by sending to Mr. A. R. Rogers, 75 Maiden Lane, New York City. Long live Beautiful Jim Key!

Regardless of any connection, by 1905, with another busy season lining up, to which Key and Key could not yet say no, Albert Rogers put out a press release in celebration of the eleventh edition of the ever-evolving booklet that had now sold over 200,000 copies. More than 600,000 members had joined the Jim Key Band of Mercy, while another one million individuals had signed the Jim Key pledge. The booklet, illustrated now with twenty-five halftones, proclaimed the inimitable A. R. Rogers, was without a doubt "as interesting as *Black Beauty*."

The year 1905 was a record-breaking one for Sarah Bernhardt, the legendary French actress with her "golden bell" of a voice, who had bewitched a generation and who was promising to spend 1906 in an unprecedented, nonstop, sixty-two-city farewell tour. Enrico Caruso and John Philip Sousa were likewise toppling competition from their musical contemporaries in the same year, while Will Rogers stepped onto the scene. In the wake of *The Great Train Robbery* and nickelodeons opening up in major cities, the motion picture era was dawning.

But 1905 was a rocky year for Beautiful Jim Key.

For starters, though Dr. Key never admitted it, his own health clearly wasn't what it had been. He began bringing a chair onstage and sitting to the side once members of the audience began their questioning. He also was a newlywed and probably wanted to be in Tennessee, where Maggie was most of that year. But Jim wouldn't hear of the possibility of retirement. And when the Doc even raised it hypothetically, the eternally energetic stallion suddenly became so depressed that he took to his stall, stumbling as he feigned the onset of lameness the way he did in their shows, and then plopped down on his side, refusing food or conversation. Not even Monk could get his attention.

The Doctor wasn't fooled. Jim was pretending that he was only pretending to be in pain. Upon examination, Bill confirmed that the sixteen-year-old superstar had been masking a lot more pain than he was letting on. The description of rheumatism in Doc Key's dependable *Bell's Hand-book to Veterinary Homeopathy* (with remedies to order from Bell's Homeopathic Pharmacy, 8 Vesey Street in New York) was straightforward: "A painful condition with tension and lameness in the affected part." Since it wasn't acute—which would have been "generally accompanied with fever, more or less, swelling"—the prognosis wasn't dire. Dr. Key certainly assured the ailing star that he was going to be fine in no time, and that no decision to retire would be made without a *Y-E-S* from Jim.

If this had been onstage, Beautiful Jim Key would have bounded back to his feet and done his own famous two-step. But this wasn't an act.

William Key watched Jim try to struggle then and there to his feet, much in the way he had as a spindly, shank-legged colt. The desperation and panic in Jim's eyes must have nearly torn him in two, but the Doc showed no worry of his own as he tried to coax him up. Doc Key reverted to the old way of communicating, turning away and back, at such a stance that asked without words: *How can I help? Teach me how to help you.*

Jim replied in gesture and gaze: *Give me a boost!* He suggested in this nonverbal way that Doc Key catch him under his tail and pull him up.

It worked. Once up on his feet, Jim was seemingly out of pain and as nimble as a youngster. And that, for the time being, put an end to any retirement plans.

The annual report from the American Humane Association meeting might have validated other reasons to carry on. The work done by Key, Key, and Rogers continued to make waves. In the past year alone, Bill read, the member societies had collectively investigated nearly seventy thousand cases of cruelty to animals and over twenty-two thousand reports of child abuse. Societies had been formed where there had been none, and the memberships of local and regional groups were swelling. More and more officers were women, a most fitting development.

So onward they forged, cutting a wider swath across the country, appearing in places they had never been and returning to many cities and states for second and third encores. Jim now had a collection of keys to cities that he kept attached to a big stallion-size wooden key and had a ceremony ready for whenever keys were presented to him. His collection included keys to Newark, Philadelphia, Boston, Cleveland, Atlanta, Omaha, Detroit, Baltimore, Kansas City, St. Louis, Birmingham, New Orleans, Charleston, Syracuse, Columbus, and Atlantic City. In addition to spending several months again at Young's Pier, the entourage was engaged for two months at Chicago's million-dollar renovated White City, a full-fledged amusement park, while also giving regular benefits there on behalf of the Illinois Humane Society.

The year's successes would have made any promoter and any champion of animal welfare proud. But Albert Rogers was not any promoter or any animal rights champion. He wanted to continue to grow, to reach higher heights, not to level off, or worse, coast on past glory. The problem, from a promotional perspective, was the press. Reporters might not have come out and said so, but it was obvious to Albert that they didn't see *his* Beautiful Jim Key as a hot news item anymore. And more and more, he was releasing defensive-sounding press statements that referred to "my horse" and "my Beautiful Jim Key." Again the resistance had to do with the sense that the Equine Millionaire had been overexposed. They had written about him from every possible angle. What more could be said? But there was another timbre he began to hear in their rejections. There was something of yesteryear about his horse, a quaint, sweet fairy tale that no one could disprove, with its message of kindness and patience, and the virtue of his missionary zeal. But this was a different day, a changing mood. Readers wanted sizzle and zing, scandal and mayhem, not sugar and rosy red apples.

A. R. Rogers was not a man to go down without a fight, and he vowed to show them all that they were wrong. But then, after he had pulled every string at his disposal to obtain new press during Jim's summer at White City, he became quite unnerved when the best he could manage was just the one article that resulted in the *Chicago Daily Journal:*

> *Beautiful Jim Key is truly a wonderful horse, and Cummins Indian Congress does some good stunts in Custer's Last Stand. But the thing that caught the crowd was the "Bumps." They must be seen first and then tried before they can be appreciated. It is Shooting-the-Chutes that have warts on them. The cars are strips of cloth and the water is a surging mass of humanity gathered around to enjoy the fun.*

The Bumps? Rogers was insulted. He envisioned this chink in the armor as potentially serious. If not halted, it could lead to the crumbling of the empire he had created. More than money was at stake. This was his reputation, his standing as a philanthropist, as the vice president of the American Humane Education Society and as Uncle Bert, president of the Jim Key Band of Mercy. As though by some sort of self-fulfilling prophecy, around this time he began to get hints that in fact the officers of the American Humane Education Society wanted him to step down. George Angell was increasingly a figurehead, turning over decisions to his board of directors, and they seemed not to trust Rogers. They patronized him and his ideas, he felt; President Stillman of the board of directors of the AHA had even questioned his motivations by dryly signing off one response: "I take it for granted that you are somewhat interested in humanitarian work for its own sake as well as in the commercial side of your exhibition."

Rogers grew more frantic as the year progressed. He wrote to complain to George Angell about the way certain individuals dragged their heels when planning a benefit, describing one society lady: "She is like a person on a raft in the middle of the ocean and don't know which way to paddle." Of course, he assured Angell, he would handle everything. Angell wrote back with his trademark encouragement, suggesting that Albert also pursue other channels.

In the midst of this flurry of correspondence, a late-breaking scandal hit the news, something with zing and sizzle—the managers of the St. Louis World's Fair were investigating allegations of wrongdoing in the awards department. The National Cash Register Company was implicated because it appeared that they had bribed an official, although that claim too was eventually tossed. Caught up in the investigation, Rogers was then accused of contract infringement, related allegedly to underreporting profits, and he was fined a whopping $2,300.

Albert Rogers cried foul as he turned his attention to the activities of the Jim Key Band of Mercy by sending out his own newsletter from "Uncle Bert." His first issue's reminder was an impassioned plea. With the conviction of one who had found religion, he wrote:

> Remember that animals feel just as keenly as human beings do, that the flesh and the bones of a dog or cat are just as tender as your own. It hurts them to be struck or handled roughly as much as it would you yourself. Try to protect all animals as much as you can. If you see anyone ill-treating them, do not hesitate to ask them to stop doing so, and tell them that you are a member of a Band of Mercy, and they will treat animals with more kindness and there will be less cruelty in the world.

Dr. Key and Jim applauded his message and the effort of the newsletter. But Doc Key didn't know what to make of the next ideas that Rogers brought to him. They were the two wildest schemes their promoter had conjured yet.

The first was a traditional kind of publicity stunt but with a twist. The plan was to buy out all the passenger seats of a Santa Fe Railroad locomotive from Dallas to San Antonio and to call it the "Beautiful Jim Key Express." Fans could purchase coaches, sleepers, and baggage cars to take the twelve-hour trip with Jim, allowing them one-on-one visits with the star in his palace car, and be part of his royal procession when he greeted the crowds along the way. It was the worst idea Dr. Key had heard from A. R. Rogers. But instead of saying so, he went along with it, proposing offhandedly that while in San Antonio he wanted to take Jim Key to the sulfur baths he knew of there.

This was the first Albert Rogers had heard of Jim's worsening condition. Now he was morose. This risky train trip could well be the last engagement he ever planned for Jim. But Doc Key calmly soothed his fears, telling him that the symptoms were periodic, and that they reasonably had another five good years of performing and touring in both of them. The main thing was to avoid cold weather in the wintertime.

Rogers then unveiled his second scheme. From March through November of 1906, he would promote a tour to rival Sarah Bernhardt's Farewell Tour. The Doctor and Beautiful Jim Key would be booked at every Music Hall or Opera House in the country and set new box office records at every stop. In an analogy to turf champions, which neither Rogers nor Key could ever resist, it would be Jim's own Triple Crown, his championship season, with each performance hall substituting for a famous track, a kind of year-long race against the likes of Bernhardt, Sousa, and Caruso, the big box office draws. There could even be bets taken before each engagement as to whether Beautiful Jim Key could break that particular record. And, no matter what, the attention created would prove to the press, once and forever, that Jim Key was truly the greatest star of the twentieth century.

William Key wasn't sure. He loved the concept. But he knew it would be grueling. Would he be putting Jim's health at risk? Or would he be giving him the opportunity to have his name placed in history? Speaking frankly, the Doc agreed to do it, but at a significant raise for himself, and for Stanley and Sam, effective immediately. Albert was apparently surprised by the amount of money and by the terms, but he didn't argue, turning his attention instead to the logistics for each of his new plans.

The first scheme turned out to be a flop. Maybe the Texas public had enough smart horses of their own, or maybe they'd all been to the St. Louis World's Fair. Whatever the reason, the Beautiful Jim Key Express that ran on October 29, 1905, failed to get any press and far from the number of tickets sold that Albert Rogers would have liked. The only good to come of it was the sulfur baths, which seemed to do wonders for Jim.

After making up some of their losses in New Orleans, Jim Key and company returned to Nashville's Union Station and prepared to part ways for the winter. As Stanley and Sam led Jim and Monk toward the train that would take the Shelbyville contingency home, Dr. Key asked Rogers if he could have a word.

Rogers, running late as was his habit, may have known that the subject the Doctor wanted to address was money. After the embarrassment in Texas and other money issues plaguing him at the time, he was in no mood. The train for Cincinnati was already boarding when, without speaking a word, he hurriedly wrote out a check and handed it to Dr. Key.

Barely looking at it, the Doc shook his head and refused to take it, saying money was what he wanted to talk about. Visibly exasperated, Rogers shrugged, put the check in his bag, pointed to his watch, and dashed off down the platform, promising over his shoulder to be in touch later.

It had been many years and a few lifetimes since anyone had caused Bill Key to lose his temper. But if there was one thing he couldn't tolerate, it was disrespect. Days later he composed the only typed letter he ever sent to Albert Rogers:

Dear Sir: Your letter in which you enclose check on Orange, N.J. bank for $250.00 was received today. I herewith return the check of $250.00 as I am satisfied there is a misunderstanding in regard to it.

My proposition to you was very plane and simple, and was this, that you pay me the sum of $2750.00 and all expenses, as heretofore, the sum of $250.00 cash to be paid upon closing contract, and $2500.00 to be paid in monthly installments from 3/1/1906 to 12/1/1906. I stated to you when you offered me the check of $250.00 and the expenses in addition at the depot, that I must have 2500.00 and all expenses in addition, to the check which I declined to take. In your haste to get on the cars at the Depot here you would not give me a chance to go into details.

In making you this proposition, my services and those of my horse, "Jim Key" will be rendered you just the same as I did at the St. Louis Exposition, and at White City, Chicago, with no privileges taken from me that I had at both St. Louis and Chicago. If you accept this proposition you must do so by the 25th of November 1905. . . . My proposition does not hold open for your acceptance letter later than Nov. 25, 1905. I also want 5 per cent on the books sold same as at White City. I will faithfully discharge my duty in talking up the book, and running the show to your interest. Yours truly, Wm Key

p.s. Stanley and Sam will write you

There was no mistaking William Key's language. Jim Key was *his* horse.

The suspense began on February 26, 1906, at the Cincinnati Music Hall. After what must have been an immediate response from Rogers, maybe followed by a trip to Shelbyville to smooth over the misunderstanding in person, a total of ten top venues were secured, at all of which a person of significant note had previously set record-breaking box office numbers.

At seventeen years old, but not looking a day over twelve, Jim Key received a headline-making reception at the train station when he strode along the platform with Monk on his back, perched there contemplating the impressive size of the waving, cheering crowd. Jim's clown, Gordon Bunch, went ahead of the group to help part the seas, as Dr. Key, flanked by Stanley and Samuel, followed behind Bunch, leading Jim.

There had obviously been much discussion between the Doc and Jim Key about the importance of enjoying themselves. The last thing the trainer wanted to do was put undue pressure on Jim or to endanger his health. The two made a pact that if, at any point, either one of them wasn't feeling up to the task, a show could be canceled, or they could finish up the tour wherever they were in the season. Did Jim understand? Dr. Key was sure he did, even though he wasn't so convinced that Jim would actually admit to being in pain. But from what the Doctor could see here at the outset, Beautiful Jim Key radiated health and vitality.

Over the next several weeks, anyone who'd been game enough to bet A. R. Rogers that Jim would fall short of expectations was forced to pay up. Jim surpassed anything Rogers could have dreamed, and made Bill Key more proud than he'd ever been. The Smartest Horse in the World, his latest moniker, stunned those he'd already stunned. He had never been wittier, never more dramatic, never wiser, never nobler. Everywhere he went, he made them laugh and he made them cry.

A new addition to the show, the pretty Miss Agnetta Floris had come from the head office of the American Humane Association in Boston to help Albert Rogers further organize the membership of the Jim Key Band of Mercy, whose numbers were soon to approach the goal of one million that Uncle Bert had set five years earlier. (One newspaper reported that Rogers had hired five secretaries and a few "minor clerks" just to respond to Jim's fan mail.) Miss Floris not only gave a short introduction onstage about humane values but also made the rounds of schools in each city they played, reinforcing the message of kindness to all creatures. Her other duties were to officiate onstage during any spelling bees and writing competitions. Her addition to the show was a smart move on the part of Rogers for several reasons, but especially because she gave reporters their new angle to write about.

Plus, Miss Floris was easy on the eyes. Whenever she was onstage, Jim bowed to her with an Ira Aldridge–styled Shakespearean flourish. When Miss Floris left the stage, he looked longingly after her before turning his attention back to the audience. When she spoke about the different ways to protect those who couldn't protect themselves, Jim had a way of scanning the audience to make sure everyone was paying attention. He had attained the elusive quality that only real superstars ever master: intimacy. He made each and every person feel a special connection to him, as though he had a secret belonging to that individual, who could then call him *my* Beautiful Jim Key. Much like a racehorse whose number they had chosen to win, his audience members had an emotional investment in his victories, and he could feel them roaring for him, egging him on.

The numbers, with an average of 50 percent of net going to humane charities, spoke for themselves:

- Music Hall, Cincinnati, Ohio—The week of February 26, 1906. Seating capacity 4,000; twenty-eight performances sold out. Broke record for paid admissions.
- Memorial Hall, Columbus, Ohio—March 4 through March 8, 1906. Seating capacity 3,000; fifteen performances sold out. Broke record for paid admissions.
- Tomlinson Hall, Indianapolis, Indiana—The week of March 12, 1906. Seating capacity 2,000; thirty performances sold out. Broke record for paid admissions.
- Convention Hall, Kansas City, Missouri—March 19 through March 21, 1906. Largest-seating auditorium in the world; Jim declared by Louis W. Shouse, manager of the Convention Hall, "to hold the world's record for drawing a greater crowd than any single attraction that was ever exhibited."

In 1905, one year earlier, Sarah Bernhardt had performed *Camille* at the Kansas City Convention Hall to an audience of 6,500.

The box office record there had been set in 1899 by John Philip Sousa, when he commanded an audience of 16,500. On March 20, 1906, Beautiful Jim Key played to 18,000, and the following night he broke his own record when he filled the massive hall with 22,000. In three days, total admissions were 52,804.

- Tootle Theatre, St. Joseph, Missouri—March 22–23, 1906. Seating capacity 1,500; ten performances. Packed houses; broke record for paid admissions. "Captured the city!"
- Omaha Auditorium, Omaha, Nebraska—March 26 through March 29, 1906. Seating capacity 3,000; sixteen performances. Broke record for paid admissions.
- Auditorium, Minneapolis, Minnesota—Week of April 2. Seating capacity of 2,500; twenty performances. "Packed every time." Broke record for paid admissions.

Jim made the editorial page of the *Omaha World Herald* in a column entitled "The Horse and the Boy," which contrasted the upbringing of the famous equine with that of Jay O'Hearn, a local boy convicted of murder:

> Suppose our boys and girls were all trained as Jim Key has been trained; suppose they were given education as fitted their needs and capacity, how many O'Hearns would there be to pay the penalty on the scaffold of mankind's amazing neglect of its most precious product.

The *Minneapolis Journal* described Jim's arrival into town by asserting that the "highest priced, most educated and most talked about horse in the world is here, to stay at Dr. Cotton's veterinary establishment 617 Fourth Avenue. Accompanying his equine majesty are his prime minister Dr. Key, and three members of his royal guard" (referring to Stanley, Sam, and Gordon Bunch). In Minneapolis, Jim missed what was alleged to be the only show he'd ever canceled because of injuries sustained in a minor train accident. The article mentioned, "Jim betrays a slight stiffness in moving about the stage, having suffered a severe shaking up in a railroad accident a short time ago." Whether this was an excuse to cover up his symptoms was never disclosed, but Dr. Key did cancel his next show. Even so, Jim energetically greeted the *Journal* writer backstage and welcomed his gift of a chocolate almond, looking for more after that, "with a persistency that lives up to his claim of being the best educated horse in the world." Indeed, that afternoon Jim was challenged by five schoolboys to a spelling match in which he bested four out of five by outspelling the next-to-the-last competitor with *A-A-R-O-N* and *I-S-A-A-C*. The fifth challenger, "Young David Jones, son of the Mayor, tied with Jim on the word 'Isaiah' and the match was declared a draw, with the $1 offered as a prize going to the boy."

The next engagement was quietly canceled, giving Jim a month to rest. But he was back in action in three weeks.

* Gray's Armory, Cleveland, Ohio—April 30 to May 5, 1906. Seating capacity 2,500; twelve performances. Broke record for paid admissions.
* Armory, Toledo, Ohio—May 6, 1906. One night; broke box office record.

But the numbers didn't tell all. Jim Key was not just a box office star. He had become a cult hero whose abilities were not simply human, but superhuman. The excitement of 45,000 fans that had come out to stand in line for his shows at Memorial Hall in Columbus took on a kind of religious fervor. The Columbus *Evening Dispatch* described Jim's show as transformational, as if being in the presence of his larger-than-life energy was to be healed of all impairments. The two-page article, subtitled "In the Audience Was Leslie Oren, Deaf, Dumb and Blind Boy," described the way that Leslie "saw" and "heard" the whole performance "by the aid of his teacher and not a point was missed by this youngster as his laughter indicated. At the conclusion the child was taken upon the stage and ran his hands over the horse's head and face. He also touched the cash register and felt over the other paraphernalia used in the performance."

The *Evening Dispatch* included a photograph of Leslie Oren at his typewriter, and ran the story that the twelve-year-old pupil at State School for the Deaf and Dumb had written for the newspaper about Jim. He noted:

I sat on his back, he did not kick or shake me off, because he is kind, and gentle, and tame. I kissed and loved the dear old horse. I patted his smooth nose. He counted and spelled and read like a little boy. . . . I love Jim Key, I love all animals. I am happy, because I saw Jim Key.

But for all the healing that his audiences seemed to receive in Jim's presence, his own impairments weren't improving. By the start of summer, Dr. Key was certain he couldn't keep Jim's aches and pains secret much longer. Probably only Monk had counted how many mornings he watched Dr. Key and the Davises having to hoist the big bay up, and the press-wary dog wasn't telling. As before, once Jim Key was up and standing, he seemed to move about just fine. But their next venue was going to be daunting. It was a whole summer at the new White City for the second year in a row, where Jim had to break his own box office record. Looking ahead, the Doc must have chosen the last night in Toledo to tell Jim that it was time to go home. He promised to build him his own amphitheater in Shelbyville so the folks could come see him there.

Jim no doubt made his indignation known. William Key struggled for days to decide what to do. As a healer, he was bound to do what he would have recommended to any one of his patients, and that was to go home. But he couldn't break his earlier promise that going home had to be Jim's choice.

They carried on with the White City engagement. Box office receipts weren't counted, but the general manager reported, "Great crowds every day." From August 28 through September 22 they were scheduled to play the whole month back in Cincinnati. Before this engagement, it seemed that Jim had suffered one of his worst episodes. This time, after he was helped up to his feet, the symptoms didn't go away. He was hurting. But he still whinnied and whined anytime the prospect was raised of canceling the rest of his tour or even one show.

Dr. Key felt obliged to keep Rogers informed about the progression of Jim's rheumatism. Maybe both men knew on some level that the month in Cincinnati would be their last for the season. Though they were booked through the end of November, once the cooler days and mornings began, it was going to be that much harder on their star. Maybe Jim had come to the same conclusion. In any event, Beautiful Jim Key rose to the occasion as never before. As the chief attraction of Cincinnati's Fall Festival, back at the Music Hall, he performed to overflow audiences show after show, day after day. On that last week, Bill Key asked him one more time if he was ready to go home, proposing one solid year of rest and healthy living in Tennessee, and then a return to public life. Jim gave him a relieved, self-satisfied nod yes.

Rogers appeared to take the news in stride. When he saw his partners off at the station, it was with the understanding that they would go out again in the spring of 1908. In the interim, he invited the Keys and the Davises to come and spend some time at Glenmere, Beautiful Jim Key's second home.

A. R. Rogers didn't linger at the station but hurried away to attend to pressing concerns related to his newest high-class attraction, Fighting the Flames, in which he had invested and was now president of the company. And as he went, he must have broken down in tears, those of a man who had just lost the greatest love of his life.

Rogers never saw the Keys or the Davises again.

The parting was understandably also very sad for the Doc and Jim, as each, in his own way, considered that Rogers had become much more than their promoter or manager or business partner. He was their friend. With all his contradictions, strange idiosyncrasies, brilliance, energy, and foibles, he was one of them.

The mix of jubilation, exhaustion, and relief that they all felt for some time to come may not have hit them until Dr. Key, Jim, Monk, Dr. Stanley Davis, and Sam Davis arrived all the way back at the Shelbyville depot, where a sizable crowd had come out as a welcoming committee, including Mrs. Maggie Key, Stanley's sweetheart Lillie Buchanan, and Sam's gal, Essie.

Bill and Jim may have experienced the same feeling that would come over them in the quiet of their Bible study time, a feeling of peace and grace that the Doctor enjoyed in the Psalms, or from one of the passages they had marked for memorization. The feeling was summed up in 2 Timothy 4:7: *I have fought the good fight. I have finished the race. I have kept the faith.*

9

All Horses Go to Heaven

> We had no word for the strange animal we got from the white
> man—the horse. So we called it sunka wakar, "holy dog." For
> bringing us the horse, we could almost forgive you for bringing
> us whiskey. Horses make a landscape more beautiful.
>
> —LAME DEER, LAME DEER SEEKER OF VISIONS,
> *quoted by Alice Walker in* Horses Make
> a Landscape Look More Beautiful

KEY, KEY, AND ROGERS WERE NOT AT ALL PREPARED to leave center stage. The forty-three-year-old promoter had the hardest time of
it. By 1907, he, Clara, and their three sons lived full-time at Glenmere,
while Mercy and Hiram purchased a home near Boston, where the
rest of the family would soon migrate. In April of that year, Rogers
took an engagement at Cincinnati's Music Hall in conjunction with
a new event, the First Annual Pure Food Drug and Confectionary
Exposition, and dared to debut his new Wonderful Educated Horse,
"Bonner the Great, the Horse with the Human Brain."

The event was entirely disappointing. At once, Rogers canceled
the search for a stand-in and proceeded with the work of the Jim Key
Band of Mercy. He issued press releases that Jim was taking a year
off and would be ready for engagements by early 1908. But when
he put off inquiries about hiring Jim, the less interest he heard. Fan
mail to the Equine Wonder trickled to a halt. Out of sight, out of
mind. Before the year was out, he began to receive letters asking if it
was true that Beautiful Jim Key had died. One such letter was from
Mrs. Colby, the president of a Springfield, Missouri, humane group.

Rogers hardly knew how to respond and was afraid to write to Dr. Key, not wanting to hear the worst.

Jim was not dead in the least, and after a brief depression he had begun to kick off a most lively existence in Shelbyville, where life at Bethany Lane agreed with him. Somewhere in this era he apparently met a mare or two that suited his celebrated tastes, as Bedford County was soon abuzz with the possibility of a future Jim Key Jr. Stud fees were not advertised but could have been sizable.

Doc and Mrs. Key hosted frequent shows in the amphitheater out back, and for a while there was a steady stream of hundreds of visitors stopping by to say *H-E-L-L-O*. As long as they came bearing gifts and could get past Monk, they were welcome. The Doc and Maggie created a room in the paneled, blanket-lined stables that was devoted to Jim's and the Doctor's extensive collection of awards, ribbons, gifts, and trophies.

Bill Key continued to read his daily newspapers, sharing items of interest with Jim, still using those discussions to keep up his prodigy's education. After a year passed, both of them had eased into their slower life. Jim's ailments came and went; the more moderate climate helped. But it was William Key whose health began to decline in late 1907. A handwritten letter he sent to Albert Rogers on December 9 of that year must have come as a shock to the younger man. Dr. Key's usually energetic clean penmanship, typically written with an ink pen, now wavered across the page without punctuation and in blurred pencil, while his grammar and spelling were failing fast:

> Mr. Rogers, This leves me well Jim Key is doing well he is in good order he is in a grasslot out at my farm he gose in and out of his stable as he wishes run around goes in stable at will and eates as much as he wishes then he gose out and runs around he dont lay down often some times he gets up with don't help When he dont want to get up we cach him up by the tail give him lift and he will get up he is not much truble to get up. . . . The horse can make the shows now if northern safeness to him in the future. I will look for you in January write me your ames for another year. Yours Truly, Wm. Key

Doc Key never told anyone what his condition actually was, with symptoms that also came and went. There is a possibility that he and Jim suffered from the same ailment. Sleeping on a cot in the stables 365 nights a year, or close to that many nights, along with the extremes of climate change, had undoubtedly taken a toll on the Good Doctor. Then again, he was almost seventy-five and not doing so poorly after all he'd lived through.

But Albert Rogers refused to accept that the letter was anything but an aberration. He immediately wrote to Mrs. Colby to allay her fears about Jim being deceased:

> I appreciate your kind letter and I am very glad to tell you that Jim Key is feeling fine. He is down on my farm in Tennessee, and I had a letter from Dr. Key a few days ago saying that Jim Key was in better condition than he had been for three or four years. I do not know where these rumors crop out every once in a while that Jim is dead, but I hear of them very often, pretty nearly every year since I have had him.

Dr. William Key and Albert Reynolds Rogers seemed to each suffer from a postfame delusional streak, as if they could feel themselves slipping out of history and refused to believe it. For the Doctor, it was partly because history was preparing to swiftly pass that time when the horse was king, and when those with horse knowledge reigned as well; and it was also because he was aging, unable to grasp hold of the changing times. For Rogers, it was more complicated, perhaps because his place in history had been attached to the destiny of a horse he never really owned.

As he waited to hear from his promoter, Doc Key began to rehearse with Jim, with the clear intention of going out on the road again. In the meantime, he looked into the prospect of breeding horses in his old age, maybe carrying on in the equine education field, and in early 1909, he had his eye on a pair of German Coach Horses that Shelbyville's J. G. Jackson was offering for stud service.

At this point, Rogers had temporarily lost his mind. It was not only his way of referring to Jim Key as *his* horse, or to Dr. Key's place in Shelbyville as *his* farm. In feverish rounds of correspondence, he almost referred to the humane cause as *his* movement, *his* creation. He bombarded the officers of the MSPCA and the AHES and the AHA with urgent missives about projects and concepts to aid the work of the organizations. Some of his ideas were brilliant, like his recommendation for a form of planned giving, complete with elegant sample letters suggesting that wealthy individuals include contributions to humane charities in their wills.

Albert's gravest concern was that the Jim Key Band of Mercy, now one million members strong, lacked adequate funding. Without money, he couldn't publish Uncle Bert's newsletter, or continue to expand the base of *his* cause. Rogers didn't mention to his fellow officers that *his* promotions business had seen a marked drop in income, though he did say that he couldn't afford to fund the Jim Key Band of Mercy himself. He did say that more funding was also needed for the American Parent Band of Mercy in order to productively harness the energy of its millions of members.

When the various officers wrote back with tersely worded replies, Rogers began making overtures to the National Humane Alliance in New York, and when no forward motion was obtained, he even occasionally dropped a plaintive line to eighty-five-year-old George Angell. A. R. Rogers knew that Angell was in poor health but either didn't want to accept it, or felt that the great Apostle of Mercy and Peace needed to be informed of the incompetence of his boards of directors.

Clara Rogers attempted to cool Albert's frenzy, suggesting that perhaps he focus his passions on the show business that he knew. Moreover, if they wanted to continue the lavish lifestyle they'd been living, they needed an income. In early 1909, Rogers opened a large-scale musical variety production, coincidentally at the Hippodrome in Boston, in which he had invested most, if not all, of his fortune. Everything that could go wrong did. The show was a bomb. Albert was sued for nonpayment of rent for an apartment leased by one of his company members; performers in his show were said to have used his name in charging meals and hosting parties across Boston. He found no relief in court and was forced to file for bankruptcy. When he next went to take out a loan, he was rejected on the grounds that, according to information from individuals at the AHES, he had hundreds of thousands socked away, not to mention that he owned Glenmere free and clear.

From his deathbed, the saintly George Angell had first written to Rogers to say that he had heard about the bankruptcy and could offer him financial assistance. Rogers refused but was honored by the offer. Straining for ideas that would redeem him, as they always had, he went to pay a visit to Mr. Angell to discuss the possibility of getting started on a project that Angell had previously approved, a new national humane education organization to be headquartered in New York under Albert's guidance. One of its first acts he proposed would be to appeal to Congress to enact a national "Be Kind to Animals Day."

Apologetic and frail, Angell announced that his directors, two in particular, were up in arms over what they saw as a competing organization. But there was more. Albert's frail old friend had apparently heard from his officers that Albert had been sued for skipping rent and restaurant charges; Angell felt compelled to be honest about expressing his disappointment. Rogers explained his side of the story; Angell accepted his explanation and promised to intervene. The new project had his blessing.

A month later, on Saturday, March 20, 1909, Albert opened his newspaper, along with the rest of the nation, to read that George Thorndike Angell "Soldier of Peace" had died. The world collapsed for Albert Rogers. He felt the loss viscerally, as if he could hear the cries of every nonhuman creature on earth mourning the passing of their protector. That is, until he struck upon an idea, an incredible idea. Swallowing his every molecule of pride, he hastily presented his vision to boards of the MSPCA, the AHES, and the AHA. He called it the "Angell Penny Fund," a fund drive to be organized by the schoolchildren throughout Boston to collect pennies in order to erect a memorial for the hero of the humane cause. The boards said no. They would erect a memorial but not via a penny drive.

Furious, Albert Rogers went ahead and publicized the Penny Fund himself, under the auspices of the Jim Key Band of Mercy. When he refused to acknowledge the many cease-and-desist letters from the directors of the boards, his very painful rift with the MSPCA and the AHES found its way into the Boston newspapers, with public advisories included that the school board would not permit the Angell Penny Fund to go forward. A memorial was to be erected, but from other sources of funding.

Then the final blow came when the secretary of the AHES wrote to thank Albert Reynolds Rogers for his years of service as a vice president and wished him well in his future endeavors. With that, Uncle Bert was banished from the movement. At his lowest and perhaps most delusional, he stormed into the offices of the MSPCA at 19 Milk Street and demanded a fair hearing. Instead, a fistfight ensued between him and one of the directors, whom Rogers later described in his failed lawsuit as a madman. The reparations he sought were not fiscal; he only wanted his vice presidency back. His last deed of desperation was to write the AHES a lengthy narrative detailing his contributions to their cause and the wrongs done to him, none more unjust than their thievery of his good name and reputation. But all in all he now saw that their behavior toward him went against the goals of mercy, kindness, justice, and peace that George Angell had stood for, and he was better off not to be in their association.

Unfortunately for all parties, Albert's idea to found a unifying international umbrella organization that would further develop humane education and policy might have been a worthy endeavor. Such an organization could have been a driving force in the future, when the issue was no longer front and center. It might have also served to better link animal welfare to the conservation and environmental movements, and perhaps even have provided a forum in which to create more cohesion within the humane movement.

On the other hand, even without the drive and innovation of Albert Rogers, the Massachusetts Society for the Prevention of Cruelty to Animals flourished and more than honored its founder throughout the decades to come. In 1912, the Angell Memorial Fountain was dedicated in Boston's Post Office Square, followed soon by the opening of the George T. Angell School (in service over five decades), and the establishment in 1915 of the Angell Memorial Animal Hospital. That same year, the first national "Be Kind to Animals Day" celebration took place, proposed by the MSPCA. No credit was given to Albert Rogers, even though he might have taken some comfort in its passage. Angell's followers went further, opening animal shelters and veterinary teaching hospitals across the state. In 1944, the S.S. *George T. Angell*, a ten-thousand-ton liberty ship, was christened, and fourteen years after, Angell Memorial Plaza was dedicated at Post Office Square.

Another one of Albert's ideas was pursued in 1956 when the MSPCA formed an alliance with Britain's RSPCA to create an international humane alliance, the ISPCA, later to be renamed WSPCA. In 1968, after celebrating the 100th anniversary of what George Angell had started and estimating that thirty-nine million animals had been helped over its first century, the MSPCA continued to grow—rescuing animals in disaster zones, campaigning against animal overpopulation and the exploitation of animal performers, and even, in 1991, sponsoring a literacy outreach program through the AHES to provide free books on humane subject matter to classrooms. In 2003, the organization changed its name to become MSPCA-Angell in recognition of its seven animal shelters and three veterinary centers. Two years earlier, the first Annual Animal Hall of Fame dinner had been held, 102 years since Beautiful Jim Key had become the first brute animal they had ever honored.

Rogers felt that he had been cast out of Eden. But with classic American entrepreneurial gumption, A. R. Rogers soon reinvented himself. In the midst of his gloom it occurred to him that the job of promoting others was far riskier and far more thankless than the job of promoting oneself and one's own ideas. Almost the moment he hung out his shingle as a marketing consultant, he was hired by planning committees of fairs and exhibitions from across the country, and in 1912 he stepped into a distinguished position as manager of New York's Grand Central Palace, where he was responsible for overseeing every aspect of the special exhibits and touring expositions it housed. On January 26, 1935, seventy-one-year-old Albert made it into the newspaper for the first time in two and a half decades when the *New York Times* ran a brief article under the headline "Gets Tercentenary Post":

> Hartford, Conn. Jan. 25—Albert R. Rogers, director of the Massachusetts tercentenary and Georgia Bicentennial celebrations, and organizer and director of many exhibitions and celebrations elsewhere, has become associated with the Connecticut Tercentenary Commission as director of celebration, the State commission announced today. Mr. Rogers, whose home is now in West Newton, Mass., is a native of Ohio and connected with the Rogers family associated with the early settlement of Connecticut.

No mention was made of Beautiful Jim Key or Albert's previous incarnation as his promoter and alleged owner. That didn't mean, however, that Rogers hadn't tried in different ways to resurrect that part of his former life. In the 1920s, he corresponded with breeders of educated horses, and in 1927, he clipped out an article in the *New*

York Times entitled "Tell of Mind Link to Horses and Dogs" by a German doctor named Karl Krall, who trained nonhumans with telepathy and hypnosis. It had to have brought into question everything that Dr. Key and Jim had convinced A. R. Rogers was true. Was Jim a hoax? Was telepathy at work? Had Dr. Key hypnotized his audience? Was Rogers himself a hoax? Or was it all true, that it was simply education with a little trickery and real hocus-pocus thrown in?

Rogers had at various points attempted to write a book about his adventures promoting the Celebrated Educated Arabian-Hambletonian, but each of the myriad drafts fell short of capturing what it had been like to be along for that ride. After he retired and moved in with Archibald and his family in Brockton, Albert returned to the project, poring often over his scrapbooks and his memories.

After the last letter he had received from Dr. Key at the end of 1907, Rogers had corresponded with Stanley for news of his former partners and to compare notes about the two known offspring of Jim Key. Old Jim had sired a pretty filly named Queen Key who went up North to live at Glenmere, where she was trained by Clarence Rogers—Albert's firstborn, and on his way to becoming a college graduate—and there was also a colt, Jim Key Jr. Dr. Davis wrote that he was "a very smart little horse" and that he hoped to train him. Unfortunately, Dr. Stanley Davis wrote early in their correspondence, Jim Jr.'s eyes bothered him quite a deal. "He has a case of periodic ophthalmia. I hope that he will get all right." Davis had been impressed that Queen Key already had her own letterhead with Clarence's name on it, promoting her education by kindness and patience. Young Doc Davis signed off that letter by cheerily saying, "I hope Clarence will have success with her as you had with Jim Key."

Inevitably, Dr. Davis had occasion to report less cheerful news. By 1909, he was already much in demand in his growing veterinary practice, which he had built after taking over Dr. Key's offices on North Main Street. This was a career that would span fifty years and earn him the love and admiration of Bedford County, black and white. But no matter how busy he was, he still stopped by daily to check on Doc Key, Jim, Monk, and Maggie. Sometimes he'd arrive on a sunny afternoon to find a little group of visitors watching the Doctor and Jim in impromptu performances. Dressed in his fine suit and boots, though hatless in the warm weather, Dr. Key obviously enjoyed the attention as much as Jim.

As beautiful and regal as ever, somewhat slimmed down at age twenty, Jim Key no longer seemed to mind the smaller audiences, as if in his equine sense memory he could conjure the old roar of the crowds and was, as ever, making sure to give them a show they would never forget. Jim was frequently draped in one of his many expensive, monogrammed blankets, like any aging star comfortably lounging in a smoking jacket and cravat, but who just happened to be a horse.

Monk was less ornery to people stopping by, not because he had succumbed to the rules of Southern hospitality, but more because he was getting up in years. When the Doc and Jim had no audience, Monk made himself available as a lifelong fan and friend by springing onto a sole chair set up in the yard just for him. Otherwise, Dr. Davis would find him on the front porch, resting in the shade next to Maggie, who was content in her reading chair, the two keeping cool under the overhang of the charming white frame house on Bethany Lane.

Stanley was one who knew that William Key's death on October 18, 1909, had been expected. The Doctor had been on the decline since the end of that summer. Even as he grew weaker, Bill Key read his newspapers and books, keeping up with the daily news as he peered into the future he would soon be leaving behind. One of the last pages he took out from the newspaper had been from the Sunday edition of the *Chattanooga Times,* an Ochs-owned paper, which had a column from Harvard's president, Charles Eliot, that had captured Dr. Key's interest. It was a list of Eliot's recommended reading for giving any man a liberal education, even if read for only fifteen minutes a day, something the Doc optimistically planned to do. Among the recommended authors were Plato, Bacon, Milton, Emerson, Browning, Marlowe, Dryden, Shelley, Plutarch, Epictetus, Tennyson, and Goethe, and specific titles included *Autobiography of Benjamin Franklin, Fruits of Solitude* by William Penn, Webster's *The Duchess of Malfi,* Middleton's *The Changeling,* Adam Smith's *Wealth of Nations, Pilgrim's Progress, Canterbury Tales,* Dante's *Divine Comedy,* Darwin's *Origin of Species,* and *Arabian Nights.*

An obituary in the *Shelbyville Gazette* referred to a few but not all of the many chapters in Dr. William Key's life, noting his enormous success with Keystone Liniment and Beautiful Jim Key, as well as his service as a veterinarian and prominent member of the community. The obituary author expressed surprise at the large numbers of individuals, both white and of color, who attended the funeral services and flocked up the hill at the Willow Mount Cemetery to witness his burial. The article stated that his comfortable estate was thought to be worth around $15,000.

William Key's comfortable estate was worth many times that estimate, but it was convenient for his heirs that outsiders didn't know the particulars. Ever the poker player, even in death, he kept those cards close to the vest. He did swear at the time he made out his last will and testament in 1904, "I am not the father of any living child and have never been." Dr. Key had been frugal but never stingy, and he had divested himself of property, trust accounts, and cash to friends and loved ones over the years, not in loans but in gifts to support individual education, to pay for funerals and the creation of businesses, and to fund charities in the areas of humane education and African-American concerns. The property and money he had at the time of his death he left mainly to Maggie and Stanley, with miscellaneous smaller gifts to various relatives on the Key, Davis, and Davidson sides, and to friends. The large acreage on Tullahoma Highway—also called Dixie Highway—later passed from Maggie to Stanley and Sam. Dr. Key left no instructions for the care of Jim in his will, perhaps because he knew that Stanley would be in charge. William Key did have one request for himself—he wished that a monument of some significance be placed at his grave.

Maggie did just that. The impressive tombstone she selected was appropriately unusual. Made of marble that was half rough-hewn and half-smooth, it appeared to be of two worlds, fitting of course because Bill was always of two worlds. With the name *KEY* prominent on its base and the word *PEACE* on its top, it bore the simple inscription: "Dr. Wm. Key, Trainer of Jim Key, 1833–1909."

Maggie, Monk, Stanley, and Sam could think of little they could do to mend Jim Key's heart. In mourning the loss of his best friend, he went into a steep decline, his rheumatism becoming more acute, now with pain, swelling, and fever. These episodes grew more frequent, when Jim could be moving about and suddenly lie down wherever he happened to be and not be able to get up without the special pulley device Dr. Davis had developed for him. But the most worrisome symptom was his apparently unstable mental state.

Then, after Monk died around this same time, Jim developed a kind of amnesia, as if he couldn't recall anything Dr. Key had ever taught him, barely recognizing Stanley or Maggie or any of those around him trying to do whatever they could muster to make him feel a little better. Jim responded to everything with a faraway, fearful look that asked: *Who are you?* And worse: *Who am I?*

Albert Rogers later wrote in one of his versions of Jim's biography that when Dr. Key died at the age of seventy-six, "it was feared that Jim Key would die also for they had never been separated, and the affection between the two was marvelous. Fortunately, for a number of years previous, Dr. Stanley Davis, a brother-in-law of Dr. Key's, had been the groom while studying to be a veterinary, and was constantly in attendance on Jim Key."

Over the next year, thanks to "everything that love, kindness and money could do to end Jim's life with every comfort," he improved noticeably. With around-the-clock supervision, he was not allowed to languish, and Dr. Davis, or "Uncle Pet" as his family members called him, put him on a diet and exercise regime that the dramatic horse soon started complaining about. A hired groom responsible for getting Jim up to his feet and taking him for his daily walk had gotten badly on Jim's nerves one afternoon when Sam and Essie Davis stopped by to check up on him and Maggie.

Essie gave Jim a rub along his neck, asking, "Well, Jim, they treatin' you all right?"

Jim glanced over at the groom to make sure he wasn't watching, then turned back to Essie and shook his head from side to side, very pointedly indicating *no*. On other days, he was himself again, an entertainer, able to demonstrate when cajoled into practicing, that he could yet be considered a scholar and model office boy.

Beautiful Jim Key turned twenty-three in early 1912, not ancient in equine years, but slowing down even more. Jim had managed to have some better days here and there, although Stanley anticipated it wouldn't be long before he was completely lame. As a last resort, Albert Rogers, back in the money at that point, offered to pay for Jim to receive treatment again at the San Antonio sulfur baths.

At least four or more versions emerged about what happened next.

In Albert's own recollection, Jim was taken to Texas, helped, and returned to Tennessee much improved, but not entirely.

In a second version that was published in the *Shelbyville Gazette*, dated September 18, 1912, with the headline "Jim Key Dies," he didn't survive the trip home from Texas and died en route, according to a dispatch from Potosi, Missouri, where the news broke. The Shelbyville paper noted:

> Jim was raised and educated here by the late Dr. Wm. Key. Pretty nearly every one here who went to the World's Fair seven years ago saw Jim. He was the educated horse that was shown in a pavilion on the Pike and was known as the smartest horse ever, which all who saw him will admit. . . . Jim was about 16 years old and his training began with his colthood. So much education was not good for him, however, and he went crazy before his death.

A third version, which appeared decades later, was that Beautiful Jim Key died of diabetes caused by an overconsumption of sugar. That was to be a warning against giving too much candy to future generations of children growing up in Bedford County, who were told the supposedly true story of the horse who could almost talk.

The other, most credible, and documented version was that Dr. Stanley Davis did not send Jim to Texas, fearing the physical and emotional stress of the journey would be worse than any benefit to be gained from the sulfur baths. He let God and nature guide Jim's course and hoped that the Celebrated Educated Arabian-Hambletonian might enjoy the passing of his last few seasons in Bedford County.

In the fall, on September 18, on one of those perfect picture postcard autumn days—that participants in the annual Tennessee Walking Horse Celebration later started coming from around the world to see—Jim Key got up on his own and came out from his stable to mosey around the front yard. He was able to hear the wind whispering down from the hills, feel the shaded sun on his flanks, and maybe have a last taste of grass or a nibble on some of the turning leaves. Then Jim lay down in the front yard and didn't get up again.

"He just passed out with all ease," wrote Dr. Stanley Davis to Albert Rogers. There was no struggle, rather a surrender. He was buried where he lay, in the front yard, in a grave raised about a foot high, over which Maggie Davis Key planted a bed of flowers.

This was the first but not the last burial place of the good bay horse who would have gone to heaven no matter his color or his goodness because, as William Key had told Jim, all horses go to heaven.

○──────────○

History happened. The world advanced and it regressed. Progressive movements lurched forward, the map of the planet changed, wars of unprecedented magnitude raged. Life went on.

Toward the end of World War II, with few momentous events happening in Shelbyville, a small delegation of citizens gathered at the train station to welcome a newsworthy arrival. On October 18, 1945, Mr. Archibald A. Rogers, Albert's youngest son, had made the trip on behalf of his ailing father to pay his respects at the graves of Dr. Key and Jim.

Dr. Davis would not have recognized the tall, outgoing forty-nine-year-old Archibald if not for his broad smile and fast gait. That was *A-R-C-H-E* all right, the same child who had toddled after his brothers Clarence and Newell when they took Stanley around Glenmere, and the same fun-loving boy of ten last seen in 1906. Their reunion, witnessed by reporters from the *Shelbyville Gazette,* was an emotional one. The two approached tentatively, shook hands, and then embraced with gusto as they might have forty years earlier. Archie could have sworn that sixty-six-year-old Stanley had barely aged a day.

After reminiscing at length about some of their shared experiences, Mr. A. A. Rogers and Dr. S. W. Davis were asked some questions by the journalists present. One reporter just had to know exactly how rich Albert Rogers had become, what with buying the horse at the Tennessee Centennial and all, plus with the expenditures of traveling over the United States, and often. What he meant to say was, "Did he make any profit?"

Archie laughed. "Yes," he said, "quite a bit. Expenses were heavy, that's true, but my father made lots of money."

Someone had to ask. "How much?"

Dr. Davis knew that line of questioning. For many years, everybody was always trying to get the lowdown on the value of Dr. Key's estate, and nobody ever seemed to have a clue. Archie Rogers didn't know how much his father ultimately made, but he did say, "The pennies from the show receipts were given to me and I had over $40,000 in my name by the time it was over." His older brothers, Clarence and Newell, received the larger coins, he said, and accumulated over $100,000 each. "Of course, my father had the major share."

The reporter noted that Albert's earnings were so profitable that Archibald Rogers was later inspired to try his hand at show business, producing "some wonderful shows in Boston and elsewhere," which were well received but not always profitable. He and his brothers went through their savings eventually and turned to other pursuits. When World War I came, his older brothers enlisted, and Newell, an aviator, was killed in action.

Archie went on to recall that after a time he left show business for the shoe business, hinting that his leather company, A&B Tanning of Brockton, Massachusetts, had been enormously lucrative. He obviously came by his entrepreneurial talents honestly.

Dr. Davis drove Archibald out to see Sam and his wife, Essie, at their home on the old Tullahoma Highway, also known as Dixie Highway. This was the large property Dr. Key had bought not long after meeting Albert Rogers at the Tennessee Centennial and striking up their partnership. Essie, the "Queen of the County" as the petite dynamo was known, later named it the Jim Key Farm. The Davis brothers, Archie, and Essie spoke sadly of the death, ten years earlier in 1935, of Maggie Davis Key, almost eighty years old at the time. Aside from the property and financial assets she passed on to Stanley and Sam and their families, Maggie bequeathed her late husband's scrapbook to Essie. When Archie mentioned that he was in possession of his father's scrapbook and files, the two made a pact to see that Jim Key's story be written down for posterity one day.

Stanley promised to get around to going through the two steamer trunks that held much more of Dr. Key's collection. For the past four decades, the trunks had been in a storage area in the back of his veterinary offices. Busy as he was, he had never gotten a chance to go through them.

Before he returned to Brockton, Archibald Rogers went with Stanley Davis to have a look at where Jim was still buried in front of the house on Bethany Lane, and Monk somewhere behind it, then on to the Willow Mount cemetery to stand at William Key's grave as Archie meditated quietly on that one, simple word: *PEACE.*

When Albert Rogers died five months later, on March 31, 1946, Archibald was grateful that he had given his father a feeling of comfort before he departed this world by delivering his fond impressions of Shelbyville, Tennessee, in the year 1945, where and when people still remembered Beautiful Jim Key.

10

After History

To THE UNSUSPECTING TRAVELER driving on the stretch of country road that meanders through Shelbyville, it's easy to miss the curious memorial about three miles south of the Bedford County Courthouse that rests on top of a low grassy grade on Himesville Road overlooking Tullahoma Highway.

Many who live in the area know nothing about either the horse or the man, even those who regularly notice the tall, colored enamel sign with its representation of a horse holding a piece of chalk in his mouth as he writes the name Jim in script upon a chalkboard. For the curious or daring who do venture out of their cars to come closer (there is some local lore about the haunted horse grave), only a hint of the remarkable history is suggested by the inscription on the large stone marker: "Famous Arabian Hambletonian Educated Horse: Beautiful Jim Key 1889–1912," or by the caption, "Be Kind to Animals," on the signpost inside a horseshoe, or the reminder on the back of the sign that says "Kindness, Justice, and Mercy to All Creatures."

The most telling feature of the site is the headstone with its engraved caption, "Jim's Dear Friends," underneath the three photographic inlaid porcelain cameos of Dr. William Key, Albert Rogers, and the scruffy stray dog Monk (shown in the plaque riding Jim). Their various gazes seem to peer at you from the past, asking you to seek out the truth of their existence, to know more, to piece together their journey here in this life, to remember them.

Though I grew up in Tennessee a hundred or so miles east of Shelbyville, and may have passed by the Jim Key memorial on more than one occasion, it took me many years and many miles to catch this story. Actually, it caught up with me a century after its main events, all the way on the other side of the country in California, where I'd been transplanted for too long. It arrived on my doorstep in the form of a casual e-mail from a cousin who sent it to me on behalf of a colleague. That man was David Hoffman, an award-winning documentary filmmaker and entrepreneur whose passions include uncovering great American stories.

Hoffman had uncovered this great American story when he paid a visit to an antique bookstore, the Coventry Bookshop in Coventry, Connecticut, in the early 1970s. The store had recently acquired the contents of an even older New Hampshire bookstore that had been around since before the Civil War. After making the wintry trek to the Coventry Bookshop on the last day of a month-long sale of its overabundant inventory, Hoffman was not disappointed and made several purchases. One of the items he bought was something that he found in a stack of yellowing papers in an otherwise overlooked upstairs back room. In that pile was a quaint pamphlet from the early 1900s; on its pale green-tinted cover was a photograph of a handsome mahogany bay in thoughtful profile. Coincidentally or not, this wasn't his first sighting of the famous turn-of-the-century horse. In fact in the early 1950s, when David was a young boy and a fledgling collector, one of the turn-of-the-century Beautiful Jim Key pennies that had been minted by the Women's Pennsylvania Humane Society had come into his possession, and he had held on to it all his life. At first he didn't make the connection between his penny and the pamphlet. But over time he did, and he also realized that some of the postcards he had collected had the same distinctive horse on them. Clearly, the story was trying to get his attention.

In and around Shelbyville, Jim's story had been similarly haunting a handful of writers and collectors who stumbled upon it every now and then, managing to stir some interest. In September 1946, one of Shelbyville's leading horse authorities, W. J. McGill, shared the scrapbook he had kept on Dr. Key and Jim with the *Gazette*, which resulted in a lengthy article. Twelve years later, the *Nashville Tennessean* brought the story out of retirement again, and it was soon picked up by the *New York Herald*. Even before that, newspaper articles in local papers and tributes during the Tennessee Walking Horse Celebration did much to air out the musty story.

But researchers were chronically blocked by the lack of documentation. This was mainly because of lost records resulting from the fact that there had been five different County Courthouse buildings over the last 150 years. The first had been Mrs. Payne's house in 1809, replaced by a bona fide courthouse in the square, which was ruined by a tornado in 1830, followed by the destruction of the next building by fire during the Civil War. In 1873, Bedford County erected one of the most impressive and expensive courthouses in the state, which endured until 1934. In December of that year, six days before Christmas, a lynch mob assembled outside the courthouse with the intent of lynching Earnest K. Harris, a twenty-two-year-old African-American who was preparing to stand trial for allegedly assaulting a fourteen-year-old white female. Prentice Cooper, later to become Tennessee's first three-term governor, had been appointed as defense attorney for young Harris and had apparently established a strong alibi for the defendant, who was said to have been at work and later at the pool hall at the time of the alleged incident. With jury selection in progress that morning—and word out that Harris might be acquitted—the seething mob had grown in numbers enough that Tennessee National Guardsmen were called in.

After tear gas was used to prevent the crowd from storming the courthouse, Cooper requested a change of venue but was denied by the judge. At noon a local police officer arrested one of the mob's organizers and held him inside the city hall, prompting the crowd to break down the main door and force his release. An hour later, the unarmed mob fought off guardsmen using tear gas, riot bombs, bayonets, and army pistols. By midafternoon, after the crowd's attempts to batter through the south and east entrances, one man had been killed and five others wounded. Inside, though jury selection had been completed, the judge finally ordered a mistrial, delaying proceedings for a month.

Aware that if Harris remained in the courthouse jail he would be murdered, Prentice Cooper forged a plan to smuggle the defendant out by disguising him in a uniform and gas mask as a guardsman. Cooper saw to it that Harris was safely transported to a Nashville jail, and a change of trial venue was subsequently arranged. A local newspaper reported:

Guardsmen left the city shortly after the Negro was taken away. They abandoned four trucks which were parked facing Shelbyville, rather than take time to turn them around. There would likely have been further violence. The trucks were a blazing bon fire a few minutes later. . . . Machine guns were mounted on upper verandas of the courthouse. They were later placed in entrances to the courthouse but were not fired, though at one time pistol and gun fire was so rapid that they sounded like machine guns.

By 7:30 that night, the mob turned its wrath on the courthouse and soon engulfed it in flames. "It is feared that most, if not all, county records are lost," the newspaper account continued. As the article reported on Thursday, December 20, 1934, "One of the finest and most imposing structures of any county in the state is today in a heap of ruins."

When Cooper was able to secure a Nashville venue for Harris's trial two months later, the defense was taken over by an N.A.A.C.P.-appointed attorney. With four hundred armed guards standing ready outside the second criminal courthouse, the alibi witnesses either were too afraid to testify or changed their stories to say he was not at work or at the pool hall that day. The jury took seven minutes to deliberate before coming back with a guilty verdict, and twenty-two-year-old Earnest K. Harris was sentenced to die in the electric chair. Despite the defense's request for a new trial—on grounds that the court officers allowed members of the jury to leave the courthouse and observe the guardsmen, thus influencing the verdict—the motion was denied. Harris was executed by electrocution on May 27, 1935.

Governor Prentice Cooper later remarked that he took on Harris's defense because he believed that Harris was entitled to a fair trial. Cooper swore then, "I don't ever want to see a time like that again." The courthouse was rebuilt at a cost of $175,000 and has managed to avoid further calamity to date.

In addition to his public service as a World War I veteran, district attorney general, state legislator, three-term Tennessee governor, and ambassador to Peru under the Truman administration, Prentice Cooper, a Shelbyville native, was a lifelong fan and friend of Beautiful Jim Key. Cooper's father, William Prentice Cooper, and his mother, Argentine Shofner Cooper (namesake of Shelbyville's Argie Cooper Public Library), were some of the most prominent names in Bedford County and had been contemporaries of Dr. William Key. Prentice, who was born in 1895, grew up with Jim Key as a local celebrity and saw him perform on several occasions in the years when the horse's star was on the rise. In 1904, nine-year-old Prentice Cooper traveled with his family to the St. Louis World's Fair, where they were welcomed by their hometown heroes and where he was able to see multiple performances by Beautiful Jim Key in his unforgettable Silver Horseshoe Building on the Pike.

It would not be an overstatement to claim that the Smartest Horse in the World had a profound, lasting influence on the future governor, who was himself educated at Webb School, Vanderbilt, Princeton, and Harvard Law School, and was, like Jim Key, a Democrat. When Prentice was raising his three sons, born to him and his wife, the beautiful Hortense Hayes Powell Cooper—who gave me a gracious welcome during a visit to the governor's mansion in Shelbyville, a historic landmark—he spoke often of the Educated Arabian-Hambletonian. In fact when I had the honor of meeting Congressman Jim Cooper in Washington, D.C., in June 2004, he recalled that his father had talked more about Jim Key than about the burning of the Bedford County Courthouse, and more than about all his experiences as governor and ambassador.

A true storykeeper of the legacy left by the horse and man from Shelbyville, Prentice Cooper died in 1969 at age seventy-four, when his son Jim was only fourteen. Jim, also a Democrat, who went on to become a champion of civil rights, literacy, and improving services for veterans, and a much-loved United States congressman now serving the Nashville area, admitted that he never knew if all those stories his father had told him were true or not. It had always sounded to him like something of a fairy tale that his father, old enough to have been his grandfather, had spun to entertain him.

The same sentiment of having heard a fairy tale was expressed by Marie Davis Harris, the daughter of Dr. Stanley Davis. Even though Stanley had witnessed Jim Key's journey from start to finish, as the years went by he had trouble convincing others that it had actually happened as he remembered it. Then, in 1967, the potential for preserving the saga was dealt a further blow with Stanley's death. He had been suffering for years from glaucoma. The father of four, including two sons whom he lost, Dr. Davis had been one of Bedford County's only veterinarians for many years and had become as beloved as Dr. Key had been in his time, an extraordinary accomplishment. But much to the anguish of his daughters, Marie and Harriette, the segregated Bedford County convalescent home of that era barred him from receiving medical treatment. Local civil rights activists, white and black, were appalled. Marie Davis Harris, the wife of Sidney Harris, a prominent black educator for whom the black high school was eventually named, was later consoled when her father was posthumously inducted into the Bedford County Hall of Fame.

With both Stanley and Sam gone, Essie Davis realized that there would be no one to tend to Jim Key's gravesite on the Bethany Lane property, which was now for sale. The Queen of the County took action. Moving quickly, she hired Thomas Johnson Sr., an employee of Uniroyal who also moonlighted as a gravedigger, to dig up Jim's bones and move them to a new grave out at her place, aka Jim Key Farm.

His then eleven-year-old son, Thomas Johnson Jr., recalled to me during my visit to Shelbyville that his dad had come in to wake him up, saying, "C'mon, June bug, we got to go dig a grave for a horse."

Young Thomas had heard fireside ghost stories from his aunt Cora Campbell, many that she swore were true, about a horse from Shelbyville who could read and write and do seemingly supernatural things that anybody with any sense knew horses couldn't do. When he went with his father to exhume the horse's remains, he hardly thought to connect Aunt Cora's stories with the white chalky bones that he helped Johnson Sr. dig up and place in a pine coffin, which they transported out to Himesville Road and Tullahoma Highway and buried on the low rise not far from Essie's house. The connection soon came, however, with a sudden wave of press coverage. And the story had only begun to haunt Thomas Johnson.

Essie Davis not only commissioned the headstone and sign to immortalize Beautiful Jim Key and his three best friends, Dr. Key, Albert Rogers, and Monk, but also made sure that her niece Essie Mott Lee, a veteran educator and writer, went to work on the biography of Dr. Key. Drawing from her aunt's personal remembrances and scrapbooks that had belonged to Dr. Key and Albert Rogers, author Lee honored her aunt's dearest wish by writing the biography that was eventually titled *Dr. William Key: The Man Who Educated a Horse*. Archibald Rogers not only made sure that Essie Lee had his father's scrapbook but also made a contribution to the Jim Key

Memorial Fund. The fund, whose purpose was to preserve the monument, was set up by Essie Mott Lee and her sister, fellow educator, writer, and musician Annie Mott Whitman. The Mott sisters were Campbells on their mother's side and were related to the Davises and Dr. Key by marriage. In another coincidence, Annie's husband, David Whitman, was related on his mother's side to Dr. Key's first two wives, the Davidson sisters. These three beautiful, brilliant, and plucky women, Essie Davis, Essie Mott Lee, and Annie Mott Whitman, deserve most of the credit for the preservation of the legacies of horse and man.

With the death of Essie Davis in 1974 and the death of Archibald Rogers in 1976, the last eyewitnesses close to the history were gone. Essie Mott Lee passed away in 1998, leaving her sister Annie to be custodian of the scrapbooks and all that was left of the family's oral histories of Dr. Key and Jim—all of which she generously contributed to my research.

In the meantime, a new generation of secondhand eyewitness reports came forward. Wonderful accounts were published in Tennessee newspapers and discussed in area historical societies with authorities like Bob Womack, a revered Middle Tennessee State professor and author, and Dick Poplin, a much-loved local historian and newspaper columnist. Bob Womack had been so steeped in Dr. Key and Jim Key stories while growing up that in writing his newspaper pieces he had accumulated several files of research about them. Dick Poplin had featured stories about the Keys and a tribute to Dr. Stanley Davis in his *Shelbyville Times-Gazette* column, inspired by his own belief in the values of kindness and tolerance, his love of animals, and the anecdotes his father had passed on to him.

In 1992, when David Hoffman and his daughter Jeannie began research on a documentary about Jim Key and first started looking into the claims of the pamphlet he had found twenty years earlier, Dick Poplin was one of the first authorities they located. He had written to David back then:

> I have always been glad my father W. A. J. (Billy) Poplin saw Jim
> at the Tennessee Centennial in Nashville in 1897 when he was 17
> years old. (He was born Dec. 1, 1879.) It made a great impression
> on him how Jim took pride in being a Democrat and could pick
> out the pretty girls.

In the spring of 2003, at the Mid-Way Café on the Murfreesboro Pike—the same road that becomes North Main Street as you head into town—David Hoffman and I had the pleasure of sitting down to talk with a group that included Dick Poplin and Bob Womack. We were not far from the property that was once a farm owned by John W. Key where William Key grew up as a slave, and even closer to the part of town where Keystone Driving Park helped bring Hambletonian blood to Middle Tennessee. The atmosphere was as warm and friendly as any I'd known growing up in East Tennessee. My impression was that Shelbyville was still as independent minded as the town had been 150 years earlier, where despite disagreements about matters political and social, people got along because they knew one another by name and could always find common ground to talk about convivially. The story of Dr. Key and Jim was our commonality, as they had been for a nation.

Bob Womack, a winning raconteur with a cherubic smile, tearfully recalled the African-American horseman who worked on his family's land and virtually raised him, and his father figure's stories of Bill and Jim Key. With the same emotion, Dick Poplin could remember how badly he felt when, as a boy, he lost his temper with his mule, something that still saddened him and made him wish for an object lesson of kindness and patience for kids growing up now.

On the way to our lunch, David Hoffman and I had passed by the stretch of North Main where William Key had purchased his first two and a half acres that became his veterinary offices and then later those of Dr. Davis.

At the Mid-Way Café, where the desserts alone are worth the trip to Bedford County and my long-lost Tennessee accent came back after only a couple bites of buttered corn bread and collard greens, I heard more recollections of these various sites from Thomas Johnson Jr. The same "June bug" who had helped his father move Jim's white chalky bones to his final resting place, and had been reared on his aunt Cora's talking-horse ghost stories, Thomas was now a collector and entrepreneur. He told me and the rest of the group how ten years earlier he had stopped by Dr. Key's former offices on North Main Street just after the demolition crew had finished tearing down the place. Looking for anything of interest, he then paid a visit to Thomas Glover, whose company did the demolition, and learned that there were a couple of steamer trunks they'd salvaged from the barn behind the offices. If Thomas wanted them, said Mr. Glover, a man in his seventies, he would sell them, but only if Thomas promised to take care of them and the items inside. The contents told the history of a great African-American whom too few remembered, Mr. Glover explained. Both leather trunks were wrapped in canvas with the crisply stamped name of "Jim Key" on them. Inside were treasures indeed, everything from the copies of *Black Beauty* that George Angell had given to Dr. Key, to his printing template for the Keystone Liniment bottle label, to the lesson plans he had written while training Jim.

Thomas Johnson Jr. soon made the connections and felt that this was more than coincidence. "God, who He is," said Thomas, "does things with purpose." The trunks' treasures have revealed to Johnson the immense respect that personified Bill Key. "He had it for people, and things, and himself. It was pride, the way he kept his things, wrapped neatly with pieces of material, made to last."

The person responsible for organizing this gathering and the definitive treasure hunter, Marilyn Wade Parker, had asked David Hoffman a crucial question before consenting to become the lead researcher and genealogist for this book and the documentary that Hoffman will produce and direct. In her seventies, Marilyn is a former beauty queen and the president of the local chapter of the DAR; she lives in a mountain-style cabin with eight dogs and three horses. She knows history, the Bible, animals, and especially horses. Though she knew very little initially about the story, her question to David Hoffman was whether he believed that horses went to heaven or not. And then before he answered, she explained that, whereas human beings had to be judged, it was written in Scripture that all creatures were of God. David didn't disagree with that, and that was enough for Marilyn Parker.

She miraculously uncovered much of the early history of Bill Key and, like a true archaeologist, helped me assemble it. "Time erases so many things," she said, somewhat wistfully. "But not everything."

Marilyn was surprised by my question about why and how the story had gotten lost. Her question was the opposite. How *didn't* this story get lost? After a catastrophic flood and with the courthouse destroyed four times, still it prevailed. It lived.

The history was never lost at all.

NOTES

An additional acknowledgment is due to David Hoffman, who initially took the research lead on this project and introduced me to many of the indispensable individuals who generously shared their discoveries and collections. Hoffman's historical insights also helped shape the narrative I created, and served as a valuable jumping-off place for my research. Our discussions reinforced my belief that context is necessary to give meaning to facts.

A list of factual and contextual sources follows. Chapter notes mainly cite quoted sources, though I have referenced general and background sources. My interviews (author's interview abbreviated as AI) were conducted either in person, on the phone, or via written correspondence. A detailed time line for Beautiful Jim Key's performances can be easily constructed from the newspaper headlines that are listed by date in the sources. It should be noted that some newspaper clippings and some items of correspondence from the William Key scrapbook (WKsb) and Albert Rogers scrapbook (ARsb) were faded or partial, or did not have dates or newspaper names available.

In mapping these chronological and geographic journeys, I hope to present a travel guide to Jim Key archaeological sites that still invite more digging.

1. Prehistory

For the account of the meeting between Alice Roosevelt and Beautiful Jim Key, I relied on the narrative supplied by

Albert Rogers in his "Information Regarding Jim Key" (various drafts, 1913–1945, unpublished article/manuscript).

For detailed description of Opening Day, Louisiana Purchase Exposition, see generally: Clifton Daniel, editorial director, *Chronicle of America* 542, "Ice cream cones, iced tea at World's Fair"; Caro Senour, *Master St. Elmo: The Autobiography of a Celebrated Dog;* David Francis, *The Louisiana Purchase Exposition;* Mark Bennett, *The History of the Louisiana Purchase Exposition;* from www.boondocksnet.com/expos extract from Marshall Everett, *The Book of the Fair,* chapter 7, "Wonders of the Pike"; *St. Louis Post-Dispatch,* 5/1/1904: "The Greatest of World's Fairs Impressively Opens" (1a), "Cooler and Perhaps Rain" (1a), "Birdseye View and Key of the Louisiana Purchase Exposition" (6–7a), "The Crowd Rushing onto the Pike Eager to Spend Money" (9a), "Truly Biggest Show That Ever Came Down the Pike" (9a), "Free Entrance to Pike Shows" (1d).

For background on Alice Roosevelt, Theodore Roosevelt, Nicholas Longworth, I relied generally on Hermann Hagedorn, *The Roosevelt Family of Saginaw Hill,* and on Betty Boyd Caroli, *The Roosevelt Women;* www.politicalgraveyard .com (Theodore Roosevelt, Nicholas Longworth); *The 20th Century: Year by Year,* general editors Fiona Courtenay-Thompson and Kate Phelps, "White House's Black Guest," 15, "Teddy Bears (and Teddy Roosevelt)," 19.

2 "Open ye gates!": David Francis, *The Louisiana Purchase Exposition,* 174.

5 "Alice, where art thou?": *Chicago Tribune* cartoon in Hermann Hagedorn, *The Roosevelt Family of Saginaw Hill,* 187.

5 "slender, supple lissome figure": referenced in Hagedorn, 265, *San Francisco Call.*

5 "I can do one of two things": Roosevelt to friend Owen Wister in Betty Boyd Caroli, *The Roosevelt Women,* 400; Hagedorn, 186.

6 "comin' down the Pike": *St. Louis Dispatch,* 5/1/1904, 9a.

8 "crime equal to treason": *Chronicle of America,* "Booker T. Washington, White House Guest," 535.

9 "Can he spell Alice Roosevelt?": Rogers, "Information Regarding Jim Key."

9 "Grin, Jim": Caro Senour, *Master St. Elmo,* 146; Essie Mott Lee, *Dr. William Key: The Man Who Educated a Horse,* 51.

10 "Nicholas Longworth!": Rogers, "Information Regarding Jim Key."

10 "Alice Roosevelt Longworth": Ibid.

10 given the underlying prehistory: David Hoffman AI, 3/3/2003; Hoffman's *Riding for America;* for early horse prehistory, generally see Anne Charlish, *A World of Horses: Evolution, History, Breeds, Sports, and Leisure;* IMAX film *Horses.*

PART ONE OF THE HISTORY

Unless otherwise noted, all quoted conversations in chapters 2 through 5 between Dr. Key and Albert Rogers come from publicity materials generated for the 1897 first edition of "He Was Taught by Kindness," later renamed "Beautiful Jim Key: How He Was Taught."

The structure and time line for chapters 2 through 5 was drawn from notes and correspondence from the Annie Mott Whitman Collection of Jim Key Materials (ARsb, WKsb). Posterity has been fortunate that Rogers had an abundance of carbon paper.

2. Inauspicious Beginnings

15 August 7, 1897: Lee, *Dr. William Key: The Man Who Educated a Horse,* 31.

15 train depot on the corner of Church and Walnut: Sherman, *A Thousand Voices,* 12.

16 eighteen-year-old Stanley Davis: Dick Poplin AI 4/3/2004; Marie Davis Harris letter to Dick Poplin 2/6/1985.

17 Jim's instincts were to trust the stranger: Monty Roberts, *The Man Who Listens to Horses,* 15.

18 "mother wit": generally defined as common sense, horse sense, sixth sense; for connection to folk medicine, see as a general reference John Lee and Arvilla Payne-Jackson, *Folk Wisdom and Mother Wit: John Lee, an African-American Herbal Healer* (Westport, Conn.: Greenwood Press, 1993).

19 "a liniment which I called 'Keystone Liniment'": more on the subject from Thomas Johnson AI 3/27/2003 and Keystone Liniment label press.

19 heyday of the patent medicine era: see generally Brooks McNamara, *Step Right Up;* David Hoffman AI 11/11/2002; "From Patent Medicines to Prescriptions," 1969 Historical Edition *Shelbyville Times-Gazette.*

21 lynchings were on the rise: see generally Howard Zinn, *A People's History,* 203–10.

22 a gray mare standing: Lee, 11.

22 Arabian blood was valued for other traits: see generally George Conn, ed., *The Arabian Horse in Fact, Fantasy and Fiction.*

23 "tongue of oil": Key and Rogers in "He Was Taught by Kindness," 1897 edition.

23 "Give the preference": E. Daumus, "The Horse of the Sahara," 1863, in Conn, *The Arabian Horse in Fact, Fantasy and Fiction,* 49.

24 "Sell, Lauretta?": Key and Rogers, various editions "How He Was Taught."

24 "'Twas a moment": Ibid.

24 "drawing such crowds": Ibid.

25 using pins and sharp tacks: David Magner, *Magner's Art of Taming and Educating Horses,* 334–37.

26 "All men are equal": attributed to Lord George Bentinck, cited in Robertson, *The History of Thoroughbred Racing in America,* 43; also Kevin Conley, *Stud,* 82, "The connection between wealth and horses goes back to the beginning of civilization."

26 geological fluke of equality: see generally for bluegrass regions, Robertson, 41; Conley, 26.

27 two varieties of limestone: 1988 *Shelbyville Times-Gazette* compilation, "Early Bedford County—Where We Live," 8; Bob Womack sample formulation; Womack AI 3/6/2003.

27 options in his home state: Tennessee as leader in Thoroughbred world, see Robertson, 41–44, 131, 282; Belle Meade Plantation Museum, visit 3/3/2003, special exhibit; Annie Whitman AI 3/7/2003 (Dr. Key links to Robert

Green, famous black jockeys); Herman Justi, ed., *Official History of the Tennessee Centennial Exposition*, "The Negro Department," 193–204.

28 Standardbred turf heroes: materials from Gail C. Cunard, Harness Racing Museum; Conley, 121–22; Stanley Dancer, introduction to chapter on harness racing in Anne Charlish, *A World of Horses*, 340–41.

29 Hambletonian was an elite name: on story, see www.harnessmuseum.com; Anne Chunko, USTA, research; Catherine Medich research; Bob Womack, *The Echo of Hoof Beats*, 39.

31 "both fine ones and fast steppers": "Keystone Driving Park," *Shelbyville Gazette*, 6/23/1887.

32 "bountiful repast of substantials": Ibid.

32 "The doctor is doing": Ibid.

33 Kentucky Volunteer: Catherine Medich research.

33 Webb School: *Shelbyville Times-Gazette* 1969 Historical Edition, "'Old Sawney' Established Nationally Known Webb Preparatory School in Bell Buckle"; *Shelbyville Times-Gazette* Bicentennial Edition 1988, "Early Bedford County Communities and Their Histories," "Bell Buckle Strives to Retain 1800s Charm."

36 "raggle-taggle, trashy man": Lee, 15 (quoting various press versions).

36 "gotten above his raisin'": Bob Scruggs AI, 3/28/2003.

3. The Human Who Could Talk Horse

For Jim's early training, I relied on Key's accounts in various press and looked at *Magner's Art of Taming and Educating Horses*, chapter 14, "Dialogue Between Man and Horse," 449–56. Generally Magner didn't espouse horse whispering techniques; also, I drew generally from Roberts's "The Man Who Listens to Horses," which echoed so much of William Key.

My main source of information for conditions affecting people of color in these years was Chase Mooney's *Slavery in*

Tennessee; the HBO Documentary *Unchained Memories* provided an emotional anchor for Mooney's statistics.

Marilyn Parker's genealogical and other research was indispensable to my telling Bill Key's early story. Marilyn Parker AI 10/3/03: "To me the will of John Key of Albemarle, son of Martin Key, I should say the tenor and implications of its contents express of possessiveness of family I have rarely seen. 'If you don't have any heirs—what you have or received from me is to go to those we do!'"

39 "Sit" . . . "Good dog": ARsb, interview with Rogers; retold to *Nashville American,* 2/12/1899.

42 reporters to note: "Jim Is Highly Educated—Can Both Spell and Figure," *Post-Standard,* 9/7/1902.

43 "Must be one of the boys": Key retelling episode to Rogers, "He Was Taught by Kindness," various editions.

44 "Doctor, Doctor!": Ibid.

46 Busbey, Offutt, and Rarey: Magner, 449–56.

47 special status: Marilyn Parker research; Annie Whitman AI 3/7/2003.

48 "as a feme solo": divorce book, Sumner County, Marilyn Parker research.

49 Richard Houston Dudley: "Chesterfield Among Horses," *Nashville American,* 2/12/1899.

50 "dangerous niggers": Mooney, 95.

50 "nigger gibberish": Ibid., 96.

53 "don't mind them darkeys": Ibid., 94.

54 the rabbit's foot: www.luckymojo.com.

54 Underground Railroad: on Dr. Key's knowledge of routes references to guiding "another darkey" north, "How He Was Educated"; *Shelbyville Times-Gazette* 1969 Historical Edition, "Union Underground Railroad Operated in Bedford County."

55 extremes of living: for a look at the treatment of animals and slaves, see Marjorie Spiegel, *The Dreaded Comparison: Human and Animal Slavery.*

55 a doctor of color: Herbert Morais, *History of the Afro-American in Medicine,* 16–17, 21–25.

57 slave-holding increasingly distasteful: *Shelbyville Times-Gazette* 1969 Historical Edition, "Study of Early Politics

Explains Secession Vote"; Mooney, "Anti-Slavery Sentiment," 66–85.

4. War Stories

Several sources were extremely helpful in my understanding
of the context in which Bill Key's war stories took place.
For dates and statistics, I referred frequently to the Web
site state.tn.us/environment/hist/PathDivided. The Ken
Burns documentary series *The Civil War* provided visual texture to the famous battles on Tennessee soil. For the war's
impact on Middle Tennessee, I was guided by the *Shelbyville
Times-Gazette* 1969 Historical Edition's entire Civil War coverage, and Bob Womack's *Call Forth the Mighty Men,* based
on diaries of Middle Tennessee Confederate soldiers. Bedford County historian Dick Poplin's writing on this era was
also significant.

Marilyn Parker's genealogical and other research provided
details of the military service of John W. Key's sons, as well
as insights from documents pertaining to other Key family
members. The name Merit appears with different spellings
in different records.

60 Doc Key paid attention: McNamara, 21–45.

61 "You are dying, Sir!": Ibid., 45.

62 "bots and colic": 1890s descriptions found in Magner,
886–94, 912–15, and *Bell's Handbook to Veterinary Homeopathy,* 11, 29.

65 The first to secede: on sequence of secessions, *Chronicle of
America, 1861,* "One by One States Join Confederacy," 364;
Zinn, 189.

66 "an unconditional Union man": *Shelbyville Times-Gazette*
1969 Historical Edition, "Anti-Secessionist 'Parson' Brownlow Detained Here by Rebel Soldiers."

68 stubbornness as with his humanity: Clara Singleton Nelson, "My Civil War Connection," *Shelbyville Times-Gazette,*
2/17/2003; Clara Singleton Nelson AI 3/28/2003.

73 "I have learned the name": for John Gumm's 4/8/1862
diary entry at Corinth, see Womack, *Call Forth the Mighty
Men,* 126.

74 In this hell: for the pattern of the three battles observed by Key, see Louis Menand, *The Metaphysical Club*, 49:

> The Civil War was fought with modern weapons and premodern tactics. The close-order infantry charge, a method of attack developed in the era of the musket, a gun with an effective range of about 80 yards, was used against defenders armed with rifles, a far deadlier weapon with a range of 400 yards. The mismatch was responsible for some of the most spectacular carnage of the war. In Pickett's charge at Gettysburg, whose failure broke the back of Lee's army, 14,000 Confederate soldiers advanced in a line a mile wide across open fields against Union guns, and only half came back. But the tactic was responsible for a lot of unspectacular carnage as well, and one of the reasons the North finally triumphed was that it found in Grant a commander unafraid to throw wave after wave of troops at entrenched Confederate positions. The North had the bigger army, but the South, for the most part, defended, and in most battles the advantage was with the defense. The Civil War was therefore an unusually dangerous war for every soldier who fought in it.

74 "keeping a close watch": ascribed to A. W. Key by Dr. Key to Rogers in "He Was Taught by Kindness," various editions.

80 When Sherman began cutting: R. W. Best AI 3/24/2003, Nashville, oral history of the Civil War.

81 "about 12 years old": 5/19/1865 diary entry of Samuel Foster, in Womack, *Call Forth the Mighty Men*, 512.

81 "mens minds can change so sudden": Ibid., 537.

82 "upon their return": notes from Mayor Dudley for 2/13/1899 *Nashville American* interview, WKsb.

82 townspeople and relatives: Lee, 6; various interviews in Shelbyville: Annie Mott Whitman, Dick Poplin, Bob Womack, Thomas Johnson, the week of 3/26/2003.

83 "When I ran my restaurant": WKsb, New Jersey newspaper clipping.

84 Most of the black citizens: Annie Mott Whitman AI 3/31/2003, Nancy Campbell Barnett AI 3/28/2003.

84 "any action looking": Freedmen's Bureau report published in *Shelbyville Times-Gazette* 1969 Historical Edition, "Social and Political Unrest Reflected Change During Reconstruction Period."

85 he had transcribed: Thomas Johnson AI 3/31/2004.

5. Higher Calling

For Rogers, I was helped immeasurably by Catherine Medich, New Jersey State Archives research as to genealogy and major biographical events; ARsb correspondence provided much insight into his inner life.

For the details of Nashville's 1897 Tennessee Centennial Exposition, I relied on the *Official History of the Tennessee Exposition,* insights from Susan Gordon of Tennessee State Library Special Collections, and materials from the Parthenon Museum in Nashville.

87 Rogers was dismayed: ARsb, correspondence with ASPCA, American Institute Fair.

88 "I do not know": http://www.lostmuseum.cuny.edu/class (The Lost Museum Classroom: Letters between P. T. Barnum and Henry Bergh of the ASPCA); also Menand's chapter on Agassiz, 97–116.

91 Clara's social sphere: http://digital.library.upenn.edu/ women/saunders/joe/joe-XIX.htm (A Celebration of Women Writers/women's reading circles, Bands of Mercy); generally on connection between women's role in philanthropy, see Jeannette M. Oppedisano, *Historical Encyclopedia of American Women Entrepreneurs.*

92 "lover of all animals": ARsb, Ida Sheehan letter.

96 one journey to Virginia: this anecdote appears in the *Post Standard* interview 9/7/1902; other news pieces quoted Dr. Key saying it was Lauretta finding the gold.

97 Doc Key had seen: *Shelbyville Times-Gazette* 1969 Historical Edition, "Bedford County Fair Was 'Biggest' Event of Year."

99 kind of trouble: *Cleveland Gazette* 5/18/1895:

> It will be remembered that at the Columbian Exposition held in Chicago it was utterly impossible for an

Afro-American to get accommodation at any restaurant on the grounds under southern management. It was the universal rule not to serve one known to have in his veins "Negro" blood. The Afro-American was tabooed. . . . The south does not recognize Afro-American gentlemen and ladies. Neither hotels, nor restaurants, nor public places of amusement, nor railroads, nor educational institutions . . . are open to the man of color common with other men.

101 a politically risky deal: Sherman, *A Thousand Voices: The Story of Nashville's Union Station*, 15.

102 "About the center": Ibid.

103 "These occasions mark": Herman Justi, ed., *Official History of the Tennessee Exposition*, speech of Professor Council, 196–98.

104 "Here are gathered": "Vanity Fair," *Nashville American*, 5/1/1897.

105 Rogers teased the press: Bobby Lawrence, *Tennessee Centennial Nashville 1897*, 86–87.

107 "because of his high office": Justi, 233.

108 "Everyone appreciated": Ibid., 236.

109 "Philadelphia, the pioneer": Ibid., 238–40.

110 "knightly chivalry": Ibid., 242.

110 "in fine, is a gem": Ibid., 245.

111 "Mr. President": Ibid., 251.

112 Jim Key for last: Ibid.; Rogers, "Information Regarding Jim Key"; *Nashville Sun* and New York newspaper (ARsb, probably *New York Sun*) 6/13/1897.

117 "It was during": *Shelbyville Times-Gazette*, 10/13/1945 (one alleged source is Mr. McGrew, from whose parents Dr. Key purchased the 240 acres for $5,000 on Himesville and Tullahoma roads).

117 A second version: Lee, 31.

121 "While at the Nashville Exposition": "He Was Taught by Kindness," 1897 edition.

122 "BEAUTIFUL Jim Key": ARsb clippings 8/15/1897 from *New York Sun* and *New York Herald*.

When quotes from press accounts have been attributed in the text, they are not included in chapter notes below.

6. Key, Key, and Rogers

For background on the animal welfare movement and biographies of Henry Bergh and George Angell, I drew mainly from Gerald Carson, *Men, Beasts, and Gods: A History of Cruelty and Kindness to Animals;* also James M. Jasper's "The American Animal Rights Movement" in *Animal Rights: The Changing Debate*, Robert Garner, ed. The MSPCA-Angell's Web site provided further information on its founder.

126 an invitation to Glenmere: Catherine Medich research.

126 sixteenth-century castle: Google search, various travel sites, including "Palace and Park of Fontainebleau. Used by the kings of France from the twelfth century, the medieval royal hunting lodge, standing at the heart of a vast forest in the Île-de-France, was transformed, enlarged and embellished in the sixteenth century by François I, who wanted to make a 'New Rome' Italianate palace combining Renaissance and French artistic traditions."

126 a new press release: ARsb, press release; quotes from *Sun* and *World*, 8/15/1897.

126 "Dear Sir": ARsb, Fynes letter.

128 most popular drama: William Lawrence Slout, *Theatre in a Tent: The Development of a Provincial Entertainment*, 39.

129 "Absolutely not": ARsb, correspondence.

129 "remarkable new play": Ibid.

130 "could have heard": ARsb, Thomas to Rogers.

131 "The perfection": ARsb, press materials, House of Refuge Dir. testimonial.

131 "Houchee Couchee": ARsb, Tomkins testimonial.

132 "The only trouble": ARsb, Williams to Rogers.

135 Stanley found more: ARsb, Dr. Stanley Davis to Rogers, recalling Glenmere stay.

136 "trained Southern horse": "Beautiful Jim Key, the Educated Horse and His Wonderful Feats," *Orange Jour-*

nal, 9/18/1897; "Beautiful 'Jim Key,'" *Orange Chronicle,* 9/18/1897.

136 showed guests around: evening at Glenmere reconstructed from Catherine Medich research; ARsb correspondence; also "Beautiful Jim Key, the Educated Horse and His Wonderful Feats," *Orange Journal,* 9/18/1897; "Beautiful 'Jim Key,'" *Orange Chronicle,* 9/18/1897; "At the Waverly Fair," *Newark Evening News,* 9/9/1897; *Newark Daily Advertiser,* 9/8/1897.

140 "prominent Orangeites": ARsb, press release, Hathaway testimonial.

140 "I have been twice": ARsb, press release, Major Pond testimonial.

142 "A good BARKER": "Beautiful Jim Key at the Inter-state Fair," *Trenton Sunday Advertiser,* 9/26/1897.

143 "has the services": Lee, 58, quoting Pittsburg clippings, WKsb.

143 "best draw we ever had": ARsb, West Pennsylvania Exposition Society testimonial.

144 "side show": WKsb, Pittsburg clippings.

144 *"Not* a Side Show": Ibid.

144 "I cannot refrain": Sousa's testimonial in Rogers, "He Was Taught by Kindness."

145 *"F-R-U-I-T-L-E-S-S"*: "Jim Is Highly Educated—Can Both Spell and Figure," *Post-Standard,* 9/7/1902.

146 "what about your claim": *Orange Journal,* 9/18/1897, WKsb clippings. This exchange quoted as printed.

147 "Those who desire": WKsb, ARsb, program excerpts as printed.

149 "Speech alone": New York *Mail and Express,* 10/25/1897; also Jim's 1897 success in Cincinnati clippings: "Little Ones: From House of Refuge and Children's Home," "Odeon, Beautiful Jim Key," "Auditorium, Beautiful Jim Key," "A Wonderful Horse."

149 "In my province": ARsb, Lykens's testimonial.

150 "A free show": Lee, 194.

151 between 1896 and 1906: David Hoffman research, inventions of the era.

152 "Take care of the pigs": Dickens cited in Gerald Carson, *Men, Beasts and Gods,* 77.

155 hindered the efforts: see generally James M. Jasper, "The American Animal Rights Movement," in *Animal Rights,* Robert Garner, ed., 130–31.

158 "a private matinee": ARsb, correspondence, Rogers to Connelly.

158 In the meantime: ARsb, correspondence, Rogers to John Haynes of AHS, George Angell of AHA.

158 "Ohio Humane Society": ARsb, correspondence, Rogers to Angell.

160 "I for one": Carson, 107, citing Angell's letter in *Boston Daily Advertiser,* 2/23/1868.

160 "a lady's name": Ibid., 108; also Jeannette M. Oppedisano reply to query, confirming role of women in shaping animal welfare movement.

164 "Patience": Rogers, "He Was Taught by Kindness."

7. Service to Humanity

167 Charles Eliot: Menand, 117.

168 lawyer made a gift: Thomas Johnson Collection, inscribed book copies.

168 "an animal act": ARsb, correspondence, rejection letter from American Institute Fair.

169 "mouth is all wet": Cincinnati clippings, "Beautiful Jim Key, Odeon"; retold in Senour, 147; retold in Lee, 55.

170 "What makes this horse": Rogers, "He Was Taught by Kindness"; ARsb, Philadelphia news clipping.

172 "most faithful man": Rogers, "He Was Taught by Kindness."

173 "Dear Sir": ARsb, Key to Rogers.

176 *"P-H-Y-S-I-C-S"*: ARsb, Baltimore news clipping.

178 had been kidnapped: ARsb, correspondence between Rogers and Key; Annie Mott Whitman AI 3/31/2003.

178 "rains last two weeks": ARsb, correspondence. The original letter, not a carbon, was apparently not mailed, and no other record of Albert's friend Louise could be located.

181 Sam Jones Union Tabernacle: for Nashville Humane Society correspondence with Reverend Jones, I relied on ARsb; Mayor Dudley's notes were found in WKsb; history of Tabernacle at Ryman Auditorium and Museum visit 4/4/2004; also, Jim Key as first solo entertainer at Ryman's Web site time line; "Object Lesson to Humanity," *Nashville American,* 2/11/1899; "Chesterfield Among Horses," *Nashville American,* 2/12/1899; "Jim Key the Famous Horse," *Nashville Banner,* 2/18/1899.

185 *Pittsburg Press* welcomed: press articles: "Humane Society Endorses the Press Animal Ambulance Fund," 10/24/1900; "Pittsburg Heartily Praises Fund," 10/25/1900; "Need of Animal Ambulance Recognized," 10/26/1900; "No City Needs Ambulance More," 10/1900; "More Money Than Was Originally Asked For," 10/1900.

186 "square roots?": ARsb.

186 "with all eyes": "Exposition Notes," *Philadelphia Inquirer,* 10/8/1899.

187 "'Charge of the Light Brigade'": "Jim Key Does Sums for 8000 People," *Minneapolis Journal,* 4/4/1906.

188 "Jim!": "Captured the City, He Broke All Records," *St. Joseph Star Special Jim Key Edition,* 3/23/1906 (Dr. Key recalled the Philadelphia 1899 incident).

188 "get the eight of clubs": "The King of All Horses, Beautiful Jim Key," *York Press,* 10/4/1898.

190 local equine gait: see generally Bob Womack, *The Echo of Hoof Beats;* also Marilyn Parker horse research: "Bell Buckle Horse History" by Betty Sain and Benvis Beachboard, compiled by Parker; Bob Womack AI 3/30/2004; Kathryn Kerby Tolle AI 4/3/2004; *Shelbyville Times-Gazette,* 1969 Historical Edition, "Heritage of Tennessee Walking Horse."

191 "Jim Key Brand": WKsb, Robinson-McGill order forms, ads; ARsb, endorsement deal ads and brochures, including office sales of Beautiful Jim Key Amberg Imperial Cabinet Letter File (Chicago, London, New York).

193 "In all my travels": ARsb press materials, Lew Parker testimonial.

194 "Pan American ??": ARsb, Key to Rogers.

196 Key told reporters: WKsb, clippings *Boston Globe, Traveler, Evening Transcript;* October–December 1901.

199 name started moving up: Ibid.

202 "scrub colt": WKsb, clipping.

202 "paper should be read": "A Letter from Jim Key," *Our Dumb Animals,* vol. 34, no. 7, 12/1901.

204 both leaders were right: for background on era, Washington, and DuBois, see Zinn, 209–10.

204 race riots exploded: Allan Morrison, "One Hundred Years of Negro Entertainment," in *Anthology of the Afro-American in the Theatre,* ed. Lindsay Patterson, 5.

206 "be the main feature": "Last Chance to See Beautiful Jim Key," *Boston Traveler,* 11/1/1901.

207 "Probably no amusement line": Slout, 23, quoting A. R. Rogers in *Billboard Magazine* on electric parks and street railway journals.

208 "This special ticket": WKsb.

209 "my people are as proud": WKsb, original copy of Booker T. Washington speech.

210 "Kindness has accomplished": WKsb, program of Providence benefit.

210 "most interesting features": Rogers, "He Was Taught by Kindness."

210 "Jim likes to hear": Ibid.

212 "The weather is very fine": ARsb, correspondence, Key to Rogers, circa spring 1902.

212 "I am in fine health": Ibid.

8. The Horse Who Could

For the history of African-Americans in popular entertainment, I relied on Langston Hughes and Milton Meltzer, *Black Magic: A Pictorial History of the Negro in American Entertainment,* along with Lindsay Patterson, ed., *Anthology of the Afro-American in the Theatre;* also Howard L. Sacks and Judith Rose Sacks, *Way Up North in Dixie.*

For the account of how Rogers obtained a concession at the Louisiana Purchase Exposition, I drew from his "Information Regarding Jim Key"; his press materials and financial records were also instructive.

Information about the 1904 Louisiana Purchase Exposition came from a variety of sources including: David Francis, *The Louisiana Purchase Exposition;* Mark Bennett, *The History of the Louisiana Purchase Exposition;* www.boondocksnet .com/expos; and coverage in the *St. Louis Post-Dispatch* on both 4/30/1904 and 5/1/1904; general background on world's fairs came from the Web site for CSU Fresno Library's World's Fair Donald G. Larson Special Collection.

Caro Senour, *Master St. Elmo,* 118–51. A detailed description of the fair and of Jim's show.

Background on Walt Disney, the Carousel of Progress, and Disney's connection to the St. Louis World's Fair was gleaned during a visit to Epcot 6/27/2003, supported by many biographical pieces on Disney.

215 Walt consciously remembered: Epcot staff AI, noting pervasive influence on nation and especially on young boy growing up in Missouri in fair's wake; compare also with observation by Erik Larson, *Devil in the White City,* 153, 373, on the 1893 Chicago Fair's "lasting impact on the nation's psyche" and Disney.

216 indebted to the animator: Epcot staff AI on importance of animals to Disney. It should be noted on the other hand that parts of *Dumbo* reinforced some of the racial stereotypes emerging in the early 1900s.

216 *theatre* was shunned: Slout, 2.

217 advent of melodrama: *Shelbyville Times-Gazette,* 1969 Historical Edition, "Activities of Thespian Club . . . in 1888," 218: "The presence of Dr. J. P. Dromgoole here . . . reminds me of the way back when we had a Thespian Club in our town that gave a weekly performance in a hall then in the rear of Evans & Shepard . . . a great deal of prejudice against the theatre and so we called it the Thespian Hall." Space had shifting scenery, trapdoors, drop curtain. Members of the company were Edmund Cooper, Dr. R. F. Evans, and Jos. H. Thompson; Cooper got all the leads, best actor and he remembered his lines, could "weep or cry at will."

217 "America's Best Bad Actor": Slout, 19.

219 "halls and reception rooms": "Last Day of Mechanics Fair," *Boston Traveler,* 10/30/1902.

220 Clever Hans, and his story: David Hoffman AI 10/11/2002, re: correspondence with Hanne Wolf on Wilhelm von Osten, Clever Hans, Morocco; 2002 *Skeptical Inquirer,* "Psychic Pets and Pet Psychics" on Pfungst.

222 would be dismissed: Portia Iversen AI 3/17/2004, about investigating/teaching alternate forms of communication with autistic students.

223 *Time* magazine: quote attributed to *Time* in Essie Mott Lee's *Dr. William Key,* 117, attributed it to "a magazine near the turn of the century."

224 "I then asked": ARsb, Palmer's letter to Ohio Humane Society.

224 "change two bits": ARsb, clipping.

226 real Negro play Uncle Tom: Langston Hughes and Milton Meltzer, *Black Magic,* 36.

227 "Dear Lincoln": ARsb, the *World*'s HDC, 11/21/1903, letter of introduction.

228 ten million readers: ARsb, press materials extract of AP story "read by ten million."

229 new Union Station: These details were informed by interviews with staff at Union Station Hotel in Nashville, where I stayed during the weeks of 3/3/2003 and 4/2/2004; also I relied on Joe Sherman, *A Thousand Voices.*

232 "The phenomenal success": ARsb, press materials.

233 "Every nation": WKsb, original speech a gift from Booker T. Washington to Dr. Key, 6/30/1904.

234 "The telephone": Senour, 146.

235 "I hope that after": Ibid., 147.

236 "A painful condition": *Bell's Handbook,* 25.

237 "my horse": ARsb, press materials; also it's interesting to note that after St. Louis, Rogers sometimes billed Jim as Wonderful Jim Key.

238 "truly a wonderful horse": "Beautiful Jim Key a Wonderful Horse," *Chicago Daily Journal,* 5/27/1905.

238 "I take it for granted": ARsb, correspondence, Stillman to Rogers.

238 "She is like a person": ARsb, correspondence, Rogers to Angell.

239 whopping $2,300: ARsb, financial records.

241 "Dear Sir": WKsb, ARsb, Key to Rogers.

242 One newspaper: ARsb, clippings, 1906.

9. All Horses Go to Heaven

For the falling-out between Rogers and the AHA, and MSPCA, I relied on correspondence between him and George Angell, as well as other officers.

248 "Bonner the Great": ARsb, WKsb.

249 "Mr. Rogers": ARsb, correspondence, Key to Rogers.

250 "I appreciate": ARsb, Rogers to Colby.

250 German Coach Horses: WKsb, flyer.

252 opened his newspaper: "Soldier of Peace: George T. Angell 1823–1909," *Boston Traveler,* 3/20/1909.

253 honored its founder: MSPCA-Angell Web site.

254 clipped out an article: ARsb, clipping: "Tell of Mind Link to Horses and Dogs," *New York Times,* 10/1/1927.

255 "smart little horse": ARsb, correspondence between Stanley Davis and Rogers.

256 Harvard's president, Charles Eliot: WKsb, clipping: "Dr. Eliot's Five Foot Library," *Chattanooga Times,* 6/29/1909.

257 "I am not the father": Will of Dr. Wm. Key, 3/14/04.

258 a kind of amnesia: Rogers, "Information Regarding Jim Key," and correspondence between Rogers and Stanley Davis.

258 "it was feared": Rogers, "Information Regarding Jim Key."

258 "everything that love": Ibid.

258 "they treatin' you": Annie Mott Whitman AI 4/3/2004; Nancy Barnett AI 3/28/2003.

259 a third version: Dick Poplin research, letter from Marie Davis Harris to Poplin.

259 "out with all ease": ARsb, correspondence, Stanley Davis to Rogers.

260 journalists present: rough draft of news piece, attributed to Mr. McGrew or to W. McGill; Bob Womack AI 4/3/2004; these quotes from that draft.

SOURCES

BOOKS AND SPECIAL PUBLICATIONS

Ades, Harry. *The Little Book of the Civil War*. London: Barnes & Noble Books, 2002.

Barber, James. *Presidents*. New York: DK Eyewitness Books in association with the Smithsonian Institution, First American Edition, 2000.

Bennett, Mark. *The History of the Louisiana Purchase Exposition*. St. Louis: 1905.

Caroli, Betty Boyd. *The Roosevelt Women*. New York: Basic Books, 1999.

Carson, Gerald. *Men, Beasts, and Gods: A History of Cruelty and Kindness to Animals*. New York: Charles Scribner's Sons, 1972.

Charlish, Anne. *A World of Horses: Evolution, History, Breeds, Sports, and Leisure*. Munich: Naturalis, 1981.

Conley, Kevin. *Stud: Adventures in Breeding*. London and New York: Bloomsbury, 2002.

Conn, George, ed. *The Arabian Horse in Fact, Fantasy and Fiction*. New York: A. S. Barnes & Co., 1959. Essays cited: "The Horse Fair," by James Baldwin, 1899; "Bedouins of the Euphrates," by Lady Anne Blunt, 1879; "A Pilgrimage to Nejd," by Lady Anne Blunt, 1881; "The Horse of the Sahara," by E. Daumus, 1863.

Courtenay-Thompson, Fiona, and Kate Phelps, general eds. *The 20th Century Year by Year*. London: Barnes & Noble Books, a Marshall Edition, 1998.

Daniel, Clifton, editorial director. Kirshon, John W., editor in chief. *Chronicle of America*. Paris: Jacques Legrand; Mount Kisco, N.Y.: Chronicle Publications, 1988.

Francis, David R. *The Universal Exposition of 1904*. St. Louis, Mo.: St. Louis Purchase Exposition Company, 1904, 1913.

Garner, Robert, ed. *Animal Rights: The Changing Debate*. New York: New York University Press, 1996.

Goodall, Jane, and Marc Bekoff. *The Ten Trusts: What We Must Do to Care for the Animals We Love*. San Francisco: HarperSan-Francisco, 2002.

Hagedorn, Hermann. *The Roosevelt Family of Saginaw Hill*. New York: Macmillan, 1954.

Hillenbrand, Laura. *Seabiscuit: An American Legend*. New York: Ballantine Books, 2001.

Hughes, Langston, and Milton Meltzer. *Black Magic: A Pictorial History of the Negro in American Entertainment*. Englewood Cliffs, N.J.: Prentice-Hall, 1967.

Jacobs, Lucile Frizzell. "The Tennessee Walking Horse." Chapter 13 in "Duck River Valley in Tennessee and Its Pioneers," 1968.

Justi, Herman, ed. *Official History of the Tennessee Centennial Exposition*. Publication committee: Dr. W. L. Dudley and G. H. Baskette. Nashville, Tenn.: 1898.

Larson, Erik. *The Devil in the White City: Murder, Magic, and Madness at the Fair That Changed America*. New York: Crown Publishers, 2003.

Lawrence, Bobby. *Tennessee Centennial Nashville 1897*. From the series *Images of America*. Charleston, S.C.: Arcadia Publishing, 1998.

Lee, Essie Mott. *Dr. William Key: The Man Who Educated a Horse*. Bloomington, Ind.: 1st Books, 1998, 2002.

Litwack, Leon F. *Been in the Storm So Long: The Aftermath of Slavery*. New York: Alfred A. Knopf, 1979.

Magner, David. *Magner's Art of Taming and Educating Horses*. Battle Creek, Mich.: Review and Herald Publishing House, 1884.

Masson, Jeffrey Moussaieff, and Susan McCarthy. *When Elephants Weep: The Emotional Lives of Animals*. New York: Delta, 1995.

McNamara, Brooks. *Step Right Up: History of the Medicine Show.* Garden City, N.Y.: Doubleday, 1976.

Menand, Louis. *The Metaphysical Club: A Story of Ideas in America.* New York: Farrar, Straus & Giroux, 2001.

Mooney, Chase C. *Slavery in Tennessee.* Westport, Conn.: Negro Universities Press, 1957.

Morais, Herbert M. *History of the Afro-American in Medicine.* International Library of Afro-American Life and History. Cornwells Heights, Pa.: The Publishers Agency, Inc., 1978.

Oppedisano, Jeannette M. *Historical Encyclopedia of American Women Entrepreneurs: 1776 to the Present.* Westport, Conn.: Greenwood Press, 2000.

Patterson, Lindsay, ed. *Anthology of the Afro-American in the Theatre: A Critical Approach.* International Library of Afro-American Life and History. Cornwells Heights, Pa.: The Publishers Agency, Inc., 1978.

Roberts, Monty. *The Man Who Listens to Horses: The Story of a Real-Life Horse Whisperer.* New York: Random House, 1997, 1998.

Robertson, William H. P. *The History of Thoroughbred Racing in America.* Englewood Cliffs, N.J.: Bonanza Books, 1964.

Rogers, Albert. "Information Regarding Jim Key." Various drafts, 1913–1945, unpublished article/manuscript.

Sacks, Howard L., and Judith Rose Sacks. *Way Up North in Dixie: A Black Family's Claim to the Confederate Anthem.* Washington, D.C.: Smithsonian Institution Press, 1993.

Senour, Caro. *Master St. Elmo: The Autobiography of a Celebrated Dog.* Chicago, Ill.: The Juvenile Book Company, 1904.

Sherman, Joe. *A Thousand Voices: The Story of Nashville's Union Station.* Nashville, Tenn.: Rutledge Hill Press, 1987.

Sights, Scenes and Wonders at the World's Fair. St. Louis, Mo., 1904.

Slout, William Lawrence. *Theatre in a Tent: The Development of a Provincial Entertainment.* Bowling Green, Ohio: Bowling Green University Popular Press, 1972.

Spiegel, Marjorie, with a foreword by Alice Walker. *The Dreaded Comparison: Human & Animal Slavery.* New York: Mirror Books/I.D.E.A., 1988, 1989.

Thuss, W. G., and A. J. Thuss. *An Art Album of the Tennes-*

see Centennial International Exposition, May 1 to October 31, 1897. Nashville, Tenn.: Marshall & Bruce Co. Publishers, 1898.

Ward, Geoffrey C., with an introduction by Ric Burns and Ken Burns. *The Civil War: An Illustrated History.* New York: Alfred A. Knopf, 1991.

Womack, Bob. *Call Forth the Mighty Men.* Bessemer, Ala.: Colonial Press, 1987.

————. *The Echo of Hoof Beats: History of the Tennessee Walking Horse.* Shelbyville, Tenn.: DABORA, Inc., 1994.

Zinn, Howard. *A People's History of the United States: 1492– Present.* New York: HarperCollins, 1980, 1995, 1998, 1999.

PAMPHLETS AND PROMOTIONAL MATERIALS

Albert R. Rogers, "He Was Taught by Kindness" aka "Beautiful Jim Key: How He Was Educated." Rogers Publications, editions 1899, 1901, 1904, 1906.

Los Angeles Public Library exhibit brochure for "The Emancipation Proclamation, January 1, 1863" on view Dec. 5–8, 2003.

Tennessee Centennial Exposition postcards, posters 1897.

"The Parthenon: A Museum Guide."

Historical Edition *Shelbyville Times-Gazette,* 1819–1969: "Physicians, Attorneys, Teachers of 1850"; "Historic Streets"; "Study of Early Politics Explains Secession Vote"; "Erwin Home Was General Hardee's Headquarters"; "Bedford Countians Took Up Arms—for Both North and South"; "Units in Which Bedford Countians Fought"; "Federal Soldier Saw Much Union Sentiment"; "HomeGuards Established During 1863"; "Shelbyville Rebels"; "Military Control of Shelbyville Changed Often During 1861–62"; "Andrews Made Plans to Steal 'The General' at Shelbyville"; "Anti-Secessionist 'Parson' Brownlow Detained Here by Rebel Soldiers"; "Bushwhacker Terrorized City"; "Bragg Set Up Defense at Shelbyville after Retreating from Murfreesboro"; "Rosecrans Outflanked Bragg at Battle of Hoover's Gap";

"English Soldier Visited Bragg's Army"; "Spy Pauline Cushman"; "Skirmish at Shelbyville, as Seen by a Soldier"; "Summary of Civil War Action in Bedford County"; "Loyalty of 80-Yr.-Old Shelbyville Woman Impressed Federals"; "S. E. Tillman Gives Insight into Civil War–Torn Bedford County"; "Forrest Escort Assembled in Shelbyville"; "Impressions of Shelbyville by a Rebel Soldier"; "Nathan Bedford Forrest: Legendary Civil War Cavalry Officer"; "Union Underground Railroad Operated in Bedford County"; "Wheeler Took Revenge in Raid on Shelbyville"; "Bedford Countians in the Civil War"; "Smalling Memoirs: Unusual Experiences Encountered by Local Confederate Officer"; "Social and Political Unrest Reflected Change During Reconstruction Period"; "Bedford County Fair Was 'Biggest' Event of Year"; "Support for Woman Suffrage Gained at 1920 Hotel Dixie Meeting"; "From Patent Medicines to Prescriptions"; "History of Negro Education in Bedford County"; "'Old Sawney' Established Nationally Known Webb Preparatory School in Bell Buckle"; "Walking Horse National Celebration: Idea That Was Successful"; "Heritage of Tennessee Walking Horse"; "Activities of Thespian Club . . . in 1888"; "Industrial Development"; "Former Slave Became Prosperous Businessman"; "Many Theories Given about Origin of Bell Buckle's Name."

Information-impressions of Shelbyville and Bedford County, *Shelbyville Times-Gazette,* spring 1988: "Bedford Votes Democratic for Governor"; "Local Theatre Was First Opera House"; "Shelbyville Depot Recommended to National Register for Historic Places"; "National Registry" (Bedford County landmarks); "Early Bedford County Communities and Their Histories"; "Bell Buckle Strives to Retain 1800s Charm"; "Shelbyville and Bedford Co. Have Close Ties to Three Members of Congress and Both Senators"; "Bedford County Can Claim Two United States Senators"; "Famous Bedford Countians"; "Summary of Some Events in Bedford Co. and Shelbyville, Tennessee, History."

"Keystone Driving Park," *Shelbyville Gazette,* 6/23/1887.

Coverage of President McKinley at Tennessee Centennial, *Nashville Sun,* Sunday, 6/13/1897.

"Beautiful Jim Key," *New York Herald,* 8/15/1897.

"Beautiful Jim Key," *New York Sun,* 8/15/1897.

"General Sporting News," *Brooklyn Eagle,* 8/18/1897.

Centennial coverage, *Nashville Daily Sun,* 8/18/1897, 8/23/1897, 8/24–26/1897.

"At the Waverly Fair," *Newark Evening News,* 9/9/1897.

Newark Daily Advertiser, 9/8/1897.

"Beautiful Jim Key, the Educated Horse and His Wonderful Feats," *Orange Journal,* 9/18/1897.

"Beautiful 'Jim Key,'" *Orange Chronicle,* 9/18/1897.

"A Pet Horse That Writes, Thinks, and Spells," New York *World,* 9/26/1897.

"A Horse That Can Count, Read, and Write," *York Press,* 9/26/1897.

"Beautiful Jim Key at the Inter-state Fair," *Trenton Sunday Advertiser,* 9/26/1897.

"Grand Expo Feature," *Pittsburg Evening Record,* 10/1897.

"The Wonderful Horse to Be Seen Exposition," *Pittsburg Daily News,* 10/1897.

"A Wonderful Horse" (Pittsburg), 10/4/1897.

"Unfere Musfteflung," *Pittsburger Beobadjter,* 10/4/1897.

Cincinnati clippings, "Little Ones: From House of Refuge and Children's Home," "Odeon, Beautiful Jim Key," "Auditorium, Beautiful Jim Key," fall 1897.

"A Wonderful Horse," *Mail and Express,* 10/25/1897.

"Jim Key a Clever Horse," *New York Times,* 12/1/1897.

"Beautiful Jim Key, The Scholar and a Model Office Boy," *Trenton Sunday Advertiser,* 2/13/1898.

"Jim Key a Great Actor," *Plainfield Courier News,* 2/26/1898.

"Jim Key Is a Scholarly Horse," *Plainfield Courier News,* 2/1898.

Daily clippings, "Amusement Notes," Plainfield Feb./March 1898.

"A Horse That Almost Talks," *Plainfield Courier News,* 3/8/1898.

"Entertained by the Scholarly Horse" (Plainfield), 3/8/1898.

"The King of All Horses, Beautiful Jim Key" (York, Pa.), 10/4/1898.

"Jim Makes His Bow," *Evening Telegram*, 11/8/1898.

"Beautiful Jim Key: First Performance of This Wonderful Horse Last Night," *Greensboro Record*, 11/8/1898.

"This Horse Will Teach People How to Spell," *Atlanta Journal*, 12/1898.

"Beautiful Jim Key to Come," *Atlanta Constitution*, 12/4/1898.

"Jim Key Performs Today," *Atlanta Constitution*, 12/9/1898.

"Jim Key's Exhibition," *Atlanta Constitution*, 12/10/1898.

"Jim Key's Power of Reasoning," Atlanta, 12/1898.

"Jim Key Performs Today," Atlanta, 12/1898.

"Wonderful Jim Key, the Educated Horse Being Exhibited by the Humane Society," *Atlanta Constitution*, 12/19/1898.

"A Tribute to Jim Key," "Jim Key the Fashion," *Atlanta Constitution*, 12/23/1898.

"Jim Key Leaves Tonight," *Atlanta Constitution*, 12/31/1898.

"Object Lesson to Humanity," *Nashville American*, 2/11/1899.

"Chesterfield Among Horses," *Nashville American*, 2/12/1899.

"Jim Key the Famous Horse," *Nashville Banner*, 2/18/1899.

"Beautiful Jim Key," *The Children's Visitor*, vol. 33, no. 3, March 1899.

"Dr. William Key, Most Successful Horse Trainer in the World," *New Orleans Item*, 1899.

"Horse Still King at the State Fair," "Jim Key to Be Awarded Blue Ribbon," "Pronounced Cleverest Horse in the World," New Orleans, August 1899.

"Exposition Notes," *Philadelphia Inquirer*, 10/8/1899.

"Beautiful Jim Key," *Temple Review*, 11/1899.

"Humane Society Endorses the Press Animal Ambulance Fund," *Pittsburg Press*, 10/24/1900.

"Pittsburg Heartily Praises Fund," *Pittsburg Press*, 10/25/1900.

"Need of Animal Ambulance Recognized," *Pittsburg Press*, 10/26/1900.

"No City Needs Ambulance More," Pittsburg, 10/1900.

"More Money Than Was Originally Asked For," Pittsburg, 10/1900.

Various Boston Food Fair ads, *Boston Globe*, 10/6–27/1901.

Boston Food Fair, *Boston Evening Transcript,* 10/19/1901.

Blurb on examination of Jim by Harvard professors, *Boston Globe,* 10/27/1901.

"Beautiful Jim Key: Horse That Reads, Writes, and Changes Money," *Boston Globe,* 11/1901.

"Last Chance to See Beautiful Jim Key," *Boston Traveler,* 11/1/1901.

"A Letter from Jim Key," *Our Dumb Animals,* vol. 34, no. 7, 12/1901.

"Jim Is Highly Educated—Can Both Spell and Figure," *Post-Standard,* 9/7/1902.

"Last Day of Mechanics Fair," *Boston Traveler,* 10/30/1902.

"Dr. Key and His Horse," *Guardian,* 11/1902.

"Beautiful Jim Key," *South Carolina Interstate & West Indian Exposition Midway Edition,* A. R. Rogers, ed., 12/28/1902.

"Beautiful Jim Key," Boston *Hampton Union,* 1903.

"Will Astonish the City," Charleston, 1902.

"Read by Ten Million People." Extract from an illustrated article that was sent out by the American Press Association; 1903 AP story (reprinted in Rogers promo materials).

"Horse, Trained by Kindness, Does Everything But Talk," *St. Louis Republic,* 4/29/1904.

Entire newspaper, precoverage of world's fair opening, *St. Louis Post-Dispatch,* 4/30/1904.

Entire newspaper, coverage of world's fair opening, *St. Louis Post-Dispatch,* 5/1/1904.

"Popular Prices the Rule on Pike," St. Louis, summer 1904.

"Jim Key's Mascot Was Once a Common Stray Dog" (clipping).

"Beautiful Jim Key a Wonderful Horse," *Chicago Daily Journal,* 5/27/1905.

"Wonderful Jim Key Has Arrived," *Columbus Evening Dispatch,* 3/6/1906.

"'Jim Key' Here Tonight," *Ohio State Journal,* 3/6/1906.

"Horse Is Winner in Spelling Bee," *Columbus Citizen,* 3/7/1906.

"'Jim Key' Makes Good Impression," *Columbus Evening Dispatch,* 3/7/1906.

"Jim Key Proves Equine Wisdom," *Ohio State Journal,* 3/7/1906.

"Wonderful Deaf, Dumb and Blind Boy Writes about 'Jim Key,'" *Columbus Evening Dispatch,* 3/8/1906.

"Captured the City, He Broke All Records," *St. Joseph Star Special Jim Key Edition,* 3/23/1906.

"The Horse and the Boy," *Omaha World-Herald,* 3/26/1906.

"Wisest Horse in the World Is Here," *Minneapolis Journal,* 3/30/1906; editorial cartoon, "The School Board Has Been."

"Jim Key Delights First Night Crowd" (Cleveland), 4/4/1906.

"Jim Key Does Sums for 8000 People," *Minneapolis Journal,* 4/4/1906.

"Is It Wrong to Slaughter Flies?" *Cleveland News,* 5/2/1906.

"Soldier of Peace: George T. Angell 1823–1909," *Boston Traveler,* 3/20/1909.

"A Negro on the 'Problem,'" "Dr. Eliot's Five Foot Library," *Chattanooga Times,* 6/29/1909.

Death notice, *Shelbyville Gazette,* 10/21/1909, "Dr. William Key, colored, died at his home last night" (d.o.d. 10/18/1909).

Clippings, obituaries, Dr. William Key, *Shelbyville Gazette,* 10/1909.

Boston clippings on Angell Memorial Fund, "Children May Give Pennies," various sources, 1909.

"Jim Key Dies," *Shelbyville Gazette,* 2/2/1911 (incorrectly reported).

Carl Krall and Wilhelm Neumann, "Tell of Mind Link to Horses and Dogs," *New York Times,* 10/1/1927.

"Gets Tercentenary Post: Albert R. Rogers to Direct Celebration Planned by Connecticut," *New York Times,* 1/26/1935.

"Beautiful Jim Key, the Educated Horse, Was the Sensation of His Day," *Shelbyville Gazette,* 9/4/1946 (from collection of W. J. McGill).

O. C. Walker, "Jim Key Foaled, Trained in Bedford, Shattered Theories of 'Dumb Animals,'" *Shelbyville-Times Gazette,* 3/21/1958.

"'Jim Key' Foaled, Trained in Bedford, Shattered Theories of 'Dumb Animals,'" New York *World* 3/21/1958.

Charles Whited, "Shelbyville's Wonder Horse," *Nashville Tennessean*, 3/23/1958.

Phil Coop, "Jim Key's Memory," *Shelbyville Times-Gazette*, 9/4/1969.

"Jim Key Wonder Horse," *31st Annual Walking Horse National Celebration Souvenir Edition*, 9/4/1969.

"Story of Jim Key Lives On," *32nd Annual Walking Horse National Celebration Souvenir Edition*, 9/1/1970.

"Memorial to Jim Key," *Shelbyville Times-Gazette*, 10/6/1970.

Dr. Bob Womack, "Jim Key . . . A Remarkable Horse," *Walking Horse Report*, 3/12/1979.

Irving Wallace, David Wallechinsky, and Amy Wallace, "The Amazing Calculating Horse," *Parade*, 6/13/1982.

Dick Poplin, "Scraps of Poplin: Bedford County's Hall of Fame" (Dr. Stanley White Davis remembered), *Shelbyville Times-Gazette*.

Dick Poplin, "The Civil War in Bedford County."

Chris Shofner, "The Smartest Horse in America," *Shelbyville Times-Gazette*, 8/27/1985.

Kay Rose, "Trunk Yields Unexpected Treasures," *Shelbyville Times-Gazette*, 2/23/2000.

Monica Whitaker, "How Kindness Made Freed Slave Famous," *Tennessean*, 2/21/1999.

Dick Poplin, "Of Cabbages and Kings," *Shelbyville Times-Gazette*, 7/17/2002.

Clara Singleton Nelson, "My Civil War Connection," *Shelbyville Times-Gazette*, 2/17/2003.

The Bell Buckle Echo: History Echoes in Bell Buckle, Tennessee, vol. 11, issue 10, October 2002; vol. 11, issue 12, December 2002; vol. 12, issue 3, March 2003.

FILM, VIDEO, AND MUSIC

The Civil War, a film by Ken Burns (episodes 1–9) PBS Gold DVD, dist. by Warner Home Video.

The Hoffman Collection: Films by David Hoffman, including *Moonshot* (4-part series, Turner Broadcasting, Peabody

Award); *Riding for America* (PBS Gold Cine—America's equestrians head for Olympics); *Barnum's Big Top* (The American Experience; the unique story of P. T. Barnum); *Sins of Our Mothers* (The American Experience; incest rumors turn to truth and truth turns to legend in Maine); *Ballad of a Mountain Man* (The American Experience; one man's quest to unearth the roots of "mountain music").

Horses: The Story of Equus, IMAX Films.

Jack Raymond compilation of early minstrel records, including "My Kickapoo Queen," "Cakewalk in Coontown," "When You Ain't Got No Money," "All I Want Is My Black Baby."

Bob Scruggs CD, "Bell Buckle Bob Plays Old Time Gospel Favorites," Texhoma Music Group.

Unchained Memories: Readings from the Slave Narratives; an HBO documentary film in association with the Library of Congress.

INTERNET RESOURCES AND WEB SITES

http//www.dbs.ohiohistory.org/africanam (5/18/1895 *Cleveland Gazette* article on treatment of blacks at Atlanta's Cotton Exposition)

http://www.165.138.44.13/civilwar/63mb.htm (Allen W. Prather, Civil War Sixth Regiment)

http://americancivilwar.com

http://www.animallaw.info/historical/articles (Annual Reports of ASPCA 1889–1904)

Animal Legal & Historical Center, Michigan University College of Law; Clara Morris, "Riddle of the Nineteenth Century: Mr. Henry Bergh," 1902

http://www.bellbuckletn.org/history.shtml

http://www.bellemeadeplantation.com

http://www.blackvoices.com (black equestrians, black jockeys)

http://www.bloodlines.net/TB/Studbook/EarlyM.htm

http://www.boondocksnet.com (world's fairs pages edited by Jim Zwick) http://chronofhorse.com (Chronicle of Horses)

http://www.clickertraining.com (horse intelligence and clicker training)

http://www.cr.nps.gov/nr/travel/undergound/opugrr.htm

http://digital.library.upenn.edu/women/saunders/joe/joe-XIX.htm (A Celebration of Women Writers/women's reading circles, Bands of Mercy)

http://dbs.ohiohistory.org/africanam/ (source of 5/18/1895 *Cleveland Gazette*)

earlyamericanhorses@yahoogroups.com (posting about early pacers and trotters)

http://www.guidehorse.org (miniature guide horses for the blind)

http://www.hall.racingmuseum.org/horse

http://www.harnessmuseum.com/harness11.htm (Hambletonian, Goshen, New York, as Cradle of the Trotter)

http://www.imh.org (International Museum of the Horse)

http://innercity.org/holt/slavechron.html

http://www.jsfmusic.com/Uncle_Tom/Tom_Article6.html (The Minstrel Show's Contribution to Folk Music)

http://www.lib.csufresno.edu/subjectresources/special collections/worldfairs

http://www.lostmuseum.cuny.edu/class (The Lost Museum Classroom: letters between P. T. Barnum and Henry Bergh of the ASPCA)

http://www.luckymojo.com (rabbit's feet and hoodoo)

http://www.mihumane.org (Michigan Humane Society)

http://mspca.techevolution.com/About+MSPCA-Angell/history/107.aspx (The Massachusetts Society for the Prevention of Cruelty to Animals Historical Time Line; biography and legacy of George T. Angell)

http://www.mtsu.edu/-library/wtn/wtn-afam.html (African-American women in Tennessee history, Ida B. Wells)

http://naid.sppsr.ucla.edu/coneyisland/articles/coasterlist.htm (background on rides promoted by Rogers, Shoot the Chutes, Loop-the-Loop, etc.)

http://nyhistory.com/central/loguen.htm (Jermain Wesley Loguen) http://www.oakridger.com/stories ("Tennessee horse population third in country" by Joe Edwards, 2/21/2000)

http://parascope.com/articles/slips/taphorse.htm ("Clever Hans" by D. Trull)

http://www.politicalgraveyard.com (miscellaneous biographies of individuals in military and elected office)

http://www.ryman.com

http://www.state.tn.us/environment/hist/PathDivided.htm

http://sunsite.utk.edu/civil-war/ung.n.html (Union generals, James Scott Negley, command div. XIV Corps at Stone's River)

http://tbheritage.com (Bonnie Scotland at Belle Meade, Luke Blackburn)

http://www.theatrehistory.com/american/barnum001.html (P. T. Barnum)

http://www.thoemmes.com/psych/pfungst.htm (Thoemmes Continuum: Classics in Psychology, Robert H. Wozniak, Bryn Mawr College—Oskar Pfungst: Clever Hans)

http://www.undergroundrailroad.org

http://www.vetcentric.com (article 9/5/2000, "Exploring the Equine Mind: Researchers Study Cognitive Abilities of Horses" by Wes Alwan, on Evelyn Hanggi, Ph.D., founder of Equine Research Foundation in Santa Cruz)

http://www.yesterland.com/progress.html (Carousel of Progress, Walt Disney)

COLLECTIONS

David Hoffman Collection:

1. Original newspapers/photography; four editions of A. R. Rogers's "Beautiful Jim Key: How He Was Taught"
2. Jim Key postcards, souvenir buttons, pins, coins
3. Program Tennessee Walking Horse National Celebration Inaugural Event (September 7–9, 1939)
4. *Shelbyville Times-Gazette* historical editions, 1969, 1988

5. Horse Sense flyer, endorsement brochure of Amberg Imperial Cabinet Letter File

The Johnson Collection: Dr. William Key/Jim Key steamer trunks:

1. souvenirs as buttons, postcards, photos, statues, and pamphlets
2. Jim Key chalkboard
3. original newspapers kept by Dr. Key
4. tintypes for photographs, promo materials
5. ledger for Keystone Liniment sales and county fair directorships
6. template for Keystone Liniment bottle label
7. college diploma, Maggie Davis Key
8. personal correspondence Dr. Key and Lucinda Davis Key, M.D.
9. tickets and stubs (thousands)

Annie Mott Whitman Collection of Jim Key Materials, Manuscripts Section, Tennessee State Library and Archives.

1. Patent medicine materials, flyer for Dr. W. C. Fair; "Bell's Handbook of Veterinary Homeopathy," 1885 edition
2. Letter from George Angell to Wm. Key, 11/1/1901, presentation of gold medal from AHES, MSPCA, Parent American Band of Mercy
3. Letter from Wm. Key to A. R. Rogers, 11/18/1905
4. Address of Booker T. Washington to National Educational Association, St. Louis, Mo., Thursday, June 30, 1904
5. Mayor Richard Dudley, handwritten notes describing Wm. Key payoff of mortgage on farm of John and Martha Key
6. Jim Key schoolhouse bell
7. Beautiful Jim Key equine honorary membership documents: American Humane Association/MSPCA, Bands of Mercy of the World, Pen and Pencil Club
8. Dr. William Key honorary membership documents and gold medal document for Band of Mercy Service to Humanity Award (bestowed 11/1/1901)

9. 1905 Robinson-McGill Mfg. Co. logo "Jim Key Brand" (order forms)
10. Jim Key Band of Mercy organizing forms (National Organizer Miss Agnetta Floris)
11. Personal reading/general clippings: "Securing Homes for Homeless Children Number," *WCTU Tidings*, Charlotte, N.C.; April 1903; subjects of African-American interest, root medicine, horses, women's suffrage; 1909 ad for Falkenfels No. 1899, German Coach Horse in stud service in Shelbyville c/o J. C. Jackson; flyer on land for sale in Chattanooga, 1890
12. Personal notes: various financial lists of costs; 1900/1901 handwritten notes on plans for Philadelphia, Washington, Pan American exhibit, carved trunk
13. Letter from Archie Rogers to Essie Mott Lee, 10/10/72

Annie Mott Whitman Collection of Jim Key Materials, Manuscripts Section, to Tennessee State Library and Archives. Albert R. Rogers scrapbooks, correspondence, souvenirs, promotional materials.

1. Marketing letters: from B. F. Keith's Amusement Ent., 8/19/1897; from American Institute Fair, fall 1897; from Allen Williams, Chief, Press Bureau Madison Square Garden, 9/13/1897; to Secretary, Danbury Fair, 9/17/1897; to Mr. Fitzpatrick from Rogers in Minn., 4/4/1906, on season; West Pennsylvania Exposition Society, 10/9/1897; Merchants Fall Festival, Springfield, Mo., 9/12/1906; letter of introduction for Rogers from J. Heekin, Heekin Coffee of Cincinnati, 10/13/1897; to T. J. Fitzpatrick, Pittsburg Exposition, pricing and misplaced props; letter of introduction for Rogers from HDC of the *World*, 11/21/1903.
2. Humane groups letters: to George Angell, 11/8/1897; John Haines of American Humane Society, 11/19/1897; to Frank Connelly, 11/23/1897; from National Humane Society Officers, 2/1899, on change of date due to cold weather; 1901 Angell to School Supt. Boston about closing schools; AHES/MSPCA, Secretary Stevens, 2/18/1905, for Angell; from New York State Convention of Societies for the Prevention of

Cruelty to Children and Animals, 1/27/1905; from American Humane Ass., 10/26/1905, commending his help; from American Humane Ass., 11/1/1905; from Minn. student organizer to Uncle Bert, 11/22/1906; from Missouri Humane Society, 9/1906; from Rogers to Angell on ideas for network of groups, 1906; from Rogers to Angell, 2/13/1906, on April Mercy Day ideas; from Angell to Rogers, 11/10/1906, on letter from San Antonio; from National Humane Alliance, 1/22/1907; Angell to Rogers, 1/31/1907, on opening New York office; Rogers to Angell on funding outreach for Bands of Mercy, 2/7/1907; from ASPCA secretary to Rogers, 2/19/1907; Rogers to Angell on fund-raising, 11/6/1907; Mr. Richardson of MSPCA/AHES to Rogers on election of valuable service, 11/20/1907; Rogers to Angell on need to unite societies, 1/6/1908; Rogers to Angell, 3/24/1908, on show at Hippodrome; Richardson to Rogers, 4/1/1908, on commendation of contribution; Rogers to Angell on lack of cooperation from Richardson, 4/1908; Rogers to Boston School Committee on Angell Memorial Fund, 3/29/1909; from secretary of Boston School Committee, 4/8/1909, circular about raising money for memorial approved

3. Letter from National Cash Register Co. (Dayton, Ohio), 1906, to J. Hazuka, Omaha, Nebraska; ads with Metropolitan Cash Register

4. Personal letters: Ida Sheehan to Rogers, 5/23/1896; formal dinner invitation from Senator Palmer, Detroit, 1905; E. S. Porter, Windsor Farms, Richmond, Va., on a "wonderful little mare," 8/12/1927; letter to Mrs. Colby from Rogers, Boston, 1/13/1909

5. Letter from Albert to "Louise," Raleigh, N.C., 10/25/1898

6. Letter from Wm. Key to A. R. Rogers, 5/3/1898, Atlantic City; from Key to Rogers noting dimensions of racks, Shelbyville; from Wm. Key to A. R. Rogers, 3/12/1900, on terms, Jim's condition; from Wm. Key to A. R. Rogers, 11/18/1905, on financial misunderstanding; from Wm. Key to Rogers, 12/9/1907, on Jim's health, interest in travel

7. Letter from St. Louis World's Fair to Rogers over legal settlement, 11/21/1904

8. Correspondence with Dr. Stanley White Davis; Davis to Rogers, 2/13/1913 and 3/10/1913, reporting Jim's death September 18, 1912

9. Letter of complaint from Rogers to American Humane Educational Society board of directors, including correspondence, 4/13/1909; note on National Jim Key Band of Mercy 1906 (700,000 members), on financial losses, 1/17/07; and letter, 1/19/1907 (posted to 1,000,000 members), on illness of Miss Floris; 2/9/1907 report on need for funds for Bands of Mercy

10. Flyers, programs: Orange Riding and Driving Club, 9/21–22/1897; program for *The Scholar and a Model Office Boy*, 10/18/1897; program for the Star Theatre Broadway bill, 12/1897; Scenic Theatre, Atlantic City; Pittsburg Exposition Sousa bill with Jim Key; Eagles Exposition/MDSPCA; Atlanta Humane Society program at 80 Whitehall St., Opera House in Shelbyville, Tenn., 1/27–28/1899; 1900 Esplanade, Export Exposition; Alhambra Pet Show and Fair, Women's Auxiliary SPCA pass; Fitzhugh Hall 12/1–6/1902, Rochester, N.Y.; Negro Day at the Exposition (Charleston 1/1/1903); Cooperstown, 9/21–23, Otsego County Fair, "McGuire's Educated Horses"; 1900 flyer for new play *The Horse of the Twentieth Century*, at the Jefferson; 1904 purchase form for "The Story of Beautiful Jim Key"; 1905 White City flyer; flyer, program (paid advertising) Omaha Auditorium, 3/26–28/1906; Columbus Memorial Hall, 3/6–8/1906 (pages of paid advertising); 4/2–7/1906 Auditorium pass for Minneapolis Humane Society; Cleveland Grays' Armory, 4/30–5/5/1906; various ads for 1900 street railway journals, children's discount tickets, press and VIP passes; First Annual Pure Food, Drug and Confectionery Exposition Cincinnati, Bonner the Great (Jim Key Band of Mercy); Toledo Humane Society to local clergy on Valentine Theatre benefit with famous horse Cresceus, owned by George Ketchum; National Jim Key Band of Mercy promotion of gold stars and copies of *Black Beauty*; newspaper composition contests; Rogers business card, "Director of Amusements"

11. Promo materials: Albert R. Rogers stationery, special promotions, letters from Uncle Bert, Jim Key Band of Mercy; Jim Key dictated letter to George Angell (10/1901); souvenir buttons "I Have Seen Jim Key"; Souvenir Young's Pier, season 1901, Albert and Albert Palmists & Astrologers; composition medals (Women's Pennsylvania SPCA); flyer for Riverview

Park, Baltimore; pass for union members at the New Bijou Theatre; "Jim Key" Special Train to San Antonio, 10/29 (1905); bill for Fighting the Flames for 9/10/1906 Cincinnati Fall Festival

12. Misc. testimonials: letter from Senator T. W. Palmer (Detroit, 5/1/1906); from W. L. Lykens (leading theatrical booking agent); W. L. Tomkins, president of the New Jersey State Fair; Mayor James M. Seymour; editors *Newark Evening News, Newark Daily Advertiser,* 1897; Wm. R. Riddle, Commander of Ohio United Boys Brigade; 10/7/1897, from M. Jenkins of New Jersey School for Deaf Mutes; 11/11/1897, Ohio Humane Society, S. Ritter, secretary; Nashville Board of Education president, Edward E. Barthell; 11/3/1899, Women's PA SPCA president Caroline Earle White; T. M. Porter, Sec., Western Pennsylvania Humane Society; Harvard president Charles Eliot, 1901; from School District Board St. Paul, Minn., schools closed for two days, 5/23/1906; Toledo Humane Society, 5/23/1906

Bob Womack Collection: loan of personal writings and clippings for research, sample formulation Keystone Liniment.

Dick Poplin Collection: various writings including article by Dick Poplin, "The Civil War in Bedford County"; letter from Marie Davis Harris (daughter of Dr. Stanley Davis) to Poplin, 2/6/1985.

VITAL RECORDS AND ARCHIVED MATERIALS

Anne Chunko, USTA: pedigree information on Rysdyk's Hambletonian.

Gail C. Cunard, director, Harness Racing Museum, Goshen, N.Y.: information on background of National Association of Trotting-Horse Breeders; "The Standard of Admission to Registration est. 1879, rev. 1887" and report on "Time Trials"; racing paper page on Trotting/Pacing, *The Horseman,* 12/13/1894; copy of "Standard Horses," reg. 2784, Kentucky Volunteer (sire Volunteer 55, dam Kentucky Girl, by Blue Bull 55) bred by John S. Biggs of Cincinnati, Ohio.

Joseph Ditta, New-York Historical Society: research on Jim Key's New York press appearances; on Rogers as director of Grand Central Palace and 1935 appointment to Connecticut Tercentenary post.

Catherine Medich, New Jersey State Archives: research on Albert R. Rogers and family-owned home Glenmere (Ridgewood, South of Montrose Ave.); 1904 listed in name of mother, 1911 in name of Clara Rogers; drawing of village of South Orange and Glenmere (from *Atlas of the Oranges,* Essex County, N.J., copyright 1911, by A. H. Mueller, Philadelphia); Mercy Adelia Reynolds Rogers genealogy, "The Life and Times of Samuel Gorton" (Rhode Island founding family); Hamilton County, Ohio, censuses for Hiram Rogers family in 1870, 1880; 1910 Boston, Mass., census for Albert Rogers and family; 1920 census for Albert Rogers in New York.

Marilyn Parker research on Dr. William Key: will of Captain John Key of Winchester, 1838; from John W. Key to Jeptha Minter, bill of sale Negroes, 10/19/1843 (William, age "about eleven," Caroline, Jack, Nancy for $1,500); 1/3/1866 property deed from William Brown of two and a half acres on Shelbyville and Murfreesboro Turnpike Rd., bought 9/22/1865; 1870, 1880 censuses Keys, Davidsons, Davises; cemetery record book Dr. Key mother-in-law Arabella Davidson (1800–9/17/1882), wife Lucy Davidson (2/1832–8/17/1885), sister Nancy McClain died 10/30/1885, Wm. Key and Lucinda Davis marriage 4/23/1888; death certificate Mrs. Lucinda Davis Key published 8/27/1896; marriage license w/Maggie Davis 3/14/1904: will of Dr. Wm. Key 3/14/04.

Marilyn Parker genealogy of Keys and Davises: cemetery records; "Colored section of Willow Mount" (Dr. William Key, Trainer of Jim Key, 1833–1909, Lucinda Davis Key, M.D., 2/24/1859–8/21/1896; Maggie Davis Key 1865–1935; funeral program for Dr. Stanley W. Davis 11/11/1967 (died 11/10/1967).

Marilyn Parker research on Strother Key: "Tennesseeans in the War of 1812"; records of service as a Volunteer Mounted Gunman; divorce of Strother and Margaret C. Graham (married 1/12/1812 in Sumner County, granted privileges of a feme sole in 1831 in Tennessee Divorces 1797–1858; Strother Key cemetery record 1787–1842).

Marilyn Parker research on John W. Key and family: genealogy of descendants of John Key Sr. of Albemarle, Va. (marriages of Goochland County, Va., 1733–1815, John Key of Albemarle and Nancy Ford); John W. Key born 1813; John Key Sr. will in will book, Sumner County, Tenn.; daughter Polly Bibb Key Blaydes and son Jesse Bibb Key "take it or leave it"; slaves deeded to sons Strother, Captain John, Richard; will of Richard Key, 1820; will of Captain John Key of Franklin County, 1838; 3/25/1840 John W. Key marriage to Martha; chancery court item 1841, a debt involving John W. Key; 1843 legal action involving John W. Key, Jeptha Minter, all of Davidson County; 1851, mother of John W. gives slave to John W. (records in court); 1852 Bedford County Court trade plus cash between John W. and Jeptha Minter, William Key returned to John W.; 7/12/1865 John W. Key Trust Deed to J. M. Minter (242 acres); offspring of John W. Key, Merit Key (M. P. Keys) and Alexander Key (A. K. Keys) in Civil War records, Eighteenth Tennessee Infantry Reg., Co. F.; 1850 census, Merit P. nine years old, Alexander W. seven, John F. five (John Franklin Key became major, died 1904 in Washington City), Louisa three; 1860 census: John W. Key forty-seven, Martha forty, M.P. nineteen, A. seventeen, J.F. fifteen, L.A. twelve, M.E. (female) eight, E.F. (female) five, W.J. (male) three, Margaret C. sixty-five (no slaves listed).

Marilyn Parker horse research: "Bell Buckle Horse History" by Betty Sain and Benvis Beachboard, compiled by Parker, Bell Buckle, Tennessee, 1986.

Dick Poplin, Bedford County Historian, columnist: Dr. Stanley White Davis materials.

Thomas J. Reider, reference archivist, Ohio Historical Society: research on Albert R. Rogers and family.

Rosedale Cemetery, Orange, New Jersey (Albert R. Rogers, died 3/31/1946).

Dave Seuss loan of *Skeptical Inquirer* 2002 research: "Psychic Pets and Pet Psychics."

Philip Shapiro research on Richard Houston Dudley: born

7/28/1836, son of Christopher Stump Dudley and Louise Pierce Bandy; elected mayor of Nashville 10/4/1897, served until 1900.

Philip Shapiro research on Davis family: 1930 census, Stanley Davis fifty-one, Lillie forty-seven, Stanley Jr. nineteen, Marie fifteen, Harriet C. thirteen, William Key six.

Philip Shapiro research on descendants of A. R. Rogers: Archibald Rogers born 6/18/1895, died 4/1974.

St. Louis Public Library, Central Library, Special Collections: copy of invitation to opening performances of Beautiful Jim Key, 4/30/1904 benefit for the American Humane Education Society.

Leilah Strachen, Harvard Student Agencies: Boston research.

Sylvia Weedman, library assistant, the Bostonian Society.

Annie Mott Whitman/Campbell family tree research: marriages of Lucy Davidson and Hattie Davidson to Dr. Key.

INDIVIDUALS, AUTHORITIES, LIBRARIES, AGENCIES, INTERVIEWS, AND QUERIES

Nancy Campbell Barnett, Shelbyville, Tennessee; oral histories on civil rights in Bedford County (niece of Essie Campbell Davis), secondhand recollections of Jim Key in later years.

Randolph Whittington Best, oral historian and student of Tennessee history, music, and Civil War; on Staff Union Station Hotel, Nashville, Tennessee.

Anne Chunko, USTA, Standardbred Equestrian Program.

Jim Cooper, Congressman, 5th district Tennessee, on Shelbyville and family history.

Dianna Dennis, author, equestrian expert, Moderator on Chronicle of the Horse Bulletin Board (*Chronicle of the Horse Magazine*); on equine intelligence, bloodlines.

Joseph Ditta, reference librarian, the New-York Historical Society; research on Jim Key's New York debut; Albert R. Rogers in New York.

Benjamin Feldman, lawyer, authority New York real estate law, author; account of work of Grand Central Palace, Lexington Avenue, A. R. Rogers era.

Stephen Fife, playwright, author, humorist; on early American theatre history, lower Broadway in 1890s, location of Maiden Lane.

Susan Gordon, Special Collections, Tennessee State Library and Archives.

David Hoffman; overall process of excavating history, notes on inventions, time period, era of world's fairs.

Portia Iversen, founder Cure Autism Now, author of *Strange Son* (Riverhead Press, due 2005), coauthor with Soma Mukhopadhyay of Rapid Prompting Method manual (Riverhead Press, due 2005); on alternative mental processes.

Janis Jones, expert US Trotters; on John H. Wallace, Wallace's Year Book registry, recommended *Master St. Elmo.*

Catherine Medich, New Jersey State Archives; Rogers genealogy, New Jersey performances, Standardbred expertise.

Megan Milford, Massachusetts Historical Society; research for Harvard study of Beautiful Jim Key.

Marilyn Wade Parker, commissary of the Tennessee Brigade of the Society of the Descendants of Washington's Army of Valley Forge.

Dick Poplin, Bedford County, Tenn., author, historian; oral history of family members who saw Jim perform.

Clara Nelson Singleton, Shelbyville, Tennessee, writer and oral historian; family members/slaves who served in the Civil War.

Nancy Stowers, Shelbyville, Tennessee; oral history of family members who saw Jim Key perform; neighbor of Essie and Sam Davis.

Kathryn Kerby Tolle, Shelbyville, Tennessee; oral history of father and uncle who saw Jim Key perform.

Annie Mott Whitman, music teacher, songwriter, author of *The Unbelievable Love: Here & Beyond* (Bloomington, Ind.: 1st Books Library, 2002).

Hanne Wolf; correspondence regarding Wilhelm von Osten, Clever Hans, Morocco.

ACKNOWLEDGMENTS

In the spring of 2002, I was at a crossroads—ready to venture off on my own after more than a dozen years of having had the good fortune to work as a coauthor and ghostwriter, but not sure how—and I was waiting for a sign. I will be eternally grateful to my cousin, Tom Wills, for sending me the e-mail that introduced this story and David Hoffman to me, and for giving me my sign. My fondest appreciation belongs to David Hoffman, for his incomparable talents as filmmaker and storyteller, his thoughtful idea-prodding, and his instincts for unearthing strange but true histories. I will always be indebted to him for allowing me to ride with *Beautiful Jim Key*.

My everlasting thanks go to my agent, the wonderful Elizabeth Kaplan, for her love of story, her buoyant energy, her gift for problem-solving made easy, and her belief from the start in this unlikely history and in me. There is no way I'll ever be able to express my gratitude sufficiently to Henry Ferris, my editor at William Morrow, for his guidance, his infectious intellectual curiosity, his good heart, and the leap of faith it took to make this dream of writing solo come true for me.

Thank you to everyone at William Morrow: to publisher Michael Morrison for his support, to marketing director Lisa Gallagher for her enthusiasm, to editorial assistant Peter Hubbard for his help, to the art department for the stunning jacket, and to the rest of the house for being a home to me.

My thanks are strewn across my home state of Tennessee, starting with the heroine of Bedford County, Marilyn Parker, who followed a genealogical trail that would have stymied any other researcher; she never stopped searching and continued to send me discoveries long after I'd turned in the manuscript. Thank you, Marilyn, for home cooking and my meeting your eight dogs and three horses, and for organizing my visits to Shelbyville, Bell Buckle, and Wartrace. Boundless gratitude goes to my other dear friend, Annie Mott Whitman, the petite dynamo who generously gave me access to the Key and Rogers scrapbooks and the oral histories about Key and Key that had passed down through her family. Though I never met her sister, the late Essie Mott Lee, or her aunt, the late Essie Campbell Davis, I am awed by their devotion to keeping the legacies of Dr. William Key and Jim alive. My lasting gratitude goes to Bob Womack, for sharing his Key collection, his youthful exuberance, and his stories from Bedford County tended over his more than eighty-one years, as well as his Civil War knowledge and Tennessee Walking Horse expertise. I offer special thanks to Thomas Johnson for Southern hospitality, for sharing highlights from his collection, and for his gift as a listener and questioner. I'm enormously grateful to the many folks in Shelbyville who also let me borrow their time and insights, stories, memories, and parts of collections: Dick Poplin, Nancy Barnett, Clara Singleton Nelson, Nancy Stowers, Bob Scruggs, Jim Bomar, Kathryn Kerby Tolle, and the Ewing Cartwright family. Thanks to Mrs. Hortense Cooper, who took time out of her busy afternoon to greet me and talk about local history, and more gratitude goes to her son, Congressman Jim Cooper, whose devotion to the important causes of our day and to Tennesseans is an inspiration. You all made me feel like family.

I am certain that divine intervention placed the amazing Susan Gordon, archivist at the Tennessee State Library and Archives in Nashville, Tennessee, in my path. My humblest, deepest thanks go to her for her labor of love performed on behalf of Jim Key, for her countless hours and help far beyond the call of the duty of research. My heartfelt thanks to Susan for shared values and for giving me a sense of the meaning of provenance that informed my work throughout. I am also indebted to Karina McDaniel, staff photographer at the Tennessee State Library.

Endless thanks are due Catherine Medich of the New Jersey State Archives for her research talents, which allowed me to step back in time and see the world that Albert Rogers inhabited, and for her Standardbred sleuthing. Throughout my research process, I was humbled by the incredible work and assistance provided me by librarians, researchers, state and local archives, historical societies, antique bookstores, and private collectors. Catherine Medich modestly said, "We are all researchers who love a good topic to search." For those who devote themselves to preserving histories, I offer my permanent admiration.

Special thanks go to everyone at the Central Library's Special Collections at the St. Louis Public Library; to Joseph Ditta of the New York Historical Society; Thomas J. Reider, Reference Archivist, at the Ohio Historical Society; to Sylvia Weedman, Library Assistant at the Bostonian Society; Megan Milford, Massachusetts Historical Society; Gail C. Cunard, director of the Harness Racing Museum; and Anne Chunko of the United States Trotter's Association. I'm grateful to research help from Leilah Strachen, Harvard Student Agencies, and my dear inquisitive friends, Dave Suess and Phil Shapiro. I'm so thankful to Di Dennis, coauthor of *Linda Allen's 101 Exercises for Jumping* and a fellow Sarah Lawrence College alumna, for her horse love and expertise, with helpful information from Sarah Tradewell and from the posting of "Cherry." I loved hearing the debates of the passionate horsey people at yahoo.com's Early American Horse group that helped refine my search for Jim Key's lineage.

There are several individuals to whom belated, profound gratitude is owed for trusting me to help with their stories and projects—experiences that helped guide me in the process of bringing the people in this story back to life. My lasting thanks go to the legendary Berry Gordy, who taught me early on that "the truth is a hit," and who nurtured my talents in ways I hope make him proud. Through his example as a leading African-American entrepreneur and philanthropist, I have better understood the journey taken by Dr. William Key. There aren't enough words to say thank you also to Della Reese-Lett, Franklin Lett, Betty DeGeneres, Victoria Principal, and Antwone Fisher. To a handful of extraordinary individuals who worked so generously to shepherd my career and my family's well-being in the past, I send thanks, especially to literary agent Jennifer Rudolph Walsh, to business manager Matt Lichtenberg, and artist's manager Sherry Robb. For ongoing PR advice and friendship, thanks to Howard Bragman, and to Dick Weaver.

Lifelong love and gratitude are owed to David Geffen—my hero—for his unbelievable generosity and support to me and my family over the years. His journey as an entrepreneur, philanthropist, and humanitarian has helped to illuminate the inner lives of many individuals in this book and has never ceased to inspire me. Lots of thanks to Priscila Giraldo at DreamWorks for steering me toward the great work of *Heads Up, Therapy with Horses,* and to all the folks at DreamWorks and the David Geffen Foundation for their kindness.

Much appreciation is sent to the many families and communities who have become my family's proverbial village. Thanks to Gene and Caroline Kimmelman, Rick Jacobs, Betsy Jasny, and the rest of my homies from Oak Ridge, Tennessee, to E. L. Doctorow for teaching me that we all have more than one story to tell, and to all my teachers, friends, and administrators from Sarah Lawrence College. Enormous admiration and gratitude go to the advocacy community that works to end domestic and other forms of violence, and to all our good neighbors in Hermosa Beach. It is just so California to thank my Pilates instructor, but without the wonderful Melanie Petri I wouldn't have made it through. My friend Kathy Cartwright also inspires me every day.

My undying gratitude goes to everyone at the Hermosa Animal Hospital, to veterinarians Kim Doane and Steve Liebl, for taking such good care of Pokey and Josey, the Educated Beautiful Jack Russell terriers who bring unconditional, unlimited joy into my life every day. Thanks to veterinarians and animal advocates everywhere, to local, state, national, and international humane groups, to animal shelters, rescue groups, and environmental organizations working to protect endangered wildlife and their habitats around the world. If readers would like to contribute to humane work to honor the memories of Beautiful Jim Key and Dr. William Key, I dearly encourage the support of local groups in dire need of funds and volunteers or any of the well-known animal protection organizations. To make an honorary gift to MSPCA-Angell.org, contributors can visit http://www.secure.ga3.org/02/honor_gift, or mail to MSPCA, Attn.: Miss Joan Stark, 350 South Huntington Avenue, Boston, MA 02130. To contribute to the fund established by Essie Mott Lee and Annie Mott Whitman, donors can mail contributions to the Jim Key Memorial Donation Fund, US Bank, 600 South Main, Goodlettsville, TN 37072; or to its Shelbyville address: US Bank, 100

North Side Square, Shelbyville, TN 37160; or to any US Bank in the country, as well as online by visiting http://www.usbank.com/.

I send love to infinity to the family that I came from: to the late Gene Eichler, to my mother, Sonya Geffen Eichler, to my sister Margrit and my brother Dan and their families, and special thanks to Great-aunt Deena. Infinite gratitude goes to the whole Rivas familia. Most of all, I thank the two guys who encourage and put up with me whenever deadlines loom, who make me laugh, and whose supply of unconditional love is unlimited. Thank you, my amazing ten-year-old son, Eli, statesman, comedian, and terrific in-house editor. Thank you, Victor, actor, athlete, author, activist, husband, friend, and love of my life. You are the big man.

INDEX

offers for purchase of,
93–95, 119, 144–45, 172,
220
offspring of, 255
parentage of, 16, 21, 22–26,
32–33, 113, 146, 190
participation in exhibitions
and shows by, xiii–xiv,
1, 4–10, 16, 42, 60–63,
87–88, 93–99, 112–18,
121–22, 131–50, 156–58,
162–72, 176–203, 206–
13, 231–34
physical appearance of,
xiii–xiv, 8–9, 42, 94, 112,
180, 186
political opinions of, 98,
115–16, 137–38, 178,
196, 206, 269
proceeds from perfor-
mances of, xiv, 131,
176–77, 260–61
professional debut of, 16,
93, 112–18
psychic abilities of, 95–96
religious instruction of,
85–86, 210–11, 247
sale of, 117–21, 260
sensitivity of, 119, 130
skepticism about feats of,
xiv, xv, 60, 64, 87, 135–
36, 145–46, 149, 168–70,
188–89, 213, 255
souvenirs of, xiv, 186, 191,
232, 264
spelling and reading of, 9–
10, 63–64, 85, 87, 95, 98,
99, 113–15, 135–39, 142,
145, 163, 170, 176–77,
180, 186, 200, 213, 245
toothy grin of, 9, 16
WK's raising and train-
ing of, xv, 37–47, 58,
59–64, 85–86, 87, 89,

93–99, 106, 113–18, 119,
137–40, 145–48, 155–57,
163–65, 167–71, 179–81,
187–89, 207–13
*Beautiful Jim Key: How He Was
Educated* (Rogers), 15
"Beautiful Jim Key Two-Step,
The" (Minoliti), 199
Beautiful Joe (Saunders), 162,
168
Bedford County Fair, 97–98
Bedford County Humane
Society, 189
Belle Meade Plantation,
27–28, 54
*Bell's Handbook to Veterinary
Homeopathy*, 38, 236
Bergh, Henry, 88–89, 152,
153–55, 159, 160
Bernhardt, Sarah, 218, 235,
240, 243
B. F. Keith's Amusements
Enterprises, 126–27
Bible, 45, 61, 85–86, 103, 168,
210, 223, 247, 271
Billboard Magazine, 207
Black Beauty (Sewell), 127–28,
161, 168, 235, 271
Blue Bull, 33
Bonner the Great, 248
Bonnie Scotland, 28
Booth, John Wilkes, 80
Boston, Mass., 166–67, 196–
204, 251
Boston Food Fair, 166–67,
187, 197, 199–201
Boston Globe, 167, 196, 200,
201
Boston Mechanics Fair, 212
Boston Traveler, 206
Bowery Boys, 154
Bragg, Braxton, 75, 78
Briggs, John S., 33
British Isles, 29–30, 153, 222

British Parliament, 24
Brooklyn Eagle, 87
Brownlow, William, 66–67,
72, 81
Bryan, William Jennings, 98,
116
Buchanan, Lillie, 247
Buchanan, T. C., 31
Buckner, Simon Bolivar, 69
Bunch, Gordon, 231, 242,
244
Busbey (horse whisperer), 46
Bushnell, Asa, 107, 108

California Mid-Winter Exposi-
tion of 1894, 109
Call Forth the Mighty Men
(Womack), 59
Camille (Dumas) 243
Campbell, Cora, 268
Campbell family, 229–30, 269
Camp Trousdale, 65
Carson, Gerald, 125
Carter's Little Liver Pills, 19
Caruso, Enrico, 235, 240
Cathcart, James A., 198
"Charge of the Light Brigade,
The" (Tennyson), 187
Charles Kent Mare, 29–30
Charleston World's Fair, 218
Chattanooga Times, 256
Chautauqua circuit, 218
Cherokee Indians, 34, 48
Chesapeake & Ohio Railroad,
108
Chicago Daily Journal, 238
Chicago Tribune, 5
Chicago World's Fair, *see*
World Columbian Expo-
sition of 1893
Chickamauga, Battle of, 96,
146
Cincinnati, Ohio, 89–90, 107,
109, 122, 127, 128–30,

131, 146–50, 169, 240,
242–43, 246–48
Eighth Street District
School in, 129
House of Refuge in, 130,
150
Odeon Theatre in, 129–30,
147–50
Cincinnati *Commercial Gazette,*
149
Cincinnati *Commercial Tribune,*
150
civil rights movement, 8, 203,
267, 268
Civil War, U.S., xiii, 27, 32, 51,
107, 153, 264, 265
battles and battlefields of,
45, 61, 73–75, 96, 112,
146
casualties of, 66, 70, 74, 80
colored regiments in,
75–76
death of horses in, 66
Lee's surrender in, 80
political, moral, and economic issues of, 65, 66,
67–68
secession of states prior to,
57, 65, 66, 68, 80
Tennessee in, 65–80, 102
WK in, xiii, 65–80, 96, 117,
183
Clarke, W. T., 109–10
Cleveland, Grover, 98
Clever Hans, 220–22, 223,
224
Clover Bottom racetrack, 27
Cody, Buffalo Bill, 193
Cole, Bob, 205, 226
Collins College for Veterinary
Surgery, 112, 190
Colored Masons, 84
Columbus *Evening Dispatch,*
245–46

Lucas, Sam, 226
Luke Blackburn, 28
Lykens, W. L., 149
lynchings, 21, 205, 265–66

McCarthy, Cormac, ix
McCarthy, Mayor, 112, 115
McClain, Henry, 83
McClain, Nancy Key, 48, 53,
    56, 83, 84
McGill, W. J., 264
McKinley, Ida, 107, 108, 109–
    11, 113, 195
McKinley, William, 98, 106–
    16, 126, 137, 155
    assassination of, 4, 195–96
    BJK's performance for,
    112–16, 178
Madame Tonson, 27
Madison Square Garden, 47,
    87, 132
Magner, D., 166
*Magner's Art of Taming and
    Educating Horses* (Mag-
    ner), 166
Malone, Thomas, 141
Man O'War, xiii
Mascot and Barney (Maguire
    Educated Horses), 220
Massachusetts Charitable
    Mechanics Association,
    212
Massachusetts Society for the
    Prevention of Cruelty to
    Animals (MSPCA), 159,
    160, 197, 199, 202, 212,
    250, 252–53, 254
*Master St. Elmo: The Autobiog-
    raphy of a Celebrated Dog*
    (Senour), 234
medicine shows, 19–20, 60–
    63, 64, 85, 217, 221
"Meet Me in St. Louis," 2, 215
Meharry Medical College, 182

*Men, Beasts, and Gods: A History
    of Cruelty and Kindness to
    Animals* (Carson), 125
Messenger, 29–30
Metropolitan Cash Register,
    227
Michton, Morris, 7
Middle Tennessee State Uni-
    versity, 269
Minneapolis Journal, 244–45
Minoliti, Giorgio, 199
minstrel shows, 19, 20, 21, 225
Minter, Jeptha, 53–54, 55, 56
Minter, J. M., 82
Mohammed (prophet), 22, 23
Monk (dog), 6, 174–75, 189,
    192–93, 204, 207, 211,
    212, 213, 224, 228, 236,
    240, 246, 247, 249, 255–
    56, 258, 263, 268
"monkey trials," 223
Monsieur Tonson, 27
Morgan, John Hunt, 75
Morgan, J. P., 195
Morocco, 222
Morrison, Allan, 214
Muggins, 31–32

Nashville, Chattanooga & St.
    Louis Railways (NC &
    St. L), 16, 101
Nashville, Tenn., 17, 27–28,
    49, 50, 52, 77, 82, 93,
    98–116, 181–85
Nashville American, 183, 185
Nashville Banner, 185
Nashville Humane Society,
    181–84
Nashville Sun, 116, 185
Nashville Tennessean, 264
Nashville World's Fair, *see* Ten-
    nessee Centennial and
    International Exposition
    of 1897

ABOVE: Together Dr. William Key and Beautiful Jim Key helped cause a change in human consciousness about whether animals feel, reason, and think—and the two went on to enlist millions in the humane movement.

LEFT: Billed as being "as interesting as Black Beauty," the twelve editions of Jim's biographical pamphlet chronicled his career from start to finish and sold more than 200,000 copies.

On breaks from his self-appointed role as Beautiful Jim Key's bodyguard, Monk loved nothing more than posing for reporters— as in this shot possibly taken in the Mirror Maze, an attraction promoted by Albert Rogers.

Monk in his familiar meditative stance atop his equine ward.

BELOW: Early in his education, Jim learned to identify different coins. By the time he graduated to his customized, gold-plated National Cash Register, he could ring up any amount requested and retrieve the correct change.

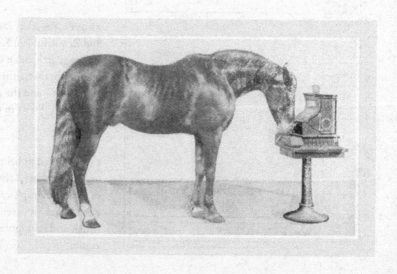

An estimated five million Americans visited the Silver Horseshoe Building on the Pike at the 1904 Louisiana Purchase Exposition in St. Louis, where Beautiful Jim Key personified the World's Fair's themes of progress and education.

COPYRIGHT 1904 BY
PACH BROS. N.Y.

Alice
Roosevelt

Nicholas
Longworth

This popular 1904 postcard appeared not long after Jim Key made his
famous prediction that romantically linked "Princess" Alice Roosevelt to
Congressman Nicholas Longworth.

This VIP pass issued for the St. Louis World's Fair opening-day performances—like the one attended by the future Alice Roosevelt Longworth—ensured packed houses and newspaper headlines, part of the promotional magic that made Jim the "Wonder of the Pike."

Unlike leaders of other humane organizations, George Thorndike Angell (1823–1909), founder of the MSPCA and the American Humane Education Society, had the vision and daring to make Beautiful Jim Key a standard-bearer for his cause.

LEFT: Dr. William Key was already sixty-four years old in 1897, around the time this publicity photograph was taken. For the next nine years, as he traveled and performed with Jim on a nearly constant basis, he became one of the most recognized and beloved African Americans of the day.

RIGHT: A 1904 photograph of Albert R. Rogers, Jim Key's brilliant promoter and manager who helped pioneer the practice of linking entertainers with charitable causes.

LEFT: Lucinda Davis Key, M.D., graduated from Howard University's medical school in 1894. The third of Bill Key's four wives, Dr. Lucinda Key was the first to discover that Jim had taught himself to say yes and no.

BELOW: The Davis brothers, Stanley and Sam, traveled with Doc Key and Jim. Later, Dr. Stanley Davis became a prominent Bedford County veterinarian while Sam and his wife, Essie Campbell Davis, established the Jim Key Farm on their property—where the educated Arabian-Hambletonian is now buried.

An interior shot of the Negro Building at the 1897 Tennessee Centennial Exposition, where Jim Key attained his proverbial big break and was discovered by promoter Rogers.

This was one of several traveling arenas that the innovative Albert Rogers devised to draw crowds.

Even though Jim, a committed Democrat, insisted he had not voted for the Republican president, William McKinley was no less effusive in his praise: "This is certainly the most astonishing and entertaining exhibition I have ever witnessed. It is indeed a grand object lesson of what kindness and patience will accomplish."

BELOW: While Rogers added sophisticated elements of staging and props to shows, Dr. Key's main focus with Jim continued to be "simply education."

ABOVE: In 1899 Dr. Key made an endorsement deal with Shelbyville's prestigious Robinson-McGill Manufacturing Company.

LEFT: Rogers negotiated a plum licensing deal with Amberg. A Beautiful Jim Key filing cabinet— a must for any modern office— could cost as much as $100.

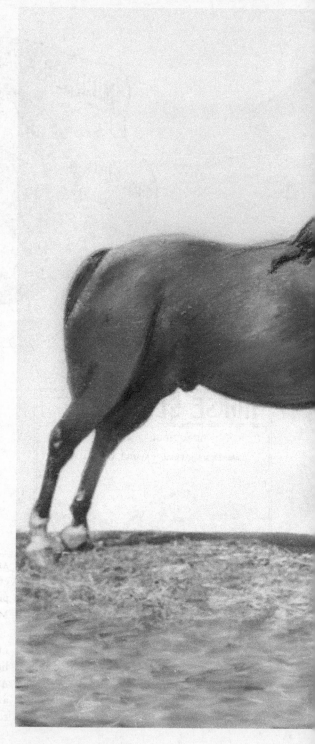

Beautiful Jim Key during a basic
demonstration of his ability to tell
time. He could also identify the days
of the week, the months of the year,
and how many days were in each—
including leap year.

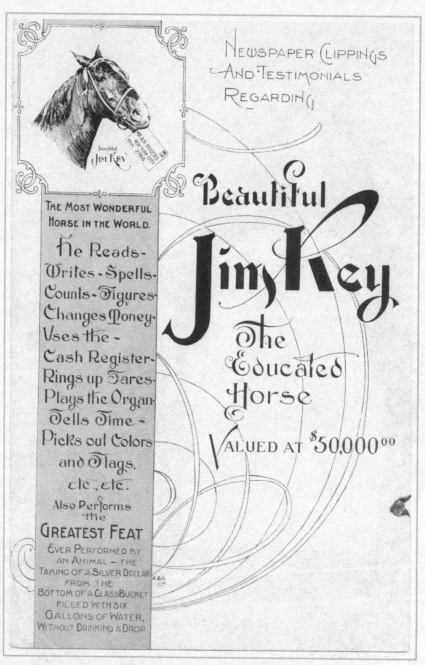

By the end of his first year in show business, Jim had become a media darling as his value went up five times his alleged selling price in 1897. Within seven years he was declared to be worth a million dollars, thus raising the bar for every other celebrity horse that followed him.

Festival Hall and Cascade Gardens at the 1904 Louisiana Purchase Exposition. Beautiful Jim Key was immortalized in a children's book that culminated with a visit by the celebrity canine St. Elmo to meet him in St. Louis.

BELOW: By 1904 the general public had embraced the principles of humane education, accepting the premise that through kindness and patience a horse could be taught to spell common and unusual names.

The burial place of Beautiful Jim Key on a hill overlooking Tullahoma Highway. The inscription reads: Kindness, Justice, Mercy to All Creatures.

CPSIA information can be obtained
at www.ICGtesting.com
Printed in the USA
LVHW041414071219
639778LV00022B/168/P

9 780060 567040